STRATEGIC MANAGEMENT

Strategic Management

[For B.Com./M.Com., and other Management Courses of All Universities]

By

VED PRAKASH

ANMOL PUBLICATIONS PVT. LTD.

NEW DELHI - 110 002 (INDIA)

ANMOL PUBLICATIONS PVT. LTD.
4374/4B, Ansari Road, Daryaganj
New Delhi - 110 002
Ph.: 23261597, 23278000
Visit us at: www.anmolpublications.com

Stratetic Management

First Published, 2005

ISBN 81-261-2162-9

PRINTED IN INDIA

Published by J.L. Kumar for Anmol Publications Pvt. Ltd., New Delhi - 110 002 and Printed at Mehra Offset Press, Delhi.

Contents

Preface

Strategic Management as a paper is being taught at the graduate and post graduate level in M.Com. and Management courses syllabus in almost all the Indian Universities and Institutions. The various courses conducted by management institutions at the Central and State level too have been considered in respect of their syllabus, course contents and requirements. Thus the material presented here would be of interest as well as great use to the students of M.Com. and other Management Courses. This book will provide complete knowledge of structure, evolution, formulation and implementation of Strategic Management.

The major topics dealt in this book are—Global Issues in Strategic Management; Strategic Decision and Planning in Business; Environmental Analysis and Diagnosis; Strategy Evolution; Strategy and Structure; Strategy Formulation; Strategy Implementation; Functional Strategies and Planning Policies; Corporate Structure; Strategic Value Analysis; Alternative Strategy; Strategy of Foreign Collaboration; Strategic Issues in International Management.

Ved Prakash

1

Global Issues in Strategic Management

"Strategic management" is the term currently used to describe the process on which the book focuses. In most businesses in earlier times (and in many smaller firms today), the focus of the manager's job was on today's decisions for today's world in today's business. Instead of focusing all their time on today, managers began to see the value of trying to anticipate the future and to prepare for it. They did this in several ways. They prepared systems and procedures manuals for decisions that must be made repeatedly. This allowed time for more important decisions and ensured more or less consistent decisions.

Budgeting and control system helped, but they tended to be based on the status quo-the present business and conditions-and did not by themselves deal well with change. These systems did provide better financial controls and are still in use. Later variations included capital budgeting and management by objectives systems.

Because of the lack of emphasis on the future in budgeting long-range planning appeared. This movement focused forecasting the future by using economic and technological tools. Long -range planning tended to be performed primarily by corporate staff groups, whose reports were forwarded to top management. Sometimes their reports and advice were heeded (when they were understood and were credible): otherwise, they were ignored. Since the corporate planners were not the decision makers, long-range planning had some impact, but not as much as would be expected if top management were involved. Then, too, they were producing first generation plans.

"First-generation planning" means that the firm chooses the most probable appraisal and diagnosis of the future environment and of its own strengths and weaknesses. From this, it evolves the best strategy for a match of the environment and the firm-a single plan for the most likely future.

Today's approach is called "strategic planning" or, more frequently, "strategic management". As we known the board of directors and corporate planners have parts to play in strategic management. But the starring roles are for the general managers of the corporation and its major operating divisions. Strategic management focuses on "second-generation planning" that is, analysis of the business and the preparation of several scenario for the future. Contingency strategies are then prepared for each of these likely future scenario.

But these are our distinctions, and the terms "long-range planning", "strategic planning", and "strategic management" have as many definitions as there are experts. Strategic management is a stream of decisions and actions which leads to the development of an effective strategy or strategies to help achieve corporate objectives. The strategic management process is the way in which strategists determine objectives and make strategic decisions. On the basis of the definition, the following are features of strategic management:

1. The various processes of strategic management may be:
   - (A) Evaluation and monitoring of the outcome of these strategies to ensure that organisational objectives are being achieved. Depending on the nature and characteristics of the organisation, some of these processes may form the part of strategic management while others may not truly form its part,
   - (B) Survellience of environment both external and internal,
   - (C) Implementation of the these strategies,
   - (D) Evaluation of the organisation's strengths and weaknesses in the light of these opportunities and threats,

(E) Identification of various opportunities offered by the environment and threats presented,

(F) Formulation of various strategies for achieving these objectives,

(G) Formulation of various objectives of the organisation.

2. Strategic management is basically a process. It has emerged out of management in other fields where the concept of management is taken as a process for achieving certain objectives of the organisation. Thus strategic management involves establishing a framework to perform various processes. The concept of strategic management must embody all general management principles and practices devoted to strategy formulation and implementation in the organisation.
3. Strategic management is basically top management function. Thus in order to ensure effective top management function, it is necessary that a distinction should be made between strategic management and operational management which emphasises day-to-day operations in the organisation, so that top management can focus more attention on the strategic aspect rather than emphasising on operational management. Since the environment of the organisation is always changing providing new opportunties and threats, top management must spend more and more time on this aspect. Thus there is a considerable change of top management function is the organisations. The change is from operational management to strategic management.
4. The focus of strategic management is on relating the organisation to its external environment. This emphasizes that there is continuous interaction between organisation and its environment taking an open systems approach. Thus the organisation must create adequate channel through which external information will pass to various points in the organisation.

5. While strategic planning helps to resolve the problem of strategic formulation on the basis of mission-and objective-setting and the analysis of environment and internal factors, it falls short of taking into account a few relevant aspects. Ansoff et al. deals with these shortcomings in terms of three variables. First, with regard to managerial problems, strategic planning considers the external linkages with the environment " under a basic assumption that the internal configuration of the organisation will remain essentially unchanged". Second, dealing with the process of resolving managerial problems, it covers only problem-solving (or planning) while assuming that implementation and control will follow. Thirdly, the variables included in strategic planning analysis are exclusively "technological-economic-informational while social and political dynamics both within and outside the organisation are assumed to be irrelevant and unaffected."

The sub-variables, which have been excluded from consideration, have a major impact on resolving strategic problems. For instance, it is essential to consider the impact that formulation of strategy, and changes in it, have on the organisation. Again, the solution of managerial problems can only be done through a comprehensive approach that not only considers formulation but also implementation and control of strategy. Factors like psychological are the mayriad of problems faced by managers.

Strategic management, a newer and broader concept of managing organisation strategically, takes into account all the aspects of managerial problems, the processes of solving them and the many variables that operate in a problem-solving environment.

ELEMENTS OF STRATEGIC MANAGEMENT PROCESS

Strategic management process consists of a number of elements, which are discreate and identifiable activities performed in logical and sequential steps. As many as twelve different elements could be identified in the models provided by various authors. From the literature on business policy, we note that most or all of the following activities are considered as parts of the strategic management process:

A. Defining business
B. Setting mission
C. Determining purpose
D. Establishing objectives
E. Performing environmental appraisal
F. Doing corporate appraisal
G. Evolving strategic alternatives
H. Exercising strategic choice
I. Formulating strategies
J. Preparing strategic plan
K. Implementing strategies; and
L. Evaluating strategies.

MODELS OF STRATEGIC MANAGEMENT PROCESS

The process of strategic management is depicted through a model which consists of different phases; each phase having a number of elements. Most authors agree on dividing the strategic management process into four phases consisting of about twelve elements.

In the following figure a vertical representation of a comprehensive model of the strategic management process is provided. In next Diagram we see the process laterally and provide a working model. Our purpose in additionally giving a working model, devoid the complexity observed in the comprehensive model, is to assist you in remembering and recalling it with ease. Here, different elements of the process are discussed as under:

(a) Business definition, mission, purpose and objectives are concerned with laying the foundation for strategic management. These relate the organisation to the society, state what it has to attain for the society, and for itself, and in the process achieve its objectives and goals. The end result of this set of elements is a hierarchy of objectives and critical success factors which serve as yardsticks and benchmarks for measuring organisational performance.

(b) Environmental and organisational appraisal deal with finding out opportunties and threats operating in the environment and the strenghts and weaknesses of the organisation in order to create a match between them. In such a manner, opportunities could be availed of and the impact of threats neutralised in order to capitalise on the organisational strengths and minimise the weaknesses.

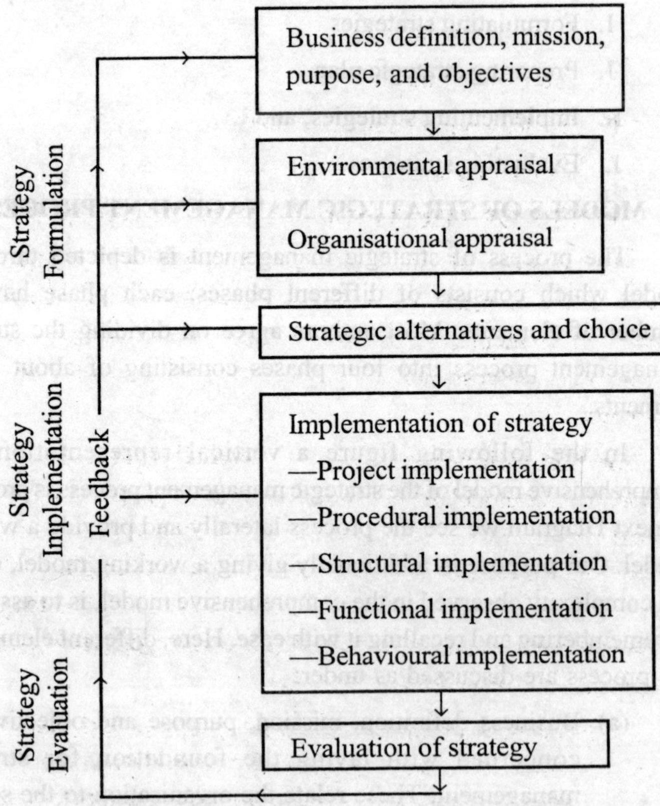

A Comprehensive Model of the Strategic Management Process

(c) Strategic alternatives and choice are required for evolving alternative strategies, out of the many possible options, and choosing the most appropariate strategy or strategies in the light of environmental opportunities and threats and corporate strengths and weaknesses. The end result of this set of elements is a strategic plan to be implemented.

(d) For implementation of strategy, the strategic plan is put into action through six sub-processes; project implementation, procedural implementation, resource allocation, structural, functional and behavioural implementation. Project implementation deals with setting up the organisation. Procedural implementation deals with different aspects or regulatory framework within which Indian organisations have to operate. Resources allocation relates to the procurement and commitment of resources for implementation. The structural aspects of implementation deal with the design of appropriate organisational structures and reorganising for matching the structure to the needs of strategy. The functional aspects relate to the policies to be formulated in different functional areas. The behavioural aspects consider the leadership patterns for implementing strategies and other issues like social responsibility, business ethics, organisational culture and corporate politics. The emphasis in the implementation phase of strategic management is on action.

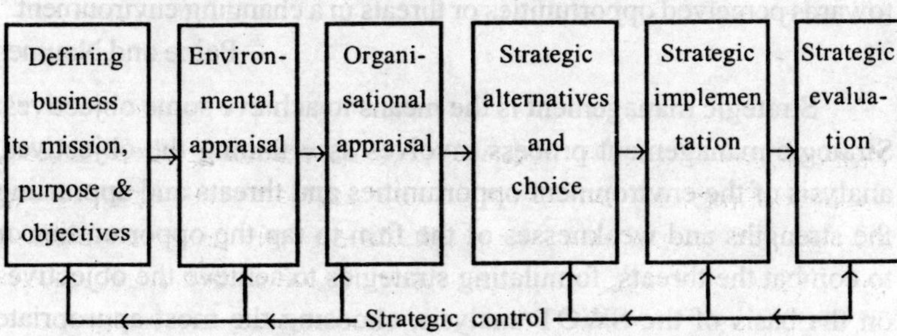

A Working Model of the Strategic Management Process

(e) The last phase of strategic evaluation appraises the implementation of strategies and measures organisational performance to exercise strategy control over the strategic management process. Strategies may be reformulated, if neacessary.

STEPS IN STRATEGIC MANAGEMENT

One can spontaneously say that the strategic management is the process of management of strategic decision-making implementation and control. It is a not a complete meaning of strategic management as it fails to cover many important aspects of strategic management. Many scholars have defined starategic management in various ways:

(i) Strategy is a "unified, comprehensive and integrated plan relating to the strategic advantages of the firm to the challenges of the environment. It is designed to ensure that the basic objectives of the enterprise are achieved. Strategic management is "that set of decisions and actions which leads to the development of an effective strategy or strategies to help achieve corporate objectives." —W.F. Glueck.

(ii) "Strategic management is the determination of the basic long-term goals and objectives of an enterprise and the adoption of courses of action and allocation of resources necessary to carry out these goals" —Alfred D. Chandler

(iii) "Strategic management involves the decision-making and the activities in an organisation which *(1)* have wider ramifications, *(2)* have a long time perspective, and *(3)* use critical resources towards perceived opportunities or threats in a changing environment." —Paine and Naumes

Strategic management is the means to achieve some objectives. Strategic management process involves ascertaining the objectives, analysis of the environment opportunities and threats and appraising the strengths and weaknesses of the firm to tap the opportunities or to combat the threats, fomulating strategies to achieve the objectives on the basis of the SWOT analysis, choosing the most appropriate strategy, implementation of strategy and reformulation of the objectives of strategy, it needs. The strategic management process is schematically personated in Fig. given below :—

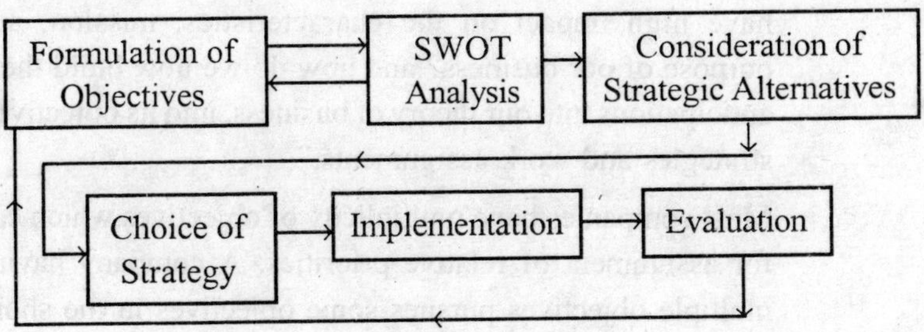

Strategic Management Process

1. **Formulation of Objectives.** A strategy is a means to achieve the ends or objectives. However, objectives should not be static, they should be dynamic. Changes in the environment and/or changes in the organisational strengths and weaknesses may call for modifications of the objectives. As Kotler remarks, "Objectives can grow obsolete because of the continuous changes occurring in the company's marketing environment. Therefore a company should appraise how well its objectives tap the firm's opportunities and resources. Dynamic companies conduct audit of their objectives and reform or reorient the objectives, to ensure that the company's objectives are the most appropriate in the given environment and the company resources. It is such appraisal and the resultant reorientation of the business which have enabled many companies to achieve remarkable successes often reflected in the prudent diversification and fast growth of business.

   Glueck has aptly remarked, "Objectives help define the organisationis its environment". Environment analysis will help find answer to the questions what should be the company's business. If 'what should be the business' is different from 'what is the business', there is a need for redesigning the business, matching the compnay resources to the environment. As Peter F. Drummer succinctly puts it, 'what will the business be' is related to "what changes in the environment are already discernible that are likely to have high impact on the characteristics, mission, and purpose of our business? and how do we now build these anticipations into our theory of business, into its objectives, strategies and work assignments."

Most companies have multiplicity of objectives which call for assignment of relative priorities. A company having multiple objectives pursues some objectives in the short-run and others on the long-term. A example, the short-run objective of market penetration may be a strategy to help achieve the long-run objective of market dominance or profit. As Kotler points out, "The Japanese are patient capitalists who are willing to wait even a decade before realizing their profits."

A company will normally pursue the secondary objectives listed as long-run objectives. This does not mean that long-term objectives are secondary objectives. Some of the long-term objectives like profit, are essentially primary objectives like development of the local community, assisting the development of the industry of which the firm is a part, serving the society, good corporate citizenship etc. are secondary objectives.

The change of some of the objectives and the definition of the business may be necessitated by environmental factors. As Drummer points out, "Very few definitions of the purpose and mission of a business have anything like expectancy of thirty, let alone fifty, years. To be good for ten years is probably all one can normally expect. The environmental trends of the last two decades indicate that the life expectancy is becoming shorter due to very fast and frequent changes in the environment, particularly in the field of technology."

2. **SWOT Analysis.** SWOT analysis is the identification of the threats and opportunities in the environment. The strengths and weaknesses of the firm is the cornerstone of business policy formulation. These factors determine the course of action to ensure the survival and growth of the firm. Though the environment might present many opportunities a company may not have the strength to exploit all of them. Similarly, sometimes a firm will not have the strength to meet the environmental threats. In such a situation it will be prudent to give it up and concentrate on such business for which the firm is most competent. The environment dynamics necessitates such restructuring. As Wells has pointed out, certain products which were exported in the early stages of the product life cycle by high income countries like the U.S.A. were later imported by them. Other countries which have acquired the technology would be able to produce them cheaper because of low above cost or would sometimes improve the technology. Thus, although the U.S. had a very dominant position in electronic products and had been exporting them in the beginning, later countries like Japan started exporting them to the U.S. and replacing the U.S. in other markets too. An analysis of products treated by countries like Japan, Korea, Taiwan etc. would show the changes in the comparative advantages.

3. **Consideration of Strategic Alternatives.** The environment opportunities and threats should be evaluated in the light of the strengths and weaknesses of the internal factors comprising finance, technology and skill, production facilities, personnel and marketing capabilities. The capability of a company to exploit the environmental opportunities or to meet the challenges depends on the strength of these factors, hence the importance of the internal resource audit. A company may be strong in respect of finance, technology, production facilities, personnel marketing

capabilities. The task is to make best use of its strategic strenghts.

4. **Choice of Strategy.** After the identification of the environmental opportunities and threats and the organisation strengths and weaknesses the next step in the strategic management process is the choice of the most appropriate strategy/strategies.

   A compnay planning market its product in foreign markets may have the following alternatives:

   (i) Manufacture the product completely in the home country and export it to the foreign market.

   (ii) Establish manufacturing facility in a free area like an export possessing zone and make exports from there.

   (iii) Manufacture the components at home and assemble the product in the foreign market.

   (iv) Contract some foreign firm for manufacturing the product and do only the marketing of it.

   (v) Establish manufacturing facility in the foreign country and undertake the complete manufacturing of the product there.

   (vi) Establish a joint venture abroad for manufacturing and marketing the product.

   (vii) Enter into licensing agreement with a firm in the foreign market.

   The choice of the strategy should invariably be based on the evaluation of the various alternatives.

5. **Implementation.** Many good strategies fail to achieve the results because of poor implementation. The term implementation has been used in a broad sense so that it encompasses also the formulation of the plan to implement the strategy.

   Formulation of different levels of strategies is an essential and important aspect of implementation in a multi-unit business. Following three levels of strategies are applicable to such a business:

(i) ***Corporate Level Strategy.*** It is the master strategy to achieve the overall corporate objectives. The other levels of strategies are designed to implement the corporate strategy, they are, therefore, formulated with reference to the corporate strategy.

(ii) ***SBU Level Strategy.*** It is the strategy to achieve the specific objectives of the strategic business unit (SBU) in order to help achieve the overall corporate objectives. According to William F. Glueck SBU is "an operating division of a firm which serves a distinct product/ market segment or a well-defined set of customers or a geographic area. The SBU is given the authority to make its own strategic decision within corporate guide-lines as long as it meets corporate objectives". The SBU is also known as 'operating division'.

(iii) ***Functional Level Strategy.*** The ultimate success of the SBU level strategy depends on the effectiveness with which it is translated to management functions like marketing, finance, production, R and D etc. For example, if some of the SBU level objectives are to be achieved by introducing a new product the R and D, production, finance and marketing departments will have to be geared up to this task.

There are only two levels of strategies in a single unit business namely. the corporate level and the functional level. Implementation involves mobilisation and deployment of resources, including personnel, needed for implementation, organising and assigning tasks to the various elements of the organisation. It is essential to formulate an implementation strategy for effective implementation of the strategy.

Besides their potential capability, motivation and high morale of people from top to bottom of the organisation are essential for successful implementation of the strategy. It is essential to formulate an implementation strategy.

6. **Evaluation.** In the words of William F. Glueck, "Evaluation of strategy is that phase of the strategic management process in which the top managers determine whether their strategic choice is implemented in meeting the objectives of the enterprise". Failure to achieve the results may be due to any one or more of the following:

   (i) Improper Implementation of the Strategy. This may be due to:

   (a) inappropriateness of the implementation strategy;

   (b) inefficieny and/or lack of commitment of the personnel in charge of implementation;

   (c) wrong assignments of the tasks; or

   (d) inadequacy of resources.

   (ii) Environmental Changes. These include increase in competition, changes in consumer preference or attitudes, technological changes which could not be anticipated while formulating the strategy etc. These may come in the way of achieving the results.

   Sometimes environment changes make the achievement of the objectives easier. The chances of environmental changes affecting the achievements of the strategy indicate the need for constant monitoring of the environment and modification or reformulation of the strategy, as and when necessary.

   (iii) Inappropriate Strategy. It may be the result of a wrong diagnosis to the environmental threats and opportunities or the internal strengths and weaknesses or of a wrong strategic choice resulting from the faulty evaluation of the alternatives.

To conclude, the key to business success is the most effective utilisation of the company's existing and additional resources and those it can mobilise and augment for any specific task. This involves the evaluation of the company's strengths and weaknesses in the light of the environmental threats and opportunities and taking appropriate measure to harness the opportunities or to combat the threats and formulation of strategies accordingly. Companies which fail to do so are often doomed to failure. As Glueck point out, "In the 50 years between 1918 and 1968, almost half of the 100 largest American firms went out of business or became significantly less important... Often a company become convinced it is almost invincible and need not examine what is happening in the market place. When the company ceases to adjust the environment to its strategy or does not react to the demands of the environment, by changing its strategy, the results are lessened achievement of the corporate objectives."

LIMITATIONS OF STRATEGIC MANAGEMENT

Strategic management has following limitations:

1. Strategic management brings rigidity in the organisation through strategic planning, it is claimed. To some extent, this can be valid and a more serious limitation of strategic management. Strategies are selected and implemented in a given set of environment, both external and internal. When these variables are taken into account, the organisation sets various parameters for its working, for example, designing of organisation structure, prescribing rules and procedures, allocating resources, etc. Over the long run, people become accustomed to these. When there is a question of making any change because of change in the strategy necessiated by the environment, it is not easy. Thus various internal inflexibilities are experienced in the organisation. These internal inflexibilities—human and procedural—may make the strategic planning ineffective, consequently demotivating the management to go for strategic management. This is a real problem in the strategic management, but this problem can be overcome by building enough flexibility in the system through an open system approach of strategic management. An open system

approach suggests that managers take into account the environmental variables, such as technological, social, cultural, legal, political and economic and also the internal variables, that is, how their organisations function in the light of these variables, thereby making continuous adjustments. Thus there is a need for concept of a moving balance among the considerations on which strategy is based, the concept to strategy that continuously envolves in the direction of the organisation's environment and its resources.

2. Problems in strategic management come because the managers are inadequately aware about its contribution to the success of the organisation and the way in which strategic management can be undertaken. For example, managers often fail to isolate the strategic work, and they use short-term outdated evaluation techniques. *(i)* the failure to isolate strategic work is very common to many managers. The problem stems from an inadequate appreciation of the need for such an appraisal. It continues with a kind of general confusion and ambiguous thinking about the concept to strategy that beguiles one into believing he is being strategic though merely he is following an arbitrary course of action and using the word strategy to describe it. Thus he is focussing his attention on operating problems ignoring more important strategic problems. *(ii)* Another problem in strategic management emerges from the fact that managers often attach importance to short-term achievement it is easy to become wedded to a financially oriented formula for measuring the performance routinely from year to year while the time required for a strategy or group of strategies to become full-blown is often much greater than the annual measurement requirement.

Both, these factors put severe limitation on the practice of strategic management but they do signify that if managers are sufficiently aware about the role and concept of strategic management, they can develop future-oriented thinking which is more valuable than merely focussing on the current operations.

3. The strategic management is essential to overcome the problems posed by complex and dynamic environment. However, this becomes a serious limitation on effective strategic management.

For strategic management, we require knowledge of the trend in the environment. However, with increasing complexity and an accelerating rate of change, it becomes more and more difficult to predict the future outcome, for example, not only there is very high level of technological and social changes in the government but there is wide variation and inconsistency in Government policies towards business in the country. Such policies are not only in terms of physical, monetary, and fiscal policies but also in terms of many regulatory measures, such as licensing, monopolies and restrictive trade practices, foreign exchange regulations, etc. Under these conditions, strategic management becomes more difficult and without sound basis.

Notwithstanding the fact that environment is more flexible and dynamic, the role of strategic management cannot be ignored. In fact, in such circumstances, the role of strategic management becomes even more crucial. The extent to which a variety of alternatives is studied in advance reduces the possibility of surprise and permits the preparation of alternative strategies for a range of possibilities. The more uncertain is the future, the more is the need for contemplating the future by assigning some probability for the events. Thus the practical problem in the way of the strategic management does not reduce its importance.

4. There are various problems in implementing a strategy. Though this aspect will be discussed at a later stage in a greater length, here it is sufficient to say that many organisational problems can not be solved by strategic management alone but require the use of the other aspects of management. Seldom corporate strategy is as clear to organisation members as is thought by its framers. Even the most persuasive, articulate, and specific strategy by the top management may not carry the same meaning throughout the organisation. The internal conflicts among departments, individuals, or organisational and personal values can not be solved by strategic management. In many of these cases, non-strategic management functions are more important.

The various limitations of strategic management should be weighed in the light of its contributions of the success of the organisation. Every action has certain limitations but it does not mean that action should not be taken. The recognition of various limitations of an action provides an opportunity to safeguard oneself against the possible counter effect of the action and places the individual in a better way to make the action more effective. For example, administering a medicine to a patient may have some side effects. But this does not mean that medicine should not be given to the patient. What is required is the administering of correct medicine and taking effective step to overcome the side effect. Similar is the case with strategic management. While going for strategic management, the managers should take into account its various limitations. Moreover, the strategic management should not be taken as panacea for all organisational problems because many of the problems are of operative nature. The role of strategic management can not be denied and various organisation have emerged as winners by following strategic management.

GLOBAL ISSUES IN STRATEGIC MANAGEMENT

In present day scenario the main emerging global trends are as follows:

1. Economic Reforms. Far reaching economic reforms have been established in communist and non-communist countries particularly in development ones. Economic liberalisation is encompassing greater scope and freedom for both domestic and foreign private enterprise. Trade liberalisation has been the centre point of these reforms. Simplification of procedures and de-bureaucratisation have also been important in countries like India.

The political and economic business environment has been fast changing all over the world. The economic reforms carried out in the erstwhile USSR, East European Countries. Cuba etc. are revolutionary. In the People's Republic of China, following one of the most conservative policies, economic reforms began as early as the 1970s. Marketing privatisation and internationalisation have been progressing in these countries at an amazing speed. Several of them have effectively eliminated state monopoly of foreign trade and have drastically reduced import controls. There has been an influx of foreign private capital and technology. The barrier of political ideology to international business is fast disappearing.

2. Global Economic Boom. Naisbitt and Aburdene point out that the world is entering a period of economic prosperity in the decade of the 1990s. There is no single factor, but an extraordinary confluence of factors behind the economic boom. The economic forces of the world are surging across national borders, resulting in more democracy, more freedom, more trade, more opportunity and greater prosperity. Although the problems, strategies and pattern of development and rates of growth may vary, all national economies are on the growth path.

Economic considerations ultimately transcend political considerations in the centrally planned economies.

The growing population, the rising income and the new conducive policy environment have attracted more investment into the developing countries. Recent figures suggest that MNCs are shifting from the developed countries to developing countries. In 1991, there was an increase of 38 per cent in the MNCs' investments in the developing countries, while there was a decline of 23 per cent in the developed countries.

3. Privatisation. The developments all over the world indicate growing economic internationalisation and privatisation. The privatisation movement ushered in the United Kingdom by Margret Thatcher spread to other developed and developing countires, including the 'communist' ones, like a wave. In India, privatisation has been accepted by the Government as an important means of industrial and economic rejuvenation. Privatisation has significant socio-political and economic implications. As the proportion of shareholders in the total population increases and as the economic lot of the workers and the poor improve, leftist parties increasingly lose their ground. Conservative Party was voted to power in Britain for the fourth consecutive period. The Labour Party remained out of power for such a long period. Since 1979 the membership of the trade unions in the U.K. has sunk by more than 25 per cent.

4. Consumerism. The consumer boom is the most conspicuous in Asia, particularly in the Pacific Rim. North America and Europe are facing more competitions from the Asian countries. Japan is moving from an export driven economy to a consumer-driven economy, shift that other Asian countries will follow in the 1990s.

Asians are the consumers of the 1990s. Wages that are increasing everywhere are creating millions of consumers. During the decade 80 million more will be added to the wealthiest Asian countries creating great opportunities for North American and Europeans, as well as for Asian producers.

5. National Strategies. Governments of different countries have been taking following measures to improve their economic competitiveness and protect their economic and none-economic interests:

(a) ***Regional Economic Groupings.*** Regional economic grouping for mutural benefits is not a new development. The EC 92 is by far the most ambitious of such schemes. Through the referendum of June 1992 Spanish people rejected the Maastricht Treaty regarding the establishment of a monetary and economic union. But the development of the European Economic Community towards economic integration, has been considerable by January, 1993. To overcome the European Fortress many companies from outside the Community have made strategic moves, including establishment of production bases within the Community.

(b) ***Free Trade Agreements.*** Several Free Trade Agreements have been in existence for quite some time now. Some important new ones took birth recently while some more are likely to come into being. The North American Free Trade Agreement of 1988 between the U.S. and Canada has been extended to Mexico, making North America a giant free trade area. The Australia-New Zealand Closer Economic Relations Trade Agreement west into effect in 1988. The ASEAN has agreed to establish a free trade area

in the year 2000. There has also been talks about a US-Japan Free Trade accord. According to Naisbitt and Aburdene, as we turn to the next century, we will witness the link up of North America, Europe and Japan to form a golden triangle of free trade with a powerful, overcharging megatrend towards world wide free trade.

(c) ***Protectionism.*** While the GATT has made some achievements in reducing the tariff barriers, there has been a substantial growth of non-tariff barriers (NTBs), often referred to as the new protectionism measure. These include voluntary export restraints and administered protection such as health and product standards, customs precedes, licensing etc. The developing countries, have been facing growing NTB to their exports to developed countries. According to a World Bank Study. NTB in major industrial countries has affected more than one-third of imports from developing countries, compared to one-forth from all countries. Several advanced countries like the USA have resorted to NTBs. The Super 301 and Special 301 of the U.S. Omnibus Trade and Competitiveness Act, 1988, have been used to make other countries to fall in line with the U.S. policies or to restrict imports to the U.S. Even Peoples Republic of China liberalised the economic policies under their threat. Protectionism has increasingly taken the covert shape in the U.S. and E.C. In these countries, there has been a growing demand for more protective measures in the wake of the challenge to their trade supremacy, particularly by the Pacific rim countries. Measures like the Super 301 have been used for covert protectionism like harassment of foreign rivals. One of the major trade rivals of the U.S. and who has been constantly facing the threat of Super 301, Japan has recently described the US as the biggest 'unfair trader' of the world. The developed countries have been using their economic supremacy to compel the developing countries to accept the Dunkel Draft of the Uruguay Round of trade negotiations under the GATT, several provisions of which are very harmful to the interest of the developing countries.

(d) ***Government Support.*** Government not only support and encourage national industries in various ways but also foreign investment. Even the centrally planned economies are now luring multinationals. Government of many non-communist developing countries also have now a more positive attitude toward domestic private sector and foreign capital and technology. In America and Europe, although there is a resentment because of the expanding foreign ownership of the economy and increased competition to established industries, government, several enterprises, and economists welcome foreign capital and technology because they bring the promise of jobs, tax revenues to cash-strapped local government and help export and import substitution.

In the light of the above trends, the major global issues in Strategic Management are discussed here under the following titles:

(i) *Globalisation.* The globalisation has become stronger today. Many multinational corporations have transformed themselves into global corporations. They are striving to enhance their competitiveness by tapping the scope for globalisation in sourcing, manufacturing and marketing. As Kotler observes, "Many companies have become truly multionational organisation. They stop thinking themselves as global marketers. The top management and staff are involved in the planning of worldwide manufacturing facilities, marketing policies, financial flows and logistical systems. The global operating units report directly to the chief executive or executive committee, not to the head of an international division. Executives are trained in worldwide operations, not just domestic or international. Management is recruited from many countries; components are supplied and purchased where they can be obtained at the least cost; and investments are made where the anticipated returns are the greatest.

Domestic operations account for only a small part of the total revenue/profit of many multinationals. In a truly multinational enterprise, not only the sales revenue is generated from many markets but product development and other operations are organised multinationally. For example, Philip's first colour T.V. set was built and sold not only in Europe but also in Canada were the market has closely followed the U.S. lead in introducing colour transmission. The list of local innovation and entrepreneurial initiatives in the company is endless. With only 8 per cent of the total sales coming from Holland, many different national subsidiaries of the company have contributed much larger share of total revenues than the parent company. Foreign operations have enjoyed relatively high organisational status compared to most companies of similar size with headquarters in the US, Japan or even the larger companies in Europe. As Drucker points out, most people think of giant companies when they hear the word 'transnational'. But, medium and even small business operate in the world economy rather than in one or two countries.

In his latest book "The Competitive Advantage of Nations" Professor Michael Porter points out that a global approach to strategy involve a number of elements. First, it clearly means selling worldwide, not just in the home market. However, international sales are viewed not as incremental business but as integral strategy. The firm builds an international brand name and establishes international marketing channels it controls. Second, a global strategy involves locating activities in order to capture local advantages, offset particular disadvantages, or to facilitate local market penetration. Third and most importantly, a global strategy involves coördinating and integrating activities on a wholewide basis in order to gain economies of scale or leasing, enjoy the benefits of a consistent brand reputation, and serve international buyers. Simply operating internationally does not equate to a global strategy unless this sort of international cooperation takes place. Advantages drawn from the global network add to home based advantages and make them more sustainable.

Porter argues that a company must move toward a global strategy as soon as its resources and competitive position allow if it is competing in a global industry. A high domestic cost of capital, high domestic factor costs, and a strong currency are no excuse in global competition. Yet competing internationally is not a substitute for improvement and innovation at home.

(ii) *Sourcing.* An important aspect of globalisation is 'global sourcing'. *i.e.*, procuring the various raw materials, components etc., from the lowest cost source available anywhere in the world. As Tom Peters points out, high speed computers and communications technology make possible the arrangement of the most exotic financing in a dozen currencies in a matter of day. This facilitates such developments in manufacturing as global sourcing. The growth of multinational subcontracting is an obvious indication of the growth of global sourcing. An important corollary of the global sourcing is the deintegration and hollowing of firms. Tasks which were routinely done inside most firms are now subcontracted to small and large, domestic and foreign outsiders.

The world sourcing market is estimated at about $ 1 trillion, forming nearly a third of the total world exports. Contributing significantly to their economic development and export earnings many South-East Asian countries have taken advantage of the growing global sourcing. However, India has almost been by passed by these developments mostly because of the conservative policies and bureaucratic hurdles.

(iii) *Joint Ventures.* There has also been a substantial increase in the joint ventures of different types. The economic reforms in the centrally planned economies and policy liberalisations in other countries have given a tremendous boost to joint venturing.

(iv) *Mergers and Acquisitions.* Mergers and acquisitions (M and A) has increased due to diversification. Many other factors like technical, strategic and financial advantages, political reasons and the fear of growing protectionism have also been behind the M and A increase. Mergers and acquisitions provide specific advantages like instant access to markets and distribution network and access to new technology or patent right.

(v) *Strategic Alliance.* Known by such names as entente, strategic alliance, coalition, etc., a new wave of competitive strategy is sweeping across the international business horizon. It seeks to enhance the long term competitive advantage of the firm by forming alliance with its existing or potential competitors, in critical areas, instead of competing with each other.

Strategic alliances enable companies to increase resources productivityand profitability by avoiding unecessary fragmentation of resources and duplication of investment. Efforts are very conspicuous in such industries as pharmaceuticals, computer, nuclear, telepathic etc. characterised by high fixed costs in R & D and manufacturing and/or high and fast changing technology.

According to Kenichi Ohmae, in a changeable world or rapidly globalising markets and industries, a world of covering consumer tastes, rapidly spreading technology, escalating fixed costs and growing protectionism, alliance is an essential tool for serving customers. Globalisation mandates alliance and makes them absolutely essential to strategy. According to Jet Magsaysay, as the business environment becomes increasingly competitive, companies will have more reasons and will find more ways to form strategic alliances. These will be a logical alternative and a key to survival in business. In the not-too-distant future, alliances will be a necessity for individiual companies as well as for orderly development of entire industries. Companies in mature, slow-growth industries will increasingly look to strategic alliances for survival.

Strategic alliances have been rapidly increasing, particularly in the internal business. They are not confined only to large firms. There are many alliances between small and large firms. Several factors like high risks and cost of R and D, fast changes and complexities of technology and the resultant imbalance in the in house technical capabilities, high cost of marketing, the need to acquire complementary technology have led to alliances.

While developing countries which, in the past, were against globalisation, have wide opened their doors for globalisation, many people in developed countries like U.S.A. are angry against globalisation. American jobs and wage levels are severely affected by the influx of cheap imports and shifting of production to low cost overseas locations. Productivity grows more quickly when countries produce goods and services in which they have comparative advantage. Living standards can go up faster. True, globalisation can benefit the developing countries in several ways. It is, however, apprehended that unregulated globalisation will cause serious problems for developing countries.

The almost universal acceptance of the market economy and the globalisation driven by private enterprise tend to aggravate most of the harmful effects traditionally attributed to neocolonialism. The global dominance of industries by MNCs is on the increase. Many countries are indiscriminate in liberalising foreign investment. Pepsi, Coke and "junk foods" are allowed even in countries like China. A number of countries allow high foreign stake even in industries where that is not really required. This could affect domestic enterprise of developing countries. There has been a large number of cases of takeover of national firms by foreign firms. In some of these cases, the domestic firms are driven to a situation of having to hand over the majority or complete equity to the foreign partners of joint ventures because of the inability of the Indian partners to bring in additional capital or some other incapability.

Replacement of traditional and indigenous products by modern products, resulting in the ruin of traditional crafts and industries and the livelihood of people in these sectors have also been happening in several countries. In a competitive environment, a firm can survive only if it is efficient. Companies all around world, including many large multinationals, have been cutting down the size of their human resources as one of the means achieving cost efficiency. The problem of over-manning is very severe in the developing countries. Unless these firms get rid of the surplus labour, they can hardly be competitive and successful. That means, The liberalisation can succeed only if the economy grows very fast to absorb the displaced labour and the new addition to the labour force.

The developing countries, in general, have been disadvantaged by the international trading system. The adverse terms of trade led to economic loss for the developing countries, in gerneral. The least developed countries have been the most deprived. It may, however, be noted that one of the reasons for the adverse terms of trade of the developing countries is the demand-supply factors. It is also estimated that the least developed countries stand to lose up to $ 600 million a year and sub-Saharan Africa $ 1.2 billion as a result of the Uruguay Round Agreement. while the developed countries are expected to gain very substantially. Multilateral trade liberalisations were mostly in respect of goods traded between industrial economies and those exported from developing to the developed nations did not benefit so much. While developing countries as a group now face tariffs 10 per cent higher than the global average, the least developed countries face tariffs 30 per cent higher, because tariffs remain high on the goods with greatest potential for the poorest countries, scuh as textiles, leather and agricultural commodities.

It should, however, be noted that a number of devloping countries have improved their export performance substantially and several of them figure in the list of the top 20 exporters.

Despite the different problems and discriminations, there are chances of developing countries benefiting from trade. Basic trade theory argues that poor people gain from trade liberalization. Developing countries have a comparative advantage in abundant, low-cost, unskilled labour. If they concentrate on goods whose production is simple and labour intensive, greater integration into global markets should increase their exports and output, raising the demand for unskilled labour and raising the incomes of the poor relative to those of the non-poor.

It is criticised that developed nations receive most of the FDI. A very small number of the developing countries, which are the relatively developed or large or fast growing in the developing world account for the lion's share of the FDI flows to his category. What the critics do not appreciate is that, as foreign investment flows are based on economic rational, it is unrealistic to expect the pattern of flow to be different.

Another criticism is that the liberalisation increases the economic inequality. Even in China, the liberalisation has created many island of affluence. If inequality increases because of the worsening of the living conditions of the poor, it certainly is unjustifiable. But, if the increase in inequality is the result of improving the economic conditions of a section, while there is no economic deterioration of any section, or because of the disproportionate benefits, the question is whether the economic progress of some sections should be curbed so that there will not be a widening of the inequality.

❒

2

Strategic Decision and Planning in Business

A strategy is defined as, "a unified, comprehensive, and integrated plan that relates to the strategic advantages of the firm to the challenges of the environment. It is designed to ensure that the basic objectives of the enterprise are achieved through proper execution by the organisation."

Alfred D. Chandler defines strategy as, "determination of the basic long-term goals and objectives of an enterprise and the adoption of the courses of action and the allocation of resources necessary for carrying out these goals."

Strategy is defined by Arthur Sharplin as, "a plan or course of action which is of vital, pervasive, or continuing importance to the organisation as a whole."

James Brain Quinn defines the term strategy as, "the pattern of plan that integrates an organisation's major goals, policies and action sequences into a cohesive whole."

The analysis of various definitions of strategy given above presents the following points:

(i) Strategy is a central understanding of the strategic management process.

(ii) Strategy is the determination of basic long-term goals and objectives of an organisation.

(iii) Determining the courses of action to attain the predetermined goals and objectives.

(iv) Developing the company from its present position to the desired future position.

(v) Set of decision-making rules making a common thread.

(vi) Allocating the necessary resources for implementing the course of action.

(vii) The common thread pulls the policies, plans, goals, objectives of the different functional areas of business such as finance, marketing, production/operations and human resources together and interweaves them as a unified comprehensive and integrated plan, action and evaluation.

(viii) Enterprise devotes its hard-won resources to projects that employ its set of core competencies, the primary skills within the organisation.

(ix) Identify factors in the political and social environment that requires careful monitoring.

(x) Set a clear direction.

(xi) Enterprise knows its strength and weaknesses compared with those of its competitors.

(xii) The competitive firm should have a rational, clear-headed notion, purged of wishful thinking of *(i)* mission *(ii)* its external competitive environment (for analyzing opportunities and threats) and *(iii)* its internal capabilities (including strengths and weaknesses).

(xiii) Recognise which competitor's actions need critical attention.

Strategy is thus, the conscious and rational management exercise which involves defining and achieving an organisation's objectives and implementing its missions. The perspective of the exercise is provided by what an organisation intends to do. The active formulation of strategy is known as strategy planning.

Effecitve formal strategy contains three essential elements *viz.*, *(i)* most important objectives to be achieved, *(ii)* the most significant policies guiding or limiting action and *(iii)* major action sequences that are to accomplish the defined goals within the limits set.

Effective strategies develop around a few key concepts and thrusts, which give them cohesion, balance and focus. Strategy deals not just with the unpredicatable but also with the unknownable. Complex business organisations have a number of hierarchically related and mutually supporting strategies.

CONCEPT OF STRATEGY

Strategy refers to decisions bearing on the future of an enterprise defining its direction and scope in the long run. These decisions ideally involve matching of resources to the changing environment, and determining what the enterprise ought to be doing in the years to come and how it should position itself to take advantage of the future market opportunities. Strategy may thus be defined as "the pattern of an organisation's responses to its environment over time". It implies that strategy may or may not involve explicit formulation of what the organisation intends to do. In other words, whether or not an organisation formulates a strategy, it is presumed to have established a relationship with its environment and hence there is a strategy which can be examined and described, even though it is not spelt out in so many words.

Thus, many business firms may be said to have a strategy even before there is explicit formulation of the strategy. Sooner or later, however, management of every organisation is required to engage in active formulation of a strategy or strategic planning. Strategy then becomes a process of taking decisions relating to the future of the organisation. This involves consideration of basic objectives, major policies and the means to be employed to achieve the objectives.

While shaping the future of an organisation, strategic decisions often mould the organisational identity and character deciding whether the organisation will continue to be in the same line of business, or combine new lines of activity with the existing business, enter new market segments, or seek to acquire a dominant position in the same market, and so on.

The concept of strategy has been defined by Vancil as follows:

> "The strategy of an ogranisation which may be expressed or implied is a conceptualisation of: *(1)* The long-term objectivés or purposes of the organisation; *(2)* The broad constraints and policies that currently restrict the scope of the organisation's activities; and *(3)* The current set of plan and near-term goals that have been adopted in the expectation of contributing to the achieving of the organisation's objectives."

Functionally, strategy may be said to provide the broad contours of a firm's business. It sets fourth specific guidelines by which the firm can conduct its search, and supplements the firm's objectives with decision rules which narrow its selection process to the most attractive opportunities. Hence, strategic decisions are primarily concerned with external rather than internal problems, and more specifically with the selection of the product-mix which the firm will produce and the markets to which it will sell, thus establishing an "impedance match" between the organisation and its environment.

Master Strategy and Programme Strategy

According to Schendel and Hatten, strategy refers to the basic goals and objectives of the organisation, the major programmes of action chosen to reach these goals and objectives, and major patterns, resource allocation used to relate the organisation to its environment. Based on this definition of strategy, a distinction may be made between "Master Strategies" and "Programme Strategies". Master strategies refer to the determination of the mission and long-term objectives of an organisation and the policies necessary for achieving the mission and objectives. Programme strategies are specific action plans drawn up to accomplish any established objectives with a timeframe. Thus, if an organisation has set the long-term objectives of growth in turnover, it may require programme strategies involving improvement in product design, or market penetration, or sales promotion.

Strategic decisions are different from operating decisions which relate to day-to-day activities or current operations, *e.g.*, resource allocation among functional areas and product lines, scheduling, operating, monitoring performance and applying controls, all aimed at maximising profitability of current operations through pricing and marketing policies, production planning and scheduling, inventory managmenet and control.

Strategic decisions also differ from administrative decisions which are concerned with structuring the firm's resources so as to create a maximum performance potential, *i.e.*, decisions concerned with establishing authority-responsibility relationships, work flows, communication, distribution channels, location of facilities as well as acquisition and development of resources, developing sources of raw materials supply, personnel training and development, financing and acquisition of plant and equipment.

IMPORTANCE OF STRAGETY

The importance of strategy is well evidenced in business history of India and other countries. There are various examples which may be cited to show that underlying the success or failure of business enterprises over time, was the ability or inability of management to formulate policies and plans to guide their destiny. Let us look into some instances.

The history of American railroad (railway) companies may be cited as a classic case of one kind. At the turn of the 20th century, these companies were at the height of prosperity. They enjoyed unprecedented loyalty of the investors. Stock prices soared and even European monarchs invested heavily in the stocks. No other form of transportation could compete with railroads in speed, flexibility, durability, economy and growth potentials. If the railroad tycoons were told by any one that in 30 years they would be flat on their backs, broke and pleading for Government subsidy, they would have thought he was a lunatic. Such a future was unimaginable. But the impossible did happen, the stock prices slumped and the companies were on the verge of bankruptcy. This was because the railroads failed to anticipate the type of changes that would take place. The stock prices crashed as new ways of meeting the transportation needs developed, and the railroads failed to capitalise on the changes.

Stewart Howe in his study of thirty firms in the Dundee jute industry found how strategic decision-making by the firms in the face of declining demand made all the difference in the results which followed. Summarising his conclusions, Howe observed, "The rapid contraction of the Dundee jute industry over the period 1967-74 in the face of competition from polypropylene was met by a variety of reactions on the part of the thirty firms which comprised the industry at the beginning of that period. The variety of strategic reactions of these firms, the fact that different strategies were adopted by similarly placed businesses, and the varying degree of success achieved by these businesses, all highlighted the way in which arriving at and implementing correct strategies can have a significant impact upon the destiny of business organisations."

The growth and diversification which have taken place over the years in Indian companies like Reliance Industries Ltd., Hindustan Lever, Transport Corporation of India, Chidambaram Group of Companies, Bajaj Auto, Arvind Mills Ltd., Ranbaxy Laboratories, and others, are clearly based on strategic management decisions about the future direction of business.

The phenomenal growth of Reliance Industries Ltd. since its inception in 1966, has made it one of India's largest private sector companies. Starting with the manufacture of high quality polyester fabrics (with the brands name 'Vimal'), its product-mix now consists of polyester fabrics, polymers, fibre intermediates, chemicals, textiles, and oil and gas.

M.A. Chidambaram, Chairman of the Chidambaram Group of Companies, started the Automobile Products of India in 1946 in Mumbai, manufacturing the well-known Lambretta scooters. He then turned his attention to the farmers, and in 1969 set up the fertilizer plant at Tuticorin under the now famous flagship company, Southern Petrochemical Industries Corporation (SPIC). The other flagship company of the group is MAC Industries. The group is now widely diversified and has a total turnover of more than Rs. 4,000 crores. Its main business include fertilizers, chemicals petrochemicals, foods, electrical machinery, transport and finance.

Companies have also faced reverses for venturing into new business ignoring the implications of such strategies. A typical case is that of Jain Group of Companies. This is the story of a very successful company's ambitions gone haywire. Jain Irrigation Systems Ltd. (JISL), the flagship company of the group, had its niche in the business of micro-irrigation systems. It grew phenomenally from a Rs. 2.5 crore turnover in 1988 to become a Rs. 250 crore integrated agri-business company within a decade. Encouraged by its immense success, the company diversified into all possible areas, such as granite, computer software and financial services, food processing and plastics, tele-communication and computer hardware. As the Managing Director of JISL put it, "We wanted to be a global corporation. Thus we diversified into all possible areas where we saw an opportunity." The misjudgment of the management led to massive losses for the year ending June 30, 1997, which cast a shadow on the future of the group. For the first time in corporate history, the chairman of the group apologised to the investors through a half-page ad in a mainline daily. It read, "I am sad that, for the first time since our inception, we have fared badly. We ventured into unknown areas like finance, information technology and granite at the cost of our core business.... I feel it is my duty to account for, to own up, to admit misjudgements, to apologise."

CRITERIA FOR EFFECTIVE STRATEGY

Although each strategic situation is unique, there are some common criteria that tend to explain an effective strategy. Criteria for effective strategy include:

(i) **Clear, Decisive Objectives.** All efforts should be directed towards clearly understood, decisive and attainable overall goals. All goals need not be written down or numerically precise but they must be understood and be decisive.

(ii) **Maintaining the Initiative.** The strategy preserves freedom of action and enhances commitment. It sets the pace and determines the course of events rather than reacting to them.

(iii) **Flexibility.** The strategy must purposely be built in resources, buffers and dimension for flexibility and manoeuvre. Reserved capabilities, planned maneuverability and repositioning allow one to use minimum resources while keeping competitors at a relative disadvantages.

(iv) Concentration. The strategy concentrates superior power at the place and time likely to be decisive. The strategy must define precisely what will make the enterprise superior in power, best in critical dimensions in relation to its competitors. A distinctive competency yields greater success with fewer resources.

(v) Coordinated and Committed Leadership. The strategy should provide responsible, committed leadership for each of its major goals. Care should be taken in selecting the leaders in such a way that their own interest and values match with the requirements of their roles. Commitment but not acceptance is the basic requirement.

(vi) Security. The organisation should secure or develop resources required, securely maintain all vital operating points for the enterprise, an effective intelligence system to prevent the effects of surprises by the competitors.

(vii) Surprise. The strategy should make use of speed, secrecy and intelligence to attack exposed or unprepared competitors at an unexpected time. Thus surprise and correct time are important.

FORMS AND KINDS OF STRATEGIES

Strategy is a plan—some sort of conciously intended course of action. Some of them may be unrealised. Some action, may emerge in the meanwhile. These two form into a realised strategy as shown in figure given below:

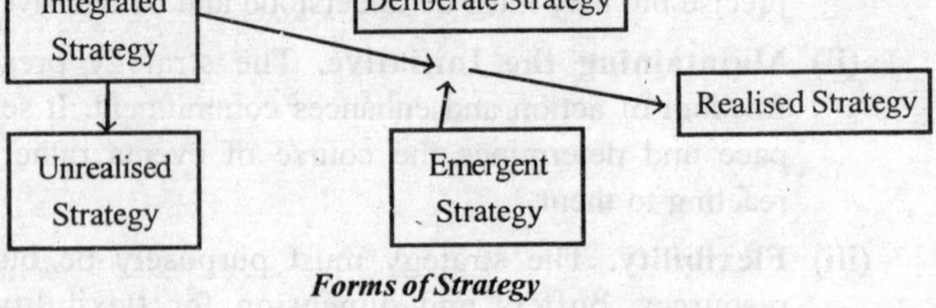

Forms of Strategy

The various forms and kinds of Strategies may be described as follows:

1. **Planned Strategy.** Precise intentions are formulated and articulated by a central leadership, and backed up by formal controls to ensure their surprise-free implementation in an environment that is benign, controllable, or predicatable (to ensure no distortion of intentions); these strategies are highly deliberate.
2. **Ideological Strategy.** Intentions exist as the collective vision of all the members of the organisation, controlled through strong shared norms; the organisation is often pro-active vis-a-vis its environment; these strategies are rather deliberate.
3. **Entrepreneurial Strategy.** Intentions exist as the personal, unarticulated visions of a single leader, and so are adaptable to new opportunities; the organisation is under the personal control of the leader and located in a protected niche in its environment; these strategies are relatively deliberate but can emerge too.
4. **Umbrella Strategy.** A leadership in partial control of organisational actions defines strategic targets or boundaries within which others must act (for example, that all new products be high priced and at the technological cutting edges, although what these actual products are to be left is to emerge); as a result, strategies are partly deliberate (the boundaries) and partly emergent (the patterns within them); this strategy can also be called deliberately emergent, in that the leadership purposefully allows others the flexibility to manoeuvre and form patterns within the boundaries.
5. **Disconnected Strategy.** Members or subunits loosely coupled to the rest of the organisation produce patterns in the streams of their own actions in the absence of, or in direct contradiction to the central or common intentions of the organisation at large; the strategies can be deliberate for those who make them.

6. **Process Strategy.** The leadership controls the process aspects of strategy (who gets hired and so gets a chance to influence strategy, what structures they work within, etc.), leaving the actual content of strategy to others; strategies are again partly deliberate (concerning process) and partly emergent (concerning content), and deliberately emergent.
7. **Consensus Strategy.** Through mutual adjustment, various members converge on patterns that pervade the organisation in the absence of central or common intentions; these strategies are rather emergent in nature.
8. **Imposed Strategy.** The external environment dictates patterns in actions, either through direct imposition (say by an outside owner or by a strong customer) or through implicity pre-empting or bounding organisational choice (as in a large airline that must fly jumbo jets to remain viable); these strategies are organisationally emergent, although they may be internalised and made deliberate.

That is why every organisation necessarily formulate strategies. it is hereby stated that strategy is necessary in view of the following reasons:

1. To have rules to guide the search for new opportunities both inside and outside the firm.
2. To take high quality project decisions.
3. To have an assurance that the firm's overall resource allocation pattern is efficient.
4. To have and develop internal ability to anticipate change.
5. To develop measures to judge whether a particular opportunity is a rare one or whether much better ones are likely to develop in the future.
6. To save time, money and executive talent.
7. To utilise the delay principle that is delay the commitment until an opportunity is on hand.
8. To identify, develop and exploit potential opportunities.

LEVELS OF STRATEGY

Analytically three levels of strategy are worthnoting:

1. Corporate-level strategy.
2. Business-level strategy, and
3. Functional-level strategy.

At the corporate level, strategic decisions relate to organisation-wise policies and are most useful in the case of multi-divisional companies or firms having wide-ranging business interests. The nature of strategic decisions at the corporate level tend to be value-oriented, conceptual and less concrete than decisions at the business or functional level. There is also greater risk, cost and profit potential as well as greater need for flexibility associated with corporate-level strategic activities. These are natural outcomes of the futuristic, innovative and pervasive character of corporate-level strategy. Major financial policy decisions involving acquisition, diversification and structural redesigning belong to the category of corporate strategy.

At the business level, decision-makers are primarily concerned with the immediate industry of product-market issues, and with policies bearing on the integration of the functional units. Business-level strategic decisions translate the general statements of direction and intent generated at the corporate level into concrete functional objectives and strategies for divisions or strategic business units (SBUs). Strategic decisions at the business level should include policies involving new product development, marketing mix, research and develpment, personnel, etc.

Corporate strategy may thus be differentiated from business strategy in two respects: Corporate strategy applies to the whole enterprise while business strategy defines the choice of product or service and market of individual business within the firm. Thus, business strategy has a relatively narrower connotation. Secondly, business strategy determines how a company will compete in a given business and position itself among competitors. Corporate strategy defines the business in which a company will compete, particularly focusing on resources to convert distinctive competence into competitive advantage.

Functional strategy involves decision-making at the operational level with respect to specific functional areas—production, marketing, personnel, finance, etc. Decisions at the functional level are often described as 'tactical' decisions. While corporate and business-level strategies are concerned with "doing the right things", functional strategies stress on "doing things right". But these decisions are necessarily guided by overall strategic considerations and must be consistent with the framework of business strategy. Thus, for example, marketing policy decisions should provide guidelines for marketing management in accordance with the chosen strategy providing the overall direction of business.

The importance of functional strategies, or operational strategies, also arises from their contribution to other levels of strategy. Particularly, such contributions may be important in terms of how an organisation seeks to be competitive. Indeed, in many cases, the success of business level strategy depends to a large extent on the decisions made and activities undertaken at the functional or operational level.

Corporate strategy has two main aspects: *(i)* Formulation of strategy or strategic planning, and *(ii)* Strategy implementation.

(I) Formulation of Strategy or Strategic Planning

Formulation of strategy involves deciding what the strategy should be. In other words, it involves decision-making by corporate management that:

(a) determines, shapes and reveals its objectives, purposes or goals;

(b) produces the principal policies and plans for achieving these goals; and

(c) defines the business the company intends to be in, the kind of economic and human organisation it intends to be, and the nature of the economic and non-economic contribution it intends to make to its shareholders, *i.e.*, the employees, customers, shareholders and the community.

Strategic planning is thus defined as "the process of deciding on objectives, on the changes in the objectives, on the resources used to attain these objectives, and on the policies that are to govern the acquisition, use and disposition of these resources." Essentially, it is the determination of the basic long-term goals and objectives in an enterprise and the adoption of courses of action and the allocation of resources necessary for carrying out these goals.

In the nature of things, strategy formulation requires *(i)* identification of opportunities and threats in the company's environment along with the estimate of risks attaching to the discernible alternatives, and *(ii)* appraisal of the company's strengths and weaknesses, and objective assessment of its actual or potential capacity to take advantage of perceived market needs or cope with the attendant risks.

The strategic alternative which results from a matching of opportunity and corporate capability at an acceptable level of risk is what is called an economic strategy. But the formulation of corporate strategy also requires consideration of what alternative is preferred by senior executives quite apart from the economic considerations. Personal values, aspirations, and ideals do influence the choice of strategy. Thus, along with the intellectual process of ascertaining what a company might be able to do in terms of environmental opportunity, and of deciding what it can do in terms of capability, what the executives want to do in terms of preferred values has also a bearing on strategic decisions. Formulation of strategy also includes consideration of the corporate obligation to segments of society, shareholders in the community. In short, then, the four major determinants of strategy may be said to consist of *(i)* external opportunities and constraints, *(ii)* internal capabilities, competence and resources, *(iii)* personal values of the executives including propensity to assume risks, and *(iv)* obligations to society and the shareholders.

The purpose of strategy is to define the nature of relationship between a firm and its environment. According to Shirley, Peters and El-Ansary, there are five key decisions which may be said to comprise the overall strategy of any company, *viz.*, *(i)* customer-mix, *(ii)* product-mix, *(iii)* geographic limits of the market to be served, *(iv)* competitive emphasis, and *(v)* objectives. Thus, the determination of strategy involves answering a set of questions in the relevant areas such as:

What is to be the target group of customers?

What are their needs and preferences? What segment of the market do they represent?

What is the geographic areas of the market to be covered? What will be the market niche?

What specific products or services should be produced?

Which products should receive the maximum emphasis? What ought to be the price-quality relationship of the product lines?

What are the distinctive characteristics of the product?

Can these characteristics be differentiated from those of similar competing products?

What are the end-uses to be served by the products?

At what point of time should the new products be launched?

What factors should be stressed by the company to secure a unique competitive advantage?

Will it be the Price, Quality, Service, Design, Special characteristics?

What else?

What could be done better than the comeptitors?

What are the basic objects to be pursued?

What is the rate of return on investment to be sought? What should be the gross profit margin of sales?

What are the growth objectives to be pursued with respect to sales, total assets, net worth or market share, and over what time period?

What is the minimum return of investment to be achieved?

The five basic decision which are essentially the components of strategy may be regarded as the 'first order' decisions to be made by executives. They are formulative rather than implemental. They define the nature of firm's relationship with the environment; they do not indicate how the relationship will be established. Once delineated, they provide direction to the lower-order implemental decisions with respect to production, marketing, finance, and other areas. From this it follows that decisions on marketing, financing, resources allocation, production processes, pricing, etc., do not constitute a part of strategy.

It should be obvious that the basic decision areas which define strategy are interrelated. A definition of the customer-mix can hardly be possible without deciding on the product-mix; similarly, determination of the product-mix presupposes the decision on the customer-mix. Likewise, objectives defining the desired profitability, growth, and market share can be formulated only in the light of the other elements of strategy because objectives which may be considered feasible in one industry may not be so in another industry. Besides, ongoing firms are usually subject to various environmental constraints (economic, financial, social and political) which have a strong bearing on the setting of objectives.

While the decisions constituting the elements of strategy are interrelated and cannot be considered piecemeal, they are also not sequential. For instance, the executives of a company perceiving their strong competitive advantage in designing products may seek to enter a new product market given the potential demand projection. Here the competitive advantage is defined before deciding on the product market to be entered. On the other hand, another company may decide to enter a new market on the basis of the perceived consumer needs and thereafter seek to develop its competitive advantage. In this case, the product-market decision precedes the definition of competitive advantage. Hence the development of strategy is stated to be an interactive, interdependent process rather than a sequential one.

(II) Strategy Implementation

Besides the formulation of choice of strategy, the organisational process related to corporate strategy also involves decision-making for implementation of the strategy. These decisions primarily comprise administrative policies regarding mobilisation of resources, designing an appropriate organisation structure, establishing the organisational process of performance measurement, compensation and maangement development, so as to accomplish the objectives. The core of strategy implementation may be said to lie in the choice of an organisational structure, organisational processes, and pattern of leadership appropriate for accomplishing the chosen strategy.

Designing an appropriate organisation structure is of crucial importance as it involves *(a)* the relative ranking of key tasks of the strategy, *(b)* assessment of the competence, working styles, and commitment of key personnel, and *(c)* determination of a hierarchical structure consistent with the distribution of formal authority and the design of an information system for the reintegration of the sub-dividend tasks. The organisational processes for implementing strategy have implications with respect to the interdependent and multi-dimensional variable like *(a)* motivation and incentives, *(b)* standards and measurement of performance, and *(c)* the system of restraints and control. The processes are of vital significance with their impact on organisational behaviour. Decisions bearing on organisational processes require consideration of such issues as the alternative criteria for determining compension, the significance of financial and non-financial incentives, the need for using different quantitative and qualitative criteria in the setting of standards and evaluation of performance, and the scope of informal social controls as well as formal control devices.

MODES OF STRATEGY-MAKING

Strategy-making is a complex process. It involves linking together of a number of important decisions to form strategies. To describe the strategy making process in terms of precise modes is difficult, for in reality company executives acting under different conditions may find it necessary to combine or alternate the modalities of decision making suited to the circumstances. However, for analytical purposes, three modes of strategy making have been distinguished. According to Henry Mintzberg, different combinations of these modes provide a more realistic description of the process.

To understand the combined or mixed modalities of strategy-making, it is first necessary to know the characteristics of the following modes:

(a) Adaptive Mode. Adaptive strategy-making process is basically remedial in nature. It is thus called 'disjointed incrementalism' involving decision by steps in the face of a complex environment. The executive in this mode is concerned with solving problems of immediate importance rather than developing long-range strategies; this may imply bargaining with suppliers, compromising with competitors, or reducing conflicts among coalitions of interest groups within the organisation. The adaptive mode is thus characterised.

(b) Planning Mode. The planning mode essentially involves decision-making in anticipation of a future state that the company wants to be in. Strategy-making in this mode is ideally based on a study of the *(i)* evaluation of the company's strengths and weaknesses, *(ii)* evaluation of the external and internal opportunities and problems, *(iii)* Fundamental socio-economic purposes of the organisation and *(iv)* values of top management. The following characteristics are thus discernible in this mode:

(i) Strategy-making depends a great deal on the role of analysts and planners as aids to the executives. This ensures application of scientific techniques and tools of analysis in the planning process and it involves a systematic and structured approach to the solution of problems as also to the task of assessing the cost and benefits of alternative proposals including analysis of risks.

(ii) It is a comprehensive process which produces a set of integrated decisions and strategies and ensures the development of a strategic direction.

(c) Entrepreneurial Mode. The entrepreneur is defined as a creative thinker, an individual who combines in himself the role of innovator and risk-bearer. He is tough and pragmatic in disposition and is motivated by a powerful need for achievement and independence. The entrepreneurial mode of strategy-making thus reflects the following characteristics:

(i) The most dominant goals in the entrepreneurial mode consist of growth and expansion in terms of assets, market share and turnover.

(ii) It is dominated by an active search for opportunities. The focus in this mode is on opportunities rather than problem solving.

(iii) With bold decisions taken in the face of uncertainty, strategy is the entrepreneurial organisation moves forward by unusual leaps and tries with corresponding gains.

(iv) In the entrepreneurial mode, power rests with one man, the chief executive, who is capable of taking bold decisions on the basis of personal power or charisma. With centralised power, the entrepreneurial personality is characterised by an unwillingness to submit to authority, an inability to work with it, and a consequent need to escape from it.

COMBINED MODES OF STRATEGY-MAKING

Even though conditioning factors might determine the appropriate strategy-making mode suited to particular organisations, it is but natural that organisations may find it useful to adopt a combination of modes suited to their respective needs at a point of time at different times. Several possible combinations may thus be distinguished as follows:

(i) Organisations usually pass through different stages in the course of their existence. A young organisation during the early stage of its life is generally prone to use the entrepreneurial mode for growth and expansion. Gradually it loses the spur due to its large size and consequent problems, including the emergence of many power-groups. The adaptive mode becomes more suited at this stage of development. With maturity and consolidation of top management it may be inclined to use the planning mode.

(ii) Executives with entrepreneurial outlook and qualities may avail of new opportunities with bold decisions at the same time having a systematic plan of growth.

(iii) This combination may be typically found in a manufacturing company which finds it beneficial to use the planning mode in financial strategy-making, the entrepreneurial mode in marketing, the adaptive mode in the personnel areas.

(iv) In a rapidly changing environment with unpredictable outcomes, an organisation may find it necessary to move one step at a time with a flexible approach to decision-making along with an underlying sense of direction towards specific goals.

(v) Typically an executive heading an organisation and having absolute power may find it difficult to achieve further growth on the basis of his own personal initiative. Instead of delegating authority he may find it convenient to take incremental decisions and avoid risk thus conforming to the adaptive mode.

STRATEGIC DECISION MAKING

Various theories have been suggested about how decisions are made. Let us examine these first. Most writers focus on three approaches: Intuitive-emotional, rational-analytical and behavioural-political:

1. Intuitive-Emotional. The opposite of the rational decision maker is the intuitive decision maker. This decision maker prefers habit or experience, gut feeling, reflective thinking, and instinct, using the unconscious mental processes. Intuitive decision makers consider a number of alternatives and options, simultaneously jumping from one step in analysis or search to another and back again.

Some who prescribe intuition of judgement as the preferred approach point out that in many cases, judgment may lead to "better" decisions than "optimizing" techniques. For example, consider sensitivity analysis on a tool such as the economic order quantity. EOQ models suggest that there is an optimal order quantity considering trade-offs of ordering and holding costs. Yet you can stray far from optimal in cost cases without a very significant impact on total cost differential. Here, then, judgement concerning other factors in the decision situation could lead to a better decision about order quantities, rather than holding fast to deciding what the rational model prescribes. In fact, the timing of when to implement a decision based on the analysis may require an intuitive feel for what the dates are telling you. In many cases, judgement such as this might be preferred stockable to relying on the analysis. Recognize, then, that analytical models are tools to help the decisions maker in improving judgement.

Those opposed to this approach argue that

(a) The rational approach ensures that adequate attentions is given to consequences of decisions before big mistakes are made.

(b) It does not effectively use all the tools available to modern decision makers.

2. Rational-Analytical. In this model, the decision maker is a unique actor whose behaviour is intelligent and rational. The decision is the choice this actor makes, in full awareness of all available feasible alternatives, to maximize advantages. The decision maker therefore considers all the alternatives as well as the consequences of all the possible choice orders these consequences in the light of a fixed scale of preferences, and chooses the altenatives that procures the maximum gain.

This is the oldest decision theory. It prescribes a rational, conscious, systematic, and analytical approach. It has been criticized because.

(a) Decision makers make decisions with more than a maximization of objectives in mind. They tend to "satisfice," that is, make a decision expected to yield a satisfactory, as opposed to an "optimal". outcome, Besides, the objectives may change.

(b) The decision maker is often not a unique actor but part of a multiparty decision situation.

(c) Decision makers are not rational enough or informed enough to consider all alternatives or know all the consequences and information is costly.

3. Political-Behavioural. A third model suggests that real decision makers must consider a variety of pressures from other people affected by their decisions. An organisation interacts with a variety of shareholders in series of interdependent exchange relationships. Unions exchange labour for decent wages and job security. Customers exchange money for products and services. Owners exchange capital for expected returns on investment. Suppliers exchange inputs for money and continued business. Government exchanges protection and economic security for taxes. Even competitors exchange information with one another through trade associations or other contacts. The list of agents and expectation goes on.

Each shareholder gives the organisation something and expects something in return. To the extent an organisation has favourable exchange relationship gets a bit more than given compared with other organization and stockholders. it has more power. More powerful stockholders have more influence over decisions because the organisation is more dependent on these stockholders. A majority stockholder can have a greater influence on decisions about reinvestment versus dividend payout than if stock is widely held by many small owners. If the firm is labour intensive more attention may be paid to union leaders demands for better wages than to the desires of stockholders for more profit, because the union might shut the firm down. Given these realities, decision makers do a juggling act to meet the demands of the various stockholders. Through political compromise they attempt to merge competing demands so that a coalition of interests emerges that will support the decision.

The mode of decision making is descriptive theory suggesting that the organisation in which the decision maker works limits the choices available. Decisions are made when the several people involved in the process agree that they have found a solution. They do this in mutual adjustment and negotiation following the rules of the game the way decisions have been made in the organisation in the past. The decision maker must consider whether the decision can be implemented politically.

ELEMENTS OF STRATEGIC DECISIONS

Strategic decision is a major choice of actions concerning allocation of resources and contribution to the achievement of organisational objectives directly. Though the various characteristics of strategic decision may vary from organisation to organisation because of their different nature, the elements of strategic decision are somewhat common to all the organisations. The strategic decision normally has three elements:

A. Commitement which directs some part of the organisation to undertake the course of action, makes the personnel involved responsible for attaining the objective and allocates to them the resources necessary for the same, the commitment element.

B. Desired result or objective to be achieved through the implementation of the decision, the result elements; and

C. Course of action or plan which specifies the work to be done to achieve the result, the action element.

Thus a strategy requires that a desired result and course of action be paired to the extent that they become completely interelated. Since business realities are quite complex, the decision making in strategic management goes through a complex process. However, a detailed descr ption of various elements of strategic decision may make the points clear.

(A) Result. Organisations are goal-directed and any organisational process including decision making, should also be goal-directed to meet the organisational objectives. Naturally, the value of a decision and the associated action is related to the dispatch with which the goal is achieved. The result element of strategic decision is a specially defined objective or statement of desired future accomplishment which will contribute to the company's overall purpose. Subsequently this becomes the basis for measuring the effectiveness of the strategy. The first test of completeness for a strategy, therefore, is whether a pertinent result element has been clearly specified . It forces the clear specification of a matching action element so that the objectives are achieved. It is quite a normal practice to express the result or objective in quantitative terms, such as, sales volume, market share, profit margin, expense reduction by certain percentage, etc. These are needed for the people at lower level in the organisation but they do not reflect why a matching action element is to be undertaken. As such the result is not related specifically to the action element of the strategic decision. The result element of strategic decision must specify what specific result is to be achieved and why. Thus the result element in strategic decision may be defined in terms of purposes that the organisation may adopt and the relationship which exists between these purposes and the various spheres of interest in organisation's business environment. Such result elements may be expressed in the form of technological leadership, market leadershiup, profitability, social contribution, employment, strengthening the national economy, and so on.

(B) Action. A stated result or objectives does not become a useful element of a strategic decision until it is paired with a pertinent action programme. Strategic decision is action-oriented and directed towards the controlling aspect of the environment. A decision may be interpreted as the intervening variable which may ultimately lead to the end result variables. The action element of strategic decision specifies what work must be done and how, in order to accomplish its matching set of results. Though there may be many alternatives opened to the organisation concerned, the various alternatives may be described in two forms: *(i)* those strategies and actions which define what type of business the organisation is to be in particularly in terms of its products and markets; and *(ii)* those strategies and actions which specify how the particular type of business is to be established, maintained and developed. These may result into a number of grand and functional strategies depending on the nature of organisation in terms of its size, age, area of operations, type of environment and management approach towards strategic management. The organisation may adopt a number of alternative strategies, such as growth strategy, stability strategy, or retrenchement strategy as grand strategies and market development, product development, financial and administration, and personnel as functional strategies depending on the situation.

(C) Commitment. A management decision is not strategic unless it has been translated into a set of action decision whereby the organisation's resources are committed for a particular course of action. Committing decision relates to both present competitive actions and the assignment of development work leading to future. Commitement of resources includes the allocation of resources on various actions and since these resources are utilised for the actions concerned, these can not be got back except in the form of their result. Since the commitment of resources involves future period, the appropriate commitemnt period should be selected. What the commitment principle implies is that long term planning is not really planning for future decision but rather planning for future impact of today's decisions. Thus a decision is a commitment, normally of funds, direction of action, or reputation. The commitment elements of the strategic decision relates to who, where, and when with respect to the proposed action. These three were to determine the assignment of responsibility, locus of action, and timing of action:

(i) Timing element is the most important element of commitment principle and development and implementation of strategy. This relates to the timing of taking action so that the organisation stands to certain benefits as compared to its competitors.

(ii) Decision regarding who will be taking up the jobs of actions is an important aspect of commitment element of strategic decision. Sometimes, this is not given adequate attention on the presumption that either organisational plan or past precedent will provide answer for the problem. However, adequate care must be taken that new strategic assignments are clarified. Such an exercise is specially required when there is : *(a)* entirely new job requirement calling for specialised skills not previously needed; *(b)* creation of separate operation whose personnel would devote full time to the new strategy area; and *(c)* need for creating internal competition as a basis for sharper evaluation of strategy.

(iii) The commitment decision should also specify where and under what circumstances implementation is to be effected. Thus locus of action element of commitment relates to what action is to be taken, who will do the work, and what are the competitive and other environmental circumstances of the strategy.

DIFFERENT ISSUES IN STRATEGIC DECISION MAKING

Being a complex process, strategic decision-making is difficult to perform. It is incomprehensible; it cannot be analysed and explained easily. Decision makers are unable to describe the exact manner in which strategic decisions are made. Like the working of the human mind, strategic decision making is fathomless. And rightly so, for it is based on complex mental processes which are not exposed to view.

For these reasons, no theoretical model, however, painstakingly formulated, can adequately represent the different dimensions of the process of strategic decision-making. Despite these limitations, we can still attempt to understand strategic decision-making by considering some important issues related to it. Following are these issues:

(A) Rationality. Rationality, in the context of strategic decision-making, means exercising a choice from among various alternative courses of action in such a way that it leads to the achievement of objectives in the best possible manner. The economists who support the maximising criterion consider a decision to be rational if it leads to profit maximisation. Behaviourists, who are the proponents of the satisfying concept, believe that rationality takes into account the constraints under which a decision maker operates. Incrementalists are of the opinion that the achievement of objectives depends on the bargaining process between different interested coalition groups existing in an organisation and therefore, a rational decision making process should take all these interest into consideration.

(B) Criteria for the process of decision-making requires objective-setting. These objectives serve as yardstick to measure the efficiency and effectiveness of the decision-making process. In this way, objectives serve as criteria for decision-making. There are three major viewpoints regarding setting criteria for decision-making:

(i) The first is the concept of maximisation. It is based on the thinking of economists who consider objectives as those attributes which are set at the highest point. The behaviour of the firm is oriented towards achieving these objectives and, in the process, maximising its returns.

(ii) The third view point is that of the concept of incrementalism. According to this, the behaviour of the firm is complex and the process of decision-making, which includes objective-setting, is essentially a continually-evolving political concensus-building. Through such an approach, the firm moves towards its objectives in small, logical and incremental steps.

(iii) The second view is based on the concept of satisfying. This envisages setting of objectives in such a manner that the firm can achieve them realistically through a process of optimisation.

(C) Individual Versus Group. Owing to the person-related factors, there are indiviual differences among decision makers. These differences matter in strategic decision-making. An organisation, possessing special characteristics, operates in a unique environment. Decision makers who understand an organisation's characteristics and its environment are in advantage position to undertake strategic decision-making. Individuals such as Chief Executives or entereprepreneurs play the most important role as strategic decision-maker. But when organisations become bigger and more complex and face an increasingly turbulent environment, individuals come together in groups for the purpose of strategic decision-making.

(D) Variability. It is a common observation that, given an identical set of conditions, two decision makers may reach totally different conclusions. This often happens during case discussion also. A case may be analysed differently by individuals in a group of learners and, depending on the differing perceptions of the problem and its solutions, they may arrive at different conclusions. Such things happen due to variability in decision-making. It also suggests that every situation is unique and there are no set formulas that can be applied in strategic decision-making.

(E) **Creativity**. To be creative, a decision must be original and different. A creative strategic decision-making process may considerably affect the search for alternatives where novel and untried means may be looked for and adopted to achieve objectives in an exceptional manner. Creativity, as a trait, is normally associated with individuals and is sought to be developed through techniques such as brainstorming. Readers may recall that one of the attitudinal objectives of a business policy course is to develop the ability to go beyond and think, which, in other words, is using creativity in strategic decision-making.

(F) **Person-related Factors.** There are a host of person related factors that play a role in decision-making. Some of these are age, education, intelligence, personal values, congnitive styles, risk-taking ability, and creativity. Attributes like age, knowledge, intelligence, risk-taking ability and creativity are generally supposed to play a positive role in strategic decision making. A cognitive style which enables a person to assimilate a lot of information, interrelate complex variables and develop an integrated view of the situation is specially helpful in strategic decision-making. Values, as enduring prescriptive beliefs, are culture-specific and important in matters of social responsibility and business ethics; issues that are important to strategic management.

APPROACHES TO STRATEGIC DECISION MAKING

As we know that strategic decision making process is complex and intriguing. Various researchers and authors have studied and described the manner in which such decision-making takes place. These different approaches have also been categorised by a few authors. We have attempted to understand the different approaches to strategic decision making under:

1. Intuitive-anticipatory. This approach is based on the intuition of, usually, a single person who is the promoter or chief executive of an organisation. He anticipates the future and takes strategic decisions accordingly. The process is implicit in the sense that the mental processes involved in decision-making are not readily evident. The basis of decision-making is intuition, judgement or hunch, which are the result of long years of experience in dealing with a variety of strategic problems. A few authors, including Herbert Simon, Rechard Cyert, James March and Henry Mintzberg have contributed to an understanding of this approach. It is difficult to provide an illustration of this approach. Owing to its inherent nature, the process of decision-making adopted under this approach is not clear and inexplicable and, therefore, cannot be reported.

2. Formal-structured. This approch involves systematic planning and set procedures. Since it is formal and structured, strategic problems are dealt with by a designated group of planners who follow a set procedure to arrive at decisions. Different types of planning system such as strategic planning, corporate planning or long-range planning are used. Most authors in strategic management use the formal-structured approach framework in their texts. As an illustration, we may consider the example of Larsen & Toubro (L & T), which adopts a formal strategic planning system. In essence, the company follows a three-stage process. The first stage is the diagnostic phase involving the setting of corporate mission, objectives and goals, and SWOT (strengths, weaknesses, opportunities and threats) analysis by each of the seven business group in the company. The second stage deals with providing directions through the choice of alternatives strategies to be adopted. The last phase is the implementation phase where the action plan is put into action.

3. Adaptive. The essence of the adaptive approach is on taking strategic decisions on the basis of how a change is perceived at a given point of time. With changing circumstances, the decisions are also reviewed. The basic for review of decisions is an estimation of the gap between the current position of the company and its objectives. Strategic decisions are meant to reduce such a gap. Circumstances are defined in terms of the environment. For an environment that is perceived to be stable, strategic decision are based on certainty. Where stability is less, and the future is risky, contingency planning systems are adopted. In an uncertain environment, the emphasis is on building up adaptive capability to respond to changes as and when they occur. This approach has been dealt with by authors like H. Igor Ansoff and Russell L. Ackoff. Many organisations exhibit the adoption of such an approach in the Indian business environment.

Mintzberg's classification of the modes of strategy making as entrepreneurial, adaptive, and planning, offers another theoretical framework which aids the understanding of the strategic decision-making process.

According to Mintzberg, three pure modes of strategy making could be defined. The entrepreneurial mode envisages an active search for opportunities by a person, usually the entrepreneur or chief executive, who takes bold and risky decisions and rapidly moves the organisation towards its objectives. In the adaptive mode, the emphasis is on solving short-term problems by adopting a reactive attitude and decisions are made in incremental steps based on negotiated settlements among different interest groups. The planning involves a systematic appraisal of the environment, assessment of internal capability and choosing courses of action in the form of meticulously formulated strategies. These three pure modes could be combined to form mixed modes like adaptive-entrepreneurial, adaptive-planning or entrepreneurial-planning modes. The method of strategy making may also differ with respect to different functional areas. Organisations may also adopt different modes at successive stages of their development.

Thus, there could be many different approaches to strategic decision-making. But to state that an organisation follows only a single approach at a time or only one approach all the time would be unrealistic. Real-life business situations offer countless examples of organisations and decision makers who adopt a combination of approaches.

4. Incremental. The incremental or, colloquially, the muddling through approach involves limiting the focus of strategic decision-making to a few alternatives at a time, that differ only marginally from one another. The choice of the best alternative is based on an iterative process of continually redefining problems so as to make them manageable. The end result is a negotiated settlement between different interest groups. Charles Lindblom has explained this approach through the concept of disjointed incrementalism. Most public sector companies in India, in their strategic decision-making, exhibit the adoption of an incremental approach. Owing to the various pulls and pressures between which public sector companies typically operate with regard to their objectives and goals, the strategic decision-making is based on negotiated settlement among different groups.

5. Entrepreneurial-opportunistic. This approach is characterised by a constant search for opportunities and exploiting them for the benefit of the organisation. Entrepreneurial strategic decision-making is based on the perception of opportunities, diagnosing them for the generation of alternatives, analysing the consequences and selecting the course of action that would best meet the objectives. Such an approach is generally adopted by entrepreneurs and family-business executives but may also be adopted by manager in organisations.

Many examples can be provided in the Indian context where this approach is adopted for strategic decision-making. The illustration of Dhirubhai Ambani, the founder-chairman of the Reliance group of companies, typifies the adoption of the entrepreneurial-opportunistic approach. Starting as a humble office member of staff in Burmah Shall, Ambani moved into spices exports and then to nylon yarn trading. It is in this business that he, in the early sixties, realised the importance of synthetic fabrics. Seizing upon the opportunity, Ambani laid the foundation of Reliance Textiles Ltd. a giant multi-product and multi-location compnay.

CONDITIONS FOR EFFECTIVE DECISION MAKING

Decision-making involves the selection of an alternative out of the several available alternatives. Thus alternative is put into action which will take place in future period. Thus, a manager is taking a decision for future conditions. In fact, long-range action is not a process of making the future decisions but a means of reflecting the future in today's decision. Conditions under which managers make decisions vary along a continuum from those of perfect certainty to those of complete uncertainty. This continuum may have three possible points depending upon the degree of certainty in the decision-making conditions: risk, uncertainty and certainty.

1. Risk. Most of the organisational decisions are made under the conditions of risk, that is, some information is available but these are not sufficient to answer all questions about the outcome of the decision. However, he has sufficient information for estimating the probability of outcomes. Probability can be defined as the percentage of times in which a particular outcome would occur if an action were repeated a very large number of times. There are three methods of estimating the probability under conditions of risk.

(a) Empirical probability is based on recording actual experience over a period of time and computing the percentage of time that each event has occurred. Managers can calculate his probability on the basis of various data available either with them or with outside the organisation. Life insurance companies generally compute probability of death on this basis.

(b) A prior probability is obtained through deductions from assumed conditions. For example, the probability of getting a head is 0.5 when a coin is tossed. Through the knowledge of the nature of coin, one can know the probability of results, though it is not possible to predict with certainty the outcome of any single toss.

(c) When the manager does not have sufficient data to calculate either a priori or empirical probability, he may estimate probability by his own exist. Such judgement, this is called subjective probability. This probability is less exact as compared to others. However, it is better to use subjective probability than just completely ignoring the probability of occurrence associated with various alternatives.

The assignment of probability is never so simple as it might appear. The decision-maker who finalises the assignment is the ultimate arbiter and different managers may assign varying estimates for various reasons. The risk preference of a manager may play key role in probability assignment. Various techniques have been developed to make decisions under the conditions of risk.

2. Uncertainty. Uncertainty conditions are those for which the manager feels he cannot develop probability estimates because he has no way of gauging the likehood of the various alternatives. Though managers assign probability to various alternatives based upon past knowledge and experience, there may be conditions where such probability assignment is not possible. In such cases, the conditional probability is assigned which suggests that the assigned probability holds true only when certain events happen:

(a) There are various alternatives for making decisions in such cases. Since the occurrence of the events is not known, the manager can apply equal probability to all states of nature of events. This is called the Laplace criterion.

(b) Maximin approach can be applied which is based on pessimism and the manager may ascertain the worst condition for each alternative.

(c) He may use optimism criterion commonly known as maximax. The manager may be optimistic in assigning the probability to various alternatives. Dealing with decisions under uncertainty is not an easy task. In the three approaches, a different strategy emerges as most favourable each time.

3. Certainty. If the manager has sufficient information about the elements affecting the outcomes of the decision, so that he can predict the otucome 100 per cent of time, the conditions of certainty exist. Such conditions exist when decisions involve actions in immediate future, and the manager has made such decisions a number of times with the same results. Under such conditions, he can use a deterministic model, the one in which all factors are assumed exact, with chance playing no role. Under such conditions of certainty, he does not need to analyse the chance elements.

Conditions for certainty exist in case of routine type of decisions in the organisation. Routine type of decisions are made in the context of day-to-day operations of the organisation. Mostly they are of repetitive type and relate to general functioning. Such decisions are taken in the conditions of certainty. For example, the allocation of resources to various product lines constitutes decision under certainty because the manager knows his resources and the amount of time it will take to process them into finished product. However, the conditions of certainty do not exist for most of the organisational decisions.

CONCEPT OF ORGANISATIONAL OBJECTIVES

Organisational objectives seek to direct the efforts of all memebers of a team while personal goals are motives of people working in the team. Efficiency is high when the two types of objectives are mutually supportive or compatible. Organisational objectives are the goals establsihed to guide the efforts of the company and each of its components. Objectives are variously referred to as purposes, goals, missions, or targets. The establishment of objectives is a very important step in planning. Planning can be effective only if objectives are carefully selected. A clear statement of purpose understood by one and all is the best guarantee of effective management. Objectives must be actionable, that is meaningful to the manager who is to achieve them. Objectives or goals must be specific and capable of accomplishment. They must be identified in such a wav that ultimate success or failure can be determined.

The foregoing description reveals the following characteristics of organisational objectives:

1. Objectives are Multiple. Every organisation has a number of economic, social and human objectives rather than a singe aim. As stated earlier, objectives are required in every area of business where the success and survival of the business is important. Every department or division has its own objectives in addition to the overall objectives of the organisation. Different objectives should be balanced with one another. A business firm has both general and specific objectives. General objectives include survival, growth, etc. while specific objectives are narrow in scope *e.g.*, to reduce absenteeism.

Organisational goals are sometimes divided into *(a)* maintenance goals, and *(b)* productivity goals. Maintenance goals are the expression of the existence of the enterprise, while productivity goals aim at improvements in performance.

2. Objectives are Basic Plans. Objectives are the standing plans which recurringly guide action. They are the basis of other plans such as policies, procedures, programmes, etc.

Objectives are the clear expressions of the purpose of an enterprise. Primary or major objective provide the principle reasons for the establishment of the enterprise while collateral objectives supplement and contribute to the primary objectives. Organisational objectives are the basis of long range planning whereas departmental objectives provide the basis for short range planning. Different organisations have different objectives and there is not universal set of objectives. Objectives must, however be practicable, consistent and clear cut. There must be proper coordination between major and derivative goals and between long range and short range objectives. Objectives should be specific, varifiable and well planned. There must be active participation of all concerned in the determination of objectives.

3. Objectives are the Ends. Objectives are the ultimate end or results towards which an organisation and its members strive at all times. All activities and resources of an enterprise are directed towards the achievement of common and specified objectives.

4. Objectives form a Chain. Objectives are arranged in a hierarchy which is known as the 'Ends and Means Chain.' Objectives of a lower order act as the means for the achievement of higher level objectives. For instance, the organisational objectives are more basic than the departmental objectives.

5. Objectives vary in Time Span. Objective may be long-term or short-term. Long term objectives refer to the objectives to be achieved over a long period of time while short-term objectives are to be achieved within a period of one to two years. Short-run objectives are steps towards long-term objectives.

SOME EXAMPLES OF OBJECTIVES

To ensure a steady growth in business so as to fulfil national expectations from BHEL and expand international operations:

(a) **Continuity.** To invest in human resources development, sustained research and development, strive for excellence in management and other long-range activities to ensure a leardership status for BHEL."

(b) **Image.** To build up a high degree of customer confidence by sustaining international excellence in product quality, performance and service, particularly in regard to supply of spares and after-sales service. To fulfil the expectation which stockholders like Government as owner, employees, customers and the country at large have from BHEL.

(c) **Profitability.** To provide a reasonable and adequate return on capital employed primarily through improvements in operational efficiency, capacity utilisation and productivity, and generate adequate internal resources to finance the company's growth.

The strategic objective formulated by another company have been stated as follows:

1. To employ the highest quality of people necessary to accomplish the prime objective and to provide them with opportunities to develop and apply their fullest abilities.
2. To ensure consistently increasing earnings per share to attain a satisfactory return on sharehoders' equity on a continuing basis and to provide consistently increasing dividends (the prime objective).
3. To have the company profit-oriented enterprise enagged in an important field of business with the ability to meet successfully the economic and social challenges of the future.

IMPORTANCE OF OBJECTIVES

Every rational human activity must have certain clear-cut objectives or goals. A manager, before performing his functions, must ask:what are the objectives of the activity he is going to manage? The answer to this question will serve many functions The objectives provide orientation by a future state of affairs which the organisation strives to realise. They set down guidelines for group activity. Objectives constitute a source of legitimacy which justifies the activities of the organisation and indeed its very existence. Moreover; objectives serve as standards for assessing the success of the organisation. Thus,objectives will check the members of the organisation from the route they have set for themselves.

Objectives are key to effective planning which is an important function of every manager. Clear objectives encourage consistency in managerial planning and decision-maketing over a period of time. An organisation having well defined objectives will not give up long-range development programmes and policies for short-term monetary gains, planning it is not related to certain objectives. It will be an empty mental exercise if it does determine what objectives are to be accomplished. Objectives represent not only the end-point of planning but also the end towards which other managerial activities like organising, directing and controlling are aimed. They provide direction not only to managerial activities but also to other activities. purchasing, production, marketing and financing are all directed towards the objectives of the enterprise.

The accpmplishment of objectives is necessary for the survival of any business enterprise. The management must specify the objectives in all areas on which the survival of the business depends. Well defined objectives in major areas of the business will help in achieving the following benefits:

(a) Managerial work with appropriate authority and capacity for independent decision is shared by a large number of managers. This may lead to disintegration in place of decentralisation unless it is a common goal. The objectives are to remove conflicts or misunderstanding of various individuals.

(b) Objectives provide the basis of control by clarifying the desired contribution of each job as well as each unit.

(c) Objectives fit individual goals into overall organisational goals and make the job meaningful and worthwhile. This stimulated human motivational.

(d) All the managers at various levels make plans of their own. Planning may lose its consistency unless all plans have the same focus of action.

GUIDELINES REGARDING OBJECTIVES

Peter Drucker has given the following guidelines regarding the objectives of a business organisation:

1. Objectives must by operational. They must be capable of being converted into specific targets and assignments. They must also be capable of becoming the basis, as wellas the motivation, for achievement.
2. Objectives must make possible concentration of resources and efforts. They must win new vistas of fundamentals among the goals of a business so that the key resources of men, money and physical resources can be concentrated. They must, therefore, be selective rather than encompass everything.
3. Objectives are needed in all areas on which the survival of the business depends. The specific targets, the goals in any objective areas, depend on the strategy of the individual business. But the areas in which objectives are needed are the same for all business, for all businesses depend on the same factors for their survival.
4. Objectives must be derived from what our business is what it will be and what is what it should be. They are not abstractions. They are the action commitments through which the mission of a business is to be carried out the standards against which performance is to be measured. Objectives, in other words, are the fundamental strategy of a business.
5. There must be multiple objectives rather than a simple objectives.

PURPOSE AND MISSION

The purpose and mission of an organisation is a general enduring statement of the organisation the intent of which embodies the decision maker's business philosophy; it implies the image which the organisation seeks to project.

An organisation's purpose and mission consists of a long-term vision of what it seeks to do and the reasons why it exists. Purpose is management's concept of the organisation and its service is mission to society. An organisation's purpose, when expressed in managerially meaningful terms, indicates exactly what activities the organisation intends to engage in present and in future. It suggests something specific about what kind of organisation it is and is to become. It depicts the organisation's business character and does so in ways what tend to distinguish the organisation from other organisations.

In this sense, purpose sets forth principles and conceptual foundation upon which the organisation rests the nature of the business in which it plans to participate, organisational mission, defined properly, offers guidance to managers in developing sharply focussed, result-oriented objectives, strategies, and policies. Therefore, a detailed understanding of organisational mission is the starting point for rational managerial action and for the design of organisation structure, processes, and procedures. Managerial effectiveness tends to begin with clarity of mission with an accurate, carefully delineated concept of just what the organisation is trying to do any why.

The concept of mission can be understood by taking the example mission of TISCO.

The fundamental mission of TISCO (Tata Iron and Steel Company Limited) is to strengthen India's industrial base through increased productivity, effective utilisation of manpower and material resources, and continued application of modern scientific managerial methods as well as through systematic growth in keeping with national aspirations. The company recognizes that while honesty and integrity are the essential ingredients of a strong and stable enterprise, profitability provides the main spark for economic activity. It affirms its faith in democratic values and in the importance of success of individuals, collective, and corporate enterprise for the economic emancipation and prosperity of the country. Guided by its basic philosophy, the company believes in discharging its responsibility towards:

1. Customers

(i) by products of proven quality at a fair price;

(ii) by fulfilling its commitments impartially and courteously in accordance with sound and strightforward business principles; and

(iii) by bearing their counting confidence in its productive ability and its technical competence to keep improving the quality for its products.

2. Community

(a) by assuming its proper share of social responsibilities in the community in which the company operates.

(b) by encouraging talent and promoting civic sense among members of the community;

(c) by availing of opportunities to develop the democratic qualities involved in collective work undertaken in the interest of the community; and

(d) by respecting the dignity· of the individual and acting according to the ideas of social justice.

3. Shareholders

(i) by protecting and safeguarding their investment; and

(ii) by ensuring to them a fair return.

4. Employees

(a) by providing adequate wages, goods working conditions, job security, effective machinery for speedy redressal of grievances, and suitable opportunities for promotion and self-development;

(b) by creating a sense of belongingness and team-spirit through their closer association with management at various levels;

(c) by promoting feelings of trust and loyalty through a human and purposeful awareness of their needs and aspiration; and

(d) by a realistic and general understanding and acceptance of their needs and rights and enlightened awareness of the social responsibilities of industry.

These missions of the company are directed towards making the company:

The best company to buy from,

(a) A leading company in the corporate field of the country.

(b) A reliable company to sell to,

(c) A sound company to invest in,

(d) A good company to work for,

The various points are indivisible. Together as a unit, they state the fundamental management philosophy to TISCO. However, most of the companies do not specify their purpose so clearly as TISCO has done. Nevertheless they do have certain purpose which is reflected in their specific objectives and actions.

A key feature of organisation's purpose is that its focus must be external rather than internal. For example, Drucker has the following suggestion:

'To know what a business we have to start with is its purpose. Its purpose must lie outside the business itself. In fact, it must lie in a society since business enterprise is an organ of society. There is only one valid definition of business purpose: to create a customer.

OBJECTIVES OF BUSINESS

As we know, the business is an economic institution operating in a socio-economic system. Therefore, objectives of business should be defined keeping in view its prevailing environment and its needs for survival and growth. Like any other institution business has several rather than a single objective. Objectives of business are multi-dimensional in nature. Business is established and it exists to achieve multiple objectives. People enter into business and stay in business because they want to earn money, social power and prestige, joy of achievement and other goals. Generally, profit motive is considered to be the primary objective of business. But profit-making is not the sole or only objectives of a business. Every business enterprise has to lay down its multiple objectives to justify its existence.

The various objectives of business may broadly be classified as follows:

1. Economic Objectives

Business is an economic activity and, therefore, its major objectives are economic. Economic objectives refer to those goals which determined a person's conduct in the business part of life. Economic objectives of business are as follows:

(a) ***Creation of Customer.*** Business can earn profits only when it provides goods or services which people are able and willing to buy. Every business enterprise is conceived in terms of a product or service that meets the needs of public. A business enterprise cannot survive unless there are enough people to buy the products and services offered by it. Customer is the generator of revenue for business. By paying for goods and services, customers determine what shall be produced and how much? In the words of Drucker, "There is only one valid definition of business purpose: to create a customer. It is the customer who determines what a business is.. The customer is the foundation of business and keeps it in existence... and it is to supply the customer that society entrusts wealth-producing resources to a business enterprise." Customers can be created only when business supplies them what they want and at the price, place and time they desire. Business earns profits by satisfying the needs of the customers. Therefore, creation and satisfaction of customers is an important objective of business. Creating customers amounts to creating the market for goods and services.

(b) ***Innovation.*** Modern business is highly dynamic and an enterprise can continue to be successful only by adapting itself to changes in its environment. A successful firm has not only to adjust itself to changing environment. It must on its own create conditions favourable to survival and growth. The highly competitive nature of modern business puts a premium on innovation and creativity which implies the introduction of new and better products, improved means of production and distribution, new technology, new methods and procedures of management, etc. To resist change is to court disaster. Profits are the result of efficient performance in marketing, innovation and productivity. Innovation results in better and cheaper products and more employment for the society. Innovation is essential for the survival and growth of business. It is through innovations that business firms perform dynamic functions of growth, diversification and change in the economy. The most progressive or excellent companies allocate large amounts of money on research and development for achieving the objectives of innovation.

2. Social Objectives

The economic objectives of business can be realised only by serving the society. Business is an organ of society and it draws its resources from the society. Therefore, it must satisfy the wants and aspirations of society. A business enterprise can survive and grow only when it caters to the needs of the society. A really successful business can be built on the foundation of social services. If a business enterprise serves the various sections of society, profits will follow automatically. Profits are, in other words, the reward which business receives by serving society. There is no conflict between profit-motive and service to society. It is through service that business earns profits.

Social objectives of business refer to the obligations of business towards customers, employees, investors, suppliers, government and the general public. The profits of business represent government and the general public. The profits of business represent a social surplus in which all stockholders must share in proportion to their contributions. The social objectives of business are as follow:

(a) ***Avoidance of Profiteering and Anti-social Practices.*** It is legitimate for a business enterprise to work legitimate profit. But it must not over-charge the customers or indulge in profiteering at their cost. It is the social obligation of a business concern not to indulge in hoarding, black-marketing, adulteration and other anti-social practices. In times of scarcity it should ensure fair and equitable distribution. Moreover, business enterprise is expected to adopt socially responsible and ethical behaviour with the suppliers, competitors, and other interacting groups of people. It should be fair in its dealing with all these groups.

(b) ***Providing Employment.*** Another social objective of business is to create opportunities for gainful employment of the people. Sometimes this objective may conflict with the economic objective of cutting down costs and improving profits by introducing mechanisation or automation. In a country like India, mechanisation may have to be deferred or implemented gradually into stages without causing loss of job to anyone.

(c) ***Quality Goods at Fair Prices.*** The first and foremost social objective of business is to provide regularly the goods and services of proper quality and quantity to consumers at reasonable prices. Today consumers are conscious of the quality of goods they buy. When goods are of sub-standard quality or adulterated, they stop patronising the enterprise and the enterprise faces eventual closure. Therefore, business units must always maintain a continuous and adequate supply of articles of standard quality. Businessmen who keep their customers satisfied are likely to earn profits.

3. Human Objectives

A business enterprise is an institution carried on by people (entrepreneurs and managers), through (employees) and for people (consumers and public). Therefore, human factor pervades all business activities. Business is not an end itself but a means towards human welfare. People are the most valuable assets of business and their well-being is its main concern. The success of a business depends upon the quality of people working in it. In order to win the co-operation of employees, business must fulfil their expectations. The human objectives of business arise from these expectations. The important human objectives of business are given below:

(a) ***Development of Human Resources.*** Business can accomplish its economic objectives of innovation and productivity only when the employees are given adequate opportunities for developing new skills and capabilities. Business should create a proper climate wherein the talents of workers are allowed to grow and mature.

(b) ***Job Satisfaction.*** It is the obligation of a business enterprise to make the jobs interesting and challenging so that employees may get job satisfaction while performing their jobs. Selection of right man for the right job and reducing unpleasantness of jobs help to offer job satisfaction which in turn ensures retention of an employee on the job for a long period. A business enterprise fulfils its human objective when it recognises the dignity of labour.

(c) ***Praticipation.*** Workers will put forth their best efforts only when they are given an opportunity to participate in making decisions redressal of employee grievances quickly and at the lowest possible level. Recognition of worker representatives and their legitimate activities helps to maintain healthy trade union practices and sound industrial relations.

(d) ***Fair Deal to Employees.*** The first human objectives of business is to pay fair wages, salaries and incentives to the employees at different levels. Fair working and living conditions and security of service are necessary for securing the whole-hearted efforts of the employees. Employee welfare is no less important than customer satisfaction.

The realisation of economic and organic objectives helps the business directly and immediately whereas the social, human and national objectives help the business indirectly and in the long run.

4. Organic Objectives

As an organic entity, a business enterprise has its own stages of infancy, childhood, adolescence, adulthood and maturity. Like a human being, the first concern of a business enterprise is to ensure its survival. When the enterprise is assured of its survival, it will aim at growth and expansion. To accomplish this objective, it will attempt to win prestige, recognition and goodwill from the society in which it operates. In order to pass through these stages in time and with strength, a business unit uses several methods, *e.g.*, ploughing back a part of its profits, attaining optimum size to avail of the economic of scale, etc. Organic objectives are the foundation for achieving all other objectives of business:

(a) ***Prestige and Recognition.*** Prestige and recognition help to ensure the survival and growth of a firm. A business enterprise with good image or goodwill can easily attract customers, investors and competent employees.

(b) ***Growth.*** Growth and diversification is one of the major objectives of business. Growth may be measured in terms of size, investment, market share, etc. Market share which a business enterprise commands reflects its standing in the market. A business enterprise may identify new customers, new products or new markets or increase its market share in the present market.

(c) ***Survival.*** First of all a business enterprise tries to maintain its existence. Survival of stability objectives implies the maintenance of a firm's competitive position or earning capacity or market standing. Unless an enterprise survives no other objectives can be accomplished.

5. National Objectives

Present day business is expected to serve as an instrument for the fulfilment of national needs and aspirations and implementation of national plans and policies in accordance with the accepted priorities. Keeping in view the overall national objective of establishing a democratic, secular and socialist society and fostering growth stability and social justice, business in India has to serve the following national objectives:

(a) ***Development of Skilled Personnel.*** Skill formation is essential for the economic growth of a country. Business can contribute to skill formation through training and development of managers and technicians.

In addition to the above objectives, business is also expected to promote national integration, balanced regional development, family planning, public health, education, sports, culture in the country.

The above description reveals that the operation of business requires reconciliation of serveral micro and macro level of objectives.

(b) ***National Self-sufficiency and Export Promotion.*** In order to enable the country to become self-reliant, it is the responsibility of business to produce such articles as have hitherto been imported. Business should aim at import substitution, specially in the case of machinery, equipment and technology. Every business should take adequate steps to boost exports and thereby augment the foreign exchange reserves of the country.

(c) ***Production According to National Priorities.*** In keeping with national plan objectives, business enterprise should manufacture and supply goods necessary for the country's development. It is also the national objective of business to manufacture and distribute cheaper varieties of essential commodities like soap, cloth, edible oils, etc, so as to help the weaker sections of the society.

(d) ***Development of Small Enterprises.*** In tune with the national policy of decentralised development, large business houses are responsible for encouraging the growth and development of small scale and cottage industries. Such industries can be used as ancillary units and their products should be patronised. Large business concerns are expected to desist from assuming monopolistic position.

(e) ***Ensuring Social Justice.*** As a responsible citizen a business enterprise is expected to remove inequalities of opportunities and to provide a fair opportunity to all to work and progress. For this purpose special attention must be given to the neglected, weaker and backward sections of the society.

WHY MISSION AND OBJECTIVES CHANGE

As strategists define their mission, they are usually urged to seek a common thread to which activities can be related. The common thread is often stated in terms of the scope of products, but markets of technologies in the domain of the enterprise are also used. The problem is that the firm might define the scope so broadly that strategic decisions or objectives tied to the mission become meaningless. On the other hand, an overly narrow mission definition can lead to the oversight of factors that are potentially important to the success of the enterprise.

If the domain of TWA is defined too narrowl.y, executives may miss important technological or competitive activities occuring outside the more limited domain of "other air carriers." As a result, the firm may risk the potential loss of a large part of its customer base.

Thus the domain must be sufficiently broad so that decision makers will be sensitive to important issues it may face in the future. Of course, overgeneralization, the opposite of myopia, may lead to a lack of focus on relevant issues as well. Should an airline view itself as being in the vocation business, it could lose sight of its basic mission. Paper Mate now views itself as in "office products" with the acquisition of Liquid Paper. A radio is product, but manufacturers of radios are in the business of providing a means of delivering audio information and or entertainment. The Bostan Consulting Group statement on this issue is instructive.

Unfortunately, there is a prevalent notion that if one merely defines one's business in increasingly general terms—such as transportation rather than railroading—The road to successful competitive strategy will be clear. Actually, that is hardly ever the case. More often the opposite is true. For example, in the case of the railroads, passengers and freight represent very different problems, and short haul *vs.* longer haul are completely different strategic issues. Indeed as the unit train demonstrates, just coal handing is a meaningful strategic issue.

Thus perhaps one of the best ways to determine a common thread is to seek out synergies which could be obtained between old and new activities. "Synergy" refers to the idea that the whole is greater than the sum of its parts (2 + 2 = 5). Here if a firm can find new activities which utilize the strengths or benefits of old activities it is likely to create more value for all activities. Hallman found synergy in its markets, products, and technologies. Another suggestion is to give careful attention to the utilities provided for customers (*e.g.*, cost, time, location convenience) by the functions performed by the enterprise. Carefull attention to categories of goods and services (rather than "products" and synergies can lead to more useful definitions of the organisation's mission and domain. For instance, Sears began its move into providing financial services to complement its existing insurance business by using its broad base of retail outlets and larger number of change customers as a point of departure. In essence, mission and business definition can change. It must be periodically evaluated as part of the strategic management process.

A final point before turning to the specificity of objectives is the idea that these issues of domain definition are stated in different terms at different levels of the organization, but similar questions emerge. For instance, the scope of question at the corporate level implies issues concerning the overall degree of diversification in the portfolio of business operations. At the SBU levels, the breadth of the product market scope a degree of vertical integration (technology scope) is the more common issue. At functional levels, the issues often are debated in terms of product-market segments. Although organizations tend toward stability, mission and objectives change over time. As discussed before, objectives could change on the basis of a rational analysis of a gap between expected and desired states. That is a normative approach. But what might lead to the determination of the stages themselves? Are there some factors which would lead to different perceptions regarding the gaps between goals and how the future goal states might be arrived at?

On the basis of the foregoing discussion of how mission and objectives are formulated, we can present some descriptive reasons why mission or objectives might change:

1. **The Aspiration Levels of Managers could Alter Goal Orientations.** They may begin to extrapolate past achievements and say that the enterprise can do more. They may look at what relevant competitors or other enterprise have achieved and decided to match or exceed these levels. The arrival of a new CDE from outside the organisation is the most prevalent condition under which mission and goals are reconsidered. New managers from the outside who are not tied or committed to past strategy and ideology are more likely to alter the mission, objective, and strategies of an organisation than are new CEOs from the inside.
2. **The mission can Change in Crisis.** When a firm's market disappears, for example, or its reason for being ceased a crisis exists. Some firms supplying equipments to the oil industry discovered this in 1974 and again in 1982 and 1986. Faced with an uncertain future, their objectives have begun to focus on flexibility. When the cure for polio was found, the mission of the National Foundation for Infantile Paralysis changed. So the attainment of objectives can also lead to a crisis. Or, new opportunities can create an identity crisis if a firm seeks to take advantage of them.
3. **Demands from Coalition Groups that make up the Enterprise can Change.** This often occurs as the memberships or leadership of groups changes or as internal

power groups change. For instance, new government or labour leaders or new competition can alter the way a business sets its goal-priorities. Similarly, if the comptroller becomes more powerful internally, the firm might begin to stress shorter-term financial goals.

4. **Normal Life-cycle Changes may Occur which Alter Goal Orientations.** Though the analogy with humans can be taken too far, there may be changes in objectives or strategies which naturally occur in the aging process. Of course, organisations may have more control over the sequencing and timing of these stages than humans. Yet it is often difficult for organization to know what stage it is in. And we're not sure that might precipitate organisational aging or movement. We do know that commitment to the past may hinder change, and new agents in coalition groups are likely to hasten it.

These four classes of factors-aspirations, crisis, demands, and development can be used to predict the likelihood that mission and objectives will remain similar to those of the past or be subject to redefinition. Thus in considering how mission and objectives are formulated, we must examine various pressures for stability or change before a gap analysis can be effectively done.

FOMULATION OF MISSION AND OBJECTIVES

We believe that mission and objectives are formulated by the corporate level strategist. But these executives do not make choices in a vacuum. Their choices are affected by several factors : the realities of the external environment and external power relationship, the realities of the enterprise's resources and internal power relationship, the value systems and goals of the top executives, and past strategy and development of the enterprise. Let us discuss each of these influencing factors then summarize.

The first factor affecting the formulation of mission and objectives is forces in the environment. The stockholders with whom the organisation has an exchange relationship will present demands or claims. These can be thought of as constraints on objectives. The stockholders may vary. The nature of their constraints can change, and their power vis-a-vis the organisation and one another may change. Taken together, they represent one set of forces within which managerial objectives must be established. The claims of the most powerful stockholders will be met, so long as the entire set of objectives falls within the constraints imposed by the set of stockholders.

Suppose that managers want to choose maximization of sales as an objective. They may have to modify this objective because of governmental regulations regarding excess profit, antitrust legislation, consumer labelling, and so on. Trade unions may require higher-than-market wage rates or fringe benefits which lead to higher costs (possibly reducing sales). Competitors may sell other products or services at unrealistically low price and spend excessive amounts on advertising. Suppliers may become monopolized and charge outrageous prices. If the organisation is more dependent on suppliers than on any other stockholder, the operative objective may very well be limited by the availability and cost of supplies. The political-behavioural realities of the the situation influence the choice of objectives.

So the prudent strategist will ask a variety of questions when establishing mission, objectives, and strategy : who are the critical stockholders? What are our critical assumptions about each stockholder? How do stockholders affect each division, business, or function at various points in time. And what changes can be expected among the stockholder groups in the future?

The second factor affecting the formulation of mission and objectives is the realities of the enterprise's resources and internal power relationships. Larger and more profitable firms have more resources with which to respond to forces in the environment than do smaller or poorer firms.

In addition to this, the internal political relationships affect mission and objectives. First, how much support does management have relative to others in the organisation? Does the management have the full support of the stockholders? For example, Paul Smucker has the support of the Smucker family stockholder to emphasize quality as an objective for his jam and preserves firm. If the management has development the support of employees and key employees groups like the professional employee's lower and middle management, then it can set higher objectives that employees will help achieve.

Mission and objectives are also influenced by the power relationship among the strategies either as individuals or as representatives of units within the organisation. Thus if there is a difference of opinion on which objectives to seek or the trade-offs among them, power relationships may help settle the difference.

A final internal factor is the potential power of lower-level participants to withhold information and ideas. To the extent that this occurs the evaluation of past goal attainment and expectation about the future can be affected. For instance, consider the sales manager who tries to hide the fact that a competitor's new products it starting to hurt sales. This might be an attempt to protect the unit, but it could mislead top managers regarding future goals and strategies, or lower-level managers might decide whether or not to forward a proposal which could lead to goal changes on the basis of what they think top management is (or is not) ready to accept. Thus the exercise of this type of informal power can play a role in the selection of objectives.

Mintzberg has advanced a theory about formulation of objectives that combines the stockholder forces described earlier with the internal power relationships. He believes that power play result from interactions of internal and external coalitions.

Six Pure Power Configurations Affecting Objectives Formulation

External	*Internal*	*Power*
Coalition	Coalition	Configuration
Dominated	Bureaucratic	The Instrument
Passive	Bureaucratic	The Closed System
Passive	Personalized	The Autocracy
Passive	Ideologic	The Missionary
Passive	Professional	The Meritocracy
Dividend	Politicized	The Political Arena

Source. *Hen*ry Mintzberg, Power in and Around Organisations (Englewood Cliffs. N.J. : Prentice-Hall, 1983). p. 307

The external coalition include owners, suppliers, unions, and the public. These groups influence the firm through social norms specific constraints campaigns, direct controls, and membership on the board of directors. Mintzberg specifies three types of external coalition.

Mintzberg says that there are six basic power configurations, as shown in above fig. In the instrument power configuration, one external influence with clear objectives typically the owner, is able to strongly influence objectives through the top manager. In a closed-system power configuration, power to set objectives rests with the top manager, who sets the objectives. This is also true in the autocracy power configuration. In the missionary power configuration, objectives are strongly influenced by past ideology and a charismastic leader. Ideology tends to dictate the objectives. In the meritocracy power configuration, the objectives are set by a census of the members, most of whom are professionals.

Thus the formulation of mission and objectives can be a simple process: the top manager sets them subjects to the environment. or more frequently, they are by a complex interplay of post and present, internal and external role players.

The third factor affecting the formulation of mission and objectives is the value system of the top executives. Enterprises with strong value systems or ideologies will attract and retain managers whose values are similar. These values are essentially a set of attitudes about what is good or bad, desirable or undesirable. These in turn will influence the perception of the advantages and disadvantages of strategic action and the choice of objectives. Exhibit given below lists the extremes of six selected values. Let's look at each of these to see how they might affect objectives:

Values Toward Various Groups in the Strategic Situation

1. Very innovative	Non-innovative
2. Risk-oriented	Risk-aversive
3. Autocratic	Participative
4. Personal goals	Shareholder goals
5. Quality	Quantity
6. Very combative	Very passive

The following list corresponds to the continuum in Exhibit given above. Each dimension is explained below:

1. Some executive believes that to succeed a firm must innovate. Others prefer to "let others make the mistakes first."
2. Some executives know that to "win big, you must take big risks."
3. Some executives believe that one should treat employees in a manner that makes them known who the boss is. Others believe that cooperation comes from a participative style.
4. Some executives believe that they should be primary beneficiaries of corporate success while others thinks the business is operated for the benefit of stockholders.
5. Some executives believe that one becomes successful by producing quality. Others go for volume.

You can see that one set of executives with the set of value on the left would be inclined to emphasize a different set or different level of objectives than those who accept the set of values on the right in Exhibit. For instance, risk-oriented innovators might see significantly larger gaps between where they want to be and where they expect to be than risk averters. Managers on the left on number 6 will avoid hostile takeovers to protect their jobs, even if it comes at the expense of shareholder loss. Corporate raiders often recognize this, and receive "greenmail" for their effort.

Prescripitively, from a "maximizing" decision perspective, those and other kinds of values ought not be considered when goals are being established. Yet some believe that it is better to recognize the inevitability of their influence on decision makers. That is, even if they are not explicity stated, value assumptions will be implicit in decision premises and the types and forms of data collected. Consequently, stating these values in the form of assumptions is one technique recommended to force these values explicity into the open. If they are included, the bases upon which decisions are made can be considered "more rational" than if decision makers pretended that these factors don't exist.

The fourth factor affecting the formulation of mission and objectives is the awareness by management of the past development of the firm. Management does not begin from scratch each year. It begins with the most recent mission and objectives. These may have been set by strong leaders in the past. The leaders consider incremental changes from the present, given the current environment and current demands of the conflicting groups. The managers have developed aspiration levels of what the objective ought to be in a future period. But by muddling through, they set the current set of objectives to satisfy as many of the demands and their wishes as they can. The momentum of the large organization and its strategies and policies are all designed to accomplish the existing mission and objectives. Just as it takes time to turn a large ship around, it usually takes time to make major corporate changes.

Mission and objectives are not the result of managerial power alone. These result from the managers' trying to satisfy the needs of all groups involved with the enterprise. These coalitions of interests (stockholders, employees, suppliers, customers, and others) sometimes have conflicting interests. As the strongest coalition group, managers try to reconcile the conflicts. Management cannot settle them once and for all. Management "bargains" with the various groups and tries to produce a set of objectives and a mission which can satisfy the groups are considered in relation to past goals. This is a very complicated, largely consensus-building process with no precise beginning or end. And at any given time, only a few specific goals can be grasped and comprehended by any single executive. Thus there appears to be a need for same grander vision as expressed by a mission definition.

Mission and objectives will become a meaningful part of the strategic management process only if corporate strategists formulate them well and communicate them and reinforce them throughout the enterprise. The strategic management process will be successful to the extent the general managers participate in formulating the mission and objectives and to the extent that these reflect the value of management and the realities of the organisation's situation. These factors also play a role in strategic choice.

How are Goals Actually Set?

In practice, goals are set by way of a complicated power-play involving various individuals and groups within and without the organisation and by reference to values which govern behaviour in general and the specific behaviour of the relevant individuals and groups. Goal-setting, in other words, involves a process of reconciliation of diverse needs of interest groups-coalitions of interests or stockholders in the organisation including the owners (shareholders), employees, suppliers, customers, Government and others. The respective stockholders often have conflicting objectives which management as the strongest coalition of interests has to resolve. The process of reconciliation is a continuous one, for conflicting group interest cannot be resolved one and for all. The acceptable set of objectives which management arrive at is the result of bargaining between the various groups at a certain point of time, but then revisions take place and incremental changes are made; the current set of objectives are dervied by management so as to satisfy as far as possible the current demands of the interest groups in the light of the existing environment and aspirations of the management about what the objectives ought to be.

Examples of Good Objective Setting

Below are given certain examples as how the organisation should define their objectives so as to provide direction for their course of action:

(1) "We strive to become leader in product innovation in our field by investing five per cent of our sales revenue on reserach and development." This provides direction to management about what the organisation wants to do in the field of innovation and how it can be achieved.

(2) "We want to make our product the number one selling brand in its field in terms of units sold." This leaves little doubt about the intended sales objectives and market standing.

(3) "We seek to produce the most durable, maintenance-free product that money can buy." This obviously focusses on

the organisation striving to become leader in respect to high quality product.

(4) "Our profit objective is to increase the earning so that we earn 12 per cent post tax return on the net world of company." This is very clear objective, easily measurable and providing direction about the quantum of profit for the organisation.

Example of Poor Objective Setting

Some organisations do not define their objectives as sharply as above statements suggest. Their objectives setting is quite poor and may not provide clear direction. Following are some example of such objectives setting:

(1) "We will go to great length to develop new ideas." This is not very precise and clear, hence fails to provide direction.

(2) "Our objective is to maximise our profit." This statement of objectives is not subject to measurement because it does not provide any yardstick for that. Therefore, the organisation can not know whether it is achieving its objective or not. Further it does not spell out the way in which the objective can be achieved. Therefore, it does not spell out commitment on the part of the management.

(3) "Our objective is to offer best and cheapest product." This statement does not provide yardstick for measuring cheapest and best product, hence fails to provide direction.

Areas of Objectives Setting

As discussed earlier, organisational objectives are of multiple character. Even major objective are multiple in nature. Thus an organisation has to set objectives in many areas. However, what objectives should be selected must meet three criteria *(i)* They must be in consistent with the values of the management in the organisation. They must pinpoint the organisational strengths and weaknesses. *(ii)* They must satisfy the external environmental forces. From these points of view, the organisation will set its objectives in several areas. For example, Peter Drucker has emphasised eight areas which an organisation must emphasise as its objectives. These are:

Physical financial resources, profitability, manager performance and development, workers performance and attitude, and public responsibility, market standing, innovation, productivity.

England and Dent have given a wide range of such objectives. There are :

(1) maximise net profit over a short period of time,

(2) maximise the company's net assets and reserves,

(3) maximise net profit over a long period,

(4) run a stable organisation,

(5) maximise the company's prestige.

(6) maximise the dividends for the shareholders,

(7) be influencial in local community decisions,

(8) create a friendly and pleasant workplace,

(9) provide high rewards and benefits to the employees,

(10) have satisfied employees,

(11) survive,

(12) be a socially responsible company,

(13) be the leading innovator in the community,

(14) be of service to the community,

(15) provide the best quality products or services possible,

(16) increase sales growth,

(17) maximise the company's rate of growth,

(18) maximise the rate of innovation of products or services,

(19) have the most satisfied customers,

(20) be a market leader, *e.g.*, first in market with new products or services,

(21) maximise the market share,

(22) keep tax payments to a minimum,

(23) keep the government out of the business,

(24) provide income or jobs for owning family members,

(25) present unionisation or further unionisation,

(26) be the most efficient firm in the industry.

STEPS IN PLANNING THE STRATEGIC BUSINESS UNITS (SBU)

The strategic business unit planning can be discussed as follows:

1. **Goal Formulation.** Goal formulation invovles reviewing and understanding the organisation's mission and then establishing goals that translate the mission into concrete terms. Because the goals chosen will take up a large amount of the organisation's resources and govern so many of its activities, this is a key step. Yet many managers hesitate to carry it.
2. **Identification of Current Objectives and Strategy.** Step 2 through 6 provide the basis for determining what must be done differently to achieve organisational goals. The first step in this series is to identify the organisation's existing objectives and strategy, which may be quite similar to its existing mission and objectives. Sometimes, however, the goal-formulation process yields a substantial change in mission and objectives; this is especially true if the organisation has been failing to meet main objectives.
3. **Resource Analysis.** The Organisation's goals and existing strategy also provide a framework for analyzing its resources. This analysis is necessary to identify the disadvantages, its strengths and weakness relative to its present and likely future competitors.
4. **Environmental Analysis.** Knowing the organisation's goals and existing strategy provides a framework for defining which aspects of the environment will have the greatest influence on the organisation's ability to achieve its objectives.
5. **Identification of Strategic Opportunities and Threats.** Identifying strateygy, analysing the environment, and analyzing the organisation's resources (Steps 2, 3 & 4)

come together in the fifth step : determining the opportunities available to the organization and the threats it faces. Opportunities and threats may arise from many factors: Land purchased for farming activities by a large agribusiness corporation may become so valuable that the company considers forming or acquiring a housing development division. In this instance, changed market conditions present a new opportunity.

6. **Strategic Decision Making.** If it appears necessary to change the strategy to close the performance gap, the next step to identify, evaluate, and select alternative strategic approaches.

7. **Strategy Impementation.** Once the strategy has been determined, it must be implemented, or incorporated into the daily operations of the organization. Even the most sophisticated and creative strategy will not benefit the organisation unless it is carried out effectively. Whether or not the strategy is recorded in a formal and detailed strategic plan, it must be translated into the appropriate operational plans.

8. **Measurement and Control of Process.** As implementation proceeds, managers must check their progress at periodic or critical stages. Company controllers often play an important role in desiging systems of strategic control (as this process is generally known).

9. **Evaluation of Strategic Alternatives.** *(1)* The strategy and its component parts should have consistent goals, objectives, and policies; *(2)* It should focus resources and efforts on the critical issues identified in the strategy formulation process and separate them from unimportant issues; *(3)* It should deal with sub-problems capable of solution, given the organisation's resources and skills; and *(4)* The strategy should be capable of producing the intended results.

❑

3

Environmental Analysis and Diagnosis

CONCEPT OF ENVIRONMENT

Just as the survival and success of any individual depend on his innate capability—such as the physiological and physiological factors—to cope with the environment and the extent to which the environment is conducive to the development of the individual, the survival and success of a business firm depend on its innate strength—resources at its command, including physical resources, financial resources, human resources, skill and organisation—and its adaptability to the environment and the extent to which the environment is favourable to the development of the organisation. The survival and success of a firm, thus, depend on two sets of factors. *viz.*, the internal factors—the internal environment—and external factors—the external environmental. However, the term business environment often refers to the external factors.

Any meaningful organisation has certain mission, objective(s) and goal(s) and a strategy to achieve them. Formulation of strategy is sometimes defined as establishing a proper firm-environment fit. Indeed, the mission/objectives/goals themselves should be based on an assessement of the external environment and the organisational factors (*i.e.*, the internal environment).

The external environment has, broadly, two components, *viz.*, business opportunities and threats to business. Similarly, the organisational environment has two components: strength and weaknesses of the organisation. Thus, strategy formulation is properly pitting the organisational factors (the internal environment) against the opportunities and threats in the external environment. In other words, business decisions are conditioned by two broad sets of factors, *viz.*, the internal environment and the external environment.

Thus, in a broad sense, the main components of environment may be classified in the following two groups:

(I) MICRO ENVIRONMENT

According to Philip Kotler, "The micro environment consists of the factors in the company's immediate environment" that affect the performance of the company. These include the supplier, marketing intermediaries, competitors, customers and the publics. Pointing out the scope of Micro environment Kotler says, "The macro-environment consists of the larger society forces that affect all the factors in the company's micro environment—namely, the demographic, economic, natural, technological, political and cultural forces."

The micro environmental factors are more intimately linked with the company than the macro factors. However, the micro forces do not affect all the firms in a particular industry in the same way. Some of the micro factors may be particular to a firm. For example, a firm depending on a supplier may have a supplier environment entirely different from that of a firm whose supply source is different. If competing firms in an industry have the same micro elements, the relative success of the firm depends on their relative effectiveness in dealing with these elements.

FACTORS OF MICRO ENVIRONMENT

1. Suppliers. Suppliers are those who supply the inputs like raw materials and components to the company. The importance of reliable sources/sources of supply are an important force in the micro environment of a company necessary for the smooth functioning of the business. Uncertainty regarding the supply and other supply constraints often compel companies to maintain high inventories causing cost increases. For example, while factories in India maintain indigenous stock of 3-4 months and imported stocks of 9 months in Japan it is for an average of a few hours to two weeks.

Many companies give high importance to vendor development due to the sensitivity of the supply. Vertical integration solves the supply problem. It is risky to depend on a single supplier because a strike, lock out or any other production problem and a change in the attitude or behaviour of the supplier may affect the company. Multiple sources of supply reduce such risks.

In a scarcity environment, As Kotler points out, "Company purchasing agents are learning how to "wine and dine" suppliers to obtain favourable treatment during periods of shortages. In other words, the purchasing department might have to "market" itself to suppliers".

2. Customer. As the major task of a business is to create and sustain customers, monitoring the customer sensitivity is a prerequisite for the business success. A company may have different categories of consumers like individuals, households, industries and other commercial establishments and government and other institutions. For example, the customers of an automobile company may include individual automobile owners, automobile manufactures, public sector transport undertakings and other transport operators. A single customer may place the company in a poor bargaining position, apart from the risks of losing business consequent to the winding up of business by the customer or due to the customers switching over to the competitors of the company. Therefore the choice of the customer segments should be made by considering a number of factors including the relative profitability, dependability, stability of demand, growth prospects and the extent of competition.

3. Competitors.

(i) Desire Competition. A firm's competitors include the other firms which market the same or similar products and also all those who compete for the discretionary income of the consumers. For example, the competition for a T.V. company may come not only from other T.V. manufacturers but also from two-wheelers, refrigerators, cooking ranges, stereo sets and so on and from firms offering savings and investment schemes like banks, Unit

Trust of India, companies accepting public deposits or issuing shares or debentures etc. Competition among these products may be described as desire competition as the primary task here is to influence the basic desire of the consumer. Desire competition is very high in countries characterised by limited disposable incomes and many unsatisfied desires and with many alternative for spending/ investing the disposable income.

(ii) ***Product Form Competition.*** If the consumer decides to go in for a T.V., he has to choose a particular form of the T.V.—black and white or colour, with remote control or without it etc. Thus, there is a product form competition.

(iii) ***Generic Competition.*** Even if the consumer decides to spend his discretionary income on recreation or education he will still be confronted with a number of alternatives to choose from like T.V., stero, two-in-one, three-in-one etc. The competition among alternative which satisfy a particular category of desire is called generic competition.

(iv) ***Brand Competition.*** The consumer also encounters the brand competition *i.e.*, the competition between the different brands of the same product form.

By implication of these different demands, marketer should strive to create primary and selective demand for his products.

4. Marketing Intermediaries. The micro environment of a company also cosists of a number of marketing intermediaries such as "firms that aid the company in promoting, selling and distributing its goods to final buyers." Marketing intermediaries are vital links between the company and the final consumers. Dislocation or disturbance of this link, or a wrong choice of the link, may cost the company very heavily.

The marketing intermediaries include middlemen such as agents and merchants who "help the company find customers or close sales with them". Physical distribution firms which assist the company in stocking and moving goods from their origin to their destination such as warehouses and transportation firms; marketing service agencies which assist the company in targeting and promoting its products to the right marketing such as advertising agencies, marketing research firms, media firms and consulting firms; and financial intermediaries which finance marketing activities and insure business risks.

5. Public. According to Kotler, "A public is any group that has an actual or potential interest or impact on an organisation's ability to achieve its interests". A company may encounter publics.

Some companies are seriously affected by such publics. For example, one of the leading companies in India was frequently under attack by the media public, particularly by a leading daily which was allegedly bent upon bringing down the share prices of the company by tarnishing its image. Environmental pollution is an issue often taken up by a number of local publics. Legal actions by local publics on this issue have caused some companies to suspend operations and/or take pollution abatement measures.

All publics are not threats to business. While some of the actions of the publics may cause problems for companies, other publics are an opportunity for the business. For example, consumerism as an opportunity for the business. The media public may be used to disseminate useful information. Cooperation between a company and the local publics may be established for the mutual benefit of the company and the local community.

(II) MACRO ENVIRONMENT

A company and the forces in its micro environment operate in a large macro environment of forces that shape opportunities and pose threats to the company. These are generally more uncontrollable than the micro forces. A picture of the important macro environment forces has been given here under.

FACTORS OF MACRO ENVIRONMENT

1. Economic Environment. Economic conditions, economic policies and the economic systems are the important external factors that consitute the economic environment of a business. The economic conditions of a country include the nature of the economy, the stage of development of the economy, economic resources, the level of income, the distribution of income and assets, etc. They are very important determinants of business strategies.

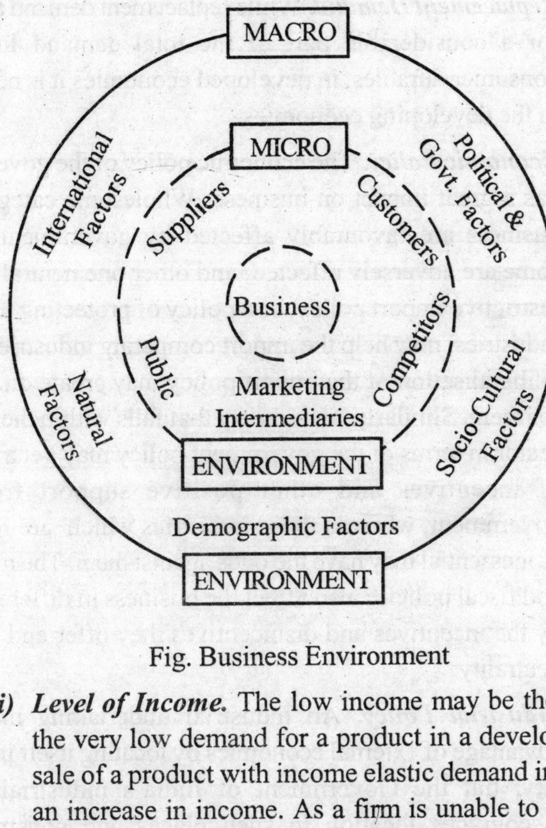

Fig. Business Environment

(i) ***Level of Income.*** The low income may be the reason for the very low demand for a product in a development. The sale of a product with income elastic demand increase with an increase in income. As a firm is unable to increase the purchase power of the people to generate a higher demand for its product, it may have to reduce the price of the product to increase the sales. The reduction in the cost of production may have to be effectd to facilitate price reduction. It may be necessary to invent or develop a new low-cost product to suit the low income market.

Business prospects are generally bright, and further investments are encouraged in countries where investment and income are steadily and rapdily rising. A number of economists and businessmen feel that the developed countries are no longer worthwhile propositions for investment because their economies have reached almost saturation levels in certain respects.

(ii) ***Replacement Demand.*** While replacement demand accounts for a considerable part of the total demand for many consumer durables, in developed economies it is negligible in the developing economies.

(iii) ***Economic Policy.*** The economic policy of the government, has a great impact on business. Wholesome categories of business are favourably affected by government policy, some are adversely affected, and other one neutral. Thus a restrictive import policy, or a policy of protecting the home industries, may help the import competing industries, while a liberalisation of the import policy may create difficulties for them. Similarly, an industry that falls within the priority sector in terms of the government policy may get a number of incentives and other positive support from the government, whereas those industries which are regarded as inessential may have the odds against them. The monetary and fiscal policies also affect the business in different ways by the incentives and disincentives they offer and by their neutrality.

(iv) ***Industrial Policy.*** An industrial undertaking may take advantage of external economies by locating itself in a large city; but the Government of India's industrial policy discourages location in such places and constrains or persuades industries to go to the backward areas. Though a backward area location may have many disadvantages, the incentives available for units located in these backward areas may to some extent compensate them for these disadvantages.

According to the industrial policy of the Government of India until July 1991, the development of 17 of the most important industries were reserved for the state. In the development of another 12 major industries, the state was to play a dominant role. In the remaining industries, co-operative enterprises, joint sector enterprises and small-scale units were to get preferential treatment over large enterpreneurs in the private sectors. Thus the government policy, limited the scope of private business. However, it has widely opened many of the industies for the private sector.

(v) ***Market Economy.*** The scope of private business depends on the economic system. There are the free market economies, and the centrally planned economies in communist countries. In between these two are the mixed economies such as in India.

Capitalist Free Market Economy. According to George N. Halm, the private enterprise has the greatest freedom in the free market economy, characterised by the following assumptions:

(i) The factors of production (labour, land, capital) are privately owned and producion occurs at the initiative of the private enterprise.

(ii) Income is received in monetary form by the sale of services of the factors of production and from the profits of the private enterprise.

(iii) The free market economy is not planned, controlled or regulated by the government. The government satisfies community or collective wants, but does not compete with private firms: nor does it tell the people where to work or what to produce.

(iv) Members of the free market economy have freedom of choice in so far as consumption, occupation, savings and investment are concerned.

However, the completely free market economy is an abstraction. Even the so-called market economies are subject to a number of government regulations.

Communist Centrally Planned Economy. The communist countries have a cerntally planned economic system. The state owns all the means of production, determines the goals of production and controls the economy according to a central master plan. Unlike the free market economy there is no consumer sovereignty in a centrally planned economy. The consumption pattern is dictated by the state. China, Soviet Union, Czechoslovakia, Hungary, Poland, etc., have centrally planned economies.

Mixed Economy. In between the capitalist and the centrally planned systems is the system of he mixed economy, under which both the public and private sectors co-exist. The extent of state participation varies widely between the mixed economies. However, in many mixed economies, the strategic and nationally important industries are fully owned or dominated by state.

Political and Government Environment

Political and government environment has close relationship with the economic system and economic policy. For example, the communist countries had a centrally planned economic system. In most countries, there are a number of laws. These cover such matters as standards of products, packing, promotion etc. to regulate the conduct of the business.

(i) ***Product Regulations.*** Some Government specifiy standards for the products to be marketed in the country, some times even prohibiting the marketing of certain products. Promotional activities are subject to various types of controls in most nations. Several European countries restrain the use of children in commercial advertisements. The advertisement of alcoholic liquor is prohibited in India. Advertisements of cigarettes must carry the statutory warning that "cigarette smoking is injurious to health", Advertisements of baby food must necessarily inform the potential buyer that breast feeding is the best. Product comparison advertisements and the use of superlatives like 'best' or 'excellent' in adverstisements is not allowed in countries like Germany. In the U.S.A. the Federal Trade

Commission is empowered to force a company to provide sufficient evidence to substantiate the claims concerning the quality, performance or comparative prices of its products. As R. Marshall puts it. "What is being asked of the drug industry and of Americn business in general is a fuller disclosure of the relevant facts about products. For drugs, food additives, some cosmetic preparations, and so forth, a full disclosure requires more knowledge of the long-range side effects of materials injected into the complex human body. For American industry as a whole, greater candour has been called for under such legislation as Truth in Lending and Fair Packaging Act, Under Administraive decrees such as the warning requirements on cigarette packages and advertising, under the threat of private damage suits using the common-law concept of warranty, and under voluntary programmes such as unit pricing and listing nutritional content of foods. The increasing complexity of products and the variety of product choice suggest furher moves away from 'caveat emptier' or 'let the buyer beware' doctrines, moves which on the whole should prove a welcome although sometimes inconvenient challenge for business.

(ii) ***Control on Competition.*** Today many countries have laws to regulate competition in the public interest. Elimination of unfair competition and dilution of monopoly power are the important objectives of these regulations. In India, the monopolistic undertakings, dominant undertakings and large industrial houses are subejct to a number of regulations which prevent the concentration of economic power to the common detriment. The MRTP Act also controls monoplistic, restrictive and unfair trade practices prejudical to public interest. Such regulation brighten the prospect of small and new firms and increase the scope of some of the existing firms to venture into new areas and business.

(iii) ***Changes in Government Policy.*** Changes in government policies such as the industrial policy, fiscal, tarrif policy

etc. have profound impact on business. Policy developments create opportunites as well as threats. A development which brightens the prospects of some enterprise may pose a threat to some others. For example the industrial policy liberalisations in India have opened up new opportunities and threats. While they have provided opportunities to large number of enterprise to diversify and to make their product mix better, they have also given rise to serious threat to many existing products by way of increased competition. Many seller's markets have given way to buyer's promotion very heavily. This has provided a splendid opportunity for the advertising industry.

(iv) Control on Monopoly. If the MRTP companies wanted to expand their business they had to convince the government that such expansion was in the public interest. If the words of T. Thomes, "Government in India has an all-pervasive and predominantly restrictive influence over various aspects of business, *e.g.*, industrial licensing which decides location, capacity and process; import licensing for machinery and materials; size and price of capital issue; loan finance; pricing; managerial remuneration; expansion plans; distribution restrictions and a host of other enactments. Therefore, a considerable part of the attention of a that Chief Executive and his senior colleagues has to be devoted to a continuous dialogue with various government agencies to ensure growth and profitability within the framework of controls and restraints.

Socio-Cultural Environment

The socio-cultural environment should be analysed while formulating business strategies. The cost of ignoring the customs, traditions, taboos, tastes and preferences, etc., of a people could be very high. The buying and consumption habits of the people, their language, beliefs and values, customs and traditions, tastes and preferences, education etc affect business. Business strategy should be appropriate in the socio-cultural environment. The marketing mix should be designed to suit the environmental characteristics of the market.

(i) ***Cultural Environment.*** Even when people of different cultures use the same basic product, the mode of consumption, conditions of use, purpose of use or the perceptions of the product attributes should differ so that the product attributes, method of presentation, positioning, or method of promoting the product may be varied to suit the characteristics of different markets.

(ii) ***Differences in Language.*** The differences in language sometimes pose a serious problem, even necessitating a change in the brand name. Preet a good brand name in India adopted 'Prestige' for the overseas markets.

(iii) ***Social Inertia.*** Social inertia and associated factors some in the way of the promotion of certain products, services or ideas. Social stigmas work in the marketing of family planning ideas, use of bio-gas for cooking, etc., Thus the success of marketing depends on the success in changing social attitudes or value systems.

(iv) ***Values and Beliefs.*** Values and beliefs associated with colour vary significantly in different cultures. Blue is considered feminine and warm in Holland, and masculine and cold in Sweden. Green is a favourite colour in the Muslim world; but in Malaysia, it is associated with illness. White indicates death and mourning in China and Korea; but in some countries, it is the colour of the wedding dress of the bride. Red is a popular colour in the communist countries; but many African countries have a national distaste for it.

(v) ***Social Responsibility.*** One must consider the social environment of the business which encompasses its social responsibility and the alternations of vigilance of the consumers and of society at large. As Barker observes, business "traditionally has been held responsible for quantities—for the supply of goods and jobs, for costs, processes, wages, hours of work, and for standards of living. Today, however , business is being asked to take on responsibility for the quality of life in our society. The expectation is that business—in additional to its traditional accountability for economic performance and results—will conern itself with the health of the society, that it will come up with the cures for the ills that currently beset us and, indeed, will find ways of anticipating and preventing further problems in these areas."

(vi) ***Education.*** As Stern succintly points out, the "more edcuated the society becomes, the more interdependent it becomes, and the more discretionary the use of it resources, the more marketing will become enmeshed in social issues. Marketing personnel are at interface between company and society. In this position, they have the resonsibility not merely for designing a competitive marketing strategy, but for sensitizing business to the social, as well as the product demand of society."

Demographic Environnment

(i) ***Demographic Traits.*** Demographic traits like the size, growth rate, age composition, sex compostion etc., of the population, family size, economic stratification of the population, educational levels, care, relation etc. are all relevant to business. The size of the population, population growth rate, age composition, life expectancy, family size, spatial dispersal, occupational status, employment pattern etc. affect the demand for goods and services.

(ii) ***Birth Rates.*** Marketing-with growing population and income are growth markets. But the decline in the birth rates in countries like the United States have affected the demand for baby products. Johnson and Johnson have overcome this problem by repositioning their products like baby shampoo and baby soap, promoting them also to the adult segment, particularly to the females. A rapidly increasing population indicates a growing demand for many products.

In Western countries labour shortage and rising wage encouraged the growth of labour-saving technologies and automation. On the other hand, most developing countries of today are experiencing population explosion and a situation of labour surplus. Therefore, the government of developing countries, encourage intensive methods of production. Capital intensive methods, automation and even rationalisation are opposed by labour and many sociologists, politicians and economists in these countries. Cheap labour and a growing market have encouraged many multinational corporations to invest in developing countries.

(iii) ***Mobilities.*** The occupational and spatial mobilities of population have implications for business. If labour is easily mobile between different occupations and regions its supply will be relatively smooth, and this will affect the wage rate.

(iv) ***Heterogeneity.*** If labour is highly heterogeneous in respect of language, caste and religion, ethnicity, etc., personnel management is likely to become a more complex task. The heterogenous population with its varied tastes, preference, beliefs, temperaments, etc., gives rise to differing demand patterns and calls for different marketing strategies.

Natural Environment

Geographical and ecological factors, and as natural resources endowments, weather and climatic conditions, topographical factors, location aspects in the global context, port facilities, etc., all influence business.

(i) ***Geographical Conditions.*** Differences in geographical conditions between markets may sometimes call for changes in the marketing mix. Geographical factors also influence the location of certain industries. For example, industries with high material index tend to be located near the raw material sources. Climatic and weather conditions affect the location of certain industries like the cotton textile industry. Topographical factors may affect the demand

pattern. For example jeeps may be in greater demand than cars in hilly areas with a difficult terrain.

(ii) ***Ecological Factors.*** Today, the depletion of natural resources, environmental pollution and the disturbance of the ecological balance have caused great concern. Government policies aim at the preservaion of environmental purity, ecological balance and conservation of non-replenishable resources etc. These have resulted in addtional responsibilities and problems for business. Some of these have the effect of increasing the cost of production and marketing.

(iii) ***Physical Factors.*** Such geographical fators as weather and climatic conditions may call for modification in the product, etc., to suit the environment because these are uncontrollable.

(iv) ***Physical Facilities.*** Business prospects depend on the availability of certain physical facilities. Many consumer durables have certain use facility characteristics. For example, the sales of television sets is limited by the extent of the coverage of the telecasting. Siimilarly, the demand for refrigerators and other electrical applicancies is affected by the extent of electrification and reliability of power supply. The demand for LPG gas stoves is affected by the rate of growth of gas connections.

Technological Environment

(i) ***Constraints.*** Technological environment sometimes poses problems. A firm which is unable to cope with the technological changes may not survive. The differing technological environment of different markets or countries may call for product modifications. Technological developments may inverse the demand for some existing products. For example, voltage stabilisers help increase the sale of electrical appliances in markets characterised by frequent voltage fluctuations in power supply. However,

the introduction of T.V.S., Fridges etc., with in-built voltage stabiliser adversely affects the demand for voltage stabilisers.

(ii) ***Advances.*** Advances in the technologies of food processing and preservation., packaging etc. have facilitated product improvements and introduction of new products.

(iii) ***Changes.*** The fast changes in technologies create problems for enterprises as they render plants and products obsolute quickly. Product-market-technology matrix generally has a much shorter life today than in the past particularly in the international marketing context.

International Environment

The international environment is very important for certain categories of business, for industries directly depending on imports to exports and import-competing industries. For example, a recession in foreign market, or the adoption of protectionist policies by foreign nations, may create difficulties for industries depending on exports. On the other hand, a boom in the export market or a relaxation of the protectionist policies may help the export-oriented industries. A liberalisation of imports may help some industries which use imported items, but may adversely affect import-competing industries.

(i) ***International Developments.*** It has been observed that major international developments have their spread effects on domestic business. The Great Depression in the U.S.A. sent its shock-waves to a number of other countries. Oil price hikes have seriously affected a number of economies.

(ii) ***Export Market.*** A goods export market enables a firm to develop a more profitable product mix and to consolidate its position in the domestic market. Export marketing facilitates the attainment of optimum capacity utilisation. A company may be able to mitigate the effects of domestic recession by exporting. However, a company which depends on the export market to a considerable extent has also to face the impact of adverse developments in foreign markets.

(iii) ***Environmentalism.*** The recent earth summit was one of the reflections of the growing concern about the environment. Environment issues have been affecting business fortunes and strategies for quite some time now. The phenomenal rise of environmental awareness as seen in the U.S. and several other, particularly European countries tend to make society marketing concept the only relevant marketing philosophy.

(iv) ***Consumerism.*** Consumerism has become a powerful social force affecting business. Its growing importance increases the relevance of the society marketing concept.

(v) ***Society Marketing Concept.*** The society marketing concept was regarded as the appropriate strategy for a forward looking company. It was regarded socially acceptable because of its focus on the consumer wants and satisfaction. However, it ignores the long-run society interest. The short-run consumer satisfaction may have adverse effects in the long run. Similarly, while considering factors like the ecological factors of the social costs of certain products may outweigh the short-run benefits to the consumers of the patents. In many cases short-term consumer benefits conflict with long-run consumer/society welfare. Many products have harmful effects on health and life. Besides there are products with high chances of accidents like certain types of polyurethane form used in bedding and mattresses which are highly inflammable.

(vi) ***Ecological Awaraness.*** There are three categories of products which causes ecological problems. Firstly, there are products whose production causes environmental problems. Secondly, there are products whose production cause depletion of natural resources. Thirdly, there are products whose consumption or use causes ecological problem. Thrown away bottles, cans and other materials have made the affluent society an effluent society. Thus the short-term convenience gives rise to a long-term problem.

All these indicate that a socially responsible company must take into account the long-run consumer and society welfare. The marketing concept should be revised incorporating the long run society welfare. As Kotler observes, "the addition of long-run consumer welfare asks the businessmen to include social and ecological considerations, in his product and market planning. He is asked to do it not only to meet his social responsibilities but also because failure to do this may hurt his long-run interest as producer."

Many regarded the society marketing concept as utopian. There are still many who consider this concept as irrelevant, particularly in situations where a seller's market prevails. However, many companies have already adopted this concept and the developments in the advanced countries indicate that companies which want to be successful in future will invariably have to imbibe this philosophy.

ENVIRONMENTAL ANALYSIS AND DIAGNOSIS

The environmental facors have a profound impact on business. Environmental analysis and diagnosis are among the first steps in the strategic management process. Business dynamics depends on the environmental dynamics. Hence environmental analysis and diagnosis are very important for strategic managment analysis.

Wm. F. Ghierk has defined environmental analysis as " the process by which strategists monitor the economic, governemntal/ legal, market/competitive, supplier/technological, geographic and social setting to determine opportunities and threats to their firms."

According to Glueck, "Environmental diagnosis consists of managerial decisions made by analysing the significance of the date (opportunities and threats of the environmental analysis."

The definition of environmental analysis has been given in the context of the strategic management process for an existing firm. This environmental analysis is the cornerstone of new business opportunity analysis. Thus environmental analysis is an essential prerequsite for strategic management decision-making. In his book 'Marketing Management' Philip Kotler has described Marketing Environmental Audit as the first component of a marketing Audit.

Thus, the prospects of a business depend both on its resources and the environment. An analysis of the strengths, weaknesses, opporunities and threats (SWOT) is very much essential for the business policy formulation. The survival and success of a business firm depend on its innate strength, the resources at its command, including physical resources, financial resources, skill and organisation and its adaptability to the environment.

Every business enterprise consists of a set of internal factors and is confronted with a set of external factors. They may be described as follows:

1. ***The Internal Factors.*** These are generally regarded as controllable factors because the company has control over these factors. It can alter or modify factors, take personal, physical facilities, organisation and functional means, such as the marketing mix to suit the environment.
2. ***The External Factors.*** These are, by and large, beyond the control of a company. These are environmental factors such as the economic factors, socio-cultural factors, government and legal factors, demographic factors, geo-physical factors etc. As these are beyond the control of a firm, its success depends, to a very large extent, on its adaptability to the environment, *i.e.*, its ability to properly design and adjust the internal controllable variable to take advantage of the opportunities and to combat the threats in the environment.

Thus every company operates within a complex network of external environmental forces both international and national. Accoridng to Barry M. Ricchmen and Melyeyn Coper, "Environment factors or constraints are largely, if not totally, external and beyond the control of individual industrial enterprise and their managements. These are essentially the 'givers' within which firms and their managements must operate in a specific country and they vary, often greatly, from country to country."

The macro environment is not simply the forces operating outside the organisation. The forces create opportunities for the business organisations for their existence and development and pose threats or challenges affecting the business adversely. The environment includes factors ouside the firm "which can lead to opportunities for or threats to the firm.

ENVIRONMENTAL ANALYSIS AND DIAGNOSIS PROCESS

Environmental analysis is the process by which strategists monitor the environmental factors to determine opportunities for and threats to their firms. Analysis also involves studying the minutes of each factors to find its nature, function and relationship. Strategic manager, essentially searches for opportunities and threats, their sources and their impact on the business. Environmental diagnosis consists of managerial decisions made by assessing the significance of the data (opportunities and threats) of the environmental analysis. Environmental analysis and diagnosis are presented in the following chart. A strategist examines the relationship between the company's strategy and the environment. Then he/she forecasts the future environment. Then, he/she compares the strategy wih the future environment. If these are the gaps, he/she reformulates the strategy after revising the business mission and objectives. Otherwise, he will continue with the present strategy as presented in fig. given below:

The Environmental Analysis and Diagnosis Process

Environment of the Organisation	*Strategists Analyse and Diagnose Gaps*
(1)	*(2)*
International Environment	***Analysis:***
General (Natiornal) Environment Economic Political Technical.	1. Identify the current strategy the firm uses to relate to the environment. What are the assumptions or predictions about the environment on which current strategy is based?
Socio-cultrual Natural Industry	2. Predict the future environmental conditions. Are the assumptions or predictions the same as in step 1? Is this a gap?

Contd.

(1)	*(2)*
Market Suppliers Competitiors	***Diagnosis :*** 3. Assess the significance of the gap between the current and future environments for the firm. Are changes in objectives needed? Do changes in strategy appear useful to consider? Will they recue the gap?

Source : Adapted from Lawrence Rs. Lauch and William F. Glueck, op. cit. p 86.

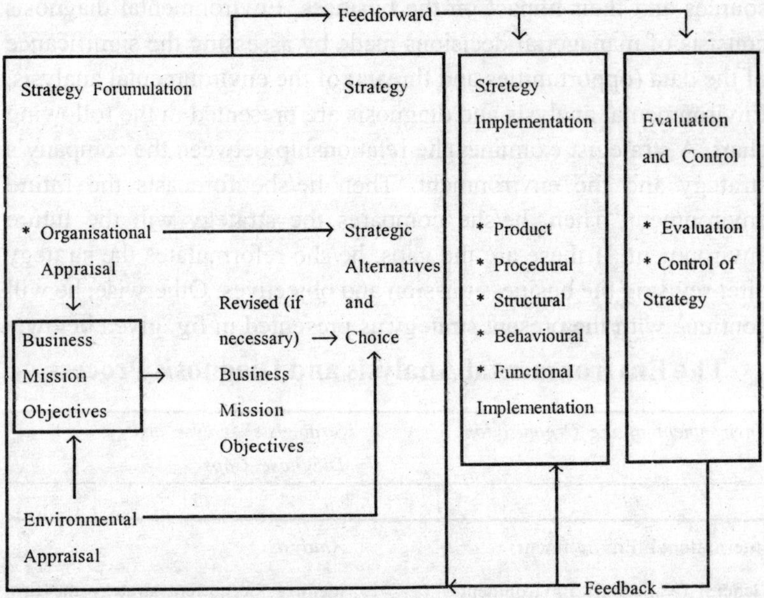

Strategic Management Process

Systematic environmental analysis and diagnosis are necessary due to the following reasons:

(1) Environmental factors are prime influences of strategy change.

(2) Environmental analysis and diagnosis provide the time to the strategist of forecast opportunities and to plan to respond aptly to these opportunities.

(3) Environmental analysis and diagnosis help strategists develop an early warning system to prevent threats to develop strategies which can convert a threat into an opportunity.

(4) They help to determine what factors in the environment present threats to the organisation's present strategy and objectives accomplishment.

(5) They also help in identifying the inherent risks involved in utilising the opportunities as normally, risks are involved in any opportunity.

(6) They help to determine what factors in the environment opportunities for optimal utilisation of resources and achievement of objectives effectively.

(7) Systematic analysis and diagnosis enable the managers, to predict the future and to have enough time for other activities. This minimises the time pressure of the managers on the unanticipated events, and

(8) They help the managers to achieve the organisational objectives effectively than other organisations.

Thus, these reasons, clearly state that environmental analysis and diagnosis are essential for effective strategic management.

PROCESS OF USING ENVIRONMENTAL ANALYSIS

The various processes or steps can be described as follows:

1. The assignment of environmental study project depends on the organisation and its practice of environmental study. If it is monitioring the environment on a continuous basis and some personnel are assigned for this purpose, these personnel can take up this job in addition to their duties. However, suitable personnel can be added to take up additional load of the work. If the organisation does not have this section, a special task force can be created for the purpose which may be termed as environmental analysis unit (EAU). The task between EAU and strategists shopuld be clearly demarcated so that exact term of reference can be fixed. The main task of EAU is to make the results of its

analysis known and understood to the strategists. It should be clear to EAU that data and analysis are only one kind of input to the strategy making process. Therefore, the analysis should not expect full use of their analysis or the power to prescribe strategy.

2. The trigger is an event or set of events that initiates strategy changes or creates need for environmental data. Events serving as triggers may take place outside the organisation, *e.g.*, a change in the Government's policy towards foreign technical collaboration or entry of new competitor with some unique features; or hiring of a new key executive. In fact, various triggers outside the organisation force managers to take environmental studies on specific project basis.
3. Direct use of environmental analysis in strategy making requires translation of environmental analysis into specific changes. When large amount of data is collected and analysed, either strategy makers can make decisions leading to strategic changes or they may create special task force whose task may be to make environmental analysis action-oriented. The task of the team will be to recommend actions to the strategy markers based on the environmental analysis. Effective translation of environmental analysis into specific strategic changes can be performed cooperatively by analysts, strategy markers, and task force if created.
3. Every organisation undertakes analysis of environment either on formal basis or informal basis depending on the size of the organisation, its managerial philosophy, the nature of its environment, etc., However, if environmental analysis is taken as on-going basis, it serves the organisational prupose in much better way. Moreover, on-going environmental study takes a much wider coverage of the environment. When an analysis is limited to specific projects, it covers only some areas in the environment

leaving blind spots in others. An on-going study can locate existing and potential impact of the environment on the organisation. This phase has to be directed by and is complementary to the phase of informal scanning. It should aim at broad coverage of the environment rather than deep analysis. This will serve two purposes it becomes complementary source for identifying perceived environmental causes for the changes in strategy, its ouput may serve as a trigger for strategy changes or for suggestion for detailed environmental analysis.

5. Triggers may be used as a means of strategy changes. However, strategy changes based on triggers alone may not give right direction for strategy changes but triggers must be used as the reasons for collecting appropriate information from the environment.
6. Data collection at this stage may be specific relating to the particular strategy which an organisation may consider seriously looking into various aspects, such as all those factors which go into choice of strategy. However, data collection and analysis can not be taken just to satisfy a strategy formation based on whims of some people at the top level of the organsiation.
7. The complete report then can be presented to those people who can make decision on it. Usually most of the organisations have certain specified groups of people who make strategic decisions. However, they can perform better if they work in closer contact with people responsible for scanning of environment.
8. As it has been pointed out earlier, environmental scanning is only one kind of inputs which goes in strategy formulation. Therefore, strategy makers may not necessarily go on the basis of report prepared by environmental scanning group. However, they are affected by the informational inputs. Therefore, environmental scanning can stimulate them indirectly to go for certain strategy.

9. Need for environmental data arises because of two factors: first, the organisation is taking up environmental analysis as an on-going process and second, when some triggers are there. While the first aspect emphasises the general study of the environment, the second emphasises on specific projects or areas to be studied.
10. Strategy makers may perceive the need for strategy changes in the light of environmental factors. This awareness of environmental forces and their impact on the organisation does not come suddenly. Moreover, this awareness fluctuates over the period of time.

TECHNIQUES OR SOURCES OF INFORMATION

First technique for environmental analysis, one normally used to gather information about potential or actual competitors, is spying. The top executive for, more likely, a middle-level executive encouraged, however, surreptitously, by a top executive employs an individual or individuals to determine trade secrets. The spy can be an employee of the competitor, one of the competitor's suppliers or customers, or a "professional" spy. Although it varies by industry and functional areas, industrial espionage appears to be increasing. This observation is based on survey data and expenditures on systems to protect trade secrets and industrial processes.

A second approach to analyzing the environment is formal forecasting. Normally it is performed by corporate planners or other staff personall or consultants at the request of top management. There is a group of consultants specializing in this called "futurists," and there are a number of journals dealing with this subject, such as *Technological Forecasting and Social Change, Jounrnal of Environment and Planning............Weekly Futures and Journal of Forecasting.*

Another solution is to design a management information system (MIS) to bring the information to the strategists. This approach formalizes the lines and staff gathering of the information desired by the strategists on a regular basis. Many experts advocates this approach, although some feel that a formal MIS fails to work properly, since information is often limited, untimely, or unreliable. Another version of an MIS is a strategic information sysems, which some firms have developed. Strategic data-bases can be developed by relying on inputs from customers, suppliers, competitors, internal managers, the sales forces, R & D units, and so on. These are often organized on the basis of answering questions which must be addressed in the strategic management process : What opportunities are available ? What environmental conditons will affect us? What competitve actions will affect us ? What strengths do we have? What weakenesses do we have? Strategic databases can be built from various infromation sources such that the strategic management process is facilitated. Problems similar to the MIS are to get managers to accept and use the SIS adequately.

Lastly of all, there is the gathering of verbal information, that is, information that we hear. This information can be gathered informally or formally for example, meetings and conferences.

Sources of verbal information include:

* Such media as radio and television.

* The firm's employees, such as peers, subordinates, and supervisors.

* Other outside the firm, including *(1)* government and university employees, *(2)* consultants, *(3)* financial executives such as bankers, stockholders, and stock analysts, *(4)* suppliers doing business with the firm, *(5)* persons in the industry channels (for example, wholesalers and brokers), *(6)* customers of the enterprise, and *(7)* competitors and their employees.

Written or documentary information is what we learn by reading from information prepared by others for various purposes. Managers read newspapers, trade journals, industry newsletters, and general publications. In some firms top managers subscribe to clipping services, which search periodicals and papers and summarize the information for them. A number of experts point out that much can be learned from reading the annual reports. The federal government requires that all firms listed on the stock exchanges must submit a 10 k to the securities and exchange commission.

There are a number of sources which can tell you where to locate information on a business if you are searching the environment as a manager or analyzing a case as a student.

FACTORS AFFECTING USE OF ENVIRONMENTAL ANALYSIS

Following are factors affecting use of environmental analysis:

1. The Nature of Information. The type of business the organisation is in or intends to be in determines the nature of information sought. Moreover, how an organisation defines its business also becomes an important factor determining the information requirements. If the organisation has defined its business narrowly, it will focus on the narrow aspect of the environment. Thus a highly diversified company may require diverse types of information. Similarly, if an organisation is conglomerate, its area of information search may be much broader.

2. The Geographic Dimension. The geographic dimension of the organisation affects the type of interaction which the organisation has with its environment. Generally greater is the area of organisation's operation, more will be its informational requirement because the environmental factors may differ from place to place. If an organisation is localised, it may require information about various aspects of the environment only as relevant to this area. However, when the area of operation increases, it may require information for those areas also. For example, the information requirement of multinationals, or organisation involved in international business is much more than that of local organisations.

3. The Organisational Growth. The age of the organisation may also determine the type of information that can be sought by it. The organisational growth over the period of time requires different type of interaction with its environment. Generally older is the age of the organisation with the more experienced managers, the narrower will be the focus on the environmental information because with the experience, managers may be able to distinguish what is relevant or irrelevant for the organisation. The necessary information may be sought and unnecessary will be screened out. Since the information can be tested to determine the organisational effectiveness by the managers, they can easily know the relevance of a particular piece of information.

4. Nature of Environment. The nature of environment, particularly in terms of homogenity and variability, will determine the type of information that managers seek from the environment. On the basis of the homogenity and variability of environment factors, the environment can be classified as follows:

(a) ***Size and Power of the Organisation.*** Size is an important factors for determining the interaction with the environment. Normally larger is the size of the organisation, more will be its interaction with its environment. When an organisation is small, it may be exempted from various legal provisions with regard to its various management practices. For example, the various labour legislations are applicable only when the organisation has achieved certain size. Similarly, the organisation is covered by MRTP Act or Industries (Development and Regulation) Act after it has achieved certain size.

(b) ***Managerial Philosophy.*** The managerial philosophy generally determines the actions which managers will take towards various factors affecting their decisions. Such factors may include the environmental forces as well as the various internal forces. If the managerial philosophy is positive, the managers are likely to take into account the various factors affecting the organisation while making decisions. In this respect, following proposition can be formulated : "All other factors being the same, the higher is the score of an organisation on the managerial philosophy index, the greater will be its concern for strategic managemental search and analysis."

The term managerial philosophy includes managers' attitudes, reactions to situations, and the way of looking at the things. If these are positive, they may go for long-term actions for which they require more information about the environment.

NEED FOR ENVIRONMENT SCANNING

The environmental scanning (appraisal) is the process by which promoters of the companies tries to monitor the economic changes, Governmnetal changes, suppliers attitude and market changes to determine new opportunities and threats if any. In simple words environmental analysis relates to identification and analysing environmental influences individually and collectively to face the future effects upon the society and business. Here the main stress is on tracing the sources of new opportunities or threats. No one can deny that it is not useful for evaluating the present strategy, new norms for future strategic decisions.

Every business fortune is influenced by social changes. Economical changes, political changes. In our country a lage number of textile mills are suffering from sickness (lesser profitability). The managerment philosophy, practice, procedures, products and technology were out of line with changes in environment.

The only surviving textile industry is Reliance which is making remarkable progress in growth and profitability. The clear reason is that Reliance took advantage of market needs and formulated strategies so that products are related to market needs.

The true management philosophy regarding expansion and growth must be alert to new opportunities arising out of new products. The management should understand the risk and accordingly should prepare its own strategies based on environmental analysis and its proper factual assessment.

What is the need of environmental analysis and appraisal ? The answer is very simple and logical as every management is concerned mostly with opportunities for more profits and growth and at the same time helps in minimisation of future threats. The future of an organisation is related with the environment in which the business is running. The growth and innovations and philosophy of change should be viewed with environmental effects. A fast changing business needs close study of facts: What are the probable threats to company. Some of the future events can be predicted by systematic scanning and follow up of environmental effects. The Environmental Scanning comprises information processing of social, economical, political, technological, product and changed market conditions.

The Research work on desirability of environmental analysis in U.S.A. has revealed that there is high degree positive correlation between environmental analysis and success of corporates. The related areas which are needed for growth due to environmental analysis needs the following considerations:

(a) Firms which had to face competition, Government regulations and healthy environment.

(b) Firms which are facing environment problems and headed by risk and uncertainty.

(c) Firms growing by mergers and thus increasing the complexity of environment.

The study revealed that corporations succeeded with little or no extra efforts at environment appraisal. The following are such firms:

(a) Firms with slow effect of environment changes and having risk prone management.

(b) Dominant firms with moderate risk-prone management.

(c) Firms with a desire of innovation of new product.

It is a considered opinion that increasing knowledge of the strategists in environment scanning there is a positive gain to the firm.

CHARACTERISTICS OF ENVIRONMENTAL ANALYSIS

Changing environment, the process of environmental analysis is very well comparable with the functions of radar. If a boat is sailing on a "sea of uncertainty", there are two essential requirements for a successful voyage. There has to be a star to steer the ship. Secondly, there must be radar to signal the existence of rocks, reefs and clear water in the uncharted sea. Thus in a business firm operating in an uncertain environment must have a vision (a guiding star) and a system of environmental analysis (the radar). From this analogy, it is possible to derive three important characteristics of the process of environmental analysis:

1. Environmental analysis is an exercise that it must comprise a total view of the environment rather than viewing trends piecemeal. A radar covers 360 degrees of the horizon, not just a segment, although it can focus on a particular segment if need be. The corporate radar must scan the whole circumference of its environment in order to minimise the chance of surprises and maximise its utility as an early warning system.
2. The analysis of environment must be a continuous process rather than being an intermittent scanning system. Like the radar, it must operate continuously in order to keep the speed of development.
3. Environmental analysis is an exploratory process. While the monitoring aspect of the system is concerned with present developments, a large part of the process seeks to explore the unknown terrain, the dimensions of possible futures, what could happen, not necessarily what will happen.

Which aspect of the environment should be management of any Organisation be concerned with? The factors that can influence future events and the sheer weight and volume or primary data be studied covering all major aspects.

Each company to set for itself the boundaries of the relevant environment and examine those variables which are critical to its own activities. This does not mean that firm engaged in manufacturing and selling products for the domestic market should monitor only the national environment, or an export firm should ignore the domestic product market conditions. For example, Reliance Textile Industries Ltd. initially focused on importing nylon yarn and polyster filaments for manufacturing fabrics primarily for the export market. The company deliberately chose not to expand its activities in the domestic market at that stage as it had identified that the market which was dominated by established leaders was not ripe for high-priced-quality products. It was in 1977 that the management realised potentiality of the internal market and decided to expand their operations on a large scale having the benefit of accumulated experience of supplying high-quality fabrics in the more competitive markets abroad.

Environmental factors are political, social, economic, legal/ regulatory and technological—may be of general specific relevance to enterprises. Further, each enterprise may perceive the relevant environment in the light of its own interest and set of circumstances which affect its functioning. Distinction may be made between three orders of environment indicators to decide upon the question of relevance. Thus, depending on the nature of environment factors to be considered, management may distinguish between:

(i) Indicators which affect all business enterprises at the national level. These indicators may be easy to identify but difficult to measure, *e.g.*, attitude of political parties towards private enterprise as reflected in election manifestoes, foreign economic relations, possibilities of armed conflicts, encounters, cold war and hostilities with neighbouring countries. etc.

(ii) Indicators relating to particular industry sectors, *e.g.*, for garment industry in India—the import-export policy of the Government of India, import restrictions in the United States and Western European countries, reservation of industries for the small-scale sector, delicensing of specific industries, and the like. These indicators may be relatively easier to measure though not so easy to identify.

(iii) Indicators relevant to individual enterprises, *e.g.*, for a company manufacturing agricultural pumpsets for irrigation—the progress of rural electrification; for a transport company—planned investment in the expansion of railway tracks and haulage capacity road construction, costs fuel and user needs for additional freight capacity.

Thus business environment may be defined as the set of external factors such as; economic factors, Geo-physical factors, Government and Legal factors which are uncontrollable in nature and affects the business decisions.

PROCESS OF ENVIRONMENTAL SCANNING

The study or scanning process is not difficult but not so easy as to which areas be covered and which should be left out. Researches conducted in the late 60s and 70s being revealed that the process of environmental analysis has been far from being systematic except with regard to information relating to current developments. Oral information from personal sources dominated the total input of information. Written and documentary information was much less frequently used by strategists. When written information were used they tended to be general information sources. Formal forecasting, if at all used, was viewed with great scepticism. Very little use was made of written studies, research reports, and meetings for environment search. Notwithstanding the above findings of research studies in the sixties and seventies and, perhaps because of these findings combined with the research findings on the beneficial effects of systematic analysis and diagnosis of external conditions the critical importance of developing as effective system of information gathering and information evaluation has been increasingly recognised over time by large enterprises.

Essentially, environmental scanning requires information inputs which can be derived from different sources:

A. **Industrial Informations.** Verbal information from such sources as the audio-visual media (radio and television); conversation among employees, managers, supervisors and subordinates; customer; distributors of the company's products (wholesalers, dealers, retailers); suppliers; competitors and their employees, financial executives in banks; stock brokers; consultants; government employees.

B. **Managerial Informations.** Information made available through the management information system which is specially designated to serve the needs of strategic planners.

C. **Written Informations.** Written and documentary information from newspapers, trade journals, industry newsletters, reports, documented clipping services;

D. **Industrial Informations.** Industrial espionage (spying) could also be a source of information about actual and potential competitors based on contacts with the employees, suppliers or customers of the competitors. Judging by survey data and expenses incurred on systems to protect trade secrets and industrial processes, it has been observed that industrial espionage and spying have been increasing in the United States. There is very little evidence in this respect about Indian industries.

Forecasting and reports based on forecasts regarding changes in economic, social and financial conditions available from governmental agencies and other specified consultancy service organisations.

ORGANISATIONAL APPRAISAL

Organisational appraisal is the process of monitoring an organisation's internal environment to identify strengths and weaknesses that may influence the firm's ability to achieve goals. The internal environment of an organisation includes forces that operate inside the organisation with specific implications for managing organisational performance. Internal environemntal factors, unlikc external environmental factors come from within. These factors, collectively define both trouble spots that need strengthening and the core competencies that the firm can build. An organisation can better analyse how much activity might add value or contribute significantly to shape an effective strategy by systematically examining its internal environment. Michael Porter has proposed a method for such an evaluation. This method is called value chain analysis. Value chain analysis can identify internal core competencies. Internal core competencies can be identified by analysing functional areas of business. The purpose of analysing an organisation's internal environment is to identify and evaluate organisational strengths and weaknesses.

STRENGTHS AND WEAKNESSES ANALYSIS

Organisational analysis requires data and information about the internal environment. SWOT analysis refines this information by applying a general framework for understanding and managing the environment under which a company operates. (The acronym SWOT stands for strengths, weaknesses, opportunities and threats). A SWOT analysis consists of evaluating a company's internal strengths and weaknesses and its external opportunities and threats. SWOT analysis underscores the basic point that strategy must produce a good fit between a firm's internal capability (its strengths and weaknesses) and its external situation (its opportunities and threats).

1. **Identifying Strengths and Weaknesses.** A strength is a strong point for the company *i.e.*, something a company is good at doing or a characteristics that gives it an important capability. A strength can be a skill, a competence, a valuable organisational resource or competitive capability or achievement that gives the company an advantage. A weakness is something the company does not have or does poorly (in comparison to competitors or standards) or a condition that put it at a disadvantageous positions. A weakness may or may not make an organisation competitively vulnerable, depending on how much it matters in the competition battle.

   A company's strengths are more significant. They can be used as cornerstones of the strategy. They are the basis for building competitive advantages. If a company does not have strengths to build competitive advantages, the management has to develop competencies quickly. These competencies can be the basis for building competitive advantages, the management has to develop competencies quickly. These competencies can be the basis for building competitive advantages.

   Successful strategists seek to exploit what a company does best—its expertise, strengths, core competencies and strongest competitive capabilities. At the same time, the successful strategists seek to correct the competitive weaknesses. Otherwise, these weaknesses hurt the company's performance, and disqualify it from pursuing an attractive opportunity. In essence, an organisation's strategy should be well-fitted to company's strengths, weaknesses and competitive capabilities. Thus, the company should built its strategy around the strengths and avoid the arena of weaknesses.

2. **Distinctive/Core Competencies.** The company should consolidate its production, technology, marketing, finance and human resource know-how into competencies to enhance its competitiveness. A distinctive or core competence is something a company does especially well in comparison to its competitors. The distinctive competence is the unique capability it gives an organisation in capitalising upon a particular opportunity; the competitive edge it may give a firm in the market place and the potential for building a distinctive competnece and making it the cornerstone of strategy. Thus, a distinctive competence is, "any advantage a company has over its competitors because it can do something which they can not or it can do something better than they can."

   Distinctive or core competencies empower a company to build competitive advantage. Core competencies include excellent quality maintenance, lowest production cost, latest technology utilisation, ability to provide required service, ability to develop new products, high credit worthiness etc.

   The benefits of core competences in formulating strategies include: *(1)* the company gets an added capability in going after a particular market opportunity, *(2)* the company gets the competitive edge it can yield in the market place, and *(3)* its potential for being cornerstone of strategy.

3. **Identifying Opportunities and Threats.** There are differences between the industry's opportunities and a firm's opportunities except in one firm industry. Some firms are in better position than other firms in the same industry, in utilising the opportunities. This situation is

based on the firm's strengths and weaknesses. The industry's opportunities most relevant to a specific firm are those that offer significant avenues for growth and those where a firm has the most potential for competitive advantages. Certain external environmental factors poses threats to a firm. These threats include: adoption of latest technology by the competitors, in-flow of high quality and improved products from foreign markets, entry of multinational and transnational corporations, change in the customer's preferences, change in governmental policies, failure of the markets, etc.

Strategy must be formulated to *(i)* purpose opportunities suited to the firm's strengths of competencies, and *(ii)* provide a defense against threats posed by the environment. The SWOT analysis should appraise a firm's strengths, weaknesses, opportunities and threats and draw conclusions about the firm's attractiveness.

4. **Strategic Cost Analysis.** One of the critical strengths of a company is its cost position relative to competitors. Cost comparison is critical particularly for those companies producing consumer goods. Therefore, assessing whether a company's costs are competitive with those of its close rivals is a necessary and crucial part of a company's internal environmental analysis. Cost differences among rivals can stem from many factors like prices of raw materials, salary levels, and cost of transportation. The lower a company's costs are below those of rivals, the company has an advantage over its competitors. Otherwise, it comes competitively vulnerable to the company. Strategic cost analysis involves comparing a company's cost position relative to key competitors, activity by activity from raw materials purchase to the price paid by ultimate customers.

Organisation requires cross-functional cooperation to collect data about present and future environments. SWOT analysis becomes a team effort performed by functional specialists from finance, human resources, marketing, production etc. Information gathered from key employees can also help managers better understand the internal environment of the organisation. Internal environmental forecasting, is a critical step in SWOT analysis. It is the process of identifying strategic issues that will affect an organisation's environment at some future time.

DETERMINANTS OF STRATEGIC ADVANTAGE ANALYSIS AND DIAGNOSIS

Strategic advantage analysis is the process by which the strategists examine the firm's resources and capabilities in the key functional areas to determine where the firm has significant strength (and weaknesses) so that it can exploit the opportunities and meet the threats in the environment. The essential purpose of each analysis is to take advantage of the distinctive competencies of the firm by way of:

Following a course of action different from those of rival firms, developing a strategy which will provide different and better outcome than those of its competitors, and making it difficult for other firms to duplicate the strategy or enter the area of opportunity if the strategy works.

It is possible to list the factors and attributes which should be of common concern to the strategists in firms operating in a competitive environment. For the purpose Stevenson listed the following groups of factors.

Categories Factors

1. Organisation

A. Top management interest and skill

B. Standard operating procedure

C. The planning system

D. The control system

E. Organisational form and structure

2. Marketing

A. Reputation

B. Product quality

C. Knowledge of the customer's needs

D. Sales force

E. Breadth of the product line

F. Customer force

3. Personnel

A. Number of employees

B. Experience

C. Employee attitude

D. Technical skills

4. Finance

A. Price-earning ratio

B. Financial size

C. Growth pattern

5. Technical

A. Basic research

B. Product development

C. Production facilities

D. Production techniques

Assessment of the strength & weakness of a firm for an analysis has following factors.

(1) Personnel. Human resource capabilities and organisational factors are closely interrelated. Together they constitute the corporate resources. The quality of managerial, technical and other employees, the organisational climate, union-management relations, personnel policies and practices and similar factors are crucial determinants of organisational effectiveness. Strengths and weaknesses relating to these resources should be analysed in terms of the following elements:

(a) ***Managerial (leadership) Style.*** What are the characteristic features of managerial style with respect to delegation, participative decision-making, communication channels, and control?

(b) ***Union-management Relations.*** Is the degree of unionisation among employees of a high order? Does the management maintain harmonious relations with the unions?

(c) ***Corporate Image.*** Is the image of the company a source of loyalty and pride of the employees?

(d) ***Organisational Climate.*** How healthy is it?

(e) ***Employee Performance Record.*** How does it compare with similar firms? Has it been consistent?

(f) ***Personnel Policies and Practices.*** Are company policies effectively implemented with respect to staffying, promotion, training and development, compensation and benefits? How do the policies compare with competing firms?

(2) Production. Production management contribute a great deal to a firm's profitability through efficient use of capital and human resources. It needs to be mentioned that production, manufacturing and related functions are closely related with the marketing and distribution functions. The following aspects of production and operations management should be considered in the assessment of capabilities:

(a) ***Cost and Availability of Material and Components.*** What is the relative level of cost of raw materials and components? Are these adequately available?

(b) ***Plant Location.*** Is the location of plant facilities congenial from the strategic point of view?

(c) ***Cost of Operations.*** How do costs of operation compare with those of competing firms? How efficient is the system of cost control?

(d) ***Purchasing and Inventory Control.*** Does the company have effective purchasing and inventory control systems?

(e) ***Production Facilities.*** Are production facilities adequate, modern, and well maintained? How do the facilities compare with those of competitors?

(f) ***Capacity Utilisation.*** Is the production capacity adequate to meet existing and potential demand? Is the capacity fully utilised? If nct, what is the extent of underutilisation?

(g) ***Operations Procedures.*** How efficient are the procedures relating to design, scheduling, testing, tooling and quality control?

(h) ***Production Control and Management Information.*** Are the management information and production control systems effective?

(3) **Finance.** The finance resources indicate to what extent the firm can make commitments to implement a strategy. Planned acquisition and utilisation of funds, expenditure control and the reporting of relevant financial and accounting information to the concerned managers as well as other parties are of crucial importance in every organisation. Assessment of the finance and accounting factors involves checking on the following aspects:

(a) ***Accounting System and Audit Procedure.*** Does the company have effective accounting systems for cost, budget and profit planning, and auditing procedures?

(b) ***Financial Planning and Budgeting.*** How efficient are financial planning and budgeting procedures?

(c) ***Financial Resources and Strength.*** Are long-term funds available or can be procured consistently with industry needs and relative to competitors?

(d) ***Tax Planning and Tax Advantages.*** Does the company enjoy tax advantages and avail of tax concessions through tax planning?

(e) ***Capital Strcuture and Cost of Capital.*** Is capital gearing planned optimally? How does the cost of capital compare with that of industry and competing firms?

(*f*) ***Relations with Owners (Shareholders).*** Are the company's devidend and profit retention policies consistent with shareholders.

(4) Research & Development. Development of new products and innovations in product design and production processes which constitute R & D functions are important parameters that often determine the success and future growth of industrial enterprises. R & D work may include exploratory (basic) research, new product or process research, improvement research, cost reduction research, and raw material adaptation research. The significance of these functions in a company lies in the competitive advantages which may accrue by way of new or improved products as also improvement in manufacturing processes leading to cost advantages. The capabilities of a company in this area can be analysed with reference to the following factors:

(i) What has been the result of R & D efforts during the last five years? How well are these efforts organised and managed.

(ii) How does the company's technical personnel compare with that of the competitor's?

(iii) Is the work environment conducive to creativity and innovation? Are the managers well disposed towards innovation and change?

(iv) What is the mix of basic, long term R & D projects and applied short term projects?

(v) Does the company have adequate R & D facilities, laboratories, equipment, tooling and testing arrangements? Are the facilities consistent with the latest scientific advancements? How efficiently are the facilities maintained and used?

(vi) What is the amount of R & D expenditure and what is the basis of investment outlay and recurring expenditure on R & D?

(5) Marketing. The marketing function is considered to be a key area not only because on its performance depends the success or failure of business activities, but also because it provides "a vital interface and communication link between the organisation and the external environment." The analysis of marketing capabilities should include the following elements:

(i) Has the advertising policy led to the establishment of a brand image?

(ii) Does the product line consists of a wide range and variety of designs and qualities?

(iii) Does the firm have a sizable market share?

(iv) How efficient and effective is the packaging and similar services?

(v) In the policy consistent with competition, consumer preference, technological change and other environmental factors?

(vi) Does the company have a separate market research unit, if so, how effective is it?

(vii) How effective is it?

(viii) Do the sales depend on a few customers?

(ix) In what phase of the life-cycle are the main products : introductory, growth, saturation or declining phase?

(x) How effective are the channels in terms of market coverage?

(6) Corporate Management. General management refers to the organisational function responsible for the overall performance of the firm. The capability of general management is thus defined as its propensity and its ability to engage in behaviour which will optimise attainment of the firm's objectives. This capability may be assessed by reference to the responsiveness of the firm to environment changes, and analysing the managers' willingness to respond and their competence, *i.e.*, ability to respond. While the managers themselves have a key role in determining their capability, the characteristics of the organisation through which they work are equally significant. Thus the managerial profit must be considered along with the organisational climate and organisational competence while diagnosing the general management capability. A profile of general management capability should therefore comprise the following aspects:

A. ORGANISATIONAL CLIMATE & COMPETENCE

(i) Culture

* Organisational attitude towards change (whether the organisation is hostile, passive or predisposed to change);
* Propensity towards risk (whether managers as a group are risk-averse, risk tolerant or risk-prone, whether they welcome novel risks or prefer only familiar risks);
* The time perspective in which the management perceives its problems (whether they rely only on past experience, prefer to deal with the present, or futuristic in outlook);
* The action perspective (whether organisational attention and energies are focussed on internal operations or external environment);
* The behavioural goals (whether thrust is on stability, efficiency, effectiveness, growth or innovation);
* What triggers change (is it crisis, unsatisfactory performance, or change is continuously sought after);
* Collective perception of the critical success factors (shared model of the world);

(ii) Power

* Distribution of power among groups with different cutlures;
* Stability of the power structure;
* Militancy of the power centres.

(iii) The organisational problem-solving skills and style (whether problem-solving is based on precedents, trial and error, optimisation of available alternatives, or generation of new alternatives);

(iv) The problem-solving process (whether compartmentalised, hierarchical, or decentralised and problem-centered); and

The management process-whether it is creative, anticipatory, or backward-looking;

(v) The information system (whether information used in managing are historical data, extrapolations, or wideranging with environmental scanning); and

The organisation structure—its flexibility and adaptability;

(vi) The technological aids to decision-making the models, computer programmes used; and

Organisational capacity.

(vii) Managerial rewards system and incentives; and how are managerial jobs defined—is it narrowly circumscribed, or open, encouraging venture and initiative;

B. MANAGERS

(i) Capacity

* Personal work capacity and
* Work habits.

(ii) Mentality

* Their relative preoccupation with external v. internal problems; and
* The past v. future times orientation;
* Perception of the critical success factors and behaviours; and
* Values, norms and personal goals of managers.

(iii) Power

* Power position of the manager in the firm and
* His ambitiousness and drive to use power.

(iv) Competence

* Talents and problem-solving skills;
* Leadership skills; and
* Knowledge about the firm and environment.

SOURCES OF DATA AND METHODS FOR ANALYSIS

As in the case of environmental scanning, the relevant data for internal resources analysis may be available from different sources including verbal messages, phblished documents, study reports, etc. Some of the data gathered during environmental analysis may also be the basis of analysing and diagnosing internal capabilities. For instance, the technological environment may indicate the relative strength or otherwise of company's R & D efforts. Besides, data generated in the normal course of business operations is a veritable source as also the data provided by the management information system. Another source of data happens to be the annual reports of companies and other supplementary statements based on the accounting and financial records of the current and preceding periods.

Following are the methods of systematic assessment of the internal resource and identifying the areas of strategic advantages (Strength) & weaknesses (disadvantages) of an organisation:

1. Strategic Advantage Profile. A profile of strategic advantages (SAP) is a summary statement which provides an overview of the advantages and disadvantages in key areas likely to affect future operations of the firm. It is a tool for making a systematic evaluation of the strategic advantages factors which are significant for the compnay in its environment. The preparation of such a profile presupposes detailed analysis and diagnosis of the factors in each of the functional areas. The relevant data for the critical areas may go as a supplement of the profile. The following Strategic Advantage Profile relates to a food processing company in India.

STRATEGIC ADVANTAGES PROFILE (SAP) OF ABC INDIA LTD.

Internal Area	*(+) Strength (–) Weakness*
(1) Corporate Resources	(+) Management team comprises young, ambitious executives.
(2) Finance	(–) No additional investment sicne 1980.
	(–) Heavy reliance on fixed deposits and bank loans.
	(+) Parent US company now interested in expansion.
(3) R & D	(–) No R & D effort so far
	(+) Backing in R & D expected from parent US company.
(4) Operations	(–) Stagnating sales performance.
	(+) Profits after tax picking up after 1993.
	(–) Plant facilities are old.
(5) Marketing	(+) Capable sales force; sales agents dispensed with.
	(–) Shinking market for most products.

The Strategic Advantage Profile is a summary statement of corporate capabilities, in summarising the functional competencies a comparative view needs to be taken in the light of external conditions and the time horizon of projections. For example, while comparing the level of inventory holding, one may find it do be relatively higher than that of competing firms; as such it should be regarded as a weakness. But if the market demand shows an upward trend, the apparent weakness should be considered a strength.

In the preparation of SAP one must also reckon the probability of the strength or advantage continuing in future and how long it can be relied upon. For, competitors are likely to be equally alert and may bridge the gap sooner or later. A company may identify its relative strength in the personnel area with highly skilled workmen and technical staff manning the production department; however, its production facilities may be old and outdated. It is obvious that the technical competence in the personnel area can hardly be regarded as a potential strength unless the company removes the weakness of obsolete production facilities.

The company should recognise the importance of its unique capabilities and capitalise the advantages rather than spreading its resources. At the same time, it must recognise the danger of relying on strengths in a particular area without simultaneously reckoning the capabilities in other interdependent units of activity. It is thus very well suggested that "a firm should develop a strategy over time which revolves around an area of distinctive advantages..., develop slack resources, and these can evolve into new areas of strength.

2. SWOT Analysis. The diagnosis of a firm's strengths and weaknesses can be fruitful only if the environmental factors and market conditions are considered along with the internal capabilities. This approach essentially involves matching of the internal capabilities with the environmental opportunities and threats, and is known as SWOT (Strengths and Weaknesses, Opportunities and Threats) analysis. In a way SWOT analysis may be said to consist of interlinking the ETOP and SAP. The extent of matching of internal capabilities and environmental conditions is reflected in the following schematic view of the position of ABC Industries Ltd.

ABC INDUSTRIES LTD.

MATCHING INTERNAL CAPABILITIES WITH ENVIRONMENTAL FACTORS

	Internal Capabilities	*Environmental Factors*
(A)	Voluntary equity participation of dealers resluting in assured commitment.	Need for identifying design changes to cater to 'shifts' in fashion.

Contd.

	Internal Capabilities	*Environmental Factors*
(B)	—cash generation on account of exports and yarn sales	Necessity of providing full range of of fabrics under one roof catering to 'family-purchase'.
(C)	—tax planning,	Restrictions in imports of fabrics.
(D)	Financial strength derived from: —ability to generate foreign exchange,	Willingness of consumers in various segments to pay high price to match the quality requirements.
(E)	Design capabilities to provide diversity of designs as also frequency of change.	Awareness of foreign fashions and wide range of designs of international standards.
(F)	Modern plant & machinery: production and technological capabilities of a high order.	Growth demand for high quality fabrics in different categories of blends.

The basic objective of this analysis is to provide a framework to reflect on the firm's ability to overcome threats and avail of the opportunities emerging in the environment. The dimensions of internal capabilities have relevance in so far as they relate to the environmental conditions. Hence, the analysis of comparative strengths and weaknesses requires linking internal capabilities with the characteristics of external environment.

Matching strengths and weaknesses with opportunities and threats requires that an organisation should direct its stengths towards exploiting opportunities and blocking threats while minimising exposure of its weaknesses at the same time. Thus, strategies, which are based on the matching of strengths and opportunities may be regarded as exploitative or developmental strategy. Those which direct strengths to threats may be called blocking strategies. If strengths are based on repair weaknesses, one may call it remedial strategy.

This analysis may provide the basis of a comprehensive approach to strategy. Capability in market research should enable an organisation to seek out market segments which are not so far identified by competitors. The same capability may be used to repair the present dependence on a narrow market segment. Cost efficiency of a firm may enable it to increase market share through an appropriate pricing strategy. With a strong financial position, the firm may imporve its production facilities or technological capability and thereby increase market share. If the weakness of a firm lies in its distribution network, or cost levels, the appropriate strategy should be to concerntrate on a market segment in which customers are less price conscious and prefer a service.

3. Functional-Area Profile and Resource-Deployment Matrix. Developed by Hofer and Schandel, this method requires the preparation of a matrix of functional areas with characteristics common to each, *e.g.*, focus of financial outlay, physical resources position, organisational system, and technological capability. It is required that the source outlay and focus of cfforts over time in the respective functional areas be presented also in the form of a matrix. Such a profile is expected to indicate how the key functional areas stand in relation to each other and as compared with the competitors with respect to the deployment of resources and the focus of efforts in the respective areas.

The functional-area profile and the resource-deployment matrix obviously determine the interpretation and diagnosis of the data and constitute the basis on which strengths and weaknesses are to be identified. While appraising the capabilities in each functional area, the strategist should consider what the policies and approaches governing the operations in the area were, are and will be. In this process, one might discover that an element of strength could become a source of weakness in future. It is necessary that the analysis takes into account the position over a period of time. This would enable the strategist to see whether areas of advantage are being further strengthened or getting dissipated.

Piecemeal analysis of the capabilities in each functional area may be misleading. The relative strengths and weaknesses of the key functional areas should be considered together. If an organisation has developed competencies in one functional area, it needs to be examined whether the capabilities in other areas have compatible potentialities. Otherwise, the imbalance may lead to a position of weaknesses for the company as a whole. The element of strength in productive efficiency had to be viewed differently in the light of the firms marketing competence.

Another important aspect of capability analysis is the comparison of strengths vis-a-vis weaknesses. Emphasising strengths rather than weaknesses is often justified for it may be useful to take advantage of an opportunity on the basis of identified strengths rather than viewing weaknesses must be considered in the light of external conditions. This is usually done but only in relation to competing firms. That is internal resources are compared with those of competing firms whereas other dimensions of the environment might be equally important to warrant consideration.

Needless to say that the choice of firms for comparison should be appropriate. It may be useful to compare the capabilities with those of a firm which are in the same phase of product life-cycle. In general, companies with similar mission statements may be chosen for purposes of comparing the internal resources. Even then, the comparative data need to be interpreted with care. For it is possible that in the case of comparable firms, there may be indicators of strength along with indicators of weakness, and it would not be proper to pick up a single indicator for comparison.

Executives are often inclined to diagnose strengths and weaknesses on the basis of operational details and the outcome of decisions on minor problems thus ignoring the more vital areas of strenghts and weaknesses which may be important for overall assessment of capabilities. To forestall this possibility executives should first identify the key areas and indicators that would be the focus of attention of top management.

FACTORS AFFECTING ENVIRONMENT SCANNING

Several factors affect the environmental scanning. These factors are classified as *(i)* Strategist related factors, *(ii)* Organisation related factors *(iii)* Environment related factors.

(i) Strategist related factors include: age, family backround, educational back ground, experience, socio-cultural background, motivational level, perception and cognitive styles, ability to face challenges, ability to cope up with stress, ability to motivate and lead the people, ability to adopt to different cultures and problem situations, ability to form and lead team work, ability to forecast, judgement, analytical and interpretation skills etc.

(ii) Organisation related factors include the nature of the business, product or services and markets, age, size and complexity of the organisation, organisation structure and its nature etc.

(iii) Environmental factors include:complexity, volatility or turbulence hostility and diversity of the environment.

The strategist may face the problem of comprehending the massive information and a number of environmental factors. Hence, the strategist should select the priority environmental factors to forecast the future or scanning the environment There are three types of scanning systems. They are:

(i) lrregular Scanning Systems. These consist of ad hoc studies in response to environmental crises.

(ii) Regular Scanning Systems. These consist of regular reviews of the environment or selected strategic environmental components. These reviews include annual planning exercises.

(iii) Continuous Scanning Systems. This is an ongoing activity. Established boundary, spanning offices often coordinate this activity. This is more future oriented system.

Environmental analysis cannot be complete without diagnosis of the results of analysis. Diagnosis of the environment actually involves assessment of the opportunities and threats identified in the process of analysis. On the basis of available data, the strategist must decide as to which sets of information to rely on and which sets to ignore, and sort out the more important from the less important information. This is indeed a difficult but nonetheless necessary task.

For large enterprise, the available information may be so diverse and so voluminous that efffective diagnosis may be all the more difficult. And yet managers must face the problem and identify the more substantive information as well as decide to act upon them.

There are three aspects of the diagnostic exercise which need to be kept in view:

1. The role and characteristics of strategists;
2. The strategists' job;and
3. Nature of the environment.

To what extent and how effectively diagnosis is carried out depend a great deal on the role and characteristics of the strategists. The strategic planners may consist of several groups, *e.g.*, the top management, the Board of Directors, corporate planners and sometimes consultants. Usually, the top management team (Chief executice and heads of functional departments and divisions) is primarily concerned with diagnosis and decision-making. Corporate planners carry out detailed analysis of the environmental factors on the basis of verbal and documentary information,forecasts and studies,and render necessary advise to the top management on the relative importance of environmental information. Consultants are sometimes engaged to advise top managers on diagnostic problems. Of all these groups the top management team has the most significant role in making diagnosis relatively more effective.

How well the diagnosis is carried out, however, depends also on the characteristics of the strategists. The more important determining factors in that respect are:

* the age and experience of the executives;
* motivation and aspiration level which are governed by *(a)* their felt needs of achievement, affiliation and power, and *(b)* the rewards for performance linked with long-run results rather than short-run attainments;
* perceptual factors, *i.e.*, pre-disposition towards the uncertainty of future conditions which include *(a)* risk-

orientation and willingness to take, risk, *(b)* ability to reflect rather than acting on impulse, *(c)* dogmatism or closed-belief, and *(d)* ability to deal with abstract concepts and ideas;

* psychological moods reflecting optimism and pessimism; and
* psychological preparedness to accept change.

A combination of certain characteristics may be congenial for and lead to better and more accurate diagnosis. Senior executives having relevant experience, an optimistic frame of mind and willingness to take risks will perceive more of opportunities than threats in the same set of data, and will be inclined to be pro-active as well as favour changes and innovation. On the other hand, diagnosis can hardly be thorough and effective if managerial rewards are based on short-run actions and results, or if managers have been accustomed to deal with problems and immediate remedies rather than diagnosing more fundamental long-run trends.

The second aspect of the diagnostic exercise relates to the stresses and strains of the job of diagnosis. The strains may be caused by a number of factors, *e.g.*,

(i) Time-pressure and preoccupation of executives with pressing duties of current significance;

(ii) Lack of discretionary powers of managers;

(iii) Inadequacy of available resources to carry out extensive search for and processing of data;

(iv) Inter personal conflict and power-play in the management team; and

(v) Information overload with the consequent breakdown of effective diagnosis.

The stresses and strains can be reduced to a great extent by effective delegation and other means like developing managerial abilities for effective diagnosis, inculcating team-spirit and group-cohesiveness in decision-making.

The quality of diagnosis depends on a third set of factors related with the characteristies of the environment. The company's dependence on suppliers, dominance of key owners (controlling investors), intensity of competition and similar environmental conditions are likely to influence the diagnosis, for management would necessarily have to attach greater importance to information pertaining to those factors. A hostile environment characterised by unfavourable factors facing the company is likely to prompt management to devote greater attention to the threats and respond quickly to the challenges. Unfavourable conditions may consist of an impending industrial recession, social values being opposed to the operations of the company, or a hostile competitive environment. Again, a volatile, dynamic environment with irregular. Less predicatable changes may cause the diagnosis of environment to be more incisive, comprehensive and timely. In a complex environment, the cost of search may also be a factor affecting the quality of diagnosis. If the firm cannot afford to bear the cost of research, diagnosis may be rendered imperfect.

ETOP : A TECHNIQUE OF DIAGNOSIS

Assessment of the environmental informational and determining the relative significance of threats and opportunities require a systematic evaluation of the information devleoped in the course of environmental analysis. For this purpose, preparation of a profile of environmental threat and opportunity (ETOP) is considered to be a useful device. As a summarised depiction of the environmental factors and their impact on future conditions the profile is a convenient means by which attention to top management may be drawn to the most critical factors and "their potential impact on the strategy of the firm as a whole and key aspects of its operations."

An illustrative profile is given below on the basis of environmental analysis carried out by Bharat Heavy Elctricals Ltd. A more detailed profile should include estimates of environmental impact on the future cost and revenue of the company.

BHEL : ENVIRONMENTAL THREAT AND OPPORTUNITY PROFILE (ETOP)

Environmental Sector		*Impact*
		(+) Opportunity (–) Threat
Socio-economic	(+)	Continued emphasis on infrastructural develop-ment which includes power supply for industry, transport, and domestic consumption.
	(–)	Severe resource constraints.
Technological	(+)	High growth envisaged in industrial production and technology upgradation.
Supplier	(–)	Sources of technology will become scarce due to formation of technology cartels.
Government	(+)	Liberalisation of technology import policy.
Competition	(–)	Customers will become more discerning in their requirments due to an increasing role of power plant consultants.
	(–)	Public sector will find it increasingly difficult to retain specialists and highly qualified personnel.

DESIGNING STRATEGIES TO OPTIMISE OPPORTUNITIES

An outcome of environment scanning is likely to be identification of available opportunities. Management should thus be concerned with designing strategies so as to avail of the opportunities with optimum results. The process of designing strategies to that effect is a difficult task. "It usually means questioning old methods, exploring unfamiliar environmental waters, facing up to an objective evaluation of strengths and weaknesses, forcing important changes on people in the firm and on organisational arrangements, and taking high risks with the firm's capital. Moreover, it has to be done in a world of rapid change, and it has to be done continuously."

In spite of the difficult nature of the task, designing strategies may be rendered manageable if the following aspects of strategic planning are given special emphasis:

(i) Selection of Issues. To start with, key planning issues likely to be critical to the success of the strategy must be identified, which will help to focus and determine the priorities to be accorded to data collection efforts relating to the issues. The issues of critical importance may include competitive domestic trends, global competition, export potential, customer or user preference, technological trends, diversification opportunities, etc.

(ii) Impact Study. The third important requirement is conducting impact studies to determine the overall consequences of implementing available alternative strategies. This will in turn require transforming environmental data into situation specific information.

(iii) Selection of Data. Selection of pertinent data needs to be done keeping in view the likely bias in personal data collection and the attendant problems of verifying and interpreting the same. Data available from public sources are comparatively more reliable. Even then, such data also need to be selected and generated for use after due consideration of their relevance, importance, manageability, variability and cost.

(iv) Flexibility of Strategic Plans. An element of flexibility needs to be incorporated in the strategies mainly because forecasting of environmental conditions cannot take care of uncertainties all the way. Flexible strategies may be designed in various ways, *e.g.*, *(a)* framing the strategy in general terms so as to give a direction but leaving some discretion in implementation; *(b)* reviewing strategies frequently; *(c)* keeping options open; or *(d)* allowing strategies to be used as rules so that exceptions may be justified.

❒

4

Strategy Evolution

EVAULATION OF STRATEGY

Strategic planning, it may be recalled, is an irregular process, though it is a continuing dynamic process of imlementating and revising policies and plans as chances occur in the capabilities, resources and environment. It is unstructured and irregular in that it comes up only when changes take place in the relevant environment or in the corporate resource position. The question of timing strategy evaluation is thus not so determinate. It may not be undertaken with any regularity of interval, nor a part of any formal system. Indeed, one point of view suggests that a comprehensive evaluation of strategy need not be a regular event; it is better undertaken only when there is a change of leadership or significant decline in financial performance. Several arguments may be advanced in favour of such a practice.

One, any activity that becomes an annual exercise is bound to be automatic and stereotyped, and hence may inhibit broad-ranging reflections called for in strategy evaluation, although an annual exercise might be helpful in developing a more efficient system of data collection and analysis.

Second, a viable strategy does not need reformulation at frequent intervals. Thus, comprehensive review of strategy is not necessary as a regular event what is needed is problem-solving in course of implementing the strategy, of course without ignoring the overall framework.

Third, frequent evaluation of a strategy may question the validity of the strategy built on the convictions and commitments of the key executives, which may seriously disturb the internal alignment of the firm.

Moreover, questioning the validity of a strategy through comprehensive review may not be desirable for competitive reasons. An unflinching, unshakeable position with regard to a firm's strategy is found to be advantegeous as a competitive strength, which tends to be weakened if the policies and plans are continually reviewed as to the advisability of the same.

What then should be then interval of time after which results should be evaluated? No doubt, a reasonable time should be allowed to pass after the implementation of strategy has commenced before results can be expected to have been achieved or evaluated. Does it mean that if goals or targets are set to be achieved in 5 years, then measurement and evaluation should take place at the end of that period? Obviously, it would be too late to take remedial action for correcting deviations, if any. Thus, a useful suggestion is that while setting targets and standards for evaluation, the specified time of desired results may be specified. Long-term targets may be broken down ito intermediate stages of progress. These would be the bench marks of progress. Thus, measurements for evaluation of results should be undertaken at periodical intervals in accordance with intermediate stages of progress relevant to the areas of operation.

Glueck and Jauch have suggested the use of a discriminating system of monitoring results analogous to the A B C system of inventory control. Environmental assumptions underlying the strategic goals may be regarded as 'A' factors-the few most important factors critical for success. Allowable variances in respect of these factors should be relatively narrow and measurement of actuals against standards should receive close attention and continuous monitoring. The majority of variables should be classfied as 'C' factors, which may provide warning signals through the progress of achievements but are not critical success factors. The tolerance limits of deviation with respect of these variables should be wider and they should be measured and evaluated periodically. The moderately large number of variables, to be classed as 'B' factors may be regarded as important but may take longer to be meaningful for evaluation; these variables should be evaluated as frequently as reliable indicators can be computed from he available data.

The purpose of strategic evaluation is to evaluate the effectiveness of strategy in achieving organisational objectives. Thus, strategic evaluation and control could be defined as the process of determining the effectiveness of a given strategy in achieving the organisational objectives and taking corrective action whenever required. From this definition, it is inferred that the nature of strategic evaluation and control process is to test the effectiveness of strategy. During the two preceding phases of strategic management process, the strategists formulate the strategy to acheive a set of objectives and then implement the strategy. Now there has to be a way of finding out whether the strategy being implemented is guiding the organisation towards its intended objectives. Strategic evaluation and control, therefore, performs the important task of keeping the organisation on the right track. In the absence of such a mechanism, there would be no means for strategists to find out whether or not the strategy is producing the desired effect. In this manner, through the process of strategic evaluation and control, the strategists attempt to answer following questions:

(i) Are the premises made during strategy formulation proving to be correct? Is the strategy guiding the organisation towards it intended objectives? Are the organisation and its managers doing things which ought to be done? Is there a need to change and reformulate the strategy?

(ii) How is the organisation performing? Are the time schedules being adhered to ? Are the resources being utilised properly? What needs to be done to esnure that resources are utilised properly and objectives are met?

The first set of questions relates to the more generalised and overarching issues of evaluation and are dealt with by the use of strategic control. The second set of question relates to issues that concern the peformance of tasks and are considered in operational control.

IMPORTANCE OF STRATEGIC EVALUATION

The process of strategic management requires that strategists lay down the objectives of the organisation and then formulate strategies to achieve them. The process of implementation of strategy starts with the identification of key managerial tasks which form the basis for the creation of organisation structure and design of system. Here, it should be reiterated that the segregation of key managerial tasks leads to a situation where individual managers are required to perform a small portion of the overall tasks required to implement a strategy. The fact that individually a manager performs a set of functions which are interrelated to the other tasks, managers elsewhere in the organisation are doing, makes it clear that the tasks have to be coordinated. The importance of strategic evaluation lies in its ability to coordinate the tasks performed by individual managers and also groups, divisions or SBUs-through control of performance. In the absence of a coordinating and controlling mechanism, individual managers may pursue goals which are inconsistent with the overall objectives of the department, division, SBU or the whole organisation

Besides the above, the importance of strategic evaluation is due to several other factors. These are: the need for feedback, appraisal and reward; check on the validity of strategic choice; congruence between decisions and intended strategy; intended strategy; successful culmination of the strategic management process.

There is need within an organisation to receive feedback on current performance so that appraisal can be done and good performance rewarded. Strategic evaluation helps to keep a check on the validity of strategic choice. An ongoing process of evaluation would, in fact, provide feedback on the continued relevance of the strategic choice made during the formulation phase.

During the course of strategy implementation, managers are required to take scores of decisions. Strategic evaluation can help to assess whether the decisions match the intended strategy requirements.

In the absence of such evaluation, managers would not explicitly know how to exercise such a discretion.

Strategic evaluation, through its process of control, feedback, rewards, and review, helps in a successful culmination of the strategic management process and the process of strategic evaluation provides a considerable amount of information and experience to strategists.

LIMITATION IN EVALUATION

The control system is an important component of strategy implementation. In the present context, the emphasis is on the evaluation of organisational units. In practice, by evaluating organisational units, one cannot avoid relying on the performance evaluation of individuals. This creates certain barriers in strategic evaluation and control. Following are the limitations:

(i) The evaluation process involves controlling the behaviour of individuals and, like any similar organisational mechanism, is likely to be resisted by managers.

(ii) By its very nature, any control mechanism presents the dilemma of too much versus too less control. It is never an easy task for strategists to decide the limits of control. Too much control may impair the ability of managers, adversely affect initiative and creativity, and create unnecessary impediments to efficient performance. On the other hand, too less control may make the strategic evaluation process ineffective and redundant.

(iii) Lastly the process of evaluation is fraught with dangers of difficulties in measurement. These mainly relate to the reliability and validity of measurement techniques used for evaluation. The control system may be distorted and may not evaluate uniformly or may measure attributes which are not inended to be evaluated.

ELEMENTS OF EVALUATION PROCESS

The process of evaluation basically deals with four steps:

A. Setting standards of performance.

B. Measurement of performance.

C. Analysing variances.

D. Taking corrective action.

These elements of the evaluation process, and how they relate to each other, are shown in the following fig. The strategy, plans, and objectives result in a set of performance standards which form the basis for evaluation through measurement of performance. The comparison of actual and standard performance leads to the analysis of variances. Feedback from this analysis results in either a check on performance, revaluation of standards, or reformulation of strategy, plans or objectives. Due to the inherent nature of operational control, corrective action is aimed mainly at performance and standard adjustment rather than the reformulation of strategy. The reformulation task is performed usually on the basis of strategic control, specially implementation control.

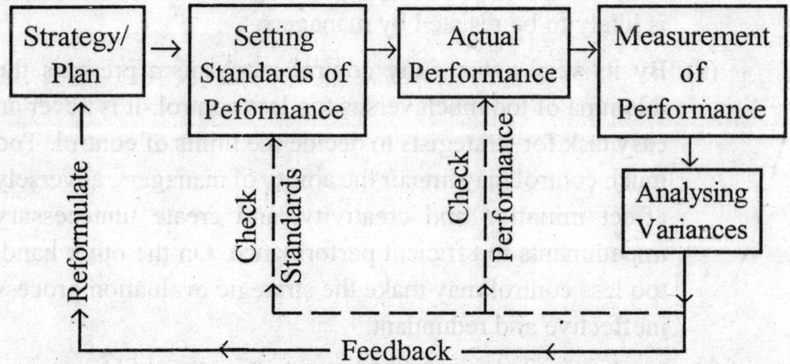

(A) Setting Standarding of Performanec. Strategists encounter the following three questions while dealing with standard setting: How to set standards? What standards to set? In what terms should standards be expressed? A three-pronged basic approach to standard-setting could be used to settle these issues.

(i) Performance indicators that best express the special requirements could then be decided upon to be used for evaluation.

(ii) The managerial tasks, derived from the strategic requirements, can be analysed for finding out the key areas of performance. Standards can then be set in each of these key areas.

(iii) The special requirements for the performance of the key tasks can help to determine the type of standards to set.

Applying this approach to the case of a company which adopts a market development strategy, it can be said that one of the key managerial tasks is to expand market presence and enhance market visibility. The special requirement is to raise the overall market share and two indicators, for instance, that could satisfy the requirements could be increased in sales revenue and efficiency of sales force.

Performance indicators—in orer to capture the reality of action—have to be set on the basis of quantitative (or objective) as well as qualitative (for subjective) criteria. Operational control can be effectively exercised through a combination of quantitiative and qualitative criteria.

(B) Measurement of Actual Performance. The evaluation process operates at the performance level as action takes place. Standards of performance act as the benchmark with which the actual performance is to be compared. It is important, however, to understand how the measurement of performance can take place. The information system is the key element in any measurement exercise. Operationally, measuring is done through accounting, reporting, and communication systems. A variety of evaluation techniques are used for measurement. Other aspects of measurement relate to the difficulties, timing, and periodicity in measuring.

If standards are appropriately set, and if means are available for measuring performance, evaluation is a fairly easy task. But there are several activities for which it is difficult to set standards and measure performance. The solution lies in developing verifiable objectives, stated in quantitative and qualitative terms, against which performance can be measured.

Timing relates to the point of time at which evaluation has to take place. In general, it could be said that delay in measurement can defeat the purpose of evaluation itself. On the other hand, measuring before timing cannot serve the purpose either. It is better to measure at critical points in a task schedule. Generally, the critical points would be at the end of a definable activity or the conclusion of the task. For instance, in a project implementation schedule, there could be several critical points at which measurement would take place.

(C) Analysing Variances. The measurement of actual performance and comparing it with the standard or budgeted performance leads to an analysis of variances. The following situations may arise:

(i) The actual performance matches he budgeted performance,

(ii) The actual performance deviates positively over the budgeted performance.

(iii) The actual performance deviates negatively from the budget performance.

The first situation is ideal but not realisitic. In practice, the actual performance rarely matches the budget performance.

The second situation is welcome as it is an indication of superior performance. But exceeding the targets continually should be considered as unusual and a check needs to be done for testing the validity of standards and the efficiency of the measurement system.

The third type of situation is alarming as it indicates a shortfall in achievement. The strategists need to pinpoint the areas where performance is below standards and go into the causes of deviation. Corrective action is taken on the basis of the analysis of the causes of deviation.

(D) Taking Corrective Action. Three causes for corrective action: checking of performance, checking of standards, and reformulating strategies, plans, and objectives are suggested here.

Initiating corrective action is not an insignificant part of the evaluation process; it involves a variety of managerial functions which are performed during strategy implementation. Performance is affected adversely due to a number of factors such as distortions in resource allocation, inappropriateness of structure and systems, and wrong leadership and motivational styles. If the evaluation process shows that performance is consistently lower than expected, the strategists would have to undertake an in-depth analysis and diagnosis of the factors that might be responsible for bad performance. Taking corrective action for checking performance, is therefore, a significant part of the day-to-day activities of managers.

Checking of standards is less frequent than a performance check but it will have to be done as soon as it is felt that there is nothing significantly wrong with performance. Standards check may result in a lowering of standards if it is concluded that organisational capabilities do not match the performance requirements. It may also lead to an elevation of standards if conditions have improved for better performance to take place. For instance, better equipment, improved systems, and upgraded skills are sure to make existing standards partly irrelevant. In such a situation, standards check would become necessary. a more radical and infrequent corrective action is to reformulate strategic plans, and objectives. Strategic, rather than operational control will lead to the conclusion that strategies need reformulation or plans need to be remodelled, or objectives have to be redefined. Reformulation of strategy will take us back to the process of strategic management where a fresh strategic choice has to be made. Remodelling of plans will entail new resource allocation pattern and subsequent changes in strategy implementation. Redefinition of objectives, however, takes us full circle to the start of the strategic management process.

STRATEGIC MOMENTUM CONTROL

These types of evaluation techniques are aimed at assuring that the assumptions on the basis of which strategies were formulated are still valid and what needs to be done in order to allow the organisation to maintain its existing strategic momentum:

(i) Generic strategies approach to strategic control is based on the assumption that the strategies adopted by firm similar to an organisation are comparable. Based on such a comparison, an organisation can study why and how other firms are implementing strategies and assess whether or not its own strategy is following a similar path.

(ii) The underlying success factors enable organisations to focus on key success factors to examine the factors that contribute to the success of strategies. By managing on the basis of the key success factors, the strategists can continually evaluate the strategies to assess whether or not there are helping the organisation to achieve its objectives.

(iii) Responsibility control centres form the core of management control systems and are of four types: revenue, expense, profit, and investment centres. Each of these centres is designed on the basis of the measurement of inputs and outputs. The study and application of responsibility centres is done in the discipline of management control systems.

STRATEGIC LEAP CONTROL

Where the environment is relatively unstable, organisations are required to make strategic leaps in order to make significant changes. Strategic leap control can assist such organisations by helping to define the new strategic requirements and to cope with emerging enviormental realities. There are four techniques of evaluation; used for exercising strategic leap control; strategic issue management, strategic field analysis, systems modelling and scenarios in this situation.

(i) Strategic field analysis is a way of examining the nature and extent of synergies that exist or are lacking between the components of an organisation. Wherever synergies exit, the strategist can assess the ability of the firm to take the advantages. Alternatively, the strategists evaluate the firm's ability to generate where they do not exist.

(ii) Scenarios are perceptions about the likely enviornment a firm would face in future. Its use could be extended to evaluation for enabling organisation to focus strategies on the basis of forthcoming developments in the environment.

(iii) System modelling is based on computer-based models that simulate the essential features of the organisation and its environment. Through system modelling, organisations may exercise pre-action control by assessing the impact of the environment on the organisational through the adoption of a particular strategy.

(iv) Strategic issue management is aimed at identifying one or more strategic issues and assessing their impact on the organisation. By managing on the basis of strategic issues, the strategists can avoid being overtaken by surprising environmental changes and design contingency plans to shift strategies whenever required.

Several of the above techniques for strategic control-except with the possible exception of responsibility centres-are of relatively recent origin. The development of these techniques is an evidence of the expanding body of knowledge in business policy and strategic management. As the use and application of strategic management gains approval, it is quite likely that organisations would start using such techniques. Operational control, however, uses more familar techniques which have traditionally been used by strategists.

CORPORATE STRATEGY

A number of criteria have been suggested by different analysts to evaluate strategy, which are qualitative measures of how well the strategy was implemented. One set of such criteria suggested by Tilles are as follows:

(a) Internal Consistency. "In a well worked-out strategy each policy fits into an integrated pattern. It should be judged not only in terms of itself, but also in terms of how it related to other policies which the company has established and to the goals it is pursuing."

(b) Consistency with the Environment. A viable strategy is expected to make for long-run success of the firm. In a dynamic environment to ensure long-run success, it is necessary to continually assess the degree to which policies previously established are consistent with the environment as it has unfolded till now, and whether current policies have taken into account the environment of the future.

(c) Appropriateness of the Strategy in the Light of Available Resources. To assess the strategy in relation to the resources of a firm the management have to identify their critical resources, *i.e.*, resources which the company has most of and which it has the least of, money, competence and physical facilities are generally considered to be the key resources of an enterprise. Monetary resources are valuable in that with adequate funds there is greatest possible flexibility or response to events as they arise. Companies aiming at reducing short-run risks may find adequancy of funds quite assuring but it may be a serious competitive disadvantage if risk investments are altogether avoided. To evaluate competence in relation to strategy there must be an appraisal of the skill profile of the firm to identify what the firm is particularly good at doing—marketing, producing. R&D. Thirdly, the strategic importance of physical facilities can be assessed by reference to the relationships of the company to its environment, *e.g.*, location of physical facilities relative to markets, to sources of labour or materials or the efficiency of facilities relative to existing or potential competitive installations. Besides, investment in the creation of physcial facilities (fixed assets) is closely connected with the technological changes.

(d) Acceptability of the Degree of Risk Involved in the Strategy. The relevant consideration in this respect is, whether, given the executive preferences towards risk, the risk involved in the strategy fits the executive preferences. This criterion does not imply that the strategy is the one with minimum risk. High returns often go with high-risk strategies. The degree of risk inherent in a strategy is dependent on three factors, *viz.*,

(i) The amount of resources (on which the strategy is based) whose continued existence or value is not assured, *i.e.*, the uncertainty of resources being available over the anticipated period which may be caused by internal or external changes.

(ii) The proportion of resources committed to a single venture, *i.e.*, the size of the stake in a particular strategy.

(iii) The time periods for which resources are committed connected with the difficulty of predicting long-run environmental changes.

The greater the magnitude of these factors, the greater is the degree of risk involved. But it is not true that inaction, or lack of changes, is a low-risk strategy. Failure to avail of opportunities and to exploit the internal resources to the fullest may well be the riskiest strategy.

(e) Appropriateness of the Time Horizon of the Strategy. A viable strategy is not only goal-bound but also time-bound in the sense of realising the goals within an appropriate time-span. For strategic goals, only if accompanied within a certain time, are meaningful. Introduction of a new product, market, or installation of a plant can be of strategic significance only if accomplished by a certain time.

(f) Workability of the Strategy. The evaluation of a strategy in terms of its workability really amounts to appraising it in terms of results achieved. If the strategy is 'working', it amounts to saying that it is an appropriate strategy and that it has been implemented with skill. If the results are not positive, one must critically examine the appropriateness of the chosen strategy and the process of implementation. In case the workability of a strategy cannot be evaluated by resutls alone, some other indicators that may be used for the purpose are suggested by Tilles as follows:

(i) The degree of consensus when exists among executives regarding corporate goals and policies.

(ii) The extent to which major areas of managerial choice are identified in advance, while there is still time to explore a variety of altenatives.

(iii) The extent to which resources requirement are discovered well on time.

PARTICIPANTS IN STRATEGIC EVALUATION

It is important to know who the participants are and what role they play in strategic evaluation and control. This will answer the question: Who evaluates the strategy and how do they do it? Going beyond the evaluators, we are also interested in knowing who the appraisers are and how they help in strategic evaluation.

The various participants in strategic evaluation and control and their respective roles are described below:

1. Middle-level and other managers may participate in strategic evaluation and control as porviders of information and feedback, as well as recipients of directions from above to take corrective actions.
2. The SBU or profit centre heads may be involved in performance evaluation at their levels and may facilitiate evaluation by corporate-level executives.
3. Theoretically, every organisation is ultimately responsible to its shareholders: lenders and the public in the case of private companies and the government in the public sector companies. The role of shareholders, in practice, however, is limited. This is specially true of the general public where the individual holding is too small to be of any effective value in strategic evaluation. Lenders such as financial institutions and banks which have equity stake are typically concerned about the security and returns on their shareholding rather than long-term assessment of strategic success. The government, through its different agencies,

does play a significant role in strategic evaluation and control of public sector companies.

4. The Board of Directors enact a formal role of reviewing and screening executive decision in the light of their enviornment, business and the functions of strategic evaluation in more generalised terms. But there is a lot of variation among Indian companies in the way through which the Board may perform its control functions. In some companies, the Board may have the real authority to oversee strategic evaluation which in others, its authority may be usurped by others like the chief executive or a higher de facto authority such as the family council, in the case of family-owned companies, or the controlling ministry in the case of public sectors companies.
5. Chief executives are ultimately responsible for all the administrative aspects of strategic evaluation and control. Ideally, a chief executive should not sit in judgement over the performance of the organisation under its control. Rather, the chief executive. Normally, the evaluation of a person should be done by an individual or a group to whom he reports. In cases where the chief executive is accountable to no one in particular, it is difficult to allocate the responsibility apart from relying on self-evaluation. But in other cases, the ownership pattern can determine who should evaluate the chief executive. Thus, the family council in family owned companies and majority shareholders in other cases could evaluate a chief executive's performance.
6. Financial controllers, company secretaries, and external and internal auditors from the group of persons who are primarily responsible for operational control based on financial analysis, budgeting and reporting.
7. Audit and executive committees, set up by the Board or the chief executive, may be charged with the responsibility of continuous screening of performance.

Barriers in Evaluation

As we know that a control system is a component of strategy implementation. In the present context, the emphasis is on the evaluation of organisational units. In practice, however, the two types of evaluation cannot be differentiated. By evaluating organisational units, one cannot avoid relying on the performance evaluation of individuals. This creates certain barriers in strategic evaluation and control. We could point out thre major types of barriers in evaluation: the units of control difficulties in measurement, and resistance to evaluation:

I. By its very nature, any control mechanism present the dilemma of too much versus too less control. It is never an easy task for strategists to decide the limits of control. Too much control may impair the ability of managers adversely affect initiative and creativity, and create unnecessary impediments to efficient performance. On the other hand, too less control may make the strategic evaluation process ineffective and redundant.

II. Secondly, the evaluation process involves controlling the behaviour of individuals and, like any similar organisation mechanism, is likely to be resisted by managers.

III. Thirdly, the process of evaluation is fraught with dangers of difficulties in measurement. These mainly relate to the reliability and validity of meaurement techniques used for evaluation. The control system may be distorted and may not evaluate uniformly or may measure attributes which are not intended to be evaluated.

How can these barriers be avoided? In this context, it apt to quote Andrews when he says: "the true function of measurement (or evaluation) is to increase perceptions of the problems limiting achievement". In Andrew's opinion, it is the attitude towards evaluation that is more important than the process of evaluation itself. The real worth of evaluation lies in its ability to throw up issues that need the attention of strategies. The next two sections describe the two types of strategic evaluation system that could be used for an effective measurement of strategic and operational performance.

TESTS FOR EFFECTIVENESS OF STRATEGY

The management can apply the following tests to judge effectiveness of the current strategy:

1. Matching Strategy Current Performance with Strategy. The central management should measure actual performance for period of time and compare it against what was planned. If comparison indicates that performance is satisfactory, the on-going strategy may be considered to be sound. However, the management before giving testimony to the soundness of the strategy should determine whether positive deviation was the outcome of mere chance or due to correct plans. Where the comparison indicates a large negative variation, the manager has to find out if the deviations have occurred because plans were wrongly formulated.

2. Organization Motivation and Strategy. An enterprise aiming at achieving leadership in the product line and embarking on a massive diversification programme will have to formulate (a) strategy which can create a stimulating climate in the organisation and encourage people to do their best and to adapt to changes of events. This calls for clear-cut objectives, goals and strategy that remove uncretainty and ambiguity and have a strong action focus. Involvement of lower level executives in decision making, freedom of job and provision of financial and non-financial incentives to those showing exceptional performance also motivate employees to contribute their best to the organisation. It is, therefore, necessary to verify if the exising strategy constitutes stimulus to organisational effort and commitment.

3. Matching Objectives with Strategy. The basic idea underlying the formulation of corporate strategy is to achieve the corporate objectives. Hence, the major criterion to evaluate the efficiency of the strategy is to determine how far it will be helpful to attain the desired results. For instance, if a firm aims at increasing its profit by 30 per cent during the next five years through augmenting sales, the central management must varify whether corporate strategy provides emphasis on market penetration, market development, product development and other measures that will help the enterprise to achieve the anticipated objectives.

Similarly, if a firm in its endeavour to fulfil social obligations sets the objectives of promoting social welfare, the management should verify how far the current strategy provides for social actions. Social responsibility concept must be embedded in the strategy, action plans and programmes of the company. Strategy not providing explicity for social welfare actions cannot be considered effective and useful to the enterprise. The central management will also have to ensure the organisational plan of the enterprise constituted at the corporate level staff department is endowed with social responsibility activities.

4. Strategy and Values of Management. Effectiveness of strategy is dependent upon the personal involvement of those at the helm of affairs. Hence, in the formulation of strategic and action plans, personal values, preference and motives of business executives must be given due consideration. Conflict between personal values of key members of the enterprise and the strategy is a sign of a danger and a harbinger of mediocre performance or failure. It is therefore, necessary for the evaluator to determine as to what extent the personal values of key executive and other executives are reflected in strategy and other plans.

5. Matching Environmental Forces with Strategy. Another important yardstick to measure effectiveness of·current strategy is to check its adequacy in exploiting existing as well as future opportunities and/or counteracting impending threats. Instances are not rare when an enterprise formulates strategy to capitalise opportunities in foreign countries while ignoring abundant opportunities existing inside the country. The management has to ensure that such sort of policy and strategy are not allowed to see the light of the day.

Further, it is also necessary to varify if the current strategy has been adapted and modified in accordance with dynamic developments in socio-economic, competitive, technological and political spheres of the country. An enterprise not bothering to interact with various environmental forces and adjust its objectives, strategies and programmes may experience disaster because external conditions may change to such an extent that even a sound plan may no longer be relevant and more of hindrance rather than help. Such a check will help the management to verify the validity of the on-going strategy.

6. Matching Strategy with Operating Plans. A strategy can achieve desired results if functional plans, action plans and programmes are consistent with it. This is why feasibility testing of sub-strategies has to be made constantly to ensure that they conform to the corporate strategic plan. If this is not done and inconsistency exists, it will be very difficult for the enterprise to achieve budgeted results within a specified period of time.

7. Matching Strategy with Organisations Strengths. A successful strategy is one which is supported by adequate resources of the enterprise. At times, the management swared by high ambitions and initial successes may be tempted to choose a path of expansion without perceptive and penetrating enquiry in to the company's past performance and present strengths. Such an over-ambitious growth plan can bring untold sufferings. To cleack the occurrence of such possibility, it will be pertinent for the central management to ensure that the strategy is consistent with the resources of the enterprise. Further, it has also to be ensured that the strategy is making maximum use of synergistics benefits.

RUMELT'S CRITERIA FOR EVALUATION

According to Richard Rumelt, while it is impossible to conclusively demonstrate that a particular strategy is optimal or to guarantee that it will work, one can, nevertheless, apply certain tests to a strategy to ascertain if it suffers from any critical flaws. The broad qualitative critieria Rumelt has suggested are the following:

1. Advantages. There are two aspects of business mission in relation to the environment. One is that the business must fit with the environment (the generic aspect), and the second is that, at the same time, business must compete with other firms that are trying to adapt to the environment. The later aspect of matching the business to its environment is the 'competitive' strategy, which focuses on the differences among firms rather than their common missions. The test of a strategy may thus be in terms of competitive advantages of which creation and/or maintenance is provided for in the strategy. Comparative advantages are generally traceable to superiority of resources, skills or position. Superior resources and superior skills enable a firm to do more and/or do it bettter than other competiting firms. The evaluation of strategy is required to analyse the specific skills and resources relevant to the competitive areas. Positional advantage may be derived from size or scale of operations, successful trade names, ownership of sources of special raw materials or long-term supply contracts, geographical location near key customers in business involving heavy investment in fixed capital and high transport costs, leadership in a service field, full-line production in a market, or reputation of reliability or dependability in the supply of any product or service.

2. Feasibility. The feasibility test of strategy really implies assessing the firm's ability to carry out the strategy. The relevant questions to be asked in this respect are:

(a) Has the organisation demonstrated that it possesses the necessary problem-solving abilities and/or competence required by the strategy?

(b) Does the organisation possess the requisite degree of coordinative and integrative skill to carry out the strategy?

(c) Does the strategy challenge and motivate key personnel and is it acceptable to those who must lend their support?

3. Consonance. The appraisal of strategy based on the matching of, or fit between the firm's mission and the environment is referred to as the test of consonance. "The key to evaluating consonance is an understanding of why the business, as it currently stands, exists at all and how it assumed its current pattern." The evaluator has thus to examine the basic pattern of economic relationships that characterise the business and determine whether or not sufficient value is being created to sustain the strategy. The business must both match and be adapted to its environment. The analysis of economic relationships and the scope or mission of business is generally carried out by looking at changing economic and social conditions over time. This is described as the 'generic' aspect of strategy. The strategy must represent an adaptive response to the external environment and the critical changes therein.

4. Consistency. The goals and policies consitute integral parts of corporate strategy. It is, therefore, essential that the strategy must not present mutually inconsistent goals and policies. And yet inconsistencies are not uncommon, where, for instance, strategy have not been explicitly formulated but have evolved in a piecemeal *ad hoc* fashion, or where strategies have been formulated on the basis of compromise arrangement between opposing power groups. Strategic consistency may be lacking and reflected in different ways. For instance, it may be manifested in the form of organisational conflict and inter-departmental bickerings, issue-based problems in co-ordination and planning despite changes in personnel, operating problems being brought to the top for resolution of policy issues. Again, the structure of objective may be inconsistent and reflected in the success of the organisational unit being, or perceived as, failure of another unit. Another type of strategic inconsistency may be noticed between organisational objectives and the values of managerial groups. Thus, the evaluation of strategy requires checking on the consistency of goal and policies in the strategy.

TYPES OF STRATEGIC CONTROL

The process of strategic management makes it clear that a strategy is formulated on the basis of serveral assumptions. These relate to the environmental and organsiational factors, which are dynamic and eventful. There is a considerable gap between the time a strategy is formulated and when it is implemented. The process of implementation is itself time-consuming. During this intervening period, there is a possibility that the assumptions made while formulating strategy do not remain valid or, at least, are no longer so valid. Strategic controls take into account the changing assumptions that determine a strategy, continually evaluate the strategy as it is being implemented, and take the necessary steps to adjust the strategy to the new requirements. In this manner, strategic controls are early warning systems and differ from post-action controls that evaluate only after the implementation is completed. (Strategic control is analogous to the continuous evaluation system used in educational institutions and differs from the end-of-the-term examination system used in traditional setups.)

The following sub-sections discuss there four strategic controls:

1. Special Alert Control. The strategic control system is the special alert control, which is based on a trigger mechanism for rapid response and immediate reassessment of strategy in the light of sudden and unexpected events. Special alert control can be exercised through the formulation of contingency strategies and assigning the responsibility of handling unforeseen events to crisis management teams. Examples of such events can be the sudden fall of a government at the central or state level, instant change in a competitor's posture, an unfortunate industrial disaster or a natural catastrophe.

2. Strategic Surveillance. The premise and implementation types of strategic controls are specific in nature. Strategic surveillance, on the other hand, is aimed at a more generalised and overchanging control "designed to monitor a broad range of events inside and outside the company that are likely to threaten the course of a firm's strategy". Strategic surveillance can be done through a broad-based, general monitoring based on selected information sources to uncover events that are likely to affect the strategy of an organisation. Aaker has suggested a "formal yet simple strategic information scanning system (that) can enhance the effectiveness of the scanning effort and preserve much of the information now lost within the organisation."

3. Implementation Control. The implementation of a strategy results in a series of plans, programmes, and projects. Resource allocation is done for implementing these. Implementation control is aimed at evaluating whether the plans, programmes, and projects are actually guiding the organisation towards its predetermined objectives or not. If at any time, it is felt that the commitment of resources to a plan, programme or project would not benefit the organisation as envisaged, they have to be revised. In this manner, implementation control may lead to strategic rethinking.

Impementation control may be put into practice through identification and monitoring of strategic thrusts such as an assessment of the marketing success of a new product after pre-testing or checking the feasibility of a diversification programme after initial attempts at seeking technological collaboration. In the first case, the company may evaluate whether the new product launch will really benefit or it should be abandoned in favour of another programme. In the second case, implementation control can help to determine whether a diversification move will actually succeed or not.

Another method of implementation control is milestone reviews, through which critical points in strategy implementation are identified in terms of events, major resource allocation, or time. This is similar to identification albeit at a smaller scale-of events and activities in PERT/CPM network. After identification of milestones, a comprehensive review of implementation is made to reassess its continued relevance to achievement of objectives.

4. Premise Control. As mentioned above, every strategy is based on certain assumptions about environmental and organisational factors. Some of these factors are highly significant and any change in them can affect the strategy to a large extent. Premise control is necessary to identify the key assumptions and keep track of any change in them so as to assess their impact on strategy and its implementation. For instance, a company may base its strategy on important assumptions related to environmental factors (*e.g.* Government policies), industrial factors (*e.g.*, nature of competition), and organisational factors (*e.g.*, breakthrough in R&D). Premise control serves the purpose of continually testing the assumptions to find out whether they are still. valid or not. This enables the strategies to take corrective action at the right time rather than continuing with a strategy based on invalid assumptions. The responsibility for premise control can be assigned to the corporate planning staff who can identify key assumptions and keep a regular check on their validity.

From the description of the four strategic controls, it might seem that strategic evaluation is complex process and requires the use of sophisticated and systematic techniques. While this may be true for large and complex organisations facing a trubulent environment, this is not fully relevant to smaller and simple firms that face a relatively stable environment. Many of the tasks require for strategic control may be performed informally in a simple way. For instance, in an enterpreneurial organisation, the owner-manager may perform strategic control through a general awareness of environmental and industry-related factors and initiate changes whenever required. This may be done through a regular scanning of business newpapers, magazines and trade journals; through attandance at seminars and conferences, and general observations. In short, whatever sources used for a environmental appraisal may also be useful for strategic control.

The basic theme of strategic control is to continually assess the changing environment to uncover events that may significantly affect the course of an organisation' strategy. As compared to strategic control, operational control has a different purpose. The next section deals with operational control.

The following table indicates the difference between strategic and operatonal control. It can be seen that the operational control is aimed at allocation and use of organisation resources through evaluation of the performance of organisational units such as division, SBUs, etc. to assess their contribution to the achievement of organisational objectives. Operational control is concerned with action or performance and this is probably the reason why it is so extensively used in organisations.

Attribute	*Operational Control*	*Strategic Control*
1. Basic question	"How are we performing?"	"Are we moving in the right direction?"
2. Aim	Allocation and use of organsational resources	Proactive continuous questioning of the basic direction of strategy

Contd.

Attribute	*Operational Control*	*Strategic Control*
3. Main concern	Action control	"Steering" the organisation's future direction
4. Focus	Internal organisation	External environment
5. Time horizon	Short-term	Long-term
6. Exercise of control	Mainly by executive or middle-level management on the direction of top management	Exclusively by top management, may be through lower-level support
7. Main techniques	Budgets, schedules and MBO	Environmental scanning information gathering, questioning and review

INFORMATION SYSTEMS OF STRATEGIC CONTROL

Accurate and reliable information about various measures of organisational performance is highly essential for successful strategic control. Organsations should develop and implement formal system to collect valid, reliable and timely information. There are two information systems *viz.*, Management Information Systems (MIS) and Management Decision Support Sysems (MDSS).

1. Management Information System (MIS)

A management information sysem is a formal computer-assisted organisational function designed to provide managers with information to help their decision-making. The important use of such information is to support strategic control.

Managers at different levels of the organisation perform different functions and therefore, they need different kinds of information. MIS should be flexible to provide different kinds of information to the managers at various levels. It presents typical activities performed by top management, middle management and junior management.

Since the success of the strategic control depends on the efficient fucntioning of MIS, the strategists should monitor the functioning of MIS continuously. The strategists should be aware of the symptoms of a malfunctioning MIS and set the MIS in the right direction and in right time.

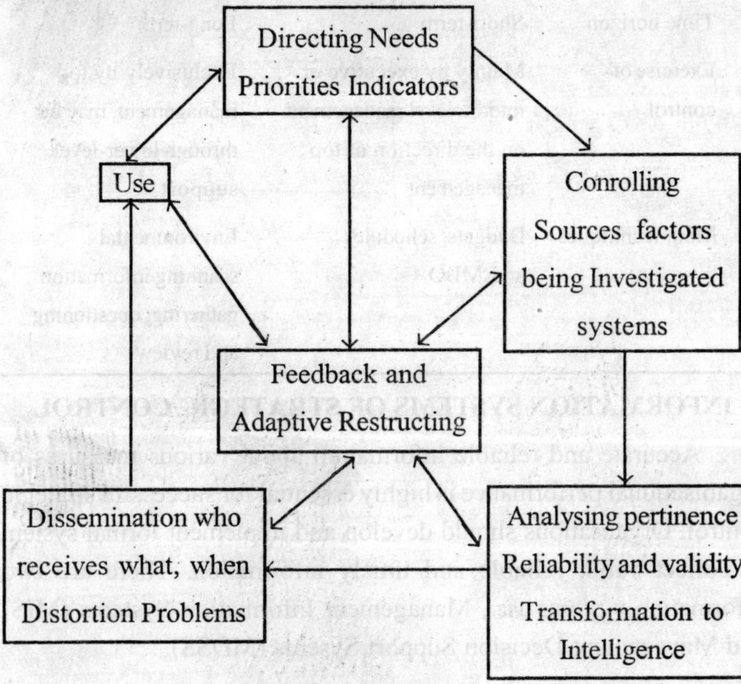

Source: Samuel C. Certo and J. Paul Peter, op. cit.,

Fig. Major Steps in operating an MIS

2. Management Decision Support System

A management decision support system is an independent set of decision aids that helps managers make relatively unstructured, perhaps nonrecurring decisions. Fig given below presents information needs of executives responsible for strategic control in their firms and the internal functions responsible for finding, interpreting and passing on critical informtion to top managers.

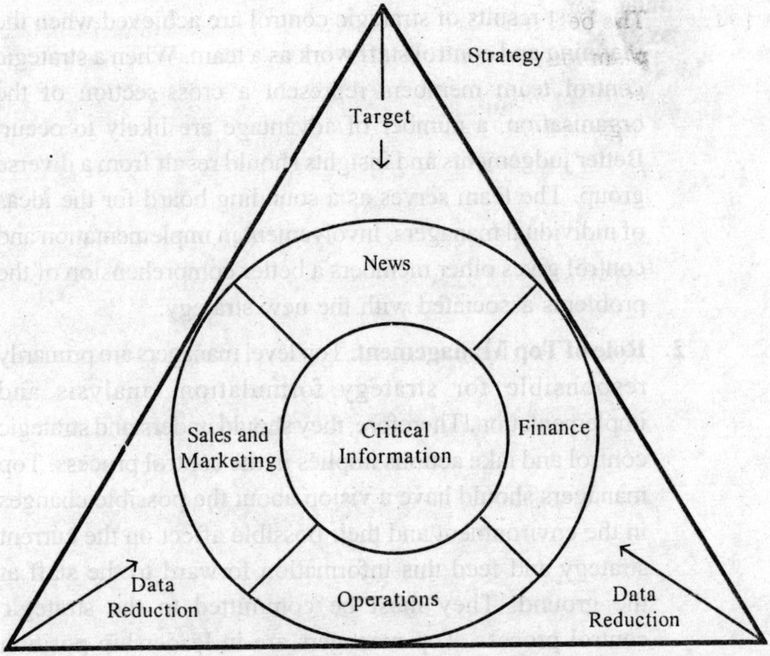

Source: Robin Matthews and Anthony Shoebridge, "EIS - A Guide for Executives," Long Range Planning, Vol.

Implementation of Strategic Control

Strategic control is the primary responsibility of the strategist who forumlated the strategy. However, it is responsibility of all members of the organisation. All employees participate in the strategy implementation. Therefore, all employees can contribute to the control of strategic implementation process.

1. **Role of the Strategy Planning Staff.** Normally the role of strategy planning, formulation, implementation and control go hand-in-hand. But, in some companies the roles of planning and control of strategy are separated. This practice is unfortunate as performing these two functions separately by two managers is too often inflexible and bureaucratic. Planning without control eliminates feed forward and control without planning eliminates feedback.

The best results of strategic control are achieved when the planning and control staff work as a team. When a strategic control team members represent a cross-section of the organisation, a number of advantage are likely to occur. Better judgements and insights should result from a diverse group. The team serves as a sounding board for the ideas of individual managers. Involvement in implementation and control gives other members a better comprehension of the problems associated with the new strategy.

2. **Role of Top Management.** Top level managers are primarily responsible for strategy formulation, analysis and implementation. Therefore, they should understand strategic control and take actions implies in the control process. Top managers should have a vision about the possible changes in the environment and their possible affect on the current strategy and feed this information forward to the staff at the ground. They must be committed to the strategic control process. Top managers are in leadership position and as such they should influence the organisation members in strategic control process.

SUCCESSFUL MAINENANCE OF STRATEGIC CONTROL

Successful maintenance of strategic control is important from the long-run point of view. Top managers must ensure that four interrelated organsational variables are consistent and complementary. They are: *(i)* organisational structure, *(ii)* reward system *(iii)* information systems, and *(iv)* organisational value systems or cultures.

Quinn argues that implementing strategy and controlling its progress are actually a series of incremental steps. Quinn suggests that the managers should do the following to implement strategic control successfully:

1. Crystallize Focus and Consensus. By controlling membership on committees, managers are able to influence, and if desired, receive the proposals wanted. Properly selected committees can broaden support for he increase commitment to new strategies.

2. Create Pockets of Committment. Executive provide broad goals, a proper climate, and flexible resource support. By allowing various groups to develop and present proposals for strategies, managers are able to build commitment among the groups to support the strategy finally selected.

3. Maintain Objectively. Managers should avoid taking a stand on issues too early in the generation and evaluation process. When managers take a position, the generation of new alternatives often ceases and the evaluation of existing alternative of often biased by the position of the top manager.

4. Eliminate Options Two Levels Down. Managers can maintain their position of neutrality and avoid rejecting proposals by encouraging discouraging, or killing options through subordinates.

5. Empower Champions. Managers are given responsibility for developing new ideas and programmes early. As the programme is evaluated and gains support, these individuals tend to become committeed to the programme or strategy. Once it is given final approval, these managers are then willing to champion the strategy and to guide it through whatever hurdles are necessary to get it operating effectively.

6. Recognize Continuing Dynamics. Strategies do not remain constant and fixed for long periods. Part of the executive's responsibility is to gain consensus and support for the new strategy, but at the same time room must be maintained to modify or terminate the strategy. Managers should use discretion in making certain that the organization does not become overcommitted to the new strategy and unwilling to change at some future point.

7. Develop Strategies Incrementally, but not Piecemeal. Part of management's responsibility is to make certain that strategies are integrated and appropriate for the environment in which the firm is operating. Strategies may be developed in incremental steps, but they must be made to fit together in a unified, integrated, and cohesive whole.

❐

5

Strategy and Structure

Whether structure is dependent upon and should follow from the strategy of an organisation has been a closely debated question since the sixties after the publication of Chandler's pioneering work. Chandler's thesis was that a change of strategy invariably required structural change to achieve economic efficiency. More specifically, he contended that the strategy of diversification usually gave rise to organisational problems which could be eventually resolved by designing a new corporate structure. Four recognisable phases were discernible in the evolution of large Amercian enterprise since the 1920s, *viz.*

(i) the development of a new structure to enable effective mobilisation of sources to meet both short-term market demand and long-term market trends,

(ii) expansion into new markets and lines to help assure the continuing full use of resources,

(iii) rationalisation of the use of sources,

(iv) initial expansion and accumulation of resources.

These four phases, Chandler found, produced three types of organisational structure:

1st Type. The accumulation of resources by a successful enterprise with an organisation of Type II led to diversification of product lines. The strategy of diversification gave rise to many administrative problems. The executives in charge of functional departments faced complex problems of coordination and control. The functional responsibilities could be delegated to subordinates, but inter-departmental comparison and control were more difficult as it was not possible to measure the profit contribution of functional heads against their performance. Problems bearing on operational issues arising at lower level of the organisation had to the responsibility of resource allocation lies, even though a strategic decision may be initiated at any level of management. The interaction between strategy and structure thus takes place in the process of strategic choice by the top management of the organisation.

2nd Type. This was a vertically integrated structure emphasising efficiency and functional coordination with one or a few related products. This type of organisation was characterised by a few managers at the top as heads of departments and the chief executive entrusted with various complex decisions. The departmental heads were too busy with the administration of particular functions and had little time to devote to the affairs of the enterprise as a whole. Having most of their activities restricted to a single functional area, they had little experience or interest in understanding the needs and problems of other departments or the total organisation.

3rd Type. The structure of this Type, the organisation reflected an extension of the interests, abilities and limitations of the chief executive, generally the owner-entrepreneur. As an entrepreneurial organisation, it was characterised by centralised decision-making and a single product line with empahsis on one function (*e.g.*, production) more than others.

It may be passed on to the functional heads for adjudication, while some of the problems might have to be resolved at the level of the chief executive. Diversification of product lines with the Type II organisation structure would have stopped organisational growth in view of the limited capability of the chief executive to cope with the new demands on his decision-making capability. Under these conditions, the management of firms were forced to make a choice of either giving up the strategy of diversification or abandoning the functional structure of organisation. Many firms decided to reorganise the structural design and established two or more product divisions with functional responsibilities delegated to the divisional managers. The firms were organisationally structured with separate, autonomous division created on a product basis, each division serving as a profit centre for control purposes. The role of the central office headed by the chief executive consisted of coordination and control with respect to finance and general staff functions like planning and research. Type III decentralised organisation enabled companies to move simultaneously to exploit opportunities in a variety of product markets, and manage a variety of unrelated activities. New products could be added and old ones dropped with only marginal effect on the organisation as a whole. Chandler's study revealed that the shift from Type II structure to Type III began in the United States in the 1920's. The several organisations the transition took place independently, *e.g.*, General Moters, du Pont, Sears Roebuck, and Standard Oil of New Jersey. Other organisations imitated the pioneers. The movement took place in many companies after the economic depression of 1930's and the second world war. In many cases, the shifts in both strategy and structure were brought about in the 1950's and 1960's.

The extent to which new structures both facilitate and spring from the development of a strategic approach is evident from Chandler's study. He noted the distinction between two types of policies : strategic and tactical. Strategic policy decisions have resource implications which require a new a revised allocation of resources. Tactical decisions relate to day-to-day management of operation and need to be consistent with a policy. Thus a strategic decision can be taken only at the top management.

From what has been noted in the studies on the growth of firms and the development of organisational forms, it may be suggested that strategy and structure are inseparable in practice. Given that policies formulated, then the very choice of strategic policy necessitates a structure design through which it can be implemented. But the very emergence of strategic awareness is linked to stages in life-cycles to products and whole enterprises... In the evolution of a company and its range of activities there emerges a stage at which internal inducements and constraints can only compel a change of organisation capable of giving a new impetus to company-wide policy and strategy review.

MATCHING ORGANISATIONAL STRUCTURE TO STRATEGY

Every strategy is grounded in its own set of key success factors and critical tasks. Therefore, the internal organisation structure should be designed around the key success factors and critical tasks. The following five-sequence procedure is a useful guide for fitting organisational structure to strategy:

1. Pinpoint the key functions and tasks necessary for successful strategy execution.
2. Reflection on how strategy-critical functions and organisational units relate to those that are routine and to those that provide staff support.
3. Determine the degrees of authority needed to manage each organisational unit bearing in mind both the benefits and costs of decentralised decision-making.
4. Make strategy-critical business units and functions for the main organisational building blocks.
5. Provide the coordination among the various organisational units.

1. Strategy-critical Activities. Some activities and skills are generally critical in the execution of a strategy. In fact, much of the activities are performed in a routine manner even in the process of strategy implementation. The critical tasks to be performed only for strategy implementation include: tight cost control when the firm adopts the strategy of low-cost producer, special promotional appeal, tight quantity control to produce zero defect products, critical skills to produce distinctly qualitative products, and special design of the produce, when the company adopts the strategy of market leader. The critical activities in high-tech industries include: research and development, product innovation, developing new products, developing new uses of existing products, taking the laboratory results into the market quickly, testing the new products in the market etc. Thus, the strategy-critical activities vary according to the nature of the firm and competitive situation of the firm.

The firm in order to decide on the type of organisation structure should know the special tasks/functions to be performed and the right time for effective strategy execution. Further, the firm should also find out the vulnerable areas where malperformance of the tasks/functions seriously endanger strategic success. This effort will enable the management concentrate on the crucial areas in organisation building efforts.

2. The Structure-Follows-Strategy Thesis. The practice of matching organisation structure to the particular needs of strategy is a fairly recent and research based management development. Alfred Chandler, in his research study found that changes in a company's strategy bring about new administrative problems, which in turn, require a new or refashioned structure for the new strategy to be successfully implemented. A company's internal organisation should be reassessed whenever strategy changes. Otherwise, internal problems would crop-up and result in failure in strategy implementation. Structure follows strategy as organisational structure is only a means to an end rather than end itself. Organisational structure is a managerial tool in the process of achievement of organisational objectives. It is easy to coordinate strategic moves across functional areas, if functions, activities and responsibilities are efficiently organised to link strategy and structure.

APPROACHES TO ORGANISATIONAL STRUCTURE AND DESIGN

There are six approaches to structure the organisation. They are: *(1)* Functional organisation structure, *(2)* Product organisation structure, *(3)* Geographical organisation structure, *(4)* Decentralised business divisions, *(5)* Strategic business units, and *(6)* Matrix organisational structure.

1. Functional Organisation Structure. Functional organisation structure is most widely used structure. Each functional departments consists of those jobs in which employees perform similar jobs at different levels. The commonly used functions are: marketing, finance and accounting, human resources, manufacturing, research and development and engineering.

Strategic Advantages. *(i)* A functional structure would be effective in single business firms where key activities revolve around well defined skills and areas of specialisation. *(ii)* Indepth specialisation and focused concentration on performing functional tasks can enhance operating efficiency and the development of core competencies. *(iii)* This type of structure promotes maximum utilisation of up-to-date technical skills and enables the firm to capitalise on specialisation and efficiency. These are strategically important considerations for single business companies, dominant product companies and vertically integrated companies. *(iv)* The functional structure is most appropriate when firm compete on the basis of technical specialisation on efficiency in a relatively stable environment. *(v)* This structure promotes common values and goals among employees of the department, facilitating coorperation and collaboration within the functional department.

Strategic Disadvantages. *(i)* The horizontal diversification of the business reduces the efficiency of the functional structure. *(ii)* The department members may see the activities from the narrow view point of the department rather than to total organisation. This aspect results in absence of inter-department coordination and cooperation. *(iii)* Interdepartmental policies further result in conflicts. This situation leads to indecision, delay in decision making or ineffective decision-making. *(iv)* Further, the narrow specialisations kill the initiative of entrepreneurs and the zeal of innovativeness and creativeness. Consequently, the firm may lose sensitiveness to the customer demands, technological changes and environmental demands. These limitations of functional structure may make the firm to reassess the suitability of the structure to the strategy and decide accordingly.

2. Product Organisation Structure. Activities are divided on the basis of individual products, product line, services and are grouped into department in product organisation structure. All important functions *viz.*, marketing, production, finance and human resource are contained within each department. This type of organisation structure overcomes many of the major limitations of functional organisational structure. Fig. given below presents the product organisation structure:

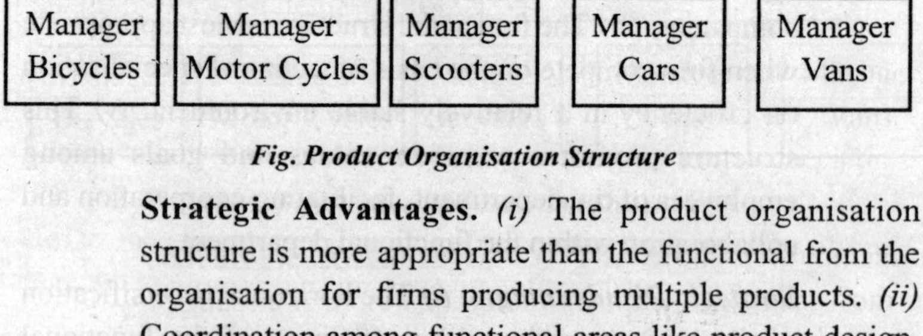

Fig. Product Organisation Structure

Strategic Advantages. *(i)* The product organisation structure is more appropriate than the functional from the organisation for firms producing multiple products. *(ii)* Coordination among functional areas like product design, producing, distributing, marketing is effective as all functions are performed in each department. *(iii)* Since, each department is independent, most of the decisions can be made at departmental level without involving the top managment in this process. It will result in fast decisions, enhancement of organisational competency to compete in rapidly changing environment. *(iv)* Responsibility and accountability for market share, sales, profit/loss is clearly fixed. Thus, either the credit for the success or blame for the failure of a product can be clearly attributed to a particular department. This advantage cannot present in case of functional organisation structure.

Strategic Disadvantages. Product organisational structure is also not free from limitations: *(i)* One of the major limitation is that unnecessary duplication of equipment and personnel among various departments. This results in loss of specialisation. *(ii)* Each department will have production, marketing, human resources, finance managers, secretarial and support staff, computers and testing equipment. As such specialised personnel and equipment cannot be produced. *(iii)* Some decisions like pay, promotion, product quality, design and pricing strategy may be inconsistent between departments. *(iv)* Interdepartmental conflicts arise regarding sharing of common resources, allocation of common and overhead expenses etc.

3. Geographical Organisation Structure. The activities or functions are grouped into department based on the activities performed in the geographical areas/regions. Each geographical unit includes all functions required to produce and market the products in a particular geographical area. Figure given below presents a geographical organisation structure. Multinational organisation, enterprise operating in diverse geographic markets or serving an expansive geographic area are organised based on the geographic structure. This strcuture is also used by chain stores, power companies, restaurant chains, dairy products, banking companies, insurance companies etc.

Strategic Advantages. The advantage of this type of organisational structure are : *(i)* Products and services are better designed to the climatic and cultural needs specific geographical regions. *(ii)* A geographical structure allows a firm to respond to the technical needs of different international area. *(iii)* Production and distributing products in different national or global locations may give the organisation to better serve the consumer needs of various nations. *(iv)* This organisation structure enables a company to adapt to varying legal systems. *(v)* It also allowed firms pinpoint the responsibility for profits or losses.

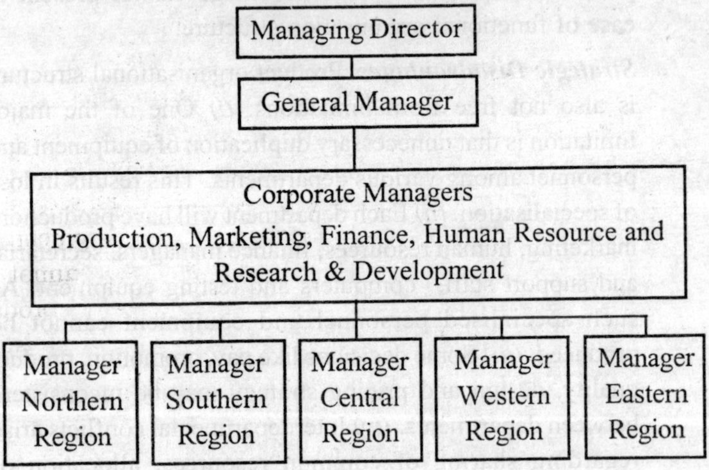

Fig. Geographical Organisation Structure

Strategic Disadvantages. This organisational structure is also not free from limitations. The limitations of the structure are similar to those of product structure. *(i)* Often more functional personnel are required. The firm cannot appoint specialist unlike in functional structure due to duplication of personnel. *(ii)* There would be duplication of equipment and facilities. *(iii)* Coordination of company-wide activities would be difficult. *(iv)* There would be a problem of imposing degree of uniformity and diversity. *(v)* It is difficult to maintain consistent company image or reputation. *(vi)* This structure adds another layer of management to run the geographic units.

4. Decentralised Business Unit Structure. Grouping activities based on product lines has been a trend among diversified companies since 1920. In a diversified firm, the basic organistional building blocks are its business units, each business is operated as a stand-alone profit centre. Fig. given below presents decentralised line of business type of organisational structure.

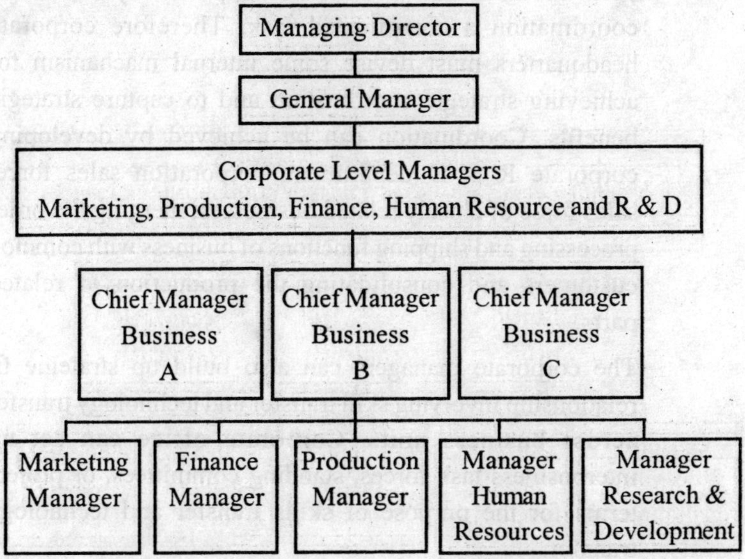

Fig. Decentralised Line of Business Type of Organisation Structure

Strategic Advantages. Functional structure and geographic structure are standard organisational building blocks in a single business firm. But, in multibusiness firms, the businensses are diversified. *(i)* Diversification is generally managed by decentralised decision-making and delegating authority and responsibility to a manager at each business unit. *(ii)* Each business unit would be managed by an entrepreneurially oriented general manager who is delegated with authority to formulate and execute business strategies. *(iii)* Each business unit operates as a stand-alone profit centre. Each business unit is structured on the bias of either functional structure or geographic structure depending upon strategy, key activities and operating requirements.

Strategic Disadvantages. The disadvantages are: *(i)* The major problem of this type of organisation structure is absence of mechanism for coordinating related activities across business units. *(ii)* General manager incharge of each business unit functions independently. It makes coordination a complicated task. Therefore corporate headquarters must devise some internal machanism for achieving strategic coordination and to capture strategic benefits. Coordination can be achieved by developing corporate R & D department, corporation sales force, sales force of closely related businesses, merging the order processing and shipping functions of business with common customers and consolidating the production of related parts.

The corporate managers can also build up strategic fit relationship involving skill transfer and technology transfer across business units. Corporate office can set up interbusiness task forces, standing committees, or project terms for the purpose of skills transfer and technology transfer.

5. Strategic Business Unit Structure. A single chief executive cannot control a number of decentralised units of a broadly diversified company. The business can be effectively controlled, if the related businesses are grouped into strategic units and the efficient and senior executive is delegated with the authority and responsibility for its management. The senior executive is delegated with the authority and responsibility for its management. The senior executive will in turn report the matter to the chief executive. This arrangement all improve strategic planning and implementation, though it adds one layer in the organisational hierarchy. Top management coordniates the interests of the diversified business units.

A strategic business unit is a grouping of business subsidiaries based on some important strategic elements common to each. The common or related elements could be an overlapping set of competitors, a closely related strategic mission, a common need to complete globally, an ability to accomplish integrated strategic planning, common key success factors and technologically related growth opportunities.

Strategic Advantages. The advantages of this structure include: *(i)* reduction of the corporate headquarter's span of control. The chief executive at the corporate headquarters has to control the general managers of the strategic business units. *(ii)* This structure permits better coordination between division with similar mission, products, markets and technologies. *(iii)* It allows strategic management to be done at the most relevant level within the total enterprise. *(iv)* It helps to allocate corporate resources to areas with greatest growth opportunities *(v)* Business units are organised based on the strategically relevant method.

Strategic Disadvantages. The strategic business unit structure also has certain disadvantages: *(i)* The first disadvantage is that corporate headquarters becomes more distant from the division. *(ii)* conflicts between/among the strategic business unit managers for greater share of corporate resources can become dysfunctional. *(iii)* Corporate portfolio analysis becomes complicated one in this structure.

6. Matrix Organisation Structure. Organisational structures discussed earlier have possessed a single chain of command. In other words, employees in the these structures reports to only one manager. But, the organisation structure possesses a dual chain of command. Both functional and project managers exercise authority over organisational activities in matrix structure. Thus personnel in this structure have two superiors *viz.*, a project manager and the manager of the functional department.

A matrix organisational structure is appropriate when:

(i) Management attention must be focused on two or more key issues (technical issues, consumer needs, functional efficiency).

(ii) Large amounts of diverse information need to be processed.

(iii) Problem solving is complex (environmental uncertainty, inter-dependence among organisational units, complex products or technology).

(iv) Economies of scale require the sharing of human resource expertise to achieve high performance.

Strategic Advantages. The matrix structure is commonly used in the firms whose technological change is rapid. The advantages of matrix structure include: *(i)* the company can have the advantages of both project type of organisational structure and functional organisation structure. *(ii)* Functional personnel are paid for their services whenever, they are used by project managers. This practice enables the management to reduce the cost. *(iii)* This structure has considerable flexibility. The personnel can be transferred from one project to the other depending upon the need of the product. *(iv)* The lower level functional employees are highly motivated and satisfied with their job as they are involved in decision making. (vi) Each project manager is incharge of a unit. Therefore, he can be developed as a general manager through performing general managerial functions.

Strategic Disadvantages. The significant strategic disadvantages of matrix organisational structure include: *(i)* greater administrative costs associated with its operation. Personnel spend much of their time in meeting and exchanging of information to coordinate functional areas with projects. *(ii)* In view of the two forms associated in this structure, they are characterised by conflicts. The most critical conflict is between functional managers and project managers. *(iii)* Functional employees experience stress by working in matrix structure. Reporting to two bosses, creates role ambiguity and role conflict. Some companies reverted their organisational structures back to traditional structures from matrix structures due to these problems.

Strategies of business are not always static. They go on changing depending upon internal and external environmental factors. Hence, a single type of organisational structure is not suitable for all times and all situations. Blending the basic forms of organisation to match the structure to strategy in the units concerned is essential. Another option is to supplement special situation devices to the basic organisational structure. Three mostly used forms are:

(i) **Project Team (or) Project Staff Approach.** Project teams are created to handle special kinds of situations with a finite life expectancy. Project teams are self-sufficient work groups. These are created to supervise the completion of a special activity. The special activities includes: setting up a new technological process, starting up a new venture, producing a new product, initiating and completion of a joint venture and the like.

(ii) **The Task Force Approach.** Interdisciplinary assignments necessitate the formation of task force. A task force consists of top level executives and specialists in different areas from the organisation. The advantages of speical task force include; increased opportunity for creativity, open communication, cross-functional authority, effective integration of talents, quick conflict resolution, collaborative approach for problem solving.

(iii) **The Venture Team Approach.** Venture team is a group of individuals. The purpose of forming this team is to bring a specific product or a new business into being. The problems of venture team are: *(i)* Difficulty of deciding the manager to whom the report should be made, *(ii)* Source of founding to the venture *i.e.*, is the source from department or business or corporation? *(iii)* methods of keeping the venture clear of bureaucratic and vested interests, and *(iv)* problem of coordinating large number of different ventures.

The suitability of structure to strategy is dependent on a number of situational factors. Absence of fit between strategy and structure leads to inefficient functioning of the company. The states of organisation development is an important factor that influence the match between strategy and structure.

ORGANISATIONAL CHANGE

Change is inevitable in a progressive culture. Change, infact, is accelerating in our society. Resolutions are taking place in political, scientific, technological and institutional areas. Sophisticated communication capabilities have increased 'telemarketing'; 'robotic' taking over some jobs currently performed by employees; man conquering the wonderland moon; are some examples that bear testimony of fastplaced, rapidly changing organisation. Organizations desire change in order to remain competitive, in order to remain in harmony with the ever-changing environment. Organizations also want to achieve internal stability because of the predictability and certainty it provides. Organisations handle the stability-change dilemma depending on the amount and type of innovation required. The organic organisation is, for example, suitable when frequent technological changes are required. Mechanistic organiszations, on the other hand, are oriented towards technological stability. Organizations, thus, resolve the stability-change dilemma by structuring in an organic way when the organization needs new ideas and frequent changes and by structuring in a mechanistic way whenever possible to obtain efficiency. The management must consider the human aspect of change before initiating any action. The man at the top responsible for the change, should take a decision of introducing change in the larger interest of the organisation and the workers but he must seek cooperation from those who are affected while managing the change.

Organisation is a social system. All parts of organisation affect all other parts. They are so interrelated that anything happening at one end is transmitting to the other end. This interrelationship develops also with the environment around it. When organisation functions for sometime, these relationship and interrelationship develops and gets established and gradually organisation obtains a systematised and orderly behaviour. An equilibrium is established in the whole system and any distrubance to such equilibrium excercises pressures on some elements which are accustomed to that way of life. In our dynamic industrial economy, several decisions are taken by the managers in performing their day to day obligation. Such decisions may involve changes in the investment pattern, organisational structure, work process, and methods of utilising the human resources of a firm or organisation to obtain the higher efficiency. But management does this only within prescribed limits established by public policies and sometimes by union agreements. People in organisation, always resist change, however well designed the change may be.

Organizations are, of course, learning to cope with the devastating rate of internal and external changes with the help of some fundamental changes in management philosophy and organizational technology. Modern organizations are highly dynamic, versatile and adaptive to the multiplicity of changes.

(i) Change basically results from *stimuli* from both outside and inside the enterprise. Organizational change refers to the alteration of structural relationships and roles of people in the organizations. It is largely structural in nature.

(ii) Change takes place in all organizations but at varying rates of speed and degrees of significance.

(iii) Finally, the enterprise can be changed in several ways. Its technology can be changed; its structure, its purpose, and other elements can be changed.

Change may affect an individual, a group, and the whole organisation. If the change is beneficial to parties affected, it may be immediately accepted. If, on the other hand, change affects no one the people will be quite indifferent but if anyhow change is detrimental to their interest, they will resist the change to their full strength. The reaction is based upon not necessarily on facts but on their perception of the situation, *i.e.*, how they perceive the change.

Response to Change

Work change does not produce a direct adjustment but instead it operates through each employee's attitudes to produce a response conditioned by feelings towards the change.

Roethlisberger confirmed through various studies made in Howthorne plant that there was no direct relationship between the change and the response but it was attitude of the people that disturbed the set pattern. Each change is perceived and interpreted by individuals according to their own attitude and respond accordingly.

The attitude or feeling of people towards change is the result of several causes:

(i) One cause of such attitudes is the personal history of the individual which refers to biological processes of people, their backgrounds and their social experiences away from the work.

(ii) A second cause of a particular attitude is the work environment itself. It reflects the fact that workers as a members of the group are influenced by its norms, codes, and patterns of the group.

(iii) The attitude of workers are mostly governed by the group interests. This effect is named as Hawthorne Effect which refers that people individually interpret change, they often show their attachment to the group by joining hand with it in some uniform response to change. At times, there may be some illogical responses though unintended, but people respond just to show their affinity with the group, they are to follow other members of the group. For example, walkout by a few persons from a meeting to express their dissatisfaction over the situation may be psychology binding others to follow the path to affirm their cohesion to the group.

EFFECT OF CHANGE ON SOCIAL SYSTEM

The dynamic force of change affects the whole social system. All its elements, *i.e.*, its people, formal organisation, informal organisation, operating environment, communication pattern, decision making and patterns of cooperation, are bound to change. There is an equilibrium in all parts of a whole society. In trying to maintain the equilibrium, group develops responses to return to its perceived best way of life whenever any change occurs. Pressure produces counter pressure within the group which results in self-correcting mechanism by which balance is established. This self-correcting characteristic of organisation is called Homeostasis, *i.e.*, people act to establish a steady state of need fulfilment and to secure themselves from disturbance of that balance. Thus it is an idea of social equilibrium.

Following are some reasons of oganisational changes:

(a) Informal organisation is a must in every formal organisation and is a very important part of our existence, because many of our motivational forces find satisfaction in these relationships, when management likes to introduce any change that disturbs the informal relationship established among people.

(b) Changes in business conditions such as change in the quality of the product, change in the marketing system or practices, business cycles, change in industrial policy etc. all create disequilibrium in the work-environment and it needs adjustment accordingly.

(c) Change in the managerial personnel in the organisation may result in disequilibrium. A personnel may retire or change place, this will all affect the policies, practice, procedure and programmes of the organisation and the people are to adjust themselves accordingly.

(d) Man is a creature of habits. He feels irritated when change occurs in methods and procedures of work of which he is accustomed to. As it takes times to adjust to the new environment, it creates disequilibrium till the complete adjustment to the new environment.

(e) Technological or mechanical changes in machines, tools and equipments may bring change in the organisation. For example installation of an automatic machinary in place of old machinary, may result in displacement or replacement of people or loss of jobs to people and may create disequilibrium.

(f) Organisations once established can be said to be good for all times. Many defects may appear with the passage of time such as extention of the plant, change in managerial functions, evolution of complex organisation relationship etc. which cause imbalance and need correction. So, change is necessary to remove such deficiencies.

(g) The formal organisation structure establishes a formal line of command of authority and reponsibility in an organisation. Along with these lines, channels of communication and interpersonal relations are established. If there is a change in this formal organisational structure, there will be a change in the formal relationship which creates disequilibrium.

Thus, the above reasons emphasise change in the organisation which create imbalance in the relationship between employer and employee, and between employee and employee. So, people generally resist the change.

FACTORS OF CHANGE

Organisational change calls for a change in the individual behaviour of the employees. Organisations survive, grow, decline or die depending on the changing behaviour of the employees. Any organisational change whether introduced through a new structural design or new technology or new training programme basically attempts to make employees change their behaviour. It is because unless the behavioural patterns of the members change the change will have a little impact on the effectiveness of organizations. But behavioural changes are the most difficult and marathon exercises. They are not expected to be brought about overnight rather they devour more time. Lewin's model provides a useful vehicle for understanding change process in the organisation.

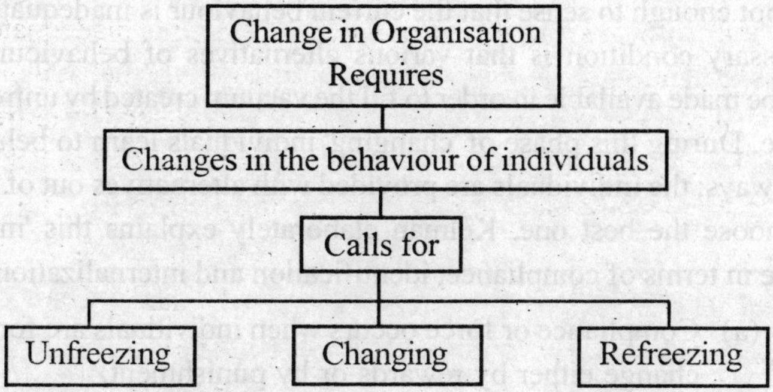

Unfreezing. It refers to making individual aware that the present behaviour is inappropriate, irrelevant, inadequate and hence unsuitables to the changing demands of the present situation. Edger Schien outlines the following elements which are vitally necessary during this unfreezing phase.

1. The physical removal of the individuals being changed from their accustomed routines, sources of information and social relationships.
2. The undermining and destruction of social support.
3. The consistent liking of reward with willingness to change and of punishment with unwilligness to change.
4. Demeaning and humiliating experience to help individuals being changed to see their old attitudes or behaviour as unworthy and think to be motivated to change.

Unfreezing is, thus, the breaking down of the existing mores, old taboos and traditions - the primitive way of doing things, so that the people are ready to accept new alternatives. It involves, discarding the orthodox and conventional methods and introducing a new dynamic behaviour that is most appropriate to the situation.

The essence of this unfreezing phase is that the individual is made to realize that his beliefs, feelings and behaviour are no longer appropriate or relevant to the current situation in the organization.

Changing. It is the phase where new learning occurs. When the individuals are convinced that their behaviour is inappropriate they happily come forward to accept the change. In order to change, it is not enough to sense that the current behaviour is inadequate. The necessary condition is that various alternatives of behaviour must also be made available in order to fill the vacuum created by unfreezing phase. During this phase of 'changing' individuals learn to behave in new ways; the individuals are provided with alternatives out of which to choose the best one. Kelman elaborately explains this 'moving' phase in terms of compliance, identification and internalizations.

(a) Compliance or force occurs when individuals are forced to change either by rewards or by punishment.

(b) Identification occurs when individuals recognize one among various models provided in the environment that is most suitable to their personality.

(c) Internalization occurs when individuals are forced to encounter a situation that calls for new behaviour.

Refreezing. During this phase individuals internalize the new beliefs, feelings and behaviour learned in the 'changing' phase. That is to say a person accepts the new behaviour as a permanent part of his behaviour repertoire. He has to practice and experiment with the new method of behaviour and see that it effectively blends with his other behavioural attitudes. It is very important for the manager concerned with the introducing change to visualize that the new behaviour is not extinguished soon. Ferster and Skinner have, in this connection, advanced the main reinforcement schedules, namely, continuous and intermittant reinforcements.

STEPS INVOLVED IN ORGANISATION WIDE CHANGE

Some changes are of such a nature that affects the whole organisation and has several consequential effects. For example, a promotion at higher level affects several hierarchical levels below. If the job of an individual is being changed, it will change his role set, also his self-concept which is in part a product of his culture, his reference groups and also his education and training. All these, he will bring in line with the formal task to display a cooperative behaviour. If the formal task role and the self-concept differ and cannot be in congruent there will be adaptive response either to leave the organisation or to make an attempt to change formal task role or to change the self-concept. In this way, any action has a chain reaction and causes a series of other changes, depending, naturally, upon the extent of its strength. Such changes that have a wide impact in the organisation, are organisation wide changes.

Any change in the organisation affects the people in terms of skills, status social relationship or otherwise but organisation wide change is just like a major surgical operation. If it remains unsuccessful, it may endanger the very existence of the organisation, and if successful, it may give a new life to the organisation. Therefore, there is a need of careful planning. Allen lists the following steps in this regard:

(i) development of clear objectives;

(ii) analysis of existing organisation;

(iii) preparation of an ideal plan;

(iv) trying out the plan;

(v) preparation of phase plan;

(vi) establihsment of uniform nomenclature.

To be on a safe side, it should be undertaken only when it is felt necessary and only with the proper planning for that we must try to understand what we have and what we would like to have. Such organisation wide changes should not be very frequent and we should have a time prospective and project into the future. This will facilitate identification of gap both in terms of men or materials and for this purpose an action plan should be prepared.

In implementing organisation wide change, it affects people throughout the organisation, so there may be many upsets and set backs. Status system titles and appellations may seriously be disturbed and designations should be immediately awarded as soon as the change is complete. Some people may be given training to re-equip them for handling new jobs. As change often evokes resistance, step should be taken to overcome them.

❐

6

Strategy Formulation

Strategy formulation is often referred to as strategic planning or long-range planning. This process is primarily analytical, not action-oriented. The strategy formulation process is concerned with developing a corporation's mission, obejctives and policy. This process involves scanning external and internal environmental factors, analysis of the strategic factors and generation, evaluation and selection of the best alternative strategy appropriate to the analysis.

Henry Mintzberg, after much research found that strategy formulation is typically not a regular, continuous process. "It is small often an irregular, discontinuous process, proceeding in fits and starts. There are periods of stability in strategy development, but also there are periods of flux, of grouping of piecemeal changes and of global change."

Performance results are generally periodic measurements of developments that occur during a given time period like return on investment, profits after taxes, earnings per share and market share. Current performance results are compared with the current objectives and with that of the previous year's performance results. If the results are equal to or greater than the current objectives and past year's results, the company will mostly continue with the current strategy otherwise, the strategy formulation process begins in earnest.

The strategic managers must evaluate the mission, objectives and policies. In fact, the strategic managers are evaluated in terms of management style, values and skills by the top management. Henry Mintzberg has pointed out that a corporation's objectives and strategies are strongly affected by top managements's view of the world. This view determines the mode to be used in strategy formulation. These modes include:

1. **Entrepreneurial Mode.** Strategy is formulated by one powerful individual. The focus is on opportunities rather than on problems. Strategy is guided by the founder's own visions of direction.
2. **Adaptive Mode.** This strategy formulation mode is characterised by reactive solutions to existing problems rather than a proactive search for new opportunities.
3. **Planning Mode.** Analysts assume main responsibility for strategy formulation. Strategic planning includes both the proactive search for new opportunities and the reactive solution of existing problems.

Strategic planning is a systemic and disciplined exercise to formulate strategies. It relates to the enterprise as a whole or to particular business units (identified as strategic business units—SBUs) of a divisionalised organisation. It consists of making risk-taking decisions—entrepreneurial decisions—for the future with the best possible knowledge of their probable outcome and effects. In short, strategic planning concerns itself with the formulation of strategic alternatives to obtain sanctions for one of the alternatives which is to be ultimately interpreted and communicated in operational terms. Thus, strategic planning is a forward-looking exercise which determines the future posture of the enterprise with special reference to its products-market posture, profitability, size, rate of innovation and external institutions.

Strategic planning differs from project planning tactical, planning and operational planning. Strategic planning is more comprehensive, for strategy is dealt with at corporate level and is concerned mainly with the long-term aspects of business. It deals with what business the company wants to be in. Project planning involves looking for new markets for xisting products, developing new products, creating demand for the same, and utilising the existing facilities if they have the capacity to meet the marketing and selling requirements of the new product. Tactical planning is done at the functional level. It is concerned more with the present than the future. It implies an ad hoc approach based on expediency with a time schedule. Operational planning, on the other hand, is essentially concerned with the existing product-market operations—the 'bread and butter lines' of the business. The scope of operational planning is restricted to the operations in the market with which the company has built up a rapport with the existing range of products through the facilities which are already in harness.

Choice activity consists of selecting the most appropriate strategy from among the alternatives. This framework is helpful in understanding the essential elements involved in strategy formulation. But the sequence of intelligence, design and choice activity may not be practised in the same order. It is possible for a strategic planner to first choose a preferred strategy, then develop other options (alternatives) to analyse for rationalising the choice.

The degree of uncertainty in tactical planning and operational planning is of a low order. It is of a higher order in project planning, while in strategic planning risk and uncertianty involved are much greater. The time span of discretion is relatively shorter in tactical and operational planning than in project planning. It is much longer in strategic planning as compared with that of project planning. Thus the value of judgment is of much greater significance in strategic planning than in project planning or operational planning.

APPROACHES TO STRATEGY FORMULATION

Possible approaches to strategy formulation are many. Gilmore has distinguished between the traditional approaches which developed during the period between World Wars I and II. and the modern approach which has evolved since the mid-1950s. The traditional approach comprised:

(a) A size-up of the situation of the company as a whole generally on the basis of size-ups of the functional departments;

(b) Determination of objectives; and

(c) Development of programme of action covering the various activities of the company in the light of direction and unity of purpose provided by the objectives.

It was an open-ended process. As Gilmore put it, "There was a definite tendency for top management to size up the situation, starting at the very base; formulate objectives and programmes of action; organise to carry out the plans; and exercise executive control; but then drift along until serious problems made it necessary to size up the situation again. In short, the traditional approach was characterised by a concern for short-term problems, sporadic diagnosis and sizing up the situations as a basis for new course of action, and adaptability to meet changes in current conditions.

The new, modern approach has evolved with emphasis on reappraisal of the existing strategy in the light of changing external conditions, constant surveillance of the environment to identify and capitalise on long-term opportunities, formulation of alternative strategies, if necessary, and choosing an appropriate strategy, all within a formalised system. In a model set-up, the process of strategy making should work as follows: "Current strategy is reappraised from time to time in the light of internal operating results, economic trends, competitors' action, and technological developments. When opportunites and threats have been disclosed, management proceeds to ask questions designed to indicate when and in what respect strategy should be changed. If a new economic mission is called for, the planners proceed to formulate a revised approach. This, in turn, calls for the revision of the competitive approach and of the programme of action. If the economic mission is considered sound, the competitive approach is questioned. If the competitive approach seems appropriate, the process continues until the appropriate area for revision is identified and a new strategy is formulated.

The method of strategy formation delineated above is a rational, normative proposition. One may also distinguish between different approaches to strategy-making on the basis of the thrusts which generate strategic alternatives and determine the effectiveness of strategic decisions. Let us examine these approaches briefly:

1. **Intuition.** The basic premise of this approach is that the strategy evolves in the mind of the chief executive without ever being explicitly stated and without the aid of formal procedures. "Intuition." Stenier has observed,· "is an excellent approach if it is brilliant." Along with intuition, personal judgment is also a necessary element in this approach. In the United States, Alfred Sloan of General Motors Corporation, Henry Ford of Ford Motor Car Company, and in India, Lala Sri Ram, Walchand Hirachand, J.R.D. Tata, G.M. Modi, Shri Anantharamakrishnan. G.D. Birla, to name a new among the pioneer industrialists, are often remembered for their imagination, drive and expansive vision, which led to corporate growth and prosperity in different fields. The strategies developed by each of them over the years may be attributed to their intuition and judgment. The very nature of strategy formation is said to provide the raison d' etre of this approach. As Anthony has put it. "Strategic planning is essentially irregular. Problems, opportunities, and 'bright ideas' do not arise accoridng to some set time table; they have to be dealt with whenever they happen to be perceived. The appropriate analytical techniques depend on the nature of the problem being analysed and currently there is no general appraoch (such as a mathematical model) that is of much help in the analysis of the types of strategic problems. Indeed, any attempt to introduce a systematic approach is quite likely to dampen the essential element of creativity.

2. **Disjointed Incrementalism.** Sometimes referred to as 'muddling through', this approach to strategy-making reflects an attitude of management having strong preference for acting only when forced to, and then considering a few convenient alternatives involving only small, non-disruptive changes in the organisation. The decisions made are of remedial nature. Only those alternatives are considered which are important, interesting and easily understandable. The strategist, instead of comprehending strictly and literally

present states of affairs or the consequences of present policies, attempt only to understand the respects in which various possible states differ from each other and from the status quo. Lindblom stressed the rationale of this appraoch on the ground that the comprehensive analytical approach to strategy-making—careful analysis of many alternatives of expected goals—is not helpful because of man's inability to cope with complex problems, the lack of information, the cost analysis, the problem of timing, and the difficulty of stating realistic goals.

3. **Entrepreneurial Approach.** The thrust underlying this approach is related with the role of the manager as an entrepreneur. Drucker has depicted the role of an entrepreneurial manager as that of a systematic risk-maker and risk-taker, looking for and finding opportunity. "Entrepreneurship is essentially the acceptance of change as an opportunity and the acceptance of 'the leadership in change' as the unique task of the entrepreneur." The role of an entrepreneur is opportunity-focused and not problem-focused. Briefly speaking this general description of the enterpreneurial manager indicates what is expected of him, but it does not enlighten us on how he should go about performing his role.

4. **Key-factors Approach.** This approach consists of determining the really significant factors that are important in the success of a particular business and concentrating major decisions on it. For instance, a new imaginative toy may be a critically strategic factor in the success of a toy company. Or, finding a propitious niche in the market where a company can give the customers an irresistible value that is not being satisfied at a relatively low cost, may again be the cornerstone of strategy formation.

5. **'Inside out' Planning.** According to Ewing. a basic approach to developing strategies could be 'inside out' planning. Straegies, he suggests, ought to be first conceived

in a thought process arising out of the unique talents and resources possessed by a company. Market forecasts should be considered later as a kind of check or constraint on strategies so conceived.

6. **Integrated Approach.** An integrative approach to the strategy-making process provides a framework which consists of the following parts:
   (a) Analysing the present internal and external conditions;
   (b) Identifying and evaluating the present strategy—the major objectives, policies and plans currently guiding the firm;
   (c) Search for strengths and weaknesses viewed within the present strategy and environment;
   (d) Considering changes in the present strategy;
   (e) Generating alternatives to resolve the problems and exploit the opportunities;
   (f) Developing alternative unified strategies by combining the various alternatives in each of the problem and opportunity area;
   (g) Evaluation of each unified strategy in terms of the enterprise objectives and choosing the strategy that best satisfies the objectives.

For an ongoing organisation, re-appraisal of the present strategy actually becomes the first phase in the total process. This requires identification of the existing strategy. It is often difficult to identify the present strategy. The strategy being followed may not be articulated. Or, there may be an articulated strategy that is not adhered to in practice. Or, again, the enterprise may not have developed any real strategy, it may be muddling through and 'being tossed about by the force of events. If no strategy is clearly indicated, it must be constructed from actual events and statements.

Identification of the present strategy is invariably accompanied by an analysis of the enterprise objective, policies, and plans in the context of the functional areas and managerial configuration of the organisation, and the external conditions. Thus, by implication, in the process of identification and description of the strategy, the evaluation of strategy, is also under way. More specifically, the effectiveness of the present strategy may be assessed on the basis of the following criteria:

(a) Past results;

(b) Its appropriateness for the future; and

(c) Its rationale, *i.e.*, by asking why the present strategy has been pursued.

Review of performance in terms of results achieved is an important basis of appraising the present strategy. But the relevant questions to be raised in this connection are: How do the results compare with the objectives of the enterprise? Have the achievements been realised within the bounds of policies established by management ? Have the results been achieved with an acceptable degree of risk? Were the achievements really the outcome of strategy, or fortuitously derived in spite of the strategy? Or, if the results have not been up to expectations, was it due to a faulty strategy or due to unforeseen changes in the environment?

Rather than the past results, what is perhaps more essential to consider is whether the present strategy would be appropriate for the future; in other words; 'consistency with the environment' should be the major criterion to assess the present strategy. In a dynamic sense, it implies judging the effectiveness of strategy with respect to the environment as it is changing, rather than with respect to the environment as it is now. If the present strategy was effective in the past, it is history. The more important question is "whether it will be a useful compass in the uncharted waters of the future."

An insight into the appropriateness of the present strategy for the future can be had also by reference to its rationale, *i.e.*, the fundamental reasons underliying the present strategy. Often the raison d' etre of a strategy lies in the personal background, needs, aspirations, and values of the owners, managers, or the strategy-makers. The appropriateness or otherwise of these factors, among other things, should be taken into account in determining the appropriateness of the strategy. Again, the genesis of the present strategy might have been the identification and exploitation of one or more opportunities perceived by management in the past. Changes in the environment may have thrown up other opportunities since then. Obviously, the present strategy needs to be judged in terms of the newly emerging environment for the future. A third possible basis of the present strategy may be the distinctive internal capacity of the firm in particular respects. To judge the appropriateness of the present strategy which stemmed from a competence or capability, one should naturally ascertain whether and to what extent the strategy is consistant with the internal resources position, the potential advantages. While it may be possible to identify the most dominant reasons underlying a strategy, it is also possible that a combination of several reasons formed the basis of the present strategy. Assessment of the strategy should, therefore, tbe governed by the appropriateness of the blend of factors leading to the strategy.

Whether a change in strategy is called for should not be difficult to decide in the light of the appraisal of present strategy. The change called for may be in the strategy itself, or in the implementation of the strategy. Change in strategy may be necessitated by one or more of the following reasons: changes in the environment; changes in the internal resource position and capabilities; resuts not measuring up to expectation in sales and profits or market shares; increased intensity of competition in the product market; changes in consumer preferences; a change in the size of the organisation; and to correct problems which are apparent.

Following evaluation of the present strategy and consideration of changes in the strategy, management has to generate alternatives, develop alternative unified strategies, and evaluate the alternative to choose an appropriate strategy. These steps are necessary assuming that reformulation of the existing strategy is called for.

TYPES STRATEGIES AND DIMENSIONS

Whatever the approaches managers adopt for identifying the strategic alternatives, they will result into a number of strategies. There are various ways of classifying the strategies:

(i) These can be classified on the basis of their scope. In such a case, the strategies may be classified as master strategies, also called as grand or root strategies and programme strategies. The former deal with the overall strategic action while later deal with strategies which may be devised to implement progamme.

(ii) The classification may be based on the level of organsiation wherein the strategies can be classfied as headquarter strategies and divisional strategies. If the latter is developed in pursuit of the former they may be called substrategies also.

(iii) The classification may be based on purpose and functions of the organisation and various strategies may be master strategies and functional strategies. Functional strategies may be for production, marketing, finance, personnel, and so on.

Even if we take master strategies for an organisation, there can be various alternatives. There may be three categories of master strategies which an organisation can follow. These are stability strategy, growth strategy, and retrenchment strategy. A combination of two or more strategies can also be followed simultaneously. A discussion of these strategies gives ideas about them.

1. Growth Strategy. Growth strategy is the much-talked and publiced in the present Indian environment. If we look at the corporate performance in the recent years, we find how the various organisations have grown both in terms of sales and profit as well as assets.

In fact, in life of any organisation, growth is necessary at some point of time. However, it is not necessary that the various stages will be uniform for all organisation. For example, many organisations may not decline even after a considerable period of time while many may die very soon even before passing through regeneration stage. This is evident by the high mortality rate of small organisations. On the other hand, Tata Iron and Steel established in 1907 is still the corporate leader. It suggests then that the strategies followed by the organisations will determine the application of various stages. If the organisations are going through growth strategy at approapriate time, they can avoid declining and regeneration stages. Growth strategy can be defined as follows:

'A growth strategy is one that an enterprise pursues when it increases its levels of objectives upward in significant increment, much higher than an exploration of its past achievement of its past achievement level. The most frequent increase indicating a growth strategy is to raise the market share and or sales objectives upward signficantly.'

Growth under growth strategy can be differentiated from normal growth which an organisation can achieve through its normal learning curve. A normal learning curve suggests the organisations will grow both in terms of sales and profitability by gaining experience of various functions. The rate of growth under such a case quite low and falls on a trend line which can be consistent throughout a period of time. However, when the organisation reaches at the level of maturity, its sales and profit may stabilise. In this growth strategy, the rate of growth is much faster than the past years owing to additional operational facilities in the organisation.

2. Stability Strategy. Stability strategy, though most frequently used by most of the organisations, often presents a confusing nomenclature. In fact, most of such organizations look for growth and do not remain stable over the long period of time. However, when they adopt some changes in their strategy postures, they try to stabilise in a particular area which is consistent with their strengths. Thus basic approach in the stability strategy is 'to maintain present course.' Stability strategy can be defined as follows:

> 'In an effective stability strategy, companies will concentrate their resources where the company presently has or can rapidly develop a meaningful competitive advantage in the

narrowest possible product-market scope consistent with the firm's resources and market requirements.'

3. Retrenchment Strategy. Retrenchment strategy, though less frequently used and publicised, has been pursued by various companies successfully. Even many experts do not agree with the present nomenclature of the strategy because of wide scope of action in this strategy. Retrenchment, as used in the field of personnel management, denotes separation of employees mainly due to decreased amount of work owing to recesion or reorganisation of work. The same word is used in the field of strategic management with a slightly different emphasis because retrenchment strategy does not always involve getting off the business. Retrenchement strategy can be defined as follows:

> 'A retrenchement strategy is one that an enterprise pursues when it decides to improve its performance in reaching its objectives by: *(a)* focussing on functional improvement, specially reduction in cost; *(b)* reducing the number of the products and markets it serves up to and including liquidation of the business, *(c)* reducing the number of function it performs by becoming a captive company.'

4. Turnaround Strategy. Turnaround strategy also known as cutback strategy, has the basic philosophy: 'hold the present business and cut the cost.' This situation is needed as no organisation is immune from internal hard time-stagnation or declining performance-no matter what the state of economy is. Traditionally, turnaround situations have been discussed either in terms of the areas of organisational performance to be improved or the time criticality of the turnaround actions. Thus the most frequent turnaround situations have been those involving improvement in declining organisational profitability coupled with decline in sales or market share. However, with increasing impact of inflation and capital cost, much attention is being given to turnaround involving improved asset utilisation. Thus turnaround strategy can be defined as follows:

> Turnaround strategy involves that strategic action which an organisation takes to complete in the same business in

turnaround situations. Turnaround, situations may be improvement in organisational lower performance caused by downward trend which is not controllable by present actions of management.

5. Divestment Strategies. Divestment (also called divestiture or cutback) strategy invovles the sale or liquidation of a portion of business or a major division, profit centre or SBU. Divestment is usually a part of rehabilitation plan and is adopted when a turnaround or restructuring plan and is adopted when a turnaround has been attempted but has proved to be unsuccessful. The option of a turnaround may even be ignored if it is obvious that divestment is the only answer.

6. Liquidation Strategies. A retrenchment strategy considered the most extreme and unattractive is liquidation strategy, which invovles closing down a firm and selling its assets. It is considered as the last resort because it leads to serious consequences such as loss of employement for workers and other employees, termination of opportunities where a firm could pursue any future activities, and the stigma of failure.

Many small-scale units, propreitorship firms, and partnership ventures liquidate frequently but medium and large-sized companies rarely liquidate in India. This is due to a variety of factors. The company management, government, and financial institutions, trade unions, and creditors and other agencies are reluctant to take a decision, or ask, for liquidation. Each party has its own reasons for doing so. While the management may hesitate to liquidate due to the fear of failure, the government may not easily allow liquidation due to the political and other risks involved. Trade unions would naturally resist the loss of employment of workers. Ceasing operations does not mean that a firm is freed from its contractual obligations to the suppliers unless of course, it is declared insolvent or bankrupt selling assets for implementing a liquidation strategy may also be difficult as buyers as difficult to find. Moreover, the firm cannot expect adequate compensation as most assets, being unusable, are considered as scrap. Besides the practical difficulties in liquidation, there is also a psychological aspect which cannot be overlooked. The prospects of liquidation create a bad impact on the company's (or business groups') reputation. For many executives who are closely associated with firms, liquidation may be traumatic experience. Despite the hesitancy on the part of all concerned with a company that intends to liquidate and the difficulties in the process of liquidation sometimes a firm may be forced to liquidate.

Liquidation strategy may be unpleasant as strategic alternative but when a "dead business is worth more than alive", it is a good proposition. When liquidation is evident, an abandonment plan is desirable. Planned liquidation would involve a systematic plan to reap the maximum benefits for the firm and and its shareholders through the process of liquidation.

7. Merger Strategies. These strategies basically involve the external approach to expansion. Basically two, or occasionally more than two firms are involved. There is not much difference in the three terms used for such types of strategies and they are frequently used synonymously. But a subtle distinction can be made. While mergers take place when the objectives of the buyer firm and the seller firm are matched to a large extent, takeovers or acquisitions usually are based on the strong motivation of the buyer firm to acquire.

8. Joint Venture. It is effective strategy when development costs have to be shared, risks spread out, and expertise combined to make effective use of resources.

Joint ventures are common within industries and in various countries. But they are specially useful for entering international markets. From the point of view of Indian organisations, the following types of joint ventures are possible:

A. Between an Indian firm and a foreign company in third country.

B. Between two firms across different industries;

C. Between an Indian firm and a foreign company in that foreign country;

D. Between an Indian firm and a foreign company in India.

It offers the advantages of achieving objectives mutually by the participating firms. Eliminating, controlling, or reducing competition may be of strategic importance and can be brought about through joint ventures. Increasing the market share can also be achieved. Diversification strategies may be adopted by paricipating firm if a joint venture is planned across different industries. If technology is a critical variable in strategy, then joint venture with foreign companies can be feasible. If legal and regulatory hurdles come in the way of external expansion, they could be subverted through a joint venture strategy of combining with a foreign firm in that foreign country or in a third country. Environmental threats within the country or opportnities abroad may cause firms to undertake joint ventures.

Strategic advantages are important for joint ventures to be set up and sustained.

9. Takeover Strategies. Takeover or acquisition is currently the popular strategy being adopted by Indian companies. During the three decades after independence, the normal route of growth was through licensing and setting up new projects. The current decade has seen an increasing use of takeover strategies (or simple takeovers) as the means of rapid growth.

Certain guidelines can be proposed for takeovers to take place systmatically. For instance, following procedure is recommended for acquisition:

1. Treat people with dignity and concern.
2. Spell out the objectives.
3. Assess managerial quality.
4. Check the compatibility of business styles.
5. Anticipate and solve problems early.
6. Indicate how the objective would be achieved.

10. Diversification and Integration Strategy. Diversification is a much-used and much-talked about strategy. In reality, it is not a strategy but a set of strategies. These strategies involve all the dimensions of strategic alternative. Diversifcation may involve internal or external, related or unrelated, horizontal or vertical, and active or passive dimensions-either singly or collectively.

Essentially, diversification involves a change in business definition either in terms of customer functions, customer groups, or alternative technologies.

The different types of diversification strategies are as follows:

(i) Vertical Integration. When an organisation starts making new products that serve its own needs, vertical integration takes place. In other words, any new activity undertaken with the purpose of either supplying inputs or serving as a costomer for outputs is vertical integration.

Vertical integration could be of two types backward and forward integration. Backward integration means moving towards the source of raw materials while forward integration involves up activities that will bring the organization nearer to the ultimate customers.

(ii) Horozontal Integration. When an organisation takes up the same types of products at the same level of production or marketing process, it is said to follow a strategy of horizontal integration. When a luggage company takes over its rival luggage company it is horizontal integration (or merger). Horizontal integration strategy may be frequently adopted with a view to geographically expand by taking up a competitor in another area, to increase the market share, and to benefit from economies of scale.

(iii) Concentric Diversification. When an organisation takes up an activity in such a manner that it is related to its existing business definition either in terms of customer groups, customers functions, or alterantive technological, it is concetric diversification. Concentric diversification may be of three types:

A. When a similars type of products is offered with the help of unrelated technology, *e.g.*, a company in the sewing machine business diversifies into kitchenware and household appliances, which are sold through a chain of retail stores to housewives.

B. When a similar type of product (or service) is provided with the help of related technology, *e.g.*, a raincoat manufacturer makes other rubber-based items such as waterproof shares and rubber gloves sold through the same retail outlets.

C. When a new type of product or service is provided with the help of related technology, *e.g.,* a leasing firm offers hire-purchase services to institutional customers and consumer financing for purchase of durables to individual customers.

(iv) Conglomerate Diversification. When an organisation adopts a strategy which requires taking up those activities which are unrelated to its existing business definition either in terms of customer groups, customer functions or alternative technologies, it is conglomerate diversification. Frequently such companies are referred to as conglomerates.

11. Modernisation Strategies. In developing countries like India, technology is often employed as a strategic and competitive tool. Modernisation, which basically involves technological upgradation, is used to achieve organisation objectives such as increased production, lower cost, efficiency, productivity. Here, modernisation is dealt with, not in an operation manner indicating technological upgradation, but in a strategic sense. With respect to the classification of strategic alternatives. Modernisation could be considered as:

A. External retrenchment if part of the organization is divested or liquidated with the aim of modernisation.

B. Internal stability strategy if the pace of modernisation is low to moderate, internal expansion strategy if the pace of modernisation is high.

C. External expansion strategy if the organisation merges with or acquires another company for the purpose of modernisation;

Internal retrenchment strategy if resources are redirected from one area to another with the aim of modernisation.

Modernisation strategies are used for different reasons. As we pointed out earlier, some of these are increasing production, lowering costs, improving efficiency and productivity. etc. Most of these objectives apparently seem to be aimed at improving the overall performance but they may also be aimed at increasing the competitive ability.

Consider these examples:

* National Organic Chemicals Industries Ltd. (NOCIL), a major manufacturer of petrochemicals in the private sector, undertook as Rs. 100 crore modernisation plan in order to compete effectively.

* Modi Industries Ltd. has planned to invest Rs 30 crore for technological upgradation of its steel unit, primarily for widening its product range.

* The corporate planning team at Steel Authority of India Ltd. (Sail) envisages as Rs. 15,000 crore captial spending programme spread over seven years to modernise its steel plants with a variety of obejctives such as lower costs, energy saving higher capacity utilisation, closing down unprofitable units. etc.

Modernisation could be used for different purposes as can be seen from the above examples. Some of these could be operational but most modernisation programmes involve a huge amount and resources and are aimed at gaining competitive and strategic strengths. Some organisations, in fact, build their strategies around technology.

12. Combination Strategies. An introduction to combination strategies is essentially a combination strategies. These are mixture of stability, expansion or retrenchment strategies applied either simultaneously (as that same time in different business) or sequentially.

It would be difficult to find any organisation that has survived and grown by adopting a single 'pure' strategy. They complexity of doing business demand that different strategies be adopted to suit the situational demands made upon the organisation. An organisation which has followed a stability strategy for quite sometime has to think of expansion. Any organisation which has been on an expansion path for long has to pause to consolidate it business. Multi-business organisations—as most large and medium Indian companies are now—have to follow multiple strategies either sequentially or simultaneously.

GROWTH STRATEGY

As pointed out earlier, growth is the necessary phenomenon of organisational life. However, it is not always beneficial to grow. For example, if a small organisation grows beyond a size and it does not remain small according to the definition by the Government, it loses many benefits and incentives which are meant for such organisations. Inspite of these, the organisations take up growth activities because this is the only way of survival in the long-run. Following are given some specifications in which organisations should look for growth strategy:

1. Notwithstanding above, the organization can grow only when the environment permits. For example in Indian business environment, there are numerous opportunities for growth because of general growth pattern of the economy but it offers more constraints to certain categories of organisations particularly those covered by MRTP Act, FERA, licensing etc. Keeping in view all these aspects, an organisation has to think for its growth much ahead to avoid delay because of certain constraints. Therefore, if the opportunity comes for the growth, the organisation should capitalise it.
2. The environment offers various concessions and incentives for growth in certain industries in certain areas. For eample, the government gives various concessions to priority sector industries and industries in backward areas. Whenever such opportunities exist, the organisation can go for growth. Moreover, in order to take the advantages of investment allowance reserve, the organization has to invest the amount

kept under this reserve. Therefore, the growth is almost a necessary condition for this.

3. When the organisation has been stabilised after the various growth or other strategies, it can look for growth either in the same field or in diversified field. For such an organisation, growth becomes the way of life : growth-stabilising-growth-stability and so on. However, an organisation should adopt growth strategy to the extent it is manageable.

REASONS FOR PURSUING GROWTH STRATEGY

The question is; why do the organization follow growth strategy? This question becomes more pertinent specially when growth strategy, particularly through diversification, is more risky while stability strategy is less risky. The answer can be that there are several reasons why the organisations opt for growth, the reasons for growth are as follows:

A. Growth offers many economies because of large scale of operations. The per unit cost of production can be very low at appropriate level of operations. This is possible because fixed costs are appropriated over large number of units. Moreover, the economies of increasing scale also afford and enhance deeper and deeper degrees of specialisation. With more people available to do the different kinds of work, greater penetration can be made into the competitive fine points of products, market segmentation applications, and marketing policies and programmes. These eventually lead to certain strategic advantages to the organization concerned.

B. There are certain intangible advantages of growth. These may be in the form of increased prestige of the organisation, satisfication to employees and social benefits. The growing organisations have always been preferred by investors of various kind. The prestige of the organization itself is advantageous in various ways. Growing organisations offer satisfaction to their employees by offering them more promotional avenues from within; stagnation in the hierarchical promotion is avoided. Thus availability of promotional avenues are motivating factor for the personnel in the organisations.

Growth strategy can be adopted in the form of expansion, vertical integration, diversification, merger, acquisition and joint venture. The basic objective in all these cases is growth but the basic problem in each case is significantly different which needs more elaborate discussion.

C. Growth strategy is taken up because of managerial motivation to do so. Managers with high degree of achievement and recognition always prefer to grow. The needs on the part of the managers push them to think as to how they can achieve their need satisfaction. The answer lies in the continuous growth of the organisation for the group of organisations as a whole. For example, managers first want recognition in a limited area. When this is achieved, they look forward for a broader area. This is never-ending chain which compels the managers to think in terms of continous growth.

D. In the long-run, growth is necessary for the very survival of the organisations themselves, particularly when the environment is quite volatile. The organization that does not grow may be pushed out of the business because of the new entrants in the field. If the organization is stabilised for very long time, it may lose its profitability because the costs may go on increasing due to higher wages, higher costs of other inputs, and lower level of efficiency because of certain obsolescence in plant and machinery, while there may not be corresponding increase in the revenue from the present products.

ADOPTION OF STABILITY STRATEGY

Stability is common for most of the organisations at some point of time. However, it is better that the organisations concerned should evaluate when they should go for change in thier strategy. In the following conditions, it is better to adopt stability strategy:

1. When there is scope for incremental improvement of functional performance in the same line of business, the organization should go for stability strategy. This is the moto of taking fullest advantages of the situation. For example, if an organisation has gone certain technological or other breakthrough, it may continue in the same line so long as it derives certain competitive advantage. The organization can look for achieving the functional improvment thereby bringing efficiency and economy in the operations which will further add to its competitive competence. This is based on the principle of learning curve which suggests that over the period, efficiency can be obtained through learning. Its business implication is that first organisation in new business is likely to reap the benefits of the learning curve first.
2. If the organisation continues to pursue same objectives, it is better to adopt stability strategy adjusting the level of achievement about the same precentage each year as it has achieved in the past. Thus stability strategy does not mean that business is stable, rather there is growth in the business, however, this growth is limited within the well specified limits and without really adding any substantial facilitie s.
3. When the organisation is serving a defined market or its segments according to its business definition it can adopt stable growth strategy. Since the organisation is serving the market and fulfilling its mission, it may continue to do so. Generally in such a case the environmental factors do not show appreciable change and the organisation is able to relate itself with the environment. This happens with most of the organisations in the short-term because their environment does not change and they can continue in the business.

REASONS FOR ADOPTING STABILITY STRATEGY

Though most of the organisations follow stability strategy for a period of time, some organisations follow it for much longer than others. It has been observed that as the companies get older, they become more conservative and more likely to pursue a stability strategy. Following are some important factors which suggest why the organisation follow stability strategy:

(A) If the organisation's past history is full of change, it will like to adopt stability so as to become efficient and manageable and to reap the rich harvest of all such past changes. In fact, stability strategy should always be followed after the growth strategy to take the best advantages of the situation.

(B) If the organisation's strategic advantages lie in the present business and market, it pursues stability strategy. For example, if organisation has high market share, it can continue in the same business and should concentrate on the internal operational efficiency.

(C) A stability is less risky in that it offers the safe business to the organisation unless there is major environmental change. If management prefers to take less risk, it can continue stability strategy.

(D) The nature of environment affects the extent to which the organisation can follow alternative strategies. For example, if the organisation wants to grow either through expansion or diversification, it has not only to appriase the environment but it has to get licence from the government for the purpose. If such a licence is not available, there is no alternative for the organisation and the organisation has to go through stability strategy. For example, the government has refused the expansion applications of various companies on the ground that they are dominant undertakings. Thus they have no alternative to choose. Many of the organisations have been forced to pursue stability strategy because of the regulatory measures of the government. Similarly if the total environmental forces are not excessively volatile, the organisation can pursue stability strategy.

(E) Some organisations are slow to change or resistant to change. Since stability strategy fits in their total framework, they often prefer not to change. Generally larger is the organisation and the more successful it has been, the greater is the resistance to change. Such organisations react to forces of environment and will change strategies only in extraordinary time.

(F) Perception of management about the performance of the organisation may motivate them to pursue stability strategy. If the managers are satisfied with present performance they will like to continue with the same. Management may not always be sure of what combination of decisions is responsible for this and, therefore, they may decide to continue the way the results are being achieved.

The stability strategy is basically defensive in its approach. It may be pursued to protect certain present organisational strength. There is not much functional change in any part of the organisation. However, it does not mean that there is not change in organisations structure and processes also. There can be organisational changes in these directions in order to bring effciency in operation.

REASONS OF ADOPTING DIVERSIFICATIONS STRATEGY

There are many reasons why organisation adopt diversification strategies. The three basic and important reasons are:

A. Diversification may be the only way out if growth in existing businesses is blocked due to environmental and regulatory factors.

B. Diversification strategies are adopted to minimise risk by spreading it over several businesses.

C. Diversification may be used to capitalise on organisational strength or minimise weaknesses.

The different types of diversification strategies described above (vertical, horizontal, concentric and conglomerate diversification) each have their own advantages and disadvantages. These are as follows:

	Advantages	*Disadvantages*
A. Horizontal	Eliminating Competitors *Access to new markets	*Increase in risk *Reduces flexibility
B. Vertical	1. Economising Operations 2. Access to and control of Supply or demand	* Risk of unfamiliar business *Less flexibility due to more commitment to a line of business.
C. Conglomerate	*Bettter management and allocation of cash flows Reducing risk by spreading investment.	*Diversion of resources leading to lack of Concentration *Risks of managing new businesses.
D. Concentric	*Attain synergy by exchange of resources and skills *Economies of scale and tax benefits.	*Additional investment in new technology *Untried Technologies

FACTORS FAVOURING DIVERSIFICATION

In some lines the customer desires to buy a variety of products from the same source. For example, a dealer in plumbing supplies must offer several types and sizes of valves to meet the needs of his customers, and he may prefer to purchase all of these from one source. If a manufacturer of valves offers him only one type, he may refuse to buy this valve because he would prefer to secure it from the same manufacturer from whom he purchases other types and sizes. Again, the retailer may desire to purchase a complete line of history from one manufacturer and may refuse to buy from a manufacturer who offers only one style of product. This attitude is most likely to be taken by the retailer who desires to use the brand name in this advertising and does not wish to incur the expense of advertising more than one brand.

If the customer buys only a small quantity of any one product at a time, it may be necessary to offer several products to the customer so that the salesman may secure sufficient sales on each call to justify the expense of making the call. For example, some bakeries operate trucks that sell bread directly to housewives. To secure an economical sales unit that will warrant the cost of the call, the salesman must offer a variety of bakery products—not just bread—to the housewife.

Products may be included in a line in order to prevent a competitor from establishing a relationship with the customer. Thus, a manufacturer of electric dishwashers may find it desirable to sell refrigerators also. Otherwise, competitors who sell both diswashers and refrigerators may develop a close business relationship with dealers through refrigerator sales, thereby including the dealer to buy both products from the same source and under the same brand name.

It may also be desirable to sell more than one product in order to decrease the severity of seasonal or cyclical fluctuations. A manufacturer of electric storage batteries, for instance, is experimenting with the production and sale of paint because it has a complementing seasonal fluctuation.

Product lines contributing to cyclical stabilization are more difficult to find. A manufacturer of automobiles may produce low-priced cars as well as high-priced cars since in the periods of depression he can secure a better sales volume on the low-priced cars.

Sometimes a company may offer additional products in order to utilize more fully the type of organisation, facilities, or other assets that it thinks desirable for operating its business efficiently. For example, a manufacturer of textiles may desire to maintain a research department to study markets, and to maintain a bureau of style and design to concentrate on product development. To justify the expense of these units, the company must secure a high volume of sales, and to obtain this volume, the company may have to add additional products. Such a procedure has led a number of concerns into serious difficulty because it is often less painful to add new products than to cut overhead expense.

Other firms diversify to spread their risks. A company highly successful with a component of missiles, for instance, sought civilian products to guard against cancellation of its military contracts. The du Pont company can risk failure on a new product because profits on other lines will provide financial support. In practice, this argument has been overworked. Companies have gone into lines they were unqualified to manage, thereby increasing their risks far more than spreading them.

The effect upon a company of increasing the number of its products. Before deciding diversification is preferable to specialization for one or more of the reasons just described, a company must consider the impact of an increase in product lines.

The typical salesman is able to sell only a few products efficiently. If he is given a large number to sell, he will usually concentrate on the sale of a new and neglect the others. For instance, a leading break fast food company added a special brand of coffee to its products line. Analysis of sales results indicated that the main line of cereals was neglected when pressure was put on the salesmen to secure coffee sales. In this particular case the coffee line was discontinued.

Usually a production organisation cannot product efficiently products of widely different quality. Manufacturers of high-grade watching have found it difficult to adjust the thinking and acting of their organisation to the production of cheaper products. An organisation manufacturing products in which a large degree of tolerance is permissible will find it difficult to manufacture products of high quality where variations from standards must be very slight. A carpenter shop cannot easily be transformed into a high-grade furniture factory.

Another of the dangers in increasing the product line is that the ability of the management to supervise activities required in selling a large number of products will be exceeded. In many cases the management of a company may be capable of supervising the sales of a few products, but if new lines of products are added with which the executives are not familiar, they may spend an amount of time administering the venture that is quite out of proportion to the importance of the new products.

A factor of major importance in determining whether to diversify is the suitability of a company's present facilities to the production and service of new products. If new products are to be manufactured in the company's plant, the additional investment required must be carefully considered. The company may lose considerably flexibility and add materially to its costs if the required investment is large. Even if the new products are to be purchased from an outside concern, management must give attention to the suitability and adequacy of storage, display, and delivery equipment for the contemplated new product.

The production of a wide number of products has a marked effect upon production costs, if they are produced at the same plant. Frequent adjustments of machinery may be required. Special dies and other tools are needed for some products; unless the article can be sold in a substantial volume, these expenses for "tooling-up" materially increase the total cost per unit. The modern trend for low-cost mass production has been possible only by production large quantities without the necessity of making frequent adjustments in equipments.

If a company sells a wide range of products, especially products of different qualities, it is likely to lose its distinctiveness. For example, a large store in an Eastern city had achieved prominence by selling high-quality, distinctive women's apparel. A new management attempted to capitalize on the firm's reputation by adding a line of medium- priced clothing, with the result that the exclusiveness of the store rapidly diminished.

We should note that many of the drawbacks of diversification just discussed can be overcome and the benefits of specialization can be obtained by creating a new separate division for the added product line. This new division might manufacture the product, or market the product, or perform all activities related to the product as a self-sufficient operation. However, the more the new line is divorced from existing operations, *(a)* the fewer will be the benefits of diversification and *(b)* the larger will be the potential volume necessary to support the new venture.

Clearly, many factors should be weighted in deciding whether to diversify or specialize. The outlook for proposed new lines and the situation existing within a company at a given time vary so much that no single answer is best for all companies. Experience does indicate that many companies have suffered from seeking to sell too many products rather than from restricting their activities to too few products.

EXPANSION OF A PRODUCT LINE

The number of products offered for sale may vary greatly among companies even in one industry. For example, one of the large meat-packing companies in the United States engages in the production and sales of numerous lines of products having both direct and indirect connection with its primary activity, that of butchering. In fact, the company has a large pharmaceutical department selling all sorts of products, such as liver extract made from hogs, cattle, or sheep. Other by-products that the company processes and sells include wool, soap, glue, and leather.

Some of these supplementary lines extend to businesses even farther removed from the original meat-packing operations. For example, the company manufactures and sells a line of sandpaper to insure a steady volume of glue consumption.

Fertilizer is another natural by-product of slaughtering operations. To market effectively its own brand of fertilizer, the company added other types of fertilizer made from materials that had to be secured from outside sources. These other lines have been expanded to such an extent that less than one tenth of the fertilizer now sold by the company is made of by-products of the packing operations. Actually the fertilizer plant has been moved to another city where it can more economically handle the products that are not derived from slaughtering.

In the production area, the company entered the ammonia business to provide the large quantities that were needed for refrigeration through out its plant. Having entered the ammonia business to provide its own requirements, the company undertook the sale of ammonia to outside concerns and thereby assured itself of economies of large-scale production.

For quite another reason it added a product line. Its refrigerator, cars, trucks, branch houses, and other marketing facilities were well adapted for handling poultry, butter and eggs. Moreover, such produce could be sold primarily to the same customers who were buying fresh meat. This company is now the largest product dealer in the country.

Here diversification has carried the company into by-products, raw materials, and products using similar manufacturing and marketing facilities. Then to assure success of these subsidiary ventures, the added lines have been expanded.

In contrast, other leading packing companies have followed a policy of selling most of their by products to independent manufacturers rather than finishing the products themselves. The managements of these companies believe that more profits can be earned by concentrating their attention upon meat-packing operations.

DANGERS OF UNWISE EXPANSION

Diversification may lead to trouble. For example, several years ago a leading watch manufacturer decided to expand into the electronics and scientific instruments businesses. The company had many of the production skills needed to make electric microscopes and similar instruments. Ever-chaning technical and scientific developments were opening up new uses for precision instruments and opportunities for manufacturers who had the technical skills to keep abreast of these changes. A new plant was acquired and three new divisions—Research and Development, Precision Products, and Eletronic Products—were formed.

The results were unsatisfactory. Two of the three divisions reported steady losses. Although sales increased, the constant demand for funds to fulfill engineering requirements and to maintain inventories for government work drained cash resources. The company had to borrow heavily from an investment bank, and control of the company went over to the bank. Then, a new chief executive decided to abandon the new lines and to concentrate on the watch business, which, though shaky, was profitable.

VARIETY OF PRODUCTS

The problem of variety of items within a line is often as pressing as the question of additional lines. Customers are continually requesting additional products, and salesmen will contend that the sales volume could be increased materially if they had a large variety of products to sell.

On manufacturer of soaps yielded to this pressure. Whenever the sales manager became convinced that competitors were offering a new soap or that a number of customers had requested a new soap that differed in colour, size, shape, fragrance, or composition, a new product meeting these specifications would be introduced. Examination of sales records showed that sales of most of these new products were satisfactory for several months but would gradully dwindle.

Apparently the initial sales were due to the enthusiasm of the salesmen for a new product and a willingness on the part of the retailers to try an original stocks to see how the product would sell. After this original distribution, however, most new products were discovered to have no unique appeal. This particular company, therefore, was found to have a large number of products for which the sales volume was inadequate to justify the cost of manufacturing, warehousing and selling. By careful study the company was able to reduce the number of items carried to comparatively few products that really had significant differences. It then concentrated its attention on selling these products rather than dissipating its efforts on new and unnecessary additions to its line.

Occasionally there may be specific reasons for a wide variety of products. A leading department store, for example, undertakes to show 300 colours of the broadloom carpet ranging over the entire colour spectrum. By so doing, the store can match any colour of wall paper, drapery, or upholstery material. Such wide variety is, perhaps, more important as a sales-promotion device than as a useful service to customers. Most stores and manufacturers believe that consumers can be adequately served with about a tenth as many colours.

A common policy is to fix a limit on the number of items. Then any proposal for a new item must be accompanied by a recommendation for dropping an existing one. while exceptions may be necessary, this plan has the advantage of forcing attention to prunning along with justifying the new item.

TURNAROUND STRATEGY

Once the organisation has decided on the type of broad turnaround strategy it should use, it needs to begin to shape the more specific aspects of its chosen turnaround strategy. These action plans will depend not only on the current strategic and operating health of the organisation but also on the exact nature of the industry in which it competes and on its strengths and weaknesses vis-a-vis other competitors in the same industry. When an organisation takes up turnaround actions usually, it involves following stages:

A. Designing Operating Turnarounds. Operating turnarounds focus on internal efficiency. The strategy an organisation can adopt in this case may be to make itself efficient in everything it does. For this purpose, there can be four alternatives-revenue-generating, cost-cutting, asset reduction, and combination strategies.

(i) ***Asset-Reduction Strategy.*** Asset-reduction strategy can be adopted if the organisation's operation is quite low as compared to its break even, say 30 to 40 per cent. In such cases, the basic question is: what assets should be sold and what should be retained. The answer will depend on the organisation's present/future strategy and saleability of different assets. As a general rule, those assets should be kept which the organisations are using currently or will be using after a year or so. However, sale of assets should not be taken in haste otherwise the assets may not fetch appropriate price. The choice of assets-reduction strategy depends primarily on the long-term prospects of the business of the orgnisation after the turnaround is completed.

(ii) ***Revenue-Generating Strategy.*** In a typical revenue-generating strategy, the organisation would focus primarily on its exising line of products, although it might be possible that these products are supplmented by products it used to make but has discontinued, provided that these products could be introduced quickly and profitably. In addition, the organisation may also take up the production of other products on a short-term basis to utilise its additional capacity but such products may not form the product line for it on a long-term basis. The greater emphasis is put on more resource-generating products. Some major efforts such as price cutting, increased advertising and increased direct sales efforts would be undertaken to stimulate the current sales level. At the same time, R & D expenditure will be low or moderate and staffing at low level as compared to sales. These are all short-term measures. However, the organisation should identify the resources and skills that it will need in order to implement its long-term strategy so that these can be protected during the short-term programme that will follow.

(iii) ***Combination Effort Strategy.*** Under combination strategy, the organisation pursues all three strategies discussed above simultaneously in relative balanced proportions. The reason for this combination effort is that the cash flow produced by a balanced effort will be sufficiently higher than that which would be produced by a narrowly focussed strategy. A combination is preferable specially when the organisation is operating quite close to its break even. If a combination strategy is adopted, it increases the complexity of managerial jobs. Therefore, it should be used only when the potential payoff more than adequately compensates for the additonal managerial complexity and operational difficulties it entails.

(iv) ***Cost-Cutting Strategy.*** It the organisation is working close to the level of break even point and it has high direct labour costs, high fixed expenses, or limited financial resources, it can adopt cost-cutting strategy. Cost-cutting is quite possible and producers results in the short-term as compared to revenue generating strategy. In fact, many companies have adopted to overcome the problem of high direct labour costs by offering voluntary retrenchment to workers on attractive compensation to take long-term advantages. Similarly, advertising costs can be cut by changing the nature of advertising from institutional to product, R & D costs can be suitably cut, personnel development costs can be minimised.

B. Change in Top Management. Before any turnaround action is to be taken, it is desirable to identify whether the present management is suitable for such an action. Though it is not necessary that the present top management can not take up such actions, a change in top management is disirable specially if it has such a strong set of beliefs about how to run the business in question and many of which are wrong. Whether the present top management should continue or change depends on type types of qualities it possesses. It has been observed that different general managers have skills of different types of managerial tasks. Consequently if the present management does not have these qualities it should be changed. Similarly, a hard-nosed, experienced cost-cutter will be required if an operating turnaround with a major cost reduction is to be pursued.

C. Designing Strategic Turnarounds. Strategic turnarounds are needed when the business has a strong current operating health but the organisation has lost its position strategically. Most turnarounds involve circumstances in which there has been a major decline in sales and/or market share position. Consequently the principle methods of differentiating among turnarounds is determined according to the magnitude of the sales and share reversal sought. Usually, three alterntives are available:

(i) Two level increase in share position, that is, movement from a dropout position to a competitor position or from a follower position to a leader position.

(ii) Maintenance or even reduction of share accompanied by the focussing on one or more defensible product/market segment or niches;

(iii) One-level increase in share position, that is, movement from a dropout position to a follower position; from a follower position to a competitor position or from competitor position to leader position.

Why to Adopt Turnaround Strategy?

Turnaround strategy, though a negative connotation of growth, is always preferable when the business is passing through lean trot. In fact, many famous organisations have adopted this strategy to overcome some of their problems. Therefore, this strategy should not be looked merely as negative one rather than a framework for pursuing growth strategy when the organisations overcome some basic problems both external and internal.

Downtrend in organisational performance is caused by both internal factors-management actions which are largely controllable-and external factors which are incontrollable. Therefore, in order to find out what turnaround strategy an organisation should follow, the following questions are more considering:

If the business is worth saving, the other question is: What is the state of current operating health as well as strategic health? This requires a detailed analysis of organisational strengths and weaknesses. Once this exercise has been taken and completed, the organisation can turn to the task of selecting the type of turnaround strategy to be pursued. It may be mentioned here that an organisation adopts two types of turnarounds: strategic and operating. Turnaround strategy involves the change in the organisation's strategy to compete in the present business. It may involve determination of organisation's share in the market-no change in the market share or change of market share by certain percentages. In the case of functional areas, most turnarounds are built around key skills in marketing production engineering, etc.

Is the business worth saving, or is it better to liquidate it now? If the answer of the former is yes, the organisation should go further for identifying what turnaround strategy it can pursue. The basic consideration in analysing this question is that the going conern value of the firm is more than its liquidated value. If the liquidated value is more, it is preferable to adopt divestment or liquidation strategy rather than to invest the substantial energies required by a turnaround for only a marginal pay off.

FACTORS INFLUENCING STRATEGIC CHOICE

Strategy formulation, according to Mintzberg, is an interplay among three basic forces:

1. A dynamic environment that changes continuously but irregularly with frequent discontinuities and wide swings in the rate of change;
2. The operating system of the organisation which seeks to stabilise its activities despite the characteristics of the environment it serves; and
3. The role of leadership mediating between the two forces so as to maintain stability of the organisation's operating system while at the same time adapting it to the environmental change.

Strategic choice involves selecting from among several alternatives the most appropriate strategy which will best serve the enterprise objectives. The choice takes place within a frame of reference consisting of different elements. and the choice (decision) made is the product of interaction of the elements in the frame of reference. Alvar Elbing has distinguished between seven categories of such elements:

(a) accumulated knowledge base,

(b) decision-making processes (intuitive versus rational, individual versus group),

(c) assumptions about causes and effect,

(d) past experiences,

(e) expectations,

(f) human needs, and

(g) culture and values.

According to Glueck, strategic choice (decisions) are made in the light of four selection factors, *viz.*,

(i) Managerial perceptions of external dependence;

(ii) Managerial awareness of past enterprise strategies;

(iii) Managerial power relationships and organisation structure;

(iv) Managerial attitudes toward risk.

More or less similar factors have been suggested by other writers but classified differently for analytical purposes. Indeed, the factors which may influence the choice of strategy are many, some of which may be 'constraints' limiting the scope of choice. The more important factors influencing the strategic choice are discussed here:

1. External Constraints. The survival and prosperity of a firm depend largely on its interaction with the elements or units in the environment—its owners (shareholders), customers, suppliers, competitors, the Government and the community. These elements constitute the external constraints, and flexibility in the choice of strategy is often governed by the extent and degree of the firm's dependence on the elements. Well established, large companies in different industries are more powerful *vis-a-vis* their environment and therefore have greater flexibility in the strategic choice than their counter parts in the respective fields. For instance, a firm which obtains bulk supply of its raw materials or components in a competitive market will have greater flexibility in its strategic chocie than another firm which has to depend for its supplies on an oligopolistic market. The strategy of competitors in the product may also restrict the choice of strategy of a firm. If majority shares of a company are owned by an individual, the executives can hardly ignore his preferences in the matter of choice.

However, external factors need not necessarily restrict the flexibility of strategic choice. It all depends on the perception of executives and their interpretation of the phenomena. Facts, it is very well said, do not speak for themselves. The executives interpret the facts in the light of their own perception of the objective condition. Thus, for instance, while considering an intensive growth strategy, the executives of one company may view the possible reactions of strong competitors as a serious problem and reject the strategy. In another company, the executives may perceive the competitors' reaction as a challenge and adopt the growth strategy along with innovative market penetration policy so as to counteract the anticipated reactions.

Research studies of Kochran, Aharoni, Salancik and Peffer have shown that the nature of a firm's decision process changes as the firm's dependence on external factors increases. Kochran found that perceived dependence led to more centralised decision-making. Aharoni in his study of Israeli managers found that higher returns of alternative opportunities were given up by managers to comply with the wishes of major customers. On the basis of his study of strategic decisions in 78 American firms. Salancik observed that firms with large government contracts were more inclined to take decisions in conformity with government requirements than otherwise. Pfeffer and Salancik in their study of dependency noted that the extent of the decision-maker's perception of dependence on any given external entity is a constraint on their choice of strategy.

2. Intra-organisational Forces and Managerial Power-relations. Within an organisation major decisions are often influenced by the power play among different interest groups. Strategic decisions are no exception. If the chief executive is in favour of a strategic option, it may be endorsed by senior managers close to him, but one or the other managerial clique may oppose it. Research findings have thrown considerable light on the impact of managerial power-relations on strategic choice. William Guth in his study of the process of strategy-making in a large U.S. corporation over a period of four years found that the decisions were significantly affected by inter-personal relations and power-relationship among members of the top management team. In their study of 25 strategic decisions. Mintzberg et al found that in 8 out of 25 decisions, power politics was a crucial factor determining the choice; in all others these factors, though less important, nonetheless influenced the strategic decisions.

Where a participative decision-making process is in vogue, the strategic choice eventually made by top management is quite often the outcome of a lot of filtering that takes place of the alternatives at lower levels of management. For instance, strategic choices made by lower-level managers may limit the strategic options considered by top management. Thus, Bower in his study of strategic decisions in a large corporation found that executives at lower levels affect the process in such a way that the final choice does not consider all the alternatives. The study of strategic decisions in medium-sized firms made by Eugene Carter showed how lower-level managers influenced the choice eventua!'y made by the chief executive. The major findings of the study were as follows:

(1) Lower-level managers suggested strategic choices that were likely to be accpeted and withheld suggestions which were less likely to be approved;

(2) The greater the uncertainty in the environment of the organisation, the larger were the number of criteria developed to make the strategic decision;

(3) While suggesting a strategic choice, different departments evaluated the strategic alternatives differently and in their own interest;

(4) The number of criteria considered in evaluating a strategic choice was directly related to the degree of uncertainty in the project's forecasts.

3. Values and Preferences and Managerial Attitudes towards Risk. The role of value systems in decision-making by managers is well established. While evaluating the strategic alternatives, different executives may take different positions because of differences in their personal values and the consequent weighing of key factors. George England et al has closely analysed how values might influence decision-making. England observed on the basis of his study that successful American managers tend to prefer more pragmatic, dynamic, interactive and achievement-oriented values, while the less successful ones are in favour of more static and passive values. On the basis of both observation and systematic studies of top management in business organisations, Guth and Tagiuri found that personal values were important determinants of the choice of corporate strategy. Six major value orientations listed by Guth and Tagiuri were:

Theoretical : an orientation toward truth and knowledge.

Economic : an orientation toward what is useful and powerful.

Aesthetic : an orientation toward form and harmony.

Political : an orientation toward power.

Religious : an orientation toward unity in the universe.

Social : an orientation toward love of people.

It was found that American executives had a major orientation toward economic, theoretical and political values rather than the other three.

Managerial attitude toward risk is another major factor that influences the choice of strategy. Individuals differ considerably in their attitude toward risk taking. Some are risk prone, others are risk averse. Conceptually, one may distinguish between the following attitudes reflecting the order of risk preferences:

(1) Risk is necessary for success;

(2) Risk is a fact of life and some risk is desirable; and

(3) High risk destroys enterprises and needs to be minimised.

Executives who are risk prone and risk takers look for high returns in high-growth less stable markets; they prefer to be pioneers or innovators, seeking early into new high-growth markets. Those who tend to be low risk-takers prefer to adopt safer options even though the payoff is not high; they prefer to be followers rather than innvoators in newer, untried fields. Those who consider some risk is desirable, balance high with low-risk choice and prefer a combined strategy. Schwartz in a study of managerial attitude toward risk found that evaluation of risky decisions by lower level managers led to the suggestion of alternatives to top management which were risky, incremental type choices, rather than risky, breakthrough decisions.

However, managerial attitude towards risk is not to be regarded as something unchangeable. It may vary in the face of fast changing industry or environmental conditions. For instance, in the event of deteriorating industry conditions, executives must of necessity decide in favour of more risky strategies so as to be able to function. Again, executives may overlook the risks involved if they perceive an opportunity with optimism, *i.e.*, where the trade-off between risk and return weighs heavily in favour of the gains from the potential opportunity.

Research studies which have thrown some light on the risk preferences of decision-makers may be cited here. The study by Vroom and Pahl showed that older managers tend to be less prone to risk taking. Sieber and Lanzetta in their study found that individuals who deal easily with risk and uncertainty are better able to cope with complex problems than those who are risk averse. Taylor and Dunnette's reseach study showed that risk-prone decision-makers limit the amount of information they consider and tend to make decisions rapidly. In a highly complex situation decisions may be taken even on impulse.

4. Impact of Past Strategy. The choice of current strategy may be influenced by the earlier strategy for a variety of reasons. Since past strategies are usually the starting point in the formation of new strategies, some alternatives may not be explored as throughly as might be otherwise expected, or certain alternatives may not be considered at all. This may be regarded as the inertia of past strategies. Another reason may be personal involvement of the decision-maker with the earlier strategy. In an experimental research study made by Barry Staw he observed that as decisions, they tended to become personally involved with the decision, thus influencing later strategic choices. Research findings of Mintzberg and others have thrown considerable light on how past strategies influence the choice of current strategy. Their findings showed that:

1. The older and more successful a strategy, the harder it is to change. The present strategy evolves from a past strategy

developed by a single, powerful leader. This original and tightly integrated strategy (a Gestalt strategy) is a major influence on later strategic choices.

2. Once a strategy gets under way, it becomes exceedingly difficult to change, and the bureaucratic momentum keeps it going. It becomes a sort of 'push-pull' phenomenon; the original decision-maker pushes the strategy, then lower management pulls it along.
3. When the past strategy begins to fall because of changing conditions, the enterprise reacts and grafts new sub-strategies on to the old and only later seeks out a new strategy.
4. If the environment changes even more radically, then the enterprise begins to seriously consider other alternative strategies which might have been previously suggested but ignored.

It is because of the lingering influence of past strategy that a change of strategy may call for replacement of the existing top executives. As Glueck and Jauch have mentioned "Strategic change is less likely if new executives are promoted from within, and it is least likely if the existing management group remains in power."

5. Time Constraints in Choice of Strategy. The time dimension of strategic chocie is another factor in the strategic decision process that may be of considerable significance. Four elements of time dimension may be worth noting. These are: *(i)* time pressure, *(ii)* time frame, *(iii)* time horizon, and *(iv)* timing of the decision.

The deadlines for making the decision create time pressures under which managers may be forced to make a choice. In the absence of time pressure, the choice might be different. The time constraint is generally imposed by others, so that executives have little discretion in the matter of choice; it has to be either 'yes or no.' Suppose, the executives of a company have a merger offer from another firm and the terms proposed are not quite favourable. If there is a deadline by which the decision has to be made, the executives may accept the offer if they feel that to wait may mean losing the opportunity; or, they may be inclined to reject it on the ground that the terms need to be examined more throughly for which more time is required. Peter Wright has observed that under such conditions, there is often a tendency to give greater weight to highly negative information, and there is a tendency to consider fewer aspects of the problem. When strategic decisions are made under time pressure, It may not be possible for the decision-maker to have all necessary information and to consider all possible alternatives.

A second aspect of time dimension is the time frame of the decision itself. *viz.*, the short-term and the long-term implications of a choice. If the reward system of a company is linked with the achievement of short-term goals, it may inhibit making strategic decisions which are likely to produce results in the long run. In other words, if the incentive compensation of executives is related to short-run earning performance, as it often is, there is every likelihood that long-term strategic conditions would be ignored.

The element of time horizon with regard to a decision refers to the period of commitment that goes with it. Stability strategy, for instance, involves immediate action and has a short gestation lag. On the other hand, diversification and growth may take a number of years to bear fruit. A long-range strategy implying commitment of resources for an uncertain future is often less acceptable than one having immediate relavance. Parkison's 'Law of Delay' may also have a bearing on the choice of strategy. The longer a decision can be delayed the lower the probability that it will ever be accepted.

The timing of a decision is yet another aspect of time dimension that may determine the quality of the strategic choice. A prompt decision may be required to make the best use of an opportunity and before the competitors have time enough to capitalise it. Similarly, the decision to enter a new product market cannot be delayed for competitors are not likely to waste any time in doing so.

6. Information Constraints. A crucial factor in the choice of strategy is the availability of information. It is on the basis of relevant data and information that executives are likely to make the decision. The degree of uncertainty and risk depends upon the amount of information that is available to the decision-makers. The lesser the amount of information available, the greater the level of uncertainty and risk. To be able to take calculated risks, managers must, therefore, ensure the availability of all information bearing on the strategic alternatives, which may be costly in terms of money and time.

7. Competitors' Reaction. Consideration of Competitors' reaction to any strategic option is often required in weighing strategic choices. Suppose the option being considered by a company is an aggressive strategy challenging a near-equal competitor. It is quite possible that the competitor would adopt a counter-strategy so as to withstand the aggressive strategy of the initiating company. It would be unrealistic for the company not to consider that possibility. The management must take into account the likelihood of the reaction, the competitor's capability to react, and its impact on the strategic choice.

GUIDELINES FOR THE CHOICE OF STRATEGY

Strategy choice is a complex process because of the impact of several factors. However, managers can reduce this problem by putting the following questions for choice of strategy.

(i) Does the strategy rush to revolutionary product to the market?

(ii) Does the strategy take into consideration the product life cycle?

(iii) Has the strategy been properly evaluated?

(iv) Is the strategy acceptable to the major constituents of the organisation?

(v) Is the strategy consistent with the environment?

(vi) Does the strategy require too much or too large of organisation's resources?

(vii) Has the strategy been tested against the appropriate criteria such as past, present, and prospective economic, political, social and technological trends?

(viii) Does identification of strategic alternatives take into consideration all relevant environmental factors honestly and impartially?

(ix) Is the payback period of the strategy acceptable in the light of changing environment?

(x) Does the strategy not conflict with other strategies of the organisation? and

Is the strategy likely to produce a minimum of new administrative problems for the organisation?

(ix) Does the organisation have sufficient resources to implement the strategy? and

Does the strategy balance the acceptable minimum risk with maximum profit potential consistent with organisation's resources and prospects?

(xii) Does the strategy fit management's values, philosophy, know-how, personality, and sense of social responsibility? and

Is the strategy consistent with the internal strengths, objectives, and policies of the organisation?

This is indeed a formidable list of questions. Not every question will be most relevant in every situation. Therefore, managers should determine which is the most pertinent question. In fact, any one may turn out to be the core question. Further, it is not necessary that every question is answered in depth.

BCG MODEL

Used by the Boston Consulting Group or Part Folio Planning method, this model aims at systematically identifying the main underlying strategic characteristics of specific business segments. It requires careful analysis of each product and market segment as a separate business (or strategic business unit) so that each business may be assigned to a specific strategy or sub-strategy. It is also known as Portfolio Planning Model. To be of any value, the model must be applied to specific segments of business-segments being defined as that combination of products, services, customers and geography with respect to which a specific competitor has absolute advantage compared with other competitors.

The BCG model is based on the application of two inter-related concepts: the experiecne curve, and the growth share matrix. The experience curve theory predicts that the unit costs of production, marketing and distribution decrease by 20 to 30 per cent each time total output doubles.

The experience curve effect can be used as the basis for developing several strategic alternatives:

The Growth Share Matrix is the second element in the BCG model. It is a framework designed to facilitate comparative analysis of business segments according to expected growth rates and relative market dominance. It is a model for analysing how market share, market growth and cash flow are related. Each product is evaluated in terms of its cash flow and growth potential and the differences determine which products represent cash investment opportunities and which represent sources of funds.

The BCG model suggests that the organisation should be managed as portfolio of business. Each of the business segments or products is assigned a strategy that best meets its competitive position and objective. The growth share matrix relates market growth or its attractiveness to a firm's relative competitive position.

The first step in the application of the model is identification of business segements or products—the strategic business units (SBUs). Each business unit so identified is then distributed into a matrix position on the basis of two criteria: *(i)* market growth potential and *(ii)* relative market share. Four possible categories of positions of the SBUs (business segments) may thus be found in the product portfolio chart as under:

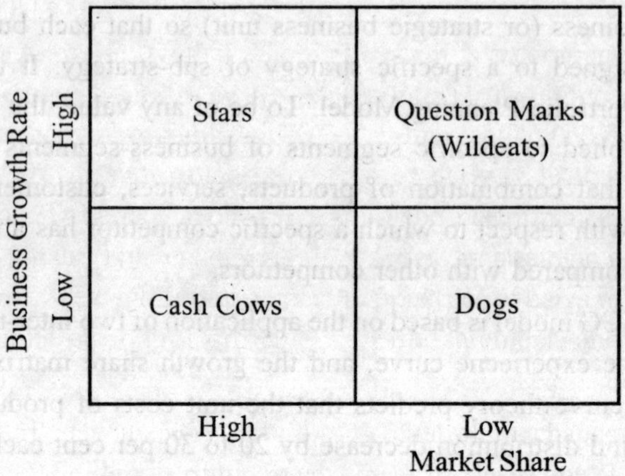

Let us explain each of the SBU categories shown in the matrix. "Dog" (Low growth/Low market share) : A business segment in this category is as a competitive disadvantage with a low-growth market. The strategy for this category should consist of cost cutting, divestment or even liquidation so as to maximise short-term cash flow.

"Question Marks : or "Wildcats" (High growth/Low market share) : Business segments in this category operating at a competitive disadvantage but having a high-growth market potential may be expanded to increase market share by taking advantage of the market growth potential. But cash demand being high and cash generation low, it may not be possible to improve the competitive position and increase market share. It would thus be desirable to withdraw from this business. In other words, the strategy in this case should be either that of aggressive growth or divestment.

"Star" (High growth/High market share): Business segments in this category are in the most favourable position with respect to both growth potential and competitive strength. Resources should be allocated to these units to grow faster than the competitors in sales and profits.

"Cash Cows" (Low growth/High Market share): Business units in this category being in a strong competitive position but with low growth potential should be managed by adopting a strategy so as to maintain the present market share while using the competitive advantage to increase the cash flow to be used in high-growth segments.

It should be clear that the growth-share matrix is a tool of analysis which may be useful to management to array all the segments of business on chart called Product Portfolio Chart. The chart is based on the relationship between market share and profitability, so that market dominance is the major strategic objective in high-growth markets. The model seeks to help management in the assignment of specific role or functions for each product and its integration into a total company strategy. The model also seeks to shift cash from mature cash-generating units to high-growth products in the early stages of life-cycle which are cash users. The use of the model involves balancing the degree of risk and profit fluctuation which is acceptable. The idea behind growth-share matrix is that high market share in rapidly growing market segments leads to higher profitability and a strong competitive position. On the other hand, for a firm operating in the slow-growth market, increasing market share may involve heavy investments often with diminishing returns. Hence, it is recommended that cash flow be shifted from slow-growth areas to high-growth market segments even at the expense of loss of market share. The strategic prescription as per the BCG model is to get rid of 'dogs'(divest) and use cash flows from 'cash cows' to support the development of 'question marks' into 'star' status.

In other words, the choice of strategy for the respective Strategic Business Areas (SBAs) ought to be on the following lines:

A. The "Wild cats" ("question marks") be analysed to see whether the investment into converting them into "stars" is worthwhile.

B. The "cash cares" should be made to control (severely) their investments and send excess cash to the headquarters'

C. The "dogs" should probably be divested, unless there are strong reasons for keeping them;

D. The "star" should be cherished and reinforced.

The BCG model is recognised as a useful technique for analysing a company's strategic alternatives.

'STOP-LIGHT' STRATEGY MODEL

The second analytical model which has been used by the General Electric Company is the 'Stop-Light' strategy model (or Business Planning Matrix) developed by General Electric and McKinsey Company in USA. The strategic planning approach in this model is based on the analogy of traffic control lights at street crossings : Green (go), Amber or Yellow (caution) and Red (stop). The model emphasises that strategic decisions ought to be made on the basis of two key variables : Business strength and Industry attractiveness. Business strength is rated considering such factors as size, growth rate, market share position, technology position, image and people. Industry attractiveness is similarly rated in the light of several factors like size, market growth and pricing, competitive structure, environmental conditions, etc. The ratings may be high, medium, or low in respect of industry attractiveness and strength of business. If the product falls in the 'green' (go) section, *i.e.*, if the business position is strong and industry is at least medium in attractiveness, the strategic decision should be to expand, to invest and grow. If the business strength is low but industry attractiveness is high, the product is in the 'yellow' zone. It needs caution, and managerial discretion is called for in making the strategic choice. A product in the 'red' (stop) zone indicates that business strength is low and so is industry attractiveness. The appropriate strategy in this case should be retrenchment, divestment or liquidation. Thus, SBUs in the 'green' section may be said to belong to the category of 'stars' or 'cash cows' in the BCG model. Those in the 'red' zone are like 'dogs' and those in the 'yellow' or 'amber' zone like 'question marks'. The planning grid constructed for the 'stop-light' strategic planning has been criticised for its inadequacy with respect to new business in new industries that are just beginning to grow. Moreover, factors which are required to be taken into account while evaluating business strength and industry attractiveness are not all precisely measurable in numerical terms. And it may not be possible to assign definite weights to those factors.

DIRECTIONAL POLICY MATRIX MODEL (DPM)

This model aims at placing each product/market unit (SBU) on a matrix according to its rating based on two variables: *viz.*, 'business sector prospects' and 'company's competitive capabilities', The various zones of the matrix are thus associated with different combinations of 'business sector prospects' and 'company's competitive strength or weakness'. The type of strategy or resource allocation which is appropriate is suggested for the product/market units falling in the respective zones. The application of this model hinges on the identification of two acts of criteria: *(A)* criteria by which the company's competitive position may be judged to be strong or weak, and *(B)* criteria by which the prospects for business sector may be judged to be favourable or unfavourable.

The key words used in this model are briefly explained below:

1. **Double or Quit.** Products in this zone with attractive sector prospects but weak competitive ability should be governed by discrete choice of strategy. Out of these products may be found some with bright futures. The strategy should be to select and back up the right product.
2. **Try Harder.** This position indicates attractive sector prospects but average competitive capability. Products located in this zone ought to be provided with necessary resources so as to move them at least to positions of equality.
3. **Leader.** The SBU which is in an enviable position of being the largest producer with the lowest unit cost and a superior technical position may be regarded as leader in the business sector. In such a position, the product needs to have absolute priority of support by way of resource allocation to hold the market share.
4. **Custodial.** A product is located in the custodial zone of the matrix when the company has a weak competitive ability

or sector prospect or both in combination. The company must bear with the situation and make good and overall position with the help of other product units.

5. **Phased Withdrawal.** The strategy of phased withdrawal is indicated where a company is in an average-to-weak competitive position in a low-growth (unattractive) business sector with little prospects of generating substantial cash. Attempts should be made in such a situation to realise the value of assets and invest the money in more profitable business segments.
6. **Disinvest.** SBUs running in losses with uncertain cash flows are located in this zone. A divestment strategy is called for in this case so that resources thereby released may be put to better use.
7. **Cash Generation.** With a strong competitive position in a sector which is unattractive from the point of view of business prospects, a company may be able to earn satisfactory profits and generate cash.
8. **Growth.** Product in this zone with average to strong competitive ability (being one among two to four major competitors) and with at least average sector prospect are suited for growth strategy supported by adequate production capacity and product R & D.

MERGER STRATEGY

Merger is an external strategy for growth of the organisation. This can be followed by merging another organisation toto or its part to increase effectiveness of both merging and merged organisations. There are various terms used for the purpose, for example, merger, absorption, amalgamation (one organisation merging another organisation), and reconstruction (two or more organisations losing their identity and forming another organisation). However, one term merger can be used for all these because it can take different forms of arrangement among the organisations considered for merger.

Recently, Indian business environment has seen lot of mergers of different kinds, for example, creation of Ambalal Sarabhai Enterprises Limited, merger of Falcon Tyres Limited and Karnataka Scooters Limited, merger of ICI controlled companies operating in India', merger of Kirlosar Pneumatic Limited and Kirloskar Tractor Limited, etc.

There are various kinds of merger and it can be classified in various ways, though the most important classification is based on industry. On this basis, Monopolies Commission, U.K. has classified merger into three groups:

1. Conglomerate merger between organisations that do not produce similar products and where neither is an actual of potential supplier of the other.
2. Horizontal merger between organisations that sell the same products or products which can be easily substituted for each other; and
3. Vertical merger between organisations of which one is an actual or potential supplier of the other.

Reasons of Merger

Merger as growth strategy is not new either to the business world or to the Indian business. There are certain reasons because of which merger is preferred as compared to internal source of growth. The preference for merger can be analysed from two angles: merging organisations's point of view and merged organisation's point of view.

Merged Organisations's Point of View

Various advantages may accrue to comapny which is being merged in another company which may be in the following directions:

I. Sometimes organisations may have imbalanced growth in which they must have acquired some distinctive advantages in one field but lack in other fields. This happens more in the case of technical people who may develop the organisation on the basis of technical competence. This competence works so long as the size of the organisation and market forces are manageable within the present capability. However, beyond that, the organisation may not progress, instead it may start declining.

II. Merger may provide growth opportunities to the business specially when future holds good but the present might not be as promising, or the business might be having some teething troubles which can not be overcome by the present management, or revival can not be taken within the framework of the existing financial and other resources of the organisation in such a case, existence and subsequently growth may be ensured by merger. In fact, such type of merger is encouraged by the the government and financial institutions which may hold sizable shares in these companies. The fates of many sick units have turned through mergers. Even the healthy units can also benefit from merger specially when there is high technological growth, high rate of product obsolescence, increasing competition which can not be met adequately without increasing the size of the operation and increasing fixed cost of staff functions.

III. Merger can be treated as a liquidation strategy from merged company's point of view. Though liquidation can be treated as a negative strategy, it is quite beneficial specially when the business is continuously a losing proposition. In such a case, merger may provide better realisation of the value of the company as compared to other methods of disposing assets. Through this process, the business can be saved and at the same time a better value can be realised.

When the declining phase starts, it compounds because the present management will analyse the problems within the framework of technology whereas the problems may lie somewhere else. Thus managerial-crisis begins, in order to overcome this crisis, the best way is to merge the organisation with another.

Merging Organisation's Point of View

Merger offers more advantages to merging organisation as compared to merged organisation. Such advantages can be analysed in the following ways:

1. Reduction in Competition and Dependence. Merger can be used to reduce competition and dependence. If the horizontal and concentric mergers are undertaken, the organisation is in a position to eliminate the competition because it may merge the organisations using same marketing channels or technology. This may happen both in developed countries as well as in under-developed countries. In developed countries, where the competition in any field is high, competitive competence can be achieved through the increased size by mergers. In underdeveloped economies, where competition may not be high except in few chosen fields, the organisation can move in a monopoly or near-monopoly position and can take the advantages. However, such advantages accrue subject to various regulatory measures which can work against the organisation. The organisation can reduce dependence on others for the supply of raw materials and disposal of its products by vertical integration. This type of merger is more profitable in the case of underdeveloped countries where supply situations of the most of the products may not be satisfactory and the operations of the organisation may hamper. Similarly, forward integration may provide opportunities for disposing off the products of the organisation which may be equally important if there is no sufficient development of the industry. For example, a yarn manufacturing company will be in a better position to dispose off its products if it merges a weaving company.

2. Diversification Advantages. Besides rapid growth, merger provides opportunities for diversification within a very short period of time. Thus the merging organisation can derive the various advantages of diversification. These advantages may be in the form of better use of resources, increased organisational capabilities through increased competitive competence, balanced portfolio of business, safety against adverse impacts of business cycles, and so on. All these can be achieved through internal diversification as well. But since merger provides these in quicker way, its contributions can be optimised much faster.

3. Faster Growth Rate. Merger can provide opportunities for faster growth rate than can be achieved by internal sources because it offers advantages in various areas. Such areas may include production, marketing and distribution, research and development, etc. Various economies of scales are achieved which ultimately result in operational efficiency, better competitive edge, better utilisation of resources, better planning of capital expenditure, and so on. All these result in much faster growth rate than what the organisation can achieve itself.

4. Quick Entry in the Business. Merger often provides the quickest way of entry into markets and industries. Entry into the fields where the expanding organisation lacks the right functional capabilities will be both risky and costly if it is taken through internal sources. Further, the benefits of start-up synergies will be absent. Merger can be considered as a good source of entry into an area which is denied for an organisation under the provisions of licensing. For example, Brooke Bond's entry in the field of shaving blade can be materialised if its proposed merger of Centron (a shaving blade manufacturing company) is materialised. Thus merger can be used as a back-door entry in the business.

5. Synergistic Advantages. Various complementary capabilities can be achieved through merger which result from 2 + 2 = 5 effect or synergistic advantages. The advantages, as discussed earlier, accrue because the system is greater than total of its parts and subparts. Following synergistic advantages may accrue because of merger:

(a) Management synergy arising from managerial competence in one business to be utilised in other business;

(b) Operation strategy resulting from higher utilisation of common facilities, personnel and overheads by various products; and

(c) Investment synergy which arises from the use of same plant, machinery, research and development facilities, better access to capital markets, and better position to negotiate terms and conditions for raising funds;

(d) Marketing synergy which may arise because both the companies can use same sales force, sales points, distribution channels, warehousing, and advertising.

6. Tax Advantages. Merger can be used as effective source of tax planning specially if merging and merged company have different tax liabilities. If one of them is tax paying company and another is having accumulated losses, the merger may result into considerable tax saving as was the case with ICI merger where ACC had accumulated losses, IEL had unabsorbed tax benefits while two other companies were tax paying companies. Thus merger resulted in substantial tax benefits. Similar benefits can accrue for investment allowance reserves which some companies have but are unable to utilise independently.

REASONS OF FAILURE

1. Often there is inadequate planning in merger and it is taken as an end in itself rather than using it as a tool for growth. In the absence of any planning for merger and subsequent programme to realise its objectives, the chances for the merger failure are very high. Therefore, managers should plan in advance of merger about how merging and merged organisations can contribute to each other. In fact, it is the mutual contribution to each other that results into various advantages of merger.

In planning merger, managers should define the contributions of merger in two ways : first, how merger can reflect a more efficient utilisation of resources and second, how greater adaptability to changing environment may be achieved. Based on these two aspects, some of the actions that can be followed may be in these directions. *(i)* An organisation that finds itself in poor growth prospect should merge with one that is in high growth area. *(ii)* If the organisation is facing the problem of unable sales and revenues, it can seek merger with one having more stable sales. *(iii)* The organisation having limited technological capability may seek merger with the one having strong research and development base. *(iv)* The organisation having weak marketing organisation may seek merger with the one having strong marketing base. These examples suggest that if merger is attempted on these lines, it will result into positive synergy.

2. Often a mistake is made in assessing the synergistic advantages which merger offers. As discussed earlier, merger offers various

types of synergistic advantages depending on the type of merger itself as well as various other factors. However, there are two types of problems which managers are likely to ignore, First, if the advantages have been perceived to be available in a particular merger but really they are not there, such advantages may turn into weaknesses as managers will become complacent over these issues. Second, synergy does not arise automatically. The opportunity may be these but the success of the mreger depends on the management's ability to take advantages of the opportunity to realise the potential economies. For example, Kintching concludes that the type of merger is not the determining factor for its success of failure but the primary cause must be sought elsewhere. Therefore, the synergistic advantages should be viewed and scrutinised more minutely that what they appear on the surface in order to provide adequate safeguard against the possible failure.

3. The last reason for merger failure is the lack of suitable managerial and other skills for the new job. In the period immediately following the merger, the quality of management determines the success or failure of the venture. It is at this stage that careful planning allows the synergy potential to be released, if it is released at all. The merger transforms the total complexion of the business specially when it results into diversification. Any failure on the part of the management to appreciate these changes in business may bring failure. Therefore, managers should ensure that the merging organisation can provide the right type of managerial and other inputs required by the merged organisation.

ACQUISITION OR TAKEOVER STRATEGY

An acquisition is one when one organisation acquires another with or without absorbing it in its own operations. Sometimes merger is effected after acquisition of another company. An acquistion may be a surprise attempt of one organisation to acquire ownership or control over the management of another against the wishes of the latter's management and some of its shareholders. In recent years, takeover strategies have been increasingly used as a means of growth, for example, takeover of Textools Limited, attempt to take over Dunlop India Limited, Bayer India Limited, etc. Some of these takeover bids have created lot of controversies in Indian corporate scene.

There are several reasons why an organisation may prefer acquisition of an existing business than launching its own grassroot development of a new business. The factors involved in an acquisition are those implicit in any 'buy or built' situation, but often the most important considerations are time and money. Acquiring existing organisations, products, technology, facilities, talent or manpower has the strong advantage of such quicker entry into the target market, while at the same time, detouring such barriers to entry as licensing, patents, technological inexperience, lack of raw material supplies, substantial economies of scale, establishment of distribution channels, etc. Internal development of all these may take time and present start-up problems. Moreover, internal expansion may result into oversupply in the market. The resultant fierce competition may affect profitability. The prospect of such situations effectively reduces the number of viable options to two : entry in the business via acquisition or no entry at all.

A. Defining Organisation's Strengths and Weaknesses. Acquisition is possible only when the organisation has resource capability to buy another organisation. Buying another organisation involves more than paying in financial terms. In fact, large number of variables work against acquisition of another organisation. Therefore, the organisation should make it sure that it has necessary capability to fight against all these forces. Since acquisition situations differ so greatly, the type of factors involved in each may vary to a very great extent. Therefore, the organisational strengths and weaknesses should be appraised in the light of these factors.

B. Defining Objectives of Acquisition. The first basic step in the acquisition process is the definition of acquisition objectives. This is necessary because it will define precisely the type of organisation to be acquired and consequently the type of efforts required in the process. Objectives of acquisition can by defined in terms of complementarity which can be achieved by acquiring an organisation, for example, entry in the field, increase in the size of the group's operation, any specific advantage offered by acquired organisation, etc.

C. Setting Task Force for Acquisition. When objectives of acquisition and organisational strengths suggest some kind of acquisition, the organisation should take effective step in the direction. Since acquisition is not a regular activity, some adhoc arrangement in the form of task force should be made. Task force may be in the form of large and complete department or section replete with functional specialists, or in small organisation, it can be a single person who obtains evaluation assistance from others. Although the form and content of this group may vary according to the nature of the merger and the size of the organisation, general functions of the group will remain the same. These functions may be of following nature:

(a) To establish a realistic time-table of necessary steps for each acquisition;

(b) To obtain the necessary evaluation, advice, and opinions from specialists, both inside and outside the organisation;

(c) To coordinate the obtaining of the expert advice into the time table and to valuate overall results of the advice and opinions of the experts; and

(d) To prepare strategy for takeover bids and negotiation for that.

Once the task force for acquisition is created, it takes over the entire responsibility for that.

D. Selection of the Target. Preliminary search of the target for acquisition may provide a number of alternatives. These alternatives may be in two forms; First, there may be profitable companies though the acquisition price may be quite high. Second, there may be sick and losing units which can be transformed into viable untis with additional resources and better management. In this case, the acquisition price may be quite low. The choice criterion that can be applied in this case is: which alternative offers better prospect of meeting acquisition objectives? A key factor for success of any acquisition is having criteria that are consistent and are rigorously applied. Otherwise, acquisition decisions are likely to be distorted by impulses and emotions, and acquisition companies victimised by the environment which typically surrounds purchase negotiations. The management must evaluate the target company on the basis of very rigorous criteria without leaving any scope of emotion. There is an apt saying : 'A buyer needs hundred eyes and seller needs not even one.' This saying is more important specially if the acquisition involves sizable amount of fund. The companies which have made successful takeover bid are characterised by their management ability to weigh the strengths and weaknesses of potential acquisition within a short period of time. Time factor is important because of two reasons. First, the takeover negotiations require certain amount of secrecy which may not be achieved if period of negotiations is long. Second, long delays may be costly specially when the shares are purchased through stock exchanges. More is the time taken in acquisition share, more is the price payable for the shares because once the news come in the market, the share prices go on higher side as is evident by many bids for takeover. Thus lack of proper criteria and time factor may result either in to the deal not to take place or if takes place, it may become costly affair to the company.

E. Preliminary Search for the Target. At this stage, the organisation can go for making a preliminary search for the organisation to be acquisition. This task becomes quite complicated because a host of factors may work against this. These may be economic, legal, and others. From economic point of view, the prospective target can be identified by putting the following questions:

(i) What the acquired organisation can do for the present organisation which it can not do itself?

(ii) What the organisation can do for the target organisation which itself can not do?

(iii) What direct and tangible savings, improvements, or efficiencies flow from merging the target?

(iv) What is the intangible value of these savings, efficiencies and improvements to the organisation?

F. Takeover Bids. After the identification of the target, the organisation should proceed to takeover it. Any organisation or group of persons wishing to obtain control of a company may accomplish its aim in one of four ways:

(a) By acquisition of sufficient shares from stock exchanges or from financial institutions who hold sizable shares because of the present terms and conditions of term loans so as to wage a successful battle of proxies with the existing management so that they are replaced by the buyer of the shares.

(b) By making a deal with the present management of the target company particularly board of directors, Whereby they may sell all their shares and resign their offices and the causal vacancies thus created being filled by the buyer of the shares.

(c) By making a general offer to the shareholders to purchase their shares sufficient to achieve control.

(d) By purchasing the company's undertaking.

Besides the economic factors, there may be legal and other factors which may affect the acquisition prospect. There is a set legal procedure for acquisition of any company in which the role of the Government and the Company Law Board is important. Every acquisition attempt may fail, if the permissions are not coming from these sectors. Even if the ensuing premissions are forthcoming, the basic problem is whether it is possible to take over the target because of the hold of the present management. Information in this regard can be collected from outside sources such as consultants, banks and financial institutions, and stock brokers.

WHY COMBINATION STRATEGY?

The combination strategy is most frequently used in multi-produced, divisionalised companies. The main process of such a strategy is optimisation of the enterprise profitability and or minimising its losses. The basic reason underlying its use is that single strategy does not fit all products or all markets. Hence, the purpose of a mixed strategy is to allocate resources to the high-growth and high-potential areas of business while reducing investments in or selling off the less profitable endeavours.

A company may pursue the combination strategy for one or more of the following reasons:

I. **Size of the firm.** It may be undesirable or impracticable to pursue growth strategy of activity at the same time, particularly when there are several opportunities and resources are not adequated to avail of all of them.

II. **Industrial recession.** When recessionary condition prevails in a product market, the strategy more suited to it is retrenchment strategy, which growth strategy may be suited to other product markets not so affected.

III. **Different products in different stages of life-cycle.** Obviously a strategy suited to a product at the initial growth stage must be different from that of a product at the nature of declining state.

Combinations strategies are most likely to be effective *(a)* for large, multi-industry firms in periods of economic transition or in periods of product/service transition in the life-cycle, and *(b)* the case of firms of which the product or market divisions have uneven performance or uneven future potentials.

COMPETITIVE STRUCTURE

The competitive structure of industries is a very important business environment. Identification of forces affecting the competitive dynamics of an industry will be very useful in formulating strategies.

According to Michael Porter's well known model of structural analysis of industries, the state of competition in an industry depends on five basic competitive forces, *viz.*,

1. Rivalry among existing firms
2. Threat of new entrants

3. Threat of substitutes
4. Bargaining power of suppliers
5. Bargaining power of buyers.

Fig. given below depicts the five forces competitive structure of industry. The diagram is a slightly modified presentation of the one provided by Porter. The arrows in the diverse directions indicate opposing forces. For example, just as the buyers and suppliers may have bargaining power over the firm, the firm may also have some bargaining power over the buyers and suppliers.

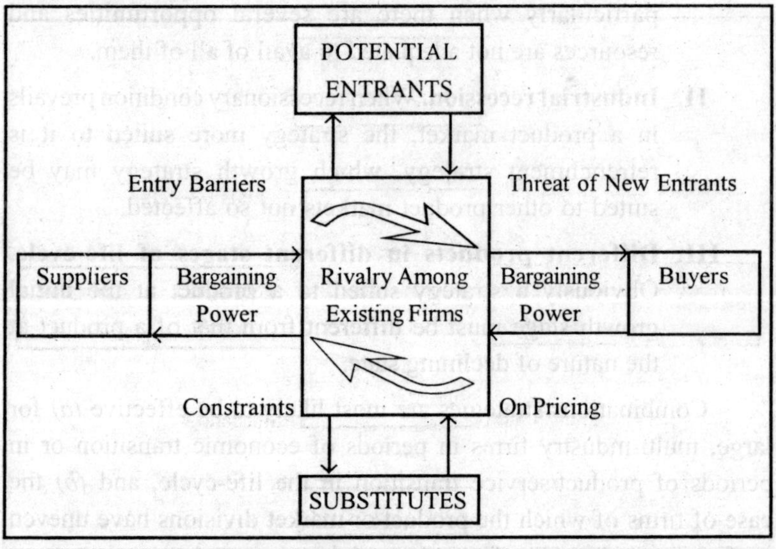

Fig. : Forces Driving Industry Competition

A growing industry often faces threat of new entrants that can alter the competitive environment. There may, however, be a number of barriers to entry. Potential competition tends to be high if the industry is profitable or critical, entry barriers are low and expected retaliation from the existing firms is not serious.

COMPETITOR ANALYSIS

Competitor analysis is necessary for formulating right strategies and determining the right positioning for the firm in the industry.

Competitor analysis seeks to find answers to certain basic questions such as:

1. Who are the competitors of the firm?
2. What are the current strategies of the competitors?
3. What drives the competitor?
4. Where is the competitor vulnerable?
5. What are their future goals and likely strategies?
6. How are the competitors likely to respond to the strategies of others?

Porter has suggested a framework for competitor analysis, consisting of four diagnostic components, *viz.*, future goals, current strategy, assumptions and capabilities.

As Porter observes, "its goals, assumptions, and current strategy will influence the likelihood, timing, nature, and intensity of competitor's reactions. Its strengths and weaknesses will determine its ability to initiate or react to strategic moves and to deal with environmental or industry events that occur."

An analysis of these components will help to formulate what Porter calls competitor's response profile, *i.e.*, answers to critical questions such as : What moves or developments will provoke the competitor and how is the competitor likely to respond or retaliate?

The competitor response profile seeks to predict the competitor's offensive moves and defensive capabilities.

Analysis of future goals would be helpful to identify the attitude and behaviour of the competitor and likely strategies. As Porter observes, "a knowledge of goals will alllow predictions about whether or not each competitor is satisfied with its present position and financial results and, thereby, how likely the competitor is to change strategy and the vigour with which it will react to outside events... or to moves by other firms?" Knowledge of competitor's goals may help to predict its reactions to strategic changes. Goals of both the business unit and corporate parent need to be examined.

In 1996, the CEO of ICI had revealed that it wanted to increase the contribution of its Asian operations from 15 per cent to 25 per cent of the total and earmarked 800 million pounds for investment in Asia, including 200 million for India. It was believed that a part of it would go for acquisitions. Similarly, the CEO of Hindustan Lever revealed the intention to raise the company's contribution to the Unilever's global turnover from about 5 percent to 10 percent within a decade. Falling in line with the parent's portfolio strategy, HLL identified the processed food business as a major thrust area. It was, thus, clear that the HLL would go for massive capacity expansion, including M & A.

It is critical to understand:

1. The competitor's assumptions about itself.
2. The competitor's assumptions about the industry and the other companies in it.

A firm may perceive itself as a socially conscious organisation, the industry leader, quality conscious firm, highly ethical etc. Such assumptions will, obviously, guide the way the firm behaves, including reactions to competitors' moves.

A firm would also have assumptions about the industry and competitors, like the industry prospects; competitors' goals, capabilities and weaknesses; competitors' possible behaviours and reactions etc.

The strategies and moves of a firm will be influenced by the above two assumptions.

Identification of the current strategies of the competitors is a very important component of competitor analysis. "A competitor's strategy is most usefully thought of as its key operating policies in each functional area of the business and how it seeks to interrelate the functions." The ability of a firm to accomplish its goals and to respond to competitor's moves depends on its strengths and weaknesses. Analysis of the strenghts and weaknesses of the competitors is, therefore, every important.

SWOT ANALYSIS

The diagnosis of a firm's strengths and weaknesses can be fruitful only if the environmental factors and market conditions are considered along with the internal capabilties. This approach essentially involves matching of the internal capabilities with the environmental opportunities and threats, and is known as SWOT (Strengths and Weaknesses, Opportunities and Threats) analysis. In a way SWOT analysis may be said to consist of interlinking the ETOP and SAP. The extent of matching of internal capabilities and environmental conditions is reflected in the following schematic view of the position of Reliance Textile Industries Ltd.

RELIANCE TEXTILE INDUSTRIES LTD.

Matching Internal Capabilties with Environmental Factors

Internal Capabilities	*Environmental Factors*
Modern plant and machinery; Production and technological capabilities of a high order.	Growing demand for high quality fabrics in different categories of blends.
Design capabilities to provide diversity of designs as also frequency of of change.	Awareness of foreign fashions and wide range of design of international standards.
Financial strength derived from: ability to generate foreign exchange	Willingness of consumers in various segments to pay high price to match the quality requirements.
tax planning.	Restrictions on imports of fabrics.
Cash generation on account of exports and yarn sales.	Necessity of providing full range of fabrics under one roof caterging to 'family purchase.'
Voluntary equity participation of dealers resulting in assured commitment.	Need for identifying design changes to cater to 'shifts' in fashion.

N.B. Adapted from S.K. Bhattacharya & N. Venkataraman, Managing Business Enterprises : Strategies and Systems, Vikas, New Delhi, 1983 p. 27.

The basic objective of SWOT analysis is to provide a framework to reflect on the firm's ability to overcome barriers (or threats) and avail of the opportunities emerging in the environment. Indeed the dimensions of internal capabilities have relevance in so far as they relate to the environmental conditions. Hence, the analysis of comparative strengths and weaknesses requires linking internal competencies with the characteristics of external environment.

An Organisation which had pioneered computer education and training in India in the early 80s found its position threatened in the mid-90s by competitors. Analysis of the changing environment and its own strengths and weaknesses led to the outlining of the organisation's SWOT as follows:

Strengths	Weaknesses	Opportunities	Threats
Value for money programmes.	Not aggressive in selling.	Growing demand for computer education.	Rise in number competitors.
Pool of trained faculty.	Course differentials not sharp.	Computer liberary becoming a necessity	High rate of technologial. absolescence.
Wide choice of course offerings.	Counsellors' enthusiasm inadequate.	Growth of niche training needs.	Commoditisa- of training.
National network of well-equipped training centries.	Customer service not focused enough.	Need for customised training modules.	Underculting of fees.

Matching strengths and weaknesses with opportunities and threats requires that a firm should direct its strengths towards exploiting opportunities and blocking threats while minimising exposure of its weaknesses at the same time. Thus, strategies which are based on the matching of strengths and opportunities may be regarded as exploitative or developmental strategy. Those which direct strengths to threats may be called blocking strategies. If strengths are used to repair weaknesses, one may call it remedial strategy. SWOT analysis may provide the basis of a comprehensive approach to strategy. Capability in market research (strength) should enable a firm to seek out market segments (geographic or customer-wise) which are not so far identified by competitors (corresponding opportunity). The same capability may be used to repair the present dependence on narrow market segment (weakness). Cost efficiency (strength) of a firm may enable it to increase market share through an appropriate pricing strategy. With a strong financial position, the firm may improve its production facilities or technological capability and thereby increase market share. If the weakness of a firm lies in its distribution network, or Research and Development, or cost levels, the appropriate strategy should be to concenrate on a market segment in which customers are less price conscious and prefer a service that can be provided without technological superiority.

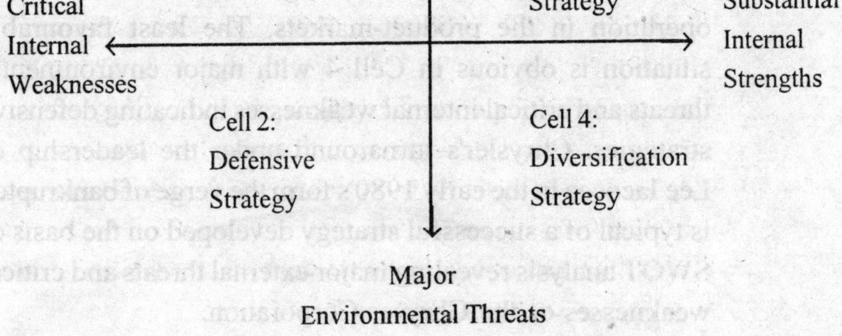

SWOT analysis can be applied in different ways in the choice of strategy:

(1) It provides a logical framework to be used for sysematic discussion of various issues bearing on the business situation, alternative strategies, and finally the choice of strategy. Indeed, it ranges across all aspects of a firm's situation. Differences in managerial perceptions of threats and opportunities, weaknesses and strengths lead to different assessments reflecting intra-organisational power relations and differing factual perspectives. Ultimate choice of strategy thus takes place through an interactive process in a dynamic setting.

(2) Another application of SWOT analysis is the structured approach whereby key external threats and opportunities may be systematically compared with internal strengths and weaknesses. Thus, the firm's internal and external situations can be matched so as to form distinct patterns, and the strategy chosen on the basis of the situation reflected in a pattern, as shown on the diagram given above.

There are four cells in the diagram, of which Cell 1 may be said to represent the most favourable situation with numerous environmental opportunities and substantial internal strengths. Aggressive growth-oriented strategies are indicated in this type of situation. On the other hand, the situation represented by Cell 4-the most unfavourable one-calls for strategies involving withdrawal or reduced operation in the product-markets. The least favourable situation is obvious in Cell 4 with major environmental threats and critical internal weaknesses indicating defensive strategies. Chrysler's turnaround under the leadership of Lee Iacocca in the early 1980's form the verge of bankruptcy is typical of a successful strategy developed on the basis of SWOT analysis revealing major external threats and critical weaknesses of the Chryser Corporation.

Cell 2 represents a mixed situation with substantial internal strengths combined with major environmental threats. Diversification strategies are indicated for this type of situation involving the use of current strengths to exploit long-term opportunities in other product-markets. A mixed situation of another kind is represented by Cell 3. A firm facing this situation has enviromental opportunities but constraints of severe internal weaknesses do not permit immediate gains to be derived from the opportunites. A two-fold strategty is thus indicated-eliminating the weaknesses along with more effective pursuit of market opportunities.

(3) The Cell-wise situations in which firms have to be actually placed often pose problems to the strategists. A business may have several opportunities but also face some serious threats in the environment. It may have likewise several weaknesses along with one or two major strengths. In such situations, the SWOT analysis guides the strategist to visualise the overall position of firm, and helps to identify the major purpose of the grand strategy being considered.

VALUE CHAIN ANALYSIS

Rather than approaching strategic analysis of internal resources across distinct functional areas, an alternative suggested by Michael Porter is the 'Value-chain as a framework. This analysis consists of identifying the series of activities which are undertaken by the firm and are strategically relevant for meeting customer demand and in respect of which the firm may potentially have an edge over its competitors. Thus the internal factors of key importance are sought to be linked with the chain of value activities through systematic identification of discrete activities as potential sources of strengths and weaknesses. There are, for most business enterprises, two broad categories of value activities: Primary activities and Support activities. The former include activities connected with the physical creation of the firm' s product or service, its marketing and delivery, and provision of after-sale support. The support activities are those which provide inputs or infratructure for primary activities to be performed.

PRIMARY ACTIVITIES

Based on technological and strategic distinctness, the primary activities are generally divisible into five basic categories as follows:

(i) **Inbound Logistics.** These are activities associated with procurement, storage, and flow of inputs to the product,like material handling, warehousing, inventory control, vehicle sheduling and returns to suppliers.

(ii) **Operations.** Activities involved in the transformation of inputs into final product, like machinning, packaging, equipment maintenance, testing, and facility operation, belong to this category.

(iii) **Marketing and Sales.** Included in this category are such activities as advertising, sales promotion, sales force management, channel selection, channel relations, and pricing.

(iv) **Outbound Logistics.** These include activities which are associated with collection, storage and physical distribution of finished goods to the customers, such as storage/ warehousing of finished goods, order processing, scheduling deliveries, operation of delivery vehicles.

(v) **Service.** These are activities aimed at providing service to enhance or maintain the value of the product, like installation, repair, training, supply of parts and product adjustment.

All the primary activities deserve attention in process of internal analysis in a systematic manner, but particular activities may require more detailed analysis depending upon the nature of industry. Thus, for example, inbound and outbound logistics generally constitute the most critical activities in food processing industry. A company engaged in running hotels should be more concerned with operations.

SUPPORT ACTIVITIES

Support activities, which provide the infrastructure for primary activities, are aslo required to be identified by isolating them on the basis of technological and strategic distinctiveness. Four categories of support activities are generally distinguished as follows:

(a) **Procurement.** Procurement activities which include purchase of materials and service inputs, equipment and machinery, etc., pervade all other activities in the value-chain, for every activity needs to use purchased inputs of some kind.

(b) **Technology Development.** Technology involved in product designing and manufacturing processes require activities to be performed for perfection and upgradation. Thus, technology development includes activities related with creating and improving the way in which various activities in the value chain are performed.

(c) **Human Resource Management.** Management of human resources-reruitment, training and development of mannpower-is involved in each and every activity in the value chain, and they constitute a distinct set of support activities.

(d) **Firm Infrastructure.** Quite distinct from the specific primary or support activities but essential to the entire chain of value activities are those activities that provide the infrastructure of the firm as a whole. They relate to general management, accounting and finance, legal affairs, strategic planning, etc.

Usefulness of Value-Chain Analysis

The framework of value-chain provides guidance for a systematic internal analysis of the firm's existing or potential strengths and weaknesses. Systematic disaggregation of a firm into certain distinct activity categories enables the strategist to identify the key internal factors for closer examination as potential sources of competitive advantage.

GENERIC COMPETITIVE STRATEGIES

Competitive strategy includes all the moves and approaches a firm has taken and is taking *(i)* to attract buyers, *(ii)* to withstand competitive pressures, and *(iii)* to improve its market position. A firm's strategy can be mostly offensive or mostly defensive depending upon the market conditions. There would be countless strategies that the firms adopt in different situations. But, all these strategies can be broadly divided into the following three categories:

1. Striving to be the overall low-cost producer in the industry (a lost-cost leadership strategy).
2. Seeking to differentiate one's product offering from rival's products (a differentiation strategy).
3. Focusing on a narrow portion of the market rather than the whole market (a focus or niche strategy).

The fig. given below depicts the distinctive features of these generic competitive strategy approaches:

1. A Low-Cost Leadership Strategy. The low-cost leader's basis for competitive advantage is lower overall costs than competitors. The low-cost strategy is a powerful approach in markets where most of the customers are price sensitive. The purposes of striving to be a low-cost producer are:

(i) to fix the price for the products at the lower level compared to that of the competitors.

(ii) to gain the maximum market share from the competitors; or

(iii) to earn high profit margin and thus maximise the profits.

Thus, this strategy will help the firm initially to gain the market share from the competitors and later to maximise the profits. The danger of this strategy is that, if the firms cut the prices abnormally to kill the competitors, the firms my end-up with problems of a cheap product.

The firm should see that their costs in all areas of production are lower than that of the competitors. There are two ways to accomplish this goal. They are:

(a) outmanaging rival on efficiency and cost control and/or

(b) finding creative ways to cut cost-producing activities out of the activity-cost chain.

These two approaches can be used independently or simultaneously. Firms to get low cost advantage should pursue cost savings exhaustively throughout the activity cost chain. All areas without exception should be taken care of.

Organisational culture of such firms should be symbolically reinforced by spartan facilities, salaries and benefits to executives and employees are based on demand and supply factors, exhaustive search for low cost materials, find the ways and means to control budget expenditure, minimisation of wastage, recycling of wastage and empowerment of employees to minimise cost.

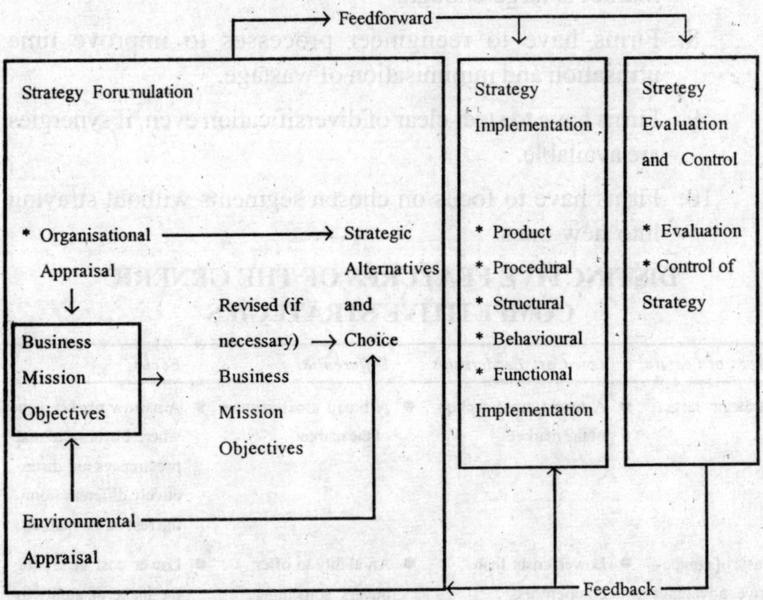

Strategic Management Process

Steps to Minimise Cost are as follows:

1. Firms intent to be a low cost producer should appraise each cost creating activity and identify the factors driving the cost of the activity.
2. Firms have to identify the controllable and uncontrollable cost, immediate and postponable costs, present and future costs etc.

3. Wherever and whenever, it is possible, firms have to eliminate whole activity from the activity cost-chain.
4. Firms have to use its knowledge about the controllable cost, postponeable costs, to manage and control these costs, month after month or year after year.
5. Firms have to control cost to keep the products affordable.
6. Firms have to forge relationships with vendors to minimise costs.
7. Firms have to build global capacities, if the domestic market is large enough.
8. Firms have to reengineer processes to improve time utilisation and minimisation of wastage.
9. Firms have to steer clear of diversification even, if synergies are available.
10. Firms have to focus on chosen segments without straying into new ones.

DISTINCTIVE FEATURES OF THE GENERIC COMPETITITVE STRATEGIES

Types of Feature	*Low-Cost Leaderships*	*Differential*	*Focus*
Strategic target	• A broad cross-section of the market.	• A broad cross-section of the market.	• A narrow market niche where buyer need and preferences are distinctively different from the rest of the market.
Basic of competitive advantage	• Lower costs than competitors.	• An ability to offer buyers something different from competitors.	• Lower cost in serving the niche or ability to offer niche buyers something customise mised to their requirements and tastes.
Product line	• A good basic product with few frills (acceptable quality and limited selection).	• Many product variations, wide selection, strong emphasis on the chosen differenting features.	• Customised to fit the specialized needs of the target segment.

Contd.

Types of Feature	*Low-Cost Leaderships*	*Differential*	*Focus*
Production emphasis	• A continuous search for cost reduction with out sacrificing acceptable quality & essential features.	• Invent ways to create value for buyers.	• Tailor-made for the niche.
Marketing empahsis	• Try to make a virtue out of product features that lead to low cost.	• Build in whatever features buyers are willing to pay for. • Charge a premium price to cover the extra costs costs of differentiating features.	• Communicate the focuser's unique ability to satisfy the buyer's specialized requirements.
Sustaining the Startegy	• Economical prices/ good value. • All elements of startegy egy aim at contributing to a sustainable cost advantage—the key is to manage cost down, year after year, in every every area of the business.	• Communicate the points of difference in credible ways. • Stress constant improvement and use innovation to stay ahead of imitative competitors. • Concentrate on a few key differentiating features; use them to create a reputation and brand image.	• Remain totally dedicated to serving the niche better than other competitors; don't blunt the firm's image and efforts by entering other segments and adding other product categories to widen market appeal.

Source. Arthur A. Thompson and A.J. Strickland, op. cit., p. 104.

ADVANTAGES OF BEING A LOW-COST PRODUCER

The low-cost producing firms get some attractive defenses against five competitive forces:

(1) Strong position to compete with rival competitors. The low-cost firm is in the strong position to compete with rival competitors, offensively based on price, to defend against price war conditions, to use the appeal of a lower price to win sales from rival competitors and earn high profits in price competitive markets.

(2) The low-cost firm has partial profit margin protection from powerful customers.

(3) The low-cost firm can prevent the entrance of potential competitors into the market through price-cuts.

(4) The low-cost firm is more insulated than competitors from powerful suppliers.

(5) The low-cost firm is better positioned than high-cost rivals against substitute products.

The low-cost leadership strategy is particularly effective when:

1. Price competition among rival sellers is dominant competitive force.
2. The industry's product is essentially standardised.
3. Most buyer use the product in the same ways.
4. Buyers shop for the best price without incurring much cost and inconvenience.
5. There are few ways to achieve product differentiation that have value to buyers.
6. Buyers are large and have significant power to bargain down prices.

Thus, heavy investments in cost-reduction activities can lock a firm into both its present technology and its present strategy, leaving it vulnerable to technological advancements and changing buyers' preferences and tastes other than a lower price. This situation is more significant in times of increase in buyers income brackets consequent upon the country's economic development.

2. Differentiation Strategies. Generally, customers' needs, taste and preferences vary from the one customer to the another customer. These differences in customers' tastes, preferences and needs can be satisfied by producing the product with different attributes. This situation results in adoption of differentiation strategy by the producer to satisfy the diversified needs of the customer by a standardised product. The producer to make this strategy successful should study the different needs, tastes and preferences of various classes of customers. Further, he should study the buying and consumption behaviour of different classes of customers. The producer, then should incorporate the features into the product offering based on the study. This will make the product much suitable to different customers compared to the competitors' offerings. Consequently, most of the customers will prefer this product to the rivals/competitors.

Competitive advantage results when more customers become strongly attached to the attributes of a differentiator's product offering.

ADVANTAGES OF EFFICIENT DIFFERENTIATION

The efficient differentiation brings the following advantages to the differentiator:

(a) The product commands a premium price for the producer.

(b) More number of units are sold as additional customers are won over by the differentiating features.

(c) Differentiation enhances the profitability when the cost of the differentiation is less than the extra price of the product.

(d) The product gains greater customer loyalty to its brand.

DISADVANTAGES OF DIFFERENTIATION

Though, differentiation brings some advantages, some times, it results in loss to the producer, They are :

(a) Differentiation is unsuccessful when the customers do not value the additional features significant enough to buy the product in profitable quantities.

(b) Differentiation results in loss when the cost of differentiation is more than the extra price of the product.

Anything a company can do to create customer value represents a potential basis for differentiation. A company should build the value creating attributes into the product at an acceptable cost after finding suitable sources of buyer values. The producer should make sure that the incorporated attributes should *(i)* raise the product's performance, or *(ii)* make the product more economical to use, or *(iii)* enhance customer satisfaction in tangible or intangible ways. Differentiation possibilities can grow out of activities performed anywhere in the activity-cost chain.

NEED FOR DIFFERENTIATION

Producers would like to differentiate their products/services as it works as an attractive strategy due to the following reasons:

(i) Differentiation provides some buffer against rival's strategies, as customers become loyal to the brand or model they like most and often like to pay higher price.

(ii) Differentiation erects entry barries in the form of customer loyalty and uniqueness that newcomers find hard to overcome.

(iii) Differentiation helps a company fend off threats from substitutes.

(iv) Differentiation mitigates the bargaining power of major customers as competitors' products are less attractive to them.

(v) Efficient differentiation creates lines of defence for dealing with competitive forces as it provides price advantage and thereby higher profit margin.

Differentiation strategy works better under the following situations:

(i) Where there are many ways to differentiate the product/service and most of the customers feel these differences as valuable.

(ii) Where the customers' tastes, preferences, needs and uses of the item are diverse.

(iii) Where the differentiation strategies are least subject to quick or inexpensive imitation by competitors. In other words, it should be difficult to competitors to copy quickly and profitably.

(iv) Where a few competitors follow differentiation strategy.

(v) Where the differentiation is based on, *(a)* technical superiority, *(b)* quality, *(c)* more customer supportive services and *(d)* more value for the money.

There is no guarnatee that the differentiation will always result in efficient competitive advantage. This is due to the limitations of the differentiation strategy. These limitations include:

(i) Buyers may perceive a little value in uniqueness of the product.

(ii) A significantly low cost strategy may defeat a differentiation strategy.

(iii) Overdifferentiating results in high cost and high price compared to that of competitors or product quality or service levels exceed customer's needs.

(iv) Trying to differentiate on the basis of something that does not lower a customer's cost or enhance a customers' well-being (as perceived by the customer).

(v) Trying to change too high a price premium (the higher the premium, the more number of customers can be lured away by lower priced competitors).

(vi) Not understanding or identifying what customers consider as value.

(vii) Ignoring the need to signal value and depending only on tangible product attributes to achieve differentiation.

DIFFERENTIATION-CUM-LOW-COST STRATEGY

Combining differentiation strategy and low-cost strategy results in giving customers more value of the money with an emphasis on more than minimally acceptable quality, service, features and performance. The purpose is to meeting or exceeding customer's expectations on different product attributes like quality, service, design, performance, features and price. Thus, the producer creates a superior value for the product. In essence, such a hybrid strategy helps a company to combine the competitive advantage appeals of both low-cost and differentiation.

Focus and Specialisation Strategies. Focusing begins by choosing a market niche where customers have distinctive preferences or requirements. Thompson and Strickland define the term 'niche' as, "geographic uniqueness, by specialised requirements in using the product or by special product attributes that appeal only to niche members." A stategist's basis for competitive advantage is either lower costs than competitors in serving the market niche or an ability to offer niche members something different from that of competitors. If the buyer's needs can be satisfied through a low cost based product compared to the rest of the market, the producer can adopt a focus strategy based on low-cost. Alternatively, if there is a customer segment that demands unique product attributes, then the producer can adopt a focus strategy based on differntiation.

A focus strategy will be efficient in the following situations:—

(i) The market segment is large enough to be profitable.

(ii) The market segment has good growth potential.

(iii) The maret segment is not significant to the success of major competitors.

(iv) The focusing producer can defend himself against challengers based on the customer goodwill he has built up and his superior ability to serve customers in the segments.

(v) The focusing producer has the skills and resources to serve the segment efficiently.

(vi) When it is costly or difficult to the competitors to meet the specialised needs to the niche.

(vii) When a company does not have enough resources to pursue a wider part of the total market.

(viii) When no other competitor is attempting to specialise in the same target segments.

(ix) When the industry has many different segments and allowing a focuser to select an attractive segment based on his strengths and capabilities.

The advantages of a focus strategy are as follows:

(i) Specialised skills of a producer adopting the focus strategy in serving the target market niche provide a basis for defending against five competitive forces.

(ii) This strategy also presents a hurdle to the producers of substitute products to enter the niche market.

(iii) The focused company's competence in serving the market niche create entry barriers for new firms. Therefore, it is harder for firms outside the niche to enter.

(iv) The niche strategy combined with low-cost and differentiation strategies will enable the producer to enhance market share and profitability.

(v) The powerful customers' bargaining power is also lowered as the competitors ability to serve their needs is less compared to the focused firm.

❐

7

Strategy Implementation

The strategy formulation and the relationship between strategy formulation and strategic implementation should be studied. This is because the formulation and implementation process are intertwined in real life. The two linkages existing between strategy formulation and strategy implementation are: *(i)* forward linkage, and *(ii)* backward linkage. The forward linkage deals with preparing the organisational activities including organisational structure, leadership, culture etc, necessary for the strategic implementation.

The backward linkage deals with the influence of implementation on strategy formulation. In other words, once the strategy is selected and implemented, it is found in the reality that there are certain deviations due to the different ground realities. These deviations force the strategist to reformulate the strategy based on the ground realities. Therefore, the past strategic actions and experiences should be taken into consideration in formulating strategies.

ISSUES AND STRATEGY IMPLEMENTATION

A number of issues are normally involved in strategy implementation. The important issues are project, procedural, organisational, structural, behaviour considerations, production/ operations, human resources, financial and marketing.

1. Project Implementation. Project is defined by the Project Management Institute of the US as, "a one-shot, time limited, goal-oriented, major undertaking, requiring the commitment of varied skills and resources." Thus, a project is a highly specific programme for which the time schedule and specific costs are determined in advance. Projects create all necessary conditions and facilities for the strategy implementation, the discipline of project management. The goals for a project are devised/derived from the plans and programmes which are based on the strategies adopted. A project passes through various phases before a set of task can be accomplished:

(i) Detailed planning related to different aspects of the projects such as infrastruture engineering designs, schedules and budgets, finance etc. has to be completed.

(ii) The phase is an extension of strategic formulation phase of the strategic management. Ideas generated during the process of strategic alternatives and choice consideration from the core of the future projects that may be undertaken by the organisation.

(iii) After a set of projects have identified and arranged according to the priority they have to be subjected to a preliminary project analysis which examines the marketing, technical, financial and economic aspects. This analysis is done to find out whether it would stand the scrutiny of the financial institutions, banks and investors. After this screening the viable projects are taken up and feasibility studies conducted.

(iv) The detailed engineering, material, awarding contracts, civil and other types of construction, etc., have to be undertaken during the implementation phase leading to the testing, trail and commissioning of the plant.

(v) The final phase deals with disbanding the project.

2. Procedural Implementation. Strategy implementation also requires executing the strategy, based on the rules, regulations and procedures formulated by the government. Though, many procedures are simplified with the liberalisation, privatisation and globalisation of Indian economy, certain procedures are still applicable in the process of strategy implementation. Therefore, the strategists should study the following procedural aspects before implementing the strategy. They are: licensing procedures, foreign collaboration procedures, Foreign Exchange and Regulation Act requirements, environmental requirements Monopolies and Restrictive Trade Practices requirements, import and export requirements, incentives and benefits, requirements of labour laws and other legislations.

3. Organisational Structures and Strategies. Companies build structures for their organisations based on their strategies. There are a number of methods/ways that the organisations can be structured. The simple strategies require simple structure whereas the growth strategies require flexible structure and complex strategies necessarily influence to build matrix structures. In fact, the stable strategies require a mechanistic organisation and a growth strategy require an organic structure.

4. Organisational Growth. Organisational structure is a means to an end of achieving organisational mission and objectives. Thus, it is an important means for strategic implementation. Organisational structure refers to the methods of allocating duties and responsibilities to individuals, and the ways what individuals are grouped together into units, departments and divisions. The formal organisational structure represents the relationships between people and functions as designated by management and conveyed in the organisation chart. It also defines the number of levles in the organisational hierarchy. The informal organisational structure represents the web of social relationships among various members of a company.

5. Entrepreneurial Structure. Generally, the small businesses and the businesses when they are started consist of an owner-manager and few employees. These types of organisations do not require an organisational chart and formal assignment of responsibilities. Organisation structure is fluid with each employee often knowing how to perform more than one task and with owner-manager involved in all aspects/areas of business.

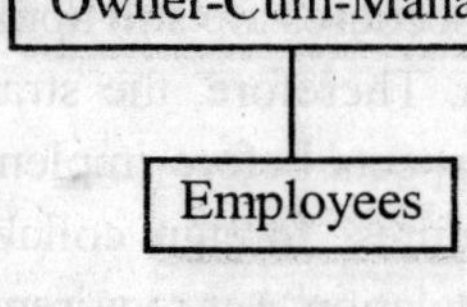

Fig. Entrepreneurial Organisational Structure (Start-up)

The small firms, if,they are successful during the first years of crucial period, it would be due to the increased demand for products or services. The entrepreneurs develop the business and increase the size of the firm to meet the increased demand. The business begins to evolve from fluidity to a status of more permanent division of labour due to the growth. The owner-manager, who was performing all functions in the initial stage now finds that he has to perform more managerial activities than operational activities. The growth demands the owner to employ new candidates and this results in assignment of specialised functions to these employees.

The business growth results in expansion of organisational structure both vertically and horizontally. The entrepreneurial organisational structure with growth is depicted in Fig. given below. As can be seen from this figure, the operative functions of manufacturing are assigned to manufacturing manager and the operative functions of marketing are assigned to the marketing manager. These two managers perform the activities with the help of employees. The owner-manager performs managerial and strategic functions.

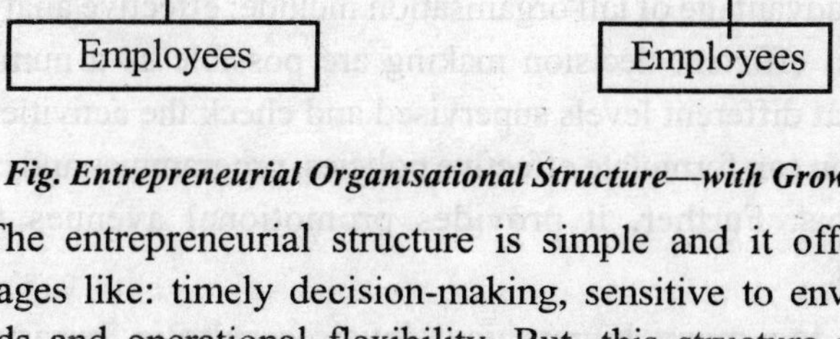

Fig. Entrepreneurial Organisational Structure—with Growth

The entrepreneurial structure is simple and it offers some advantages like: timely decision-making, sensitive to environment demands and operational flexibility. But, this structure results in excessive depending on owner-manager who is normally not a professional manager. This structure cannot respond to the increasing demand beyond a point. Thus, this structure is mostly suitable to the strategy catering to the needs of a local market by being small.

6. Vertical/Tall Organisations. Vertical/Tall organisations refer to increase in the length of the organisation's hierarchy chain of command. The hierarchical chain of command represents the company's authority— accountability relationship between superiors and subordinates. Authority and responsibility flows from the top to the bottom through all the levels of the hierarchy, accountability from the lowest level to the highest level. Fig. given below shows the vertical/tall organisation. Employees at each level should report to their superior, who in turn should report to his boss. Thus, the activities are reported to the top. Authority is more centralised in tall organisation.

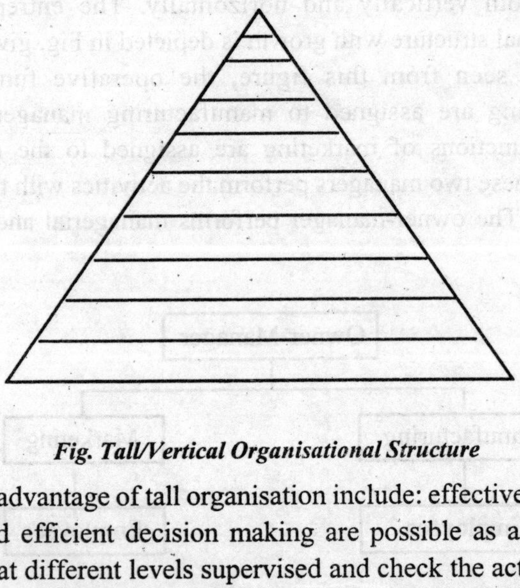

Fig. Tall/Vertical Organisational Structure

The advantage of tall organisation include: effective analysis of factors and efficient decision making are possible as a number of managers at different levels supervised and check the activities. The organisation can formulate effective policies, programmes and control mechanisms. Further, it provides promotional avenues to the employees.

But, too many hierarchical levels results in bureaucratic characteristics rather than commercial characteristics to the business firm. Tight operational control delays the decision making process. This process makes the organisation incompetent. Too many controls may reduce the cost of operation.

Tall and centralised organisations allow for better communication of company's mission, goals and objectives to all employees. It also enhances coordination of functional areas to ensure that each area will work closely witht the other functions. Since, all employees are centrally directed, coordination become possible.

Tall organisational structure is appropriate for the firms having bleak growth opportunities, problem children and dogs. Further, firms with cost minimisation strategy and firms in maturity stage can adopt tall organisations. Thus, this type of structures are well suited for environments that area relatively stable and predictable.

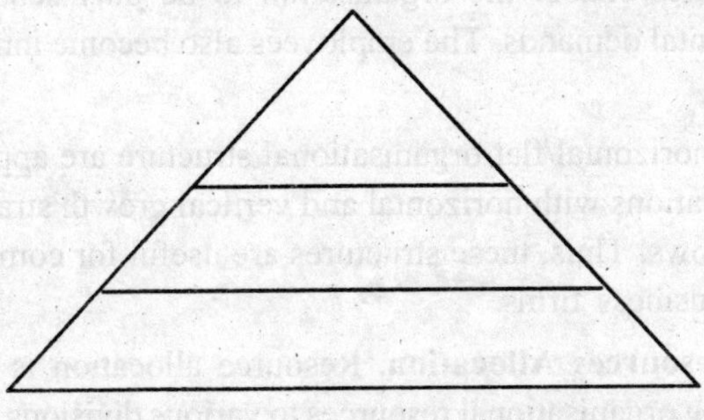

Fig. Flat/Horizontal Organisational Structure

7. Horizontal/Flat Organisations. Horizontal/flat organisations refer to an increase in breadth of an organisation's structure. Fig. given above presents the model of horizontal/flat organisation. The number of levels in the organisational hierarchy are a few. The span of control is relatively large.

The increasing bio-professionalisation and multi-professionalisation and wide acceptance for empowerment allowed even the large business firms to reduce the number of hierarchical levels of their organisations. Consequently, large sized firm also started adopting horizontal/flat organisation by delayering. In fact, this structure is well suited for the small size business firms.

Authority is more decentralised in relatively flat structures. Managers with broad span of the control must grant more authority to his subordinates. Decisions are more likely to be made by the employees who are at the helm of affairs and more familiar with the situations and ground realities. Organisational activities are mostly performed informally. Professional managers are treated as real profession lists.

The major advantage of flat structure is quick decision-making. Thus, it enables the management to take decisions in right time. Other advantages of this structure include: low adminsitrative costs, freedom and autonomy to the managers to operate, decision making by the managers who are at helm of affairs and empowerment of managers. These benefits motivate the managers to accept responsibility and commit themselves towards organisational objectives. Further, these characteristics enable the organisation to be duly sensitive to the environmental demands. The employees also become innovative and creative.

The horizontal/flat organisational structure are appropriate for the organisations with horizontal and vertical growth strategies, stars and cash cows. Thus, these structures are useful for competitive and dynamic business firms.

8. Resources Allocation. Resource allocation is the process of allocating organisational resources to various divisions, department and strategic business units (SBUs). Resource allocation deals with the procurement and commitment of financial, physical and human resources to strategic tasks for the achievement of organisational objectives. Resource allocation is a powerful means of communicating the strategy of the organisation as it gives the desired signals to all concerned. It will demonstrate what strategy really is in operation. If the resource shift is not in line with the official strategy, the latter will remain only as a paper strategy.

Resource allocation decisions are linked to the objectives. Several questions have to be dealt within resource allocation. What sources can be tapped for resources? What fact affect resource allocation? What different approaches could be adopted?

How does resource allocation take place? Decision about dividend is important in relation to objectives and long-term ability of the company to attract capital. How to distribute the expected profits among investors, employees and the company's own needs is an important resource allocation decision from the viewpoint of long-term implementation of the strategy.

Methods for resource allocation are *(i)* B.C. G. Matrix, *(ii)* Budgeting systems.

9. Functional Policies. Functional policies provide guidelines to operating managers, so that *(a)* coordination across functional units take place. Once the strategy of the company is decided, modificational functional policies may become necessary to meet the demands of the new business. *(b)* similar situations are handled consistently *(c)* strategies are implemented and *(d)* executive time in decision making is reduced.

10. Communication of Strategy. Communication of strategy covering the mission objectives market scope, technology and all the issues relating to implementation, to different level in organisation is very important for its success. This is so because strategy is implemented through people who ought to be clear about the roles they have to play in relation to each other.

11. Leadership. Developing appropriate leaderships is one of the most important elements in the implementation of a strategy. Appropriate leadership is necessary, though not a sufficient condition for developing effective structure and systems for the success of strategy. Leadership is the key factor for developing and maintaining right culture and climate. There are several aspects of leadership styles and skills, some of them appropriate to the context, content of strategy, while others are desirable attributes in general for the success of an organisation. The challenges of leaderships is in implementation are the gravest as leadership in most scare resources.

12. Challenge of Change. The strategy implementation process generally invovles a change. The change can be minor or major. If it affected a large number of people, cuts into deeper issues like beliefs, values etc., it is major change. The process of change has three stages namely infreezing, moving and refreezing.

13. Pre-Implementation Evaluation of Strategy. Before the implementation of strategy it is advisable to go for a final scrutiny so as to avoid failure due to weaknesses in the analysis, if any and to ensure that strategy decided for the organisation is optimal. It is something like checking all the electrical connections before switching on the circuit. There are several check-points that may be used for evaluation.

The process of strategy formulation is referred to in current literature as 'Strategic planning' and is distinguishable from Management Planning and Control for strategy implementation. Strategic planning is defined as "the process of deciding on the objectives of the organisation, on the changes in the objectives, on the resources used to attain these objectives, and on the policies that are to govern the acquisition, use and disposition of these resources. It involves matching of the external economic, political and social environments to corporate capabilities and setting the long-term objectives and goals of the organisation as well as the policies and strategies to achieve the objectives. As Anthony has put it. "Strategic planning is a process having to do with the formulation of long-range strategic plans and policies that determine or change the character or direction of the organisation. In an industrial company, this process includes planning that effects the objectives of the company; the acquisition and disposition of major facilities, divisions, or subsidiaries; policies of all types, including policies as to management control and other processes, the markets they serve and distribution channels for serving them, the organisation structure, research and development of new product lines, sources of new permanent capital, and dividend policy; and so on."

As distinguished from strategic planning, the system of 'management planning and control' is associated with the ongoing administration of an enterprise. It is the process by which managers assure that resources are obtained and used effectively and efficiently in the accomplishment of the organisation's objectives. It accepts the corporate objectives evolved by strategic planning as 'givens' and attempts to relate the organisational resources to the objectives in order to arrive at a time-phased statement of the corporate goals and objectives and operational plans. Thus, the management planning and control system may be regarded as the medium through which the strategic objective, policies and plans are translated into more specific, measurable, attainable and meaningful goals and plans. Conceptually, it is a part of the total concept of strategy—a segment of the strategy implementation phase.

The management planning system involves the preparation of annual plans formalising the overall corporate goals and objectives in terms of sales, costs, margins, profits and return on capital, broken up, as necessary, in relation to products, operations, and geographic location of the activities. It may also involve the development of longer term (say, five-yearly) 'action' plans defining the possible ranges of sales and market share, cost, profits, capital expenditure, expected return on investment, and the operational plans in terms of money, men and materials which would be required over the time span in order to achieve the pre-determined corporate objectives. The formal planning system should ensure that the executives, with participation from managers at lower levels, break down the institutional objectives into functional and divisional objectives, thus translating strategic considerations into management considerations for specific time periods. The planning and control system to be effective requires the organisation structure to be such that it defines authority and responsibility in terms of jobs to be accomplished.

For effective implementation of strategy, the essential elements of the planning and control system should consist of:

(a) an appropriate organisation structure that defines authority and responsibility in terms of the job to be accomplished;

(b) a reporting system that can quickly diagnose deviations from the desired results, particularly in those areas which represent key variables in operations;

(c) goals and targets of organisational units based on the input-output relationship in the relevant operations;

(d) participation and support of all levels of management and supervisory personnel;

(e) a follow-up mechanism to ensure prompt remedial action by proper analysis, review and coordinated action.

The planning device commonly used to implement strategy is the budget. As an instrument for putting plans and policies into effect. The budget enables management to formalise goals and targets in quantitative/financial terms. Moreover, budgeting requires the participation of managers at different levels in the development of plans and policies. A motivational force is thus built into the process of planning and control, which is a vital necessity for successful implementation of the strategy. Its usefulness, notwithstanding budgeting has also its inherent limitations. But on balance many of the limitations may be found to lie not in the budget or the process of budgeting but in the lack of management awareness of the limitations, or the improper use of budgets.

RELATIONSHIP BETWEEN STRATEGY FORMULATION AND IMPLEMENTATION

The relationship between strategy formulation and implementation can best be described by their interdependence. These have been divided primarily from the point of view of orderly study as well as the skill requirements for these two aspects of strategic management. The requirement of strategy formulation is primarily conceptual and analytical skills while that of implementation is administrative skills. But in real life, the processes of formulation and implementation are interwined. Both can be thought of reiterative in the sense that both are affected by each other. For example, the strategy is formulated in a particular environment which is dynamic. The feedback from the operations, a result of strategy implementations, gives notices of the changing environmental factors to which strategy should be adjusted. Thus this is on-going process which should be seen in continuity rather than in discrete form. The formulation of strategy does not end where its implementation begins; both should be taken as a continuous process.

The interdependence of formulation and implementation of strategy does not, however, mean that managers should not distinguish between the two. While interdependence helps management to take corrective action in the light of the feedback given by the implementation, the distinction between the two helps in putting right perspective on organisational resources, both human and physical. Strategy formulation should not be assigned to management below certain level because of its dependence on contingent factors; implementation can be assigned to this level of management. This is possible because once the overall strategic decisions are made, detailed implementation plans can be developed for the various functional areas of operations. Thus various levels of management come into the picture of strategic management. As will be seen later, when the strategy is put into action through the process of development of internal plans, the feedback mechanism emphasises the need to continually assess implementation of strategy and organisational performance in order to determine any change required in the strategy. Thus those who are responsible for strategy formulation can not be relieved from the task of its implementation.

TECHNIQUE FOR STRATEGY FORMULATION

I. Scenarios. Scenario generation is one of the methods which strategic planners have found useful for the interpretation of a fluid, rapidly changing business environment with an uncertain future. Scenarios constitute an effective device for sensing, interpreting, organising and bringing to bear diverse information about the future in planning and strategic decision-making. Simply stated, scenarios may be regarded as stories about the future. But more precisely speaking, these are descriptions of plausible alternative futures of the macro-environment. The primary purpose of scenario generation is to delimit the range of uncertainties in the most critical factors in an environment. Typical scenarios include qualitative and quantitative descriptions of uncertainties in the most critical factors in an environment. Typical scenarios include qualitative and quantitative descriptions of the more important social, political, economic, demographic, technological and other conditions. They often describe the basic trends, assumptions, conditions and dynamics of the factors relating to the future period that the scenario covers. As such scenarios are not forecasts or predictions. Probability estimates are hardly associated with the elements of the scenario. Hence scenarios are said to be fuzzy, too imprecise and hard to apply. Also scenario generation is an expensive process. There is no doubt that scenarios represent a significant departure from the traditional methods of forecasting like the single or multiple variable extrapolation and regression methods. However, most of the environmental factors are not amenable to easy prediction on account of their complexities and the rapidity of changes. Under the circumstances scenarios are found to be an ideal complement to the various other methods of forecasting and planning.

II. Gap Analysis. The basic question that strategic planners have to face with regard to environmental forecasting is how far ahead will they look, that is about the time horizon for forecasting. For, to respond strategically to a perceived environmental change in future, the strategic decisions have to be taken well in advance. It may be a matter of technology of production envisaged by the planners. Thus, for instance, it will take a considerably longer period to create production facilities for computer hardware than for production (say) a newly designed software. A technique which has been found useful in determining the time horizon for environmental forecasting is that of 'Gap Analysis'. Application of this technique will be clear from the following diagram which depicts a typical situation.

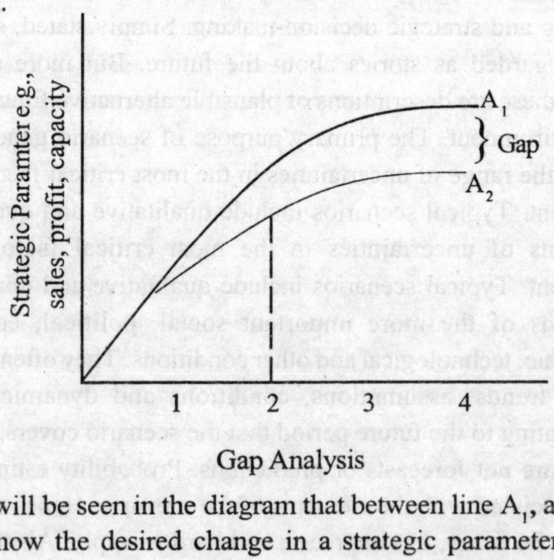

Gap Analysis

It will be seen in the diagram that between line A_1, and line A_2, which show the desired change in a strategic parameter like sale, profit, etc. and what will happen if there is no change in strategy, respectively, a gap has emerged by the second year. The gap widens with the passing of time. The planners should know how long it will take for current decisions to begin to fill the gap. If it is a question of creating capacity for computer hardware, two years will be too short a period for the purpose unless it is decided to acquire an existing plant.

Once the time horizon for forecasting is determined it is necessary that objective data should be processed and then analysed for making forecasts, taking into account the probabilities of occurrence and the risks involved. One or more of the following forecasting techniques may be adopted in this context:

(1) Unstructured Inexpert Opinion techniques such as person-in-the-street interviews, brainstorming, etc.

(2) Structured Inexpert Opinion techniques include use of questionnaire, interviews and surveys.

(3) Structured Expert Opinion techniques which include 'delphi' technique, highly structured interviews, and on-line Computer Interaction.

(4) Multivariate Interaction Analysis which includes mehtods involving the use of Input-output Models, Probability Networks, Factors Analysis, and regression Analysis.

(5) Mapping which includes Relevance Trees and Morphology Analysis.

(6) Theoretical Limit Envelopes which include methods such as Worst-Case Analysis, High and Low Limits Estimation, and Sizing Calculations.

(7) Unstructured Expert Opinion techniques such as "What if" Interviews, Role Playing, use of Consensus Panels, and Scenario Generation Forecasting technology change in particulary rendered easier by scenario generation.

(8) Dynamic Models which include Historical Analogues, Time-lags, and Stochastic Modelling.

(9) Single variable extrapolation : Variants of this techniques include linear extrapolation, life-cycle curves, power-series expansion, exponential smoothing, and others, Single varibale extrapolation is found useful if it is possible for the firm to identify a key environmental variable, on the assumption that the past is a guide to the future. However, a single environmental variable is generally insufficient. Thus, multiple regression techniques may have to be used.

RESOURCE ALLOCATION

A strategic plan is the representation of hopes and aspirations of strategists. Project implementation is for the creation of infrastructure to enable them to put such a plan into action. Procedural implementation provides the 'go-ahead' signal. But nothing really happens until resources are procured and allocated to tasks for accomplishment of objectives. Resources allocation deals with the procurement and commitment of financial, physical, and human resources to strategic tasks for the achievement of organisational objectives. Resource allocation is both a one-time and a continuous process. When a new project is implemented, it would require resources. An on-going concern would also require periodic allocation of resources. Strategy implementation should deal with both these types of resources allocation. Several questions have to be dealt with in resources allocation; what sources can be tapped for resources? What factors affect resource allocation? What different approaches could be adopted? How does resource allocation take place? and, finally, what difficulties are encountered? We deal with these questions in the following sub-sections.

Factors Influencing Resource Allocation

Resource allocation deals with the commitment and distribution of resources. Since resources are almost always scare, the process of resource allocation is quite complex. The basic question before the strategists is how to allocate scarce resources to competitive strategic tasks that lead to the accomplishment of organisational objectives. It would be easier for strategists to allocate resources to the strategic priorities are clear. But setting clear priorities practically is often a daunting task. This is so because a variety of factors affect the process of resource allocation. These factors would be the objectives of the organisation preference of dominant strategists, internal politics, and external influences.

There are a number of objectives. Some are official while others are operative (or implicit). Employees of any organisation tends to judge the importance given by strategists to tasks on the basis of the amount of resources allocated to them. If the chairperson of a company, while presenting the annual report, waxes eloquently on the virtues of human resources but the actual resource allocation does not reflect the importance given to these resources, then human resources development is certainly not a priority strategic task. Operative objectives tend to affect the pattern of resource allocation to the maximum extent.

The dominant strategists-most often the chief executive, tend to affect the process of resource allocation. Their preference are reflected in the way how resources get allocated. Except SBU, divisional and departmental heads know that such preferences matter and try to present their demands in line with them or attempt creating interest in the dominant strategists for their demands so that resources can be attracted easily.

Resources are often misconstrued as power. Those department units which are able to attract more resources are considered more powerful. Executives who are in a position to affect the process of resources allocation in their favour are perceived to be more effective. These perceptions make resource allocation a rational-political process. Internal policies within the organisation, therefore, affects the process of resource allocation.

Apart from internal politics, external influences also affect resource allocation. These influences arise due to government policy and stipulations, the demands of external shareholders, financial institutions, community and others. For instance, conditions imposed in the letter of intent issued to a company may require additional investments in pollution control and safety equipments before its conversion to an industrial licence. The shareholders may expect a higher dividend or bonus shares and resources may be to be diverted to them. Financial institutions may impose restrictions or require companies to invest in technology upgradation. The discharging of social responsibilities such as contribution to community services may require allocation of funds. Thus, external influences affect the process of resources allocation considerably.

Procurement of Resources

The different types of resources-financial, physical, and human-are derived from different sources. But finance is generally considered to be the primary source; it is used for creation and maintenance of other resources. We deal with sources of finance here. Basically, there are two types of finances-long term and short-term. Long-term finance is required for creation of capital assets. Short-term finance is for working capital. Both types of finances can be procured form internal and external sources.

Internal sources include retained earnings, depreciation provisions, taxation provisions, and other types of reserves like development rebate and investment allowance reserves. External sources consist of equity and loans (generally for long-term finance) and bank credit, hire-purchase debt, trade credit and fixed deposits (generally for short-term finances). While both internal and external sources carry benefits as well as disadvantages, given a choice, a business firm would prefer the internal sources. But much depends on management policy related to financing. The cost of capital from different sources has to be considered.

When modernisation, expansion, and diversification strategies lend to the creation of a new company or require additional investments, and when external sources of financing are tapped, certain important issues have to be considered. There are the requirements for the Controller of Capital Issues and financial institutions, and the stipulations, stock exchanges. The Controller of Capital Issues would consider the total capital most outlays and the scheme of finance for project, debt-equity ratio, and equity-preference ratio. The financial institutions have their own norms and specific areas and types of financing. The primary support for working capital is provided by commercial banks.

Having procured financial resources, the strategists set out to implement the strategies in right earnest. The first task is to distribute the resource within the organisation to different SBUs, divisions, departments, functions, tasks and individuals.

MEANS OF RESOURCE ALLOCATION

1. BCG-based Budgeting. The BCG matrix can also be used for resources allocation. In a BCG matrix, SBUs or products are identified as 'stars', 'question marks', 'cash cows' and 'dogs'. Investment and cash flow decisions can be made on the basis of the type of SBU. For instance, resources can be diverted from a 'cash cow' to a 'questions mark' or a 'star'. The BCG matrix, can, therefore, play a useful role in a multi-SBU-division or department company where resources have to be allocated.

2. Strategic Budgeting. Budgeting is a common technique used as a planning coordination, and control device in management. Its use is widespread in organisations. The topic of budgeting is covered exhaustively in texts in the area of financial management. But apart from traditional budgeting where stress is on accounting, a budget increasingly being used as a dynamic management tool. The difference lies in the way budgeting exercise is carried out in an iterative manner between different managerial levels and the assumptions made before the formulation of budgets. Position papers on different aspects such as environment, distinctive competence, marketing, past performance, etc are prepared and presented to the top management which uses them in formulating corporate policy guidelines and stating long-and short-term goals. The operating management meanwhile prepares operational plans and sets targets which are coordinated with the corporate objectives through the executive management. Based on resources availability and corporation guidelines the strategies budget is prepared by the executive-level committee and presented to the top management for approval and sanctions. The strategic budget then communicated down the line and the tasks of implementation taken up.

As can be seen from the above description, strategic budgeting is an iterative process involving a multi-level, organisation-wide effort and, therefore, needs to carry the approval of all concerned. More importantly, it takes into account strategic factors such as environmental changes and their likely impact on the implementation of strategies, and the corporate distinctive competencies and their probable effect on the objective achieving capability of the organisation. This is the reasons why it is termed as a strategic budget. Besides, this type of budgeting, there are also other means of resource allocation.

3. Zero-Based Budgeting. Zero-based budgeting is an operation planning and budgeting process that requires each strategist to justify resource allocation demand not on the basis of previous years' budget but on "ground zero", which is based on a fresh calculation of costs each time a plan is to be implemented. The strategic plan is divided into operational plans, goals and activities, and resource requirements are calculated everytime a budget is prepared. ZBB can be used for effective resource allocation among competing units on the basis of strategic priorities since costs are related to benefits for each strategic task undertaken.

4. PLC-Based Budgeting. Resources allocation could be linked to the different stages in a product's (or SBU's) lie cycle. A product in the introduction and growth stages may attract more resources and these resources may be diverted from the high-profit yielding products that have reached the maturity stage of their life cycle.

5. Capital Budgeting. Resources allocation for new projects or products could be done on the basis of capital budgeting. Existing projects, in cases of restructuring and modernisation, could also use capital budgeting for resources allocation.

6. Parta System. The parta sysem is an indigenous form of control device used for exercising management control. Though essentially, parta is a control tool used for the daily assessment of net cash inflow from operations before tax and dividends, the budgeted parta is a pre-determined amount agreed upon between the chairperson of the company and the business unit in charge. The total parta sysem is a daily budgeting and reporting system.

Difficulties in Resources Allocation

The previous sub-section described the factors that affect the process of resource allocation. These factors, combined with the fact that the resource allocation process is highly complex, create several difficulties for the strategists.

The first difficulty arises due to a scarcity of resources. Financial physical, and human resources are hard to find. Firms will usually face difficulties in procuring finance. Even if finance is available, the cost of capital is a constraint. Those firms which enjoy investor confidence and high credit-worthiness process a distinctive competence as it increases their resource-generation capability. Physical resources would consist of assets such as land, machinery and equipment. In a developing country like India many capital goods have to be imported. The government can provide a limited amount of foreign exchange and this places a restriction on firms wishing to procure physical resources. Human resources are seemingly in abundance but the problem arises due to the non-availability of skills that are specially required. Computer professionals, advertising personnel, and chemical engineers are currently scarce in India. This places severe restrictions on firms wishing to attract and retain personnel. In sum the availability of scarce resources is a very real problem faced in resource allocation. Within organisations, there are several difficulties encountered in resource allocation. The usual budgeting for existing SBUs, divisions, and departments places restrictions on generating resources for newer units and those with a greater potential for growth. Overstatement of needs is another frequent problem in a bottom-up appraoch to resource allocation. The budgeting and corporate planning departments may have to face the irks of those executives who do not get resources according to their expectations. Such negative reactions may hamper the process of strategic planning itself. When strategic budgeting is used for resource allocation, powerful units may be divested of resources for reallocation to potential units. "Budget battles" may ensue if resource allocation affects vested interests. It must be pointed out, however, that the chief executive has a major role to play in managing the process of resource allocation. Strategic management, based on participative mode, and communication of stratgic plan to all executives creates a congenial environment where the resource allocation decisions may be taken amicably.

APPROACHES TO RESOURCE ALLOCATION

1. First alternative approach is the product life cycle system of budgeting resources which suggests that resource allocation should be in tune with the stages in the product life cycle. The basic proposition in this approach is that resources needs vary at different stages in the life-cycle of a product and the strategic choice is also influenced by changes in the state of its life cycle. Thus, for instance, with retrenchment strategy assigned to a product division, one may suggest that it would be useful to adopt zero-base budgeting which implies that resource allocation should depend on the budget requests being justified in detail from scratch and not being considered in the light of allocations of the previous period. Even as a general approach to resource allocation, zero-base budgeting may help management to evaluate expenditure proposed and make trade-offs among current operations, development needs, and profits.

2. The second approach is the analytical conceptual models used for strategic choice (the Growth-Share matrix, 'Stop-light', and Directional Policy matrix models) are considered to be useful for resource allocation in multi-divisional firms. The Growth-Share Matrix suggests that business segments with low growth/high market share position should be allocated resources so as to maintain the present market share and the cash flow generated to be shifted to segments with high-growth/low market share. Thus, resources allocation may be governed by considerations of competitive capabilities/market share/business strengths of

the one hand, and growth prospects/industry attractiveness of business segments on the other.

3. A third approach to management decisions on resources allocation is provided by the budgeting system carefully geared to the chosen strategy.

   As the first step in the process, the corporate objectives and strategy are stated along with the environmental and competitive conditions to be communicated to the SBUs (organisational units), which in turn draw up preliminary budgets after defining the unit-wise objectives and strategies. The preliminary budgets are reviewed by top management and approved if found consistent with the strategy. Summary budgets are then prepared and subsidiary budgets developed including the operating budget, financial and expenses budget. The process involves a series of negotiations among managers at the SBU and corporate levels. For instance unit managers having defined the objectives and strategy of the unit prepare premises and forecasts which are sent for approval by top management. Tentative allocation of resources take place at the corporate level and budget proposals are called for on that basis. The preliminary budgets indicate changes in the resources requirements as compared with the previous period. Only on approval of the preliminary budgets the units draw up their plans and programmes. In large organisations the budget department at the headquarters provide all information to the SBUs and advises them in connection with preparation of budget proposals.

UNSUCCESSFUL IMPLEMENTATION OF STRATEGY

Before going into the details of how a chosen strategy is implemented, it is desirable to identify the factors which cause unsuccessful implementation of strategy so that managers can take adequate safeguard against these factors. There are several such factors:

1. First factor that can lead to unsuccessful implementation of a strategy is the defect in the strategy formulation itself. For example, if a strategy is beyond the capability of the organisation, it can not be successfully implemented. In such a case, the implementers may face serious problems and the organisation may lead to bankruptcy. Therefore, the strategic choice should always be correlated with the organisation's ability to implement it. While formulating and implementing a strategy, adeuqate precuations should be taken against these factors. In the light of these factors, various tools of strategy implementation should be adopted.
2. Unsatisfactory coupling of the strategy to the actions necessary to implement it both within the organisation and in the external decision situations with which it is concerned may cause unsuccessful implementation of the strategy. This type of difficulty can result from a number of causes and conditions. For example, unsatisfactory coupling of the new strategy may be due to the lack of explicit decoupling from previous strategy and commitment with the organisation itself. This decoupling may be caused, in turn, by the existence of a sizeable group of people within the organisation who are convinced that the new strategy is not practical and that the previous ways and activities are best. Another factors responsible for this unsatisfactory coupling may be misperceptions by the strategists of the impact of the newly proposed initiatives on the organisation and its people. It is sometimes assumed that the new initiatives will be accepted by the organisation with a minimum of time and effort from all those who are involved. In actual practice, however, much more work is necessary to ensure that the strategy is accepted and implemented than to prepare it in the first instance. Another reasons for unsuccessful coupling may be cause of different perspectives of strategists and implementers. In most cases, majority of people are concerned with the current operations. Their primary task is to ensure that these operations are

conducted smoothly and efficiently. Their perspective is involved with the avoidance of change and of the factors that could interfere with the operations in their area of responsibility. Strategies, in other hand, seek out changes and determine whether it can be used to the advantage of the organisation. These different perspectives can result in the two groups becoming alienated from each other. For successful implementation of the strategy, a link between these two groups is necessary.

3. Another major factors causing unsuccessful implementation of the strategy is insufficient attention to the negotiation of outcomes in the external decision situations. It is a tendency to assume, once the strategy is formulated, that all that is necessary for the success of the organisation is the aggressive pursuit of the strategy. However, this assumption holds good only so long as there is no change in the decision situations. If these situations change, there should be correpsonding change in the strategy also. For this is essential that the structure of the strategic decision situations in which the organisation is involved should be kept clearly in view throughout the implementation. If this is done, changes in the conditions surrounding those decision situations can be taken in stride. Contingency strategy made during the strategy formulation process can be brought ino operation when appropriate.

❐

8

Functional Strategies and Planning Policies

All organisations, irrespective of their size, nature and scope of business must perform the functions like production/operations, finance, marketing, human resource and research and development. Careful planning, execution and coordination of these functions are highly essential for efficient strategic planning, implementation and control. The strategic managers at functional level should understand the interrelationship of these functions in formulation of the strategies at functional levels. The activities of all the functional areas are interwoven in attaining their purposes as well as the purpose of the total firm as shown in fig given below. In fact, these functional areas of a firm are like different organs of a human body. Therefore, it is needless to say that the organisational strategies are implemented at the functional levels.

1. Production/Operations. The basic objectives of production/operations management is to ensure that the outputs produced have a value that exceeds the combined costs of the inputs and the transformation process. In other words, it should added the value to the inputs in the process of transformation.

STRATEGIES FOR SMALL BUSINESS UNITS

(i) Small business units that complete with the niche-low-cost strategy go for low initial investments in their plant, equipment, building outlets etc.

(ii) These business units also go for low investments in semi-variable and variable costs.

(iii) Small business units that adopt the niche-differentiation strategy select strategies that yeild superior quality. These units, in some situation may go for hand-crafting processes to differentiate the product and produce according to the customer's preferences.

(iv) Small business units adopting niche-low-cost/differentiation strategy go for strategies that simultaneously lower costs and increase differentiation. This strategy, though, initially involves higher costs, it will result in cost savings and quality improvement in the long-run.

STRATEGIES FOR LARGE BUSINESS UNITS

Large business units can take advantage of a number of factors. The major advantage is the reduction in cost per unit of output that occurs as a firm gains experience in producing a product or rendering a service. Production/operations costs may be systematically reduced through larger sales volume. The experience curve concept is based on three variables *viz.*, learning, economies of scale and capital labour substitution possibilities. Learning refers to the idea of specialisation and its advantages. Economies of scale refer to reductions in costs per unit of output as volume of output increases. Capital-labour substitution is substituting capital for labour and *vice versa*. This is possible with the increase in the volume of operations, the three variables, put together, will result in decrease in cost per unit as business gains greater market share as it takes the advantages of experience curve.

The business with low cost strategy are prticularly vulnerable to business units that are also able to attain quality in addition to low cost.

Adopters of differentiation as a generic strategy are vulnerable to competition that offer alternative products, but at lower, or even predatory prices. However, managers of the business units that adopt differentiation strategy do not actively capiatalise on the opportunities presented by lower costs.

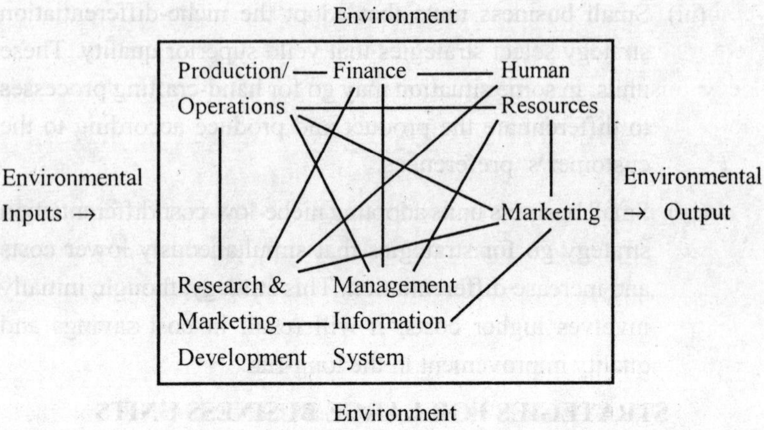

Fig. Interrelationships Among Functional Areas

Regardless of the generic strategy adopted, large business units may have to bear the risk of experience curve. These risks are due to technological innovations. Consequently, plant and machinery will be obsolete. Crores of rupees of investment may have to be written off.

1. Quality Considerations. Maintenance of superior and total quality brings the advantages as follows:

(a) Producing a quality product reduces the quantity of defects, which causes yeild to increase.

(b) Producing product right the first time reduces the number of rejects and time and money spent on network.

(c) Making the operative employees responsible for quality eliminates the need for inspection.

(d) Improvement of quality converts the waste of employee hours and machine time into the manufacture of good product and better service. Improvement in quality naturally and inevitably begets improvement of productivity. This process is essential for business unit adopting the niche-low-cost/differentiator or low-cost-differentiation generic strategies.

Every business unit would like to have a surplus of internally generated cash beyond expenditure, to allow it to reinvest. However, companies may go for borrowed funds, when strategic decisions require cash beyond the generated funds. Long-run capital investment decisions focus on the allocation of resources and are linked to corporate and business unit strategies.

Business units that adopt the niche-low-cost or low-cost generic strategies pursue financial strategies that are intended to lower their cost of capital, cost of borrowings, cost of purchase of plant and machinery, cost of purchase of material, cost of imports etc.

Business units that compete with the niche-differentiation or differentiation generic strategies pursue financial strategies that fund quality improvements. They upgrade their plants, machinery, production processes to maintain the quality above the level of the competitors and invest finances in these areas. These businesses place the top strategic priority on quality maintenance and improvements.

The businesses that compete with the niche-low-cost differentiation, low-cost-differentiation, or multiple strategies use their financial function to lower costs, on one hand, and promote quality improvements on the other hand.

2. Research and Development. The two basic areas of research and development are: *(i)* product/service R & D, and *(ii)* process R & D. Product/service R & D refers to efforts that ultimately lead to improvements or innovations in the firms products/services. Process R & D refers to reducing the costs of operations and making them more efficient.

Business units that adopt the niche-low-cost and low-cost strategies emphasise process R & D with a view to reduce the cost of operation. Business units that adopt the niche-differentiation and differentiation strategies give emphasis on product/service R & D to produce improved and innovative product models. Businesses that adopt niche-low-cost/differentiation, low-cost differentiation, and multiple strategies simultaneously emphasise both on product/service R & D and process R & D.

3. Marketing. The strategic considerations of marketing are: products/services, place of markets/location of outlets, channels of distribution, price and promotional activities. The business units that adopt the niche-low-cost and low-cost generic strategic produce no-frills products/services. Business units that adopt generic strategies of differentiation and low-cost differentiation pursue different marketing strategies. Marketing unique, quality products/services that are distinguishable from that of competitors are some of the strategies followed by these businesses.

The business units with compete with niche-differentiation and niche-low-cost/differentiation strategies tend to offer specialised, high quality to highest products to meet the particular needs of a relatively small market.

4. Human Resources. Human resources management function includes the major activities like designing and analysing jobs based on the future organisational needs, planning for future human resource needs, recruiting, selecting and employing people based on the needs of the organisation, training and developing employees to develop their human resources, appraising their performance and move the employees among different levels based on organisational needs and employee career goals, fixing and maintaining the compensation package, maintaining conducive human relations, and creating and maintaining high quality of work life.

In addition to these activities the firm adopting growth strategies go for the human resource development, creating and maintaining harmonious organisational climate, team building organisational development, empowering the employees, management of diversified cultures and the like. Companies adopting stability strategy do not bring signficant changes in human resources management. Companies adopting retrenchment strategies cut the size of human resources, cut the compensation package etc.

5. Information Systems. All functional areas of the business can be benefited by a well designed information system. A computer-based decision support system that contains a central data base permits each functional area to access information its need and to communicate electronically with the other functional departments as necessary. This facility helps each department to keep abreast of what other departments are doing and coordinate its efforts accordingly.

Information systems of most organisations evolve through four stages of growth. At the first stage, companies use electronic data for cost reduction, accounting applications, etc. Computer applications, in the second stage spread into all functional areas. The activities include: forecasting, inventory control, cash flow, personnel records and sales analyses. The third stage focuses on certain control activities such as in purchasing and scheduling. The final stage is the most sophisticated, involving decision support applications such as planning models, simulations, and on-line uses in human resources, cost analyses and order entries. This stage, enables management to develop competitive advantages.

MARKETING POLICY

From a practical point of view, marketing includes activities through which an organisation tries to satisfy the needs of human beings through exchange process. Organisations come into existence and grow as a result of their ability to satisfy the needs of their customers. They must be able to identify and satisfy these needs by producing the required goods and services. This process involves large number of activities which require policy decisions. Below is given a list of such activities and factors determining the performance of each which will help managers to develop policies in marketing area.

1. **Inventory Levels.** Demand pattern, customer service level, plant and warehouse location, production planning and scheduling, financial strengths.
2. **Credit and Discount.** Channel intermediaries requirements, cash flow requiements.
3. **Physical distribution.** Plant location, transportation mode, customers location, customer geographic distribution service level requirements.

4. **Marketing Research and Information System.** Financial strengths, production equipment and facilities, financial and accounting information.

5. **Promotion.** Promotion capacity, financial strengths, channel intermediaries capacity, availability of promotional avenues.

6. **Price.** Cost structure, product quality, stage of product life cycle, nature of competition, target market share, functional discounts, quality discounts, return on investment objectives.

7. **Product Packaging.** Product characteristics material and product handling equipment, middlemen needs, transportation modes.

8. **Distribution Channel Structure.** Nature of market, product characteristics, availability of middlemen and other channel specialists, financial requirements, firm's market position.

9. **Product Research and Development.** Financial strengths of the organisation, marketing feasibility, product technology.

Thus major policy issues in the area of marketing include the competitive tactics to be used in the marketing mix.

Whether a firm will sell its product or service directly to the consumers or make use of intermediaries (middlemen) for the purpose constitutes a major policy issue. For certain service service organisations, direct sale to consumers is invariably called for, like, for instance, civil airways, banks, consultancy firms, passenger and freight transport services. But for most manufactures of goods, selection of the channel of distribution involves a choice of great significance. For one thing, on channel decisions depend the firm's pricing decisions, advertising decision and sales force decisions. Pricing decisions depend upon whether it chooses wholesalers or retailers for distribution of its products; the firm's advertising decision depend upon the degree of co-operation from the agencies in the channel of distribution; the sales force decisions also depend upon whether the firm choose to sell to retailers or uses its own representatives. Secondly, the significance of channel decisions lies in that they involve long-term commitments to and dependence on other firms.

Channel decisions refer to the managerial decision on the selection of he most suitable route for distribution of goods from the producers to the users. Following are the important reasons which place channel decision in policy decision areas:

(a) If the choice of channels is proper, fluctuations in production may be reduced. The manufacturer can obtain date regarding sales and stock of the middlemen and exercise control wherever he feels necessary. The stability of production will help to ensure steady employment and proper budgetary control.

(b) The channels chosen involve the firm in relatively long-term commitments to other firms or middlemen. The relations between the manufacturer and the middlemen depend mainly on the choice of appropriate channels of distribution. Therefore, it is necessary that channel decisions are taken with great care.

(c) The channels selected for the firm's product affect every other marketing decision like pricing, promotion, physical distribution and the cost involved in the use of trade channels enter the price of the product that the ultimate consumer has to pay. If the costs of trade channels are very high the firm may draw public criticism.

The choice of the appropriate channels of distribution is not a simple job. While taking a decision in this regard, management should carefully consider the following factors:

(1) Market Considerations. The nature of the market is a key factors influencing the choice of channels of distribution. The following features of the market should be analysed to determine the channels:

(a) Consumer or industrial market.

(b) Number of potential customers.

(c) Size of order.

(d) Customer buying habits and expectations.

(e) Geographical concentration of market.

(2) Product Consideration. The type and naure of the product influences the number and type of middlmen to be chosen for distributing the product. The important factors with regard to the product are as follows:

(i) Product line.

(ii) Standardised product.

(iii) Unit value.

(iv) Persihability.

(v) Bulk and weight.

(vi) Technical nature.

(3) Company Considerations. The nature and size of the business firm have an important impact on the selection of channels of distribution. Following factors are important in this regard:

(i) Services provided by sellers

(ii) Experience and competence of management.

(iii) Financial resources.

(iv) Volume of production.

(v) Desire for control of channels.

A manufacturer who wants to control the distribution of his product will select a short channel of distribution. He may do so even though the distribution cost is higher if he feels that he can give his product more aggressive promotion.

(4) Middlemen Considerations. Certain factors related to the middlemen which influence the channel selection are as follows:

(i) Competition and legal constraints.

(ii) Cost.

(iii) Sale potential.

(iv) Attitude of middlemen.

(v) Financial ability.

(vi) Availability of desired middlemen.

PRODUCTION POLICY

Production functions involve the transformation of a set of inputs to predetermined outputs in accordance with objectives of the organisation. Production management encompasses the design, implementation, operation and control of system made up of workers, materials, capital equipment, information and money to accomplish some set of objectives. Following are the major production/operations policy decisions with their determinants:

1. **Process Planning and Job Design.** Forecast of demand, product engineering, product technology, labour force, design stability.
2. **Raw Material and Work-in-progress Inventory.** Forecast of demand, cash flow, supplier reliability.
3. **Facilities Layout.** Medium and long-term forecast of demand and stability of product line. Production technology physical facilities constraints, safety considerations.
4. **Planning of Aggregate Output.** Short-range forecast of demand finished goods inventory level, cash flow, employment policy, plant capacity, state of production/operation system at the time of decision.
5. **Plant Location and Capacity.** Long-range forecast of the size and location of the market, capital structure, environmental conditions, state of operations and logistic system production technology.

The basic objective of policy decision in the area of production operations is the effective utilisation of organisational resources.

Alongwith the policy decisions on production activity policies need to be formulated also on production processes. Following are different aspects of the choice *viz.*,

(A) Division of Labour. The volume of production and the extent of standardisation of products determine whether and how far line operations could be sub-divided and entrusted to different operatives. Division of labour has been the characteristic features of large-scale manufacturing works since the industrial revolution. Routinisation of operations is known to produce monotony, boredom, lack of motivation and low morale due to 'anomie' (aloneness among many). Job enlargement is recognised now as a superior means of securing higher productivity and efficiency.

(B) Choice of Technology. The technology to be used is uniquely given in the case of certain industries (products). Airlines may use aircrafts of different types to service particular regions. On the choice of technology depends the divisions regarding equipment, personnel, methods of operation and organisation. In the service organisations, too, the process to be used may require a choice to be made out of different alternatives.

(C) Policy on Mechanisation and Automation. Technological advances over the last half a century have enlarged the scope of mechanisation and automation in many industries, *e.g.*, the use of tractor and harvesters in agriculture, automatic spinning and weaving in textile mills, packing and packaging of products, loading and unloading of cargo, automatic signalling in the railways, assembly line operations, etc.

(D) Size and Location of Production Units. For large enterprise, the decision with respect to the size of plant needs to be examined with two alternatives in view, *viz.*,

(i) Large size with centralised location, and

(ii) Dispersal of operating units with small size of plan capacity.

Most consumer goods as well as industrial goods are procured or produced in anticipation of demand. Sales are made out of stocks carried. On the other hand, in some industries, procurement and production take place on the basis of order booked. Manufacture of heavy mechinary, quality furniture, aircrafts, ships and trawlers, indeed all products to be supplied according to customer specifications fall in this category. However, even in these cases, it may be possible to carry standard parts and components in stock, and only the final assembly operations may be done on the basis of orders received. It is sure that holding inventories in anticipation of customer demand involve certain risks, *e.g.*, the risk of obsolesence, demange and deterioration; it also involves locking up of capital, and incurring storage costs. Procuring inventories in accordance with sales orders may reduce the risks and costs involved. However, procurement of inventories for stock may enable managment to take advantage of the economy of large-scale operations, quantity discounts, and prompt delivery, as well as to avail of the vendor's services. Contrarily, purchasing small lots corresponding to orders booked may result in slow delivery and higher costs.

Thus, the coordination of purchasing and production with sales is essentially related to the timing of procurement. It is not a question of either buying in anticipation or oders or wating until orders are in hand. Rather it is a question of the extent to which procurement for stock should be combined with procurement 'to order'. The policy on this issue depends on the following considerations:

(a) **Minimum Inventory of Raw Materials and Finished Goods that is to be Carried.** This should be adequate to meet unforeseen contingencies like delay in getting supply from the vendor, or the actual use being more than the anticipated requirement, or any possible delay in production operations. The level of finished goods inventory at which replenishment should be ordered, *i.e.*, the re-ordering point, must take care of the sales during the lead time (or period required for replacement). In the case of raw materials, orders should be placed for replenishment of stock at that point where the level of inventory is adequate to meet the production requirements during the period which the vendor may take to execute the order.

(b) Recorder Quantity. The size of the purchase order for replenishment of stocks is primarily dependent on the economical production runs which can be estimated in terms of the number of days or weeks or months' requirement. On the other hand, there are cost implications of buying large lots and small lots. With large order size the number of purchase orders is likely to be fewer and hence clerical expenses (ordering costs) may be lower; freight charges and handling costs are also likely to be less; further, quantity discount may reduce the cost of purchase. But large order size also involves corresponding large investment in working capital and interest obligations, as also higher carrying costs (cost of storage space, insurance, damage and deterioration, if not obsolescence). Ordering small quantities will imply a larger number of orders. Hence higher ordering costs (clerical expenses), but reduced capital investment and interest, freight charges and handling costs, as well as lower carrying costs. The concept of 'economic lot size' or 'economic order quantity' may be used to resolve the question or order size. The most economical lot size or reorder quantity should be that which minimises the average cost taking into account the aggregate of carrying costs and ordering costs. With different order sizes, the ordering costs will tend to decline and carrying costs go up as the order size is increased. The aggregate cost would be minimum when the two types of costs are going up and the other coming down) are equal. Thus, the most economical order size is given by the equation.

$$Q = \sqrt{\frac{2AS}{i}}$$

Where a company decides to make or produce rather than buy material/components, the total cost of inventory can be minimised by modifying the EOQ (Economic Order Quantity) formula to take into account the fact that only a part of the production goes into inventory while the remaining part is used concurrently in the production process or sold. It is assumed that the production rate may be equal to a greater extent than the consumption or demand rate. The 'Economic Run Length' (ERL) which is a modified form of EOQ is thus calculated wherein the 'ordering cost' is replaced by 'product set-up cost'. The set up cost is the fixed cost representing one-time cost of machine adjustment, work scheduling, etc. ERL is calculated by using the formula:

$$\text{ERL} = \sqrt{\frac{2cs}{I\left(1-\frac{d}{p}\right)}}$$

c where, c is the annual consumption in units

s is the set-up cost (Rs. per set-up)

I is the carrying cost per unit

d is the consumption/demand rate in units per day

p is the production rate in units per day.

(c) Fluctuations in Sales. Purchase and production in the face of seasonal and cyclical fluctuation in the volume of sales may lead to over-stocking or under-stocking of inventory at different times.

The problem can be overcome by *(i)* adjusting purchases and production in harmony with sales volume, *(ii)* maintaining a level rate of production, purchasing and producing for stock during the slack period and using the same to meet peak demand, or *(iii)* sub-contracting instead of expanding production during periods of peak demand, or *(iv)* levelling out the impact of periodic fluctuations in demand.

The first option, that is, adjusting purchase and production in accordance with the sales volume, is found useful in the case of products which are subject to periodic changes in customer tastes and fashions, *e.g.*, ready-made garments, ladies handbags, footwear, etc. In these cases, it may be advisable not to carry inventories in excess of the sales needs. But it implies higher costs on account of ideal facilities and plant capacity, loss of skilled personnel, and discontinuity of operations. Level production (the second option) involves production in excess of demand during slack periods and building up inventory to be available for sale during peak demand. The policy may help the company to retain skilled personnel and enable full use of the production facilities, plant and equipment throughout the year. But it involves additional financial and storage costs to be incurred during the slack season, along with the risks of obsolescene and deterioration. In industries subject to rapid technological changes, level production may lead to a competitive disadvantage for the company. Moreover, it may not be easy to predict the extent of fluctuations in demand. The third option of subcontracting may not permit procurement of adequate quantities during the busy season and hence lead to loss of customers. The fourth option (levelling out the impact of fluctuating demand) may be acted upon in different ways, *e.g.*, adding new products that have complementary seasonal fluctuations. Allowing off-season discounts on sale, or by changing the time of introducing new models as was done by automobile manufactures in the United States.

(d) Fluctuation in Prices. Should the reorder quantity be adjusted in anticipation of price changes? One normally expects that order quantity should be currently increased if prices are likely to rise, and correspondingly it should be reduced if prices are expected to fall. In other words. stocks should be built up in anticipation of a price rise, and cut down in anticipation of a decline in prices. But there are two problems to be taken care of. One is that of forecasting price changes. The other relates to the availability of supply. With anticipatory rise of prices and brisk business conditions procurement is likely to take longer time in view of higher demand. It may be easier to redcue order quantities in anticipation of fall of prices. Besides speculative buying, *i.e.*, building up stocks in anticipation of a price rise is risky, particularly on account of the difficulty of accurately forecasting price trends. The policy of adjusting the size of purchase orders and timing thereof should therefore be governed by two considerations: *(a)* predictability of price changes, and *(b)* estimation in advance of volume of demand of particular items of inventory.

Just-in-time (JIT) Inventory System

Just-in-time inventory system is a cost saving mechanism relevant to organisations where materials are purchased and finished goods delivered without any waiting time. It involves materials being procured more frequently and in small lots 'just-in-time' to be used, and finished produce being turned out 'just-in-time' to be sold. Thus, if a situation prevails where goods are produced at the time when needed and in the quantity that is needed, the inventories of work in process and finished goods would be almost nil. Likewise if supplies of raw materials can be obtained just at the time and in the quantities required, there will be virtually zero inventory. Actually JIT system does not require storage of materials as the materials procured lie on the shop in between the consecutive manufacturing operations.

The concept of JIT inventory was originally introduced in Toyata Motor Company, Japan, and later adopted by many American companies producing automotive and electronics goods. The system may result in considerable savings in cost. But its application to be fruitful need two pre-conditions to be satisfied: *(1)* There has to be close rapport between workers and management as well as between suppliers and the company; *(2)* There has to be strict self-discipline.

NATURE OF PERSONNEL POLICY

Personnel management is primarily concerned with human resources with the organisation. Therefore, policy issues in the areas of personnel management should be concerned with *(a)* manpower planning, recruitment, selection and placement *(b)* training and developments of manpower *(c)* transfer, promotion, demotion, and separation; *(d)* working conditions and employee service; *(e)* communication, consultation and negotiation; *(f)* human and social implications of change in the internal organisation and methods of working of economic and social change in the community at large. The basic objectives of personnel policies is to ensure adequate and effective manpower at the right to implement the strategy. Besides the organisation has to forumulate policies in other areas which can support the implementation of basic strategy through the performance of main functions. Such areas may be research and development, legal, and public relations. *(g)* terms of employment, methods and standard of remuneration.

The signficance of personnel policy in strategy implementation hardly needs any elaboration. Both physical and human resources are crucial to the achievement of strategic goals. The basic objective of personnel policy in an organisation is to ensure consistency of action and equity in its relations with employees. These policies constitute the basis for sound personnel practices. They provide the yardstisk by which implementation of strategic plans and programmes can be appraised. Besides, personnel policies are an integral part of the whole policy structure of an enterprise. Any weakness in personnel policy may thus weaken the other functional policies.

The close interrelation between the quality of personnel and strategic managment requires the top executives to be concerned with the following policy issues.

Recruitment Policy. The appropriate match between strategic goals to be achieved and the kind of people employed require two different but related aspects of staffing to be examined.

On the one hand, there is the necessity of recruiting and maintaining the required number of work people and on the other it is retired, experienced persons available for employment and others employed in other organisation but seeking a change for better prospects. External recruitment obviously provides a wider choice from among personnel to select those with skill, training, education and experience required by the firm. For a firm which needs personnel for implementing growth strategy, the process of recruitment from external sources must be planned well in advance. The problems of external recruitment consists of the relatively higher turnover of new recruits and the demoralising effect of outside recruitment on the existing work organisation.

Sources of Recruitment

A. Internal Sources

Internal sources refer to the employees currently working in an enterprise. As and when a post falls vacant, someone already working in the enterprise is transferred or promoted to it.

While a promotion or transfer does not result in any increase or decrease in the number and kinds of persons working in the enterprise, it may leave a significant effect on this working of the departments effected by it.

B. External Sources

(i) Advertisements, Personnel Consultants, and Jobbers and Contractors.

(ii) Employement Exchange and Educational Institutions.

(iii) Field Trips, Miscellaneous.

CHARACTERSTICS OF A GOOD TRAINING AND DVELOPMENT POLICY

A good training policy must be based on the following principles:

(1) ***Relevance to Job Requirements.*** To be effective, a training programme must be related to the requirements of the job for which it is intended. For this, a thorough analysis of each job is essential.

(2) ***Allowance for Individual Difference.*** A good training programme should take into account the difference in ability, learning capacity, interests and temperamental and emotional make-up of trainees.

(3) ***Management Support.*** Top managers should actively support all training programmes. It is the nature of subordinates to look to their superiors for an indication on

what to support and what to ignore. It is futile to expect subordinates to be serious about their training of their bosses themselves because they are indifferent about it.

(4) ***Suitable Incentives.*** There should be provision for suitable monetary and non-monetary incentives to motivate trainee, so that they take training seriously.

(5) ***Determination of Training Needs.*** Training needs of employees should be determined carefully and the methods chosen for the purpose should be effective.

(6) ***Compensation and Supplementary Benefits.*** Policies with regard to wage and salary administration and policy on supplementary benefits are vital components of personnel policy because it is mainly on the basis of satisfactory compensation schemes that company is able to attract and retain capable personnel. In the absence of sound policy with respect to the compensation structure, wages and salaries are likely to be based on personalised arbitrary decisions and thus fall short of the essential elements of adequacy and equity in compensation plans. A satisfactory policy frame is invariably conducive to high morale and minimum frictions among individuals and groups of employees. For apart from the adequacy of the level of compensation, inequities in the pay structure happen to be the most common causes of dissatisfaction and grievances among employees.

The basic issues to be resolved while formulating the compensation policy are those relating to:

(a) Incentive pay

(b) Recognition or relative efficiency of performance;

(c) The internal structure of compensation or internal alignment of pay for different job so as to ensure that pay rates are equitable;

(d) The level of pay and its adequacy.

PROMOTION POLICY

Promotion refers to the advancement of an employee to a higher job involving greater responsibility, more pay and better status. It is the movement of an employee to a position of better remuneration, higher status and greater responsibility. A mere increase in pay or working conditions without an increase in status and responsibility is called upgrading or dry promotion. Demotion is the opposite of promotion.

The policy of filling vacancies at higher levels through promotion of lower level employees has several advantages: *(a)* Employees have an opportunity for improving their status and earnings. Promotion, therefore, improves he motivation and morale of employees. *(b)* It creates sense of royalty among employees. By satisfying the basic urge for advancement, it reduces industrial disputes, labour turnover and absenteeism *(c)* It improves the quality of performance. Reduction in waste and indiscipline results in lower costs. "The company that has no recognised promotion policy likely to have frustrated and restless employees as they have no opportunity for advancement."

However, all higher level vacancies need not necessarily be filled through promotion. Sometimes, lower level staff may be fit for promotion. Moreover, recruitment from outside brings new blood and independent thinking. The basic aim should be to obtain the best possible personnel irrespective of wherefrom they come.

BASIS OF PROMOTION—MERIT *VS.* SENIORITY

There are two bases of promotion, *i.e.*, seniority and merit. Employees generally favour merit, while employees and their unions prefer seniority as the basis of promotion.

Seniority means length of recognised service. It is counted from the date of joining the organisation or from the date of confirmation. Seniority can be calculated in several ways. It is lost due to certain events. *e.g.*, frequent absence from duty.

Seniority is the oldest and most widely used basis of promotion. Promotion on the basis of seniority is justified on following grounds:

(a) It is an objective basis. It prevents favouritism and arbitrary action as there is no room for discretion or prejudices.

(b) It is very simple and practicable as seniority can be measured easily and accurately.

(c) It reduces labour turnover as employees try to remain in the firm to accumulate seniority,

(d) Every employee has a definite idea at all times of his place in the group. He feels secured and develops a sense of loyalty to the organisation. Promotion based on seniority is reward for loyalty.

(e) Length of service is an approximate measure of experience and ability.

(f) Seniority is acceptable to trade unions and gives a feeling of satisfaction to employees.

If a man has been in service for a long time he ought to be better than a newcomer, unless he has been dodging work. Seniority also fits with the cultural expectations for social customs of India.

Seniority as the sole basis of promotion has, however, the following demerits:

(a) Rules for the accumulation of seniority have to be laid down with particular reference to the impact of suspension, lay-off, strike, discharge, etc.

(b) Rigid adherence to seniority makes it difficult to recruit and retain capable personnel.

(c) Employees with longer service are not necessarily more competent. Seniority overvalues experience and premium on merit.

(d) The quality and quanity of work suffers as employees try to stick around and do not make full use of their capabilities.

(e) It lowers the morale of ambitious and meritiorius employees as they get no recognition. When less competent lose interest in efficiency.

(f) Seniority provides performance and inefficiency, as no differentiation is made beween efficient and inefficient employees.

Advantages refer to the efficiency and ability of an employee. Promotion on the basis of merit has following advantages: *(a)* It provides a powerful incentive to work hard and make continuous improvement in efficiency *(b)* There is an overall improvement in operations and the profit of the enterprise. *(c)* Ambitious and hard working employees are duty rewarded. They feel satisfied and contributed maximum to the success of the organisation.

Merit has been criticised due to following limitations: *(a)* Employees feel insecure and become discontented. *(b)* The morale of employees is low when they find that their juniors are promoted before them it causes frustration and loss of interest and loyalty for the organisation. Moreover, merit does not indicate an employee's promotability. An individual may be quite competent for the present job, but his overall personality may not be suitable for higher positions.

Thus, neither absolute seniority nor exclusive merit is a sound basis of promotion. A sound promotion policy should be based on a judicious balance between the two in practice, seniority is given more weightage but merit should also be given due consideration. None of two should be exclusive criterion for promotion. Seniroity can be the deciding factors when two persons are equally meritiorious. Similarly, out the two equally senior employees the more competent one should be promoted first. If senior-most employee is incompetent to do the job well junior employees with merit should be promoted.

Essentials of a Sound Promotion Policy

A sound systematic promotion policy should consist of the following:

(1) The report of each employee should be prepared by his superior but subject to the approval of the departmental head.

(2) The policy management regarding filling of vacancies through promotion or from outside should be clearly stated.

(3) Accurate and uptodate records of seniority and merit should be kept. All employees should be kept informed of their record and opening for promotion.

(4) Promotion policy should be based on job analysis to define job requirement. Employees should know clearly what is expected of them in higher jobs, so that they can prepare themselves for advancement.

(5) Objective and systematic plans of performance appraisal should be set up to identify promotable employees. This is necessary to avoid unfairness in promotions.

(6) Lines of promotion should be clearly defined. For each job a schedule of jobs to which promotion can be made should be prepared.

(7) The basis of promotion should be clearly defined. The relative weight to be given to merit and seniority should be specified.

Industrial Relations Policy

The personnel policies and practices of a firm in many ways are influenced by the state of union-management relations. To what extent the basic philosophy of top management *vis-a-vis* their human resources is subordinated to the bargaining power of employee union depends upon the company's policy with regard to the nature of relation with the union, recognition the support of the union organisatin, the scope of collective bargaining and settlement of industrial disputes. Ideally, harmonous relation between management and employee union should develop on the basis of mutual co-operation. But company executive are often inclined to adopt a policy of belligerency toward union activities. This approach is born out of strong dislike and mistrust of the union by the executives, who refuse to recognise the union as a bargaining agent of when forced to negotiate, do it grudgingly with a house-trading approach. With a hostile attitude to management toward the union, the relationship is inevitably vitiated by mutual suspicion, and there is increasing militancy on the part of the union leaders.

CHARACTERISTICS OF A GOOD TRANSFER POLICY

To be effective, the transfer policy should possess the following characteristics:

(1) If a transfer is going to result in any change in the rate of remuneration this should be made sufficiently clear.

(2) How a transfer is going to affect the seniority of the person concerned should be spelt out in clear terms.

(3) It is quite likely that requests for transfer to the same job, or to the same shift, are received from many employees. In such cases, a decision should be taken in keeping with the predetermined policy.

(4) The deparments or units within which transfers have to be made should be decided in advance.

(5) If transfers become necessary because there is surplus of labour force in one department of unit and shortage in another it should be ensured that workers in their new positions are not given completely new kinds of jobs.

(6) There should be accurate and complete job description of the jobs to which transfers are under consideration. Requirements as to training of the new jobs should be clearly laid down. Also, the workers to be transferred should be clarly informed about the time during which they are supposed to adjust themselves to the requirements of their new jobs.

(7) Responsibility for recommending and approving transfer should be clearly defined.

FEATURES OF A GOOD PERSONNEL POLICY

Every enterprise should relate its personnel policy to the economic legal, social and technological factors present in the society in which it operates. This means it has to keep on adjusting and adpating personnel policy to suit and change in these factors.

A good personnel policy should possess the following features:

(1) **Proper Communication.** It should enjoy acceptability among the people for whom it has been formulated.

(2) **Acceptability.** It should enjoy acceptability among the people for whom it has been formulated.

(3) **Integrative.** It must fully take into account the differing amenities, capabilities, interests, desires, aspirations, beliefs and temperamental make-up of the people for whom it is intended.

(4) **Uniformity.** It should be uniformly applicable to all members and units of the enterprise.

(5) **Stability.** Even though personnel policy has to be consistently adjusted and adapted to suit any changes in economic, legal, and technology factors, it should be reasonably stable and permanent.

(6) **Flexibility.** It should not be so rigid and inflexible that it can not be adjusted and adapted to changes in economic, legal, social and technological factors.

(7) **Responsiveness to Prevailing Trends.** Personnel policy should be adjusted to the prevailing norms and trends in ways. For example, if the current thinking is in favour of involving the management process, the policy should be against.

(8) **Precision and Certainty.** It should be clear to the point and complete in every respect. It should not lead to varying and conflicting inerpretations.

(9) **Promotion of Enterprise Policies.** It should fit into the basis of overall policies of the enterprise.

(10) **Protection of the Interests of All Parties.** It should take into account the interests of all parties associated with the enterprise, *i.e.*, workers enrepreneurs, consumers, government and the community.

NEED FOR FUNCTIONAL POLICIES

For effective implementation, strategists have to provide direction to functional managers regarding the plans and policies to be adopted. In fact, the effectiveness of strategic management depends critically on the manner in which strategies are implemented. In this section, we see the nature of functional plans and policies, why they are needed, and how they are developed.

In terms of the levels of strategy formulation functional strategies operate below the SBU or business-level strategies. Within functional strategies there might be several sub-functional areas. Thus, a company might have a textile division among its several SBU or business areas. Within the textile division, there might be functional areas such as marketing, production, research and development, etc. Further, the functional area of marketing may have sub-functions such as product development, advertising and sales promotion, marketing research, etc.

Functional strategies, or more appropriately, functional plans and policies as they actually are plans or tactics to implement businesss strategies—are made within the guidelines set at higher levels. Plans are made to select a course of action while policies are required to act as guidelines to action. Functional plans and policies, therefore are operational plans and tactics to make a strategy work.

Functional managers need guidance from the business strategy in order to make decisions. Operational plans tell the functional managers what has to be done while policies state how the plans are to be implemented.

Glueck suggests five reasons why functional plans and policies are needed. Functional plans and policies are developed to ensure that:

1. There is a basis available for controlling activities in the different functional areas of business:
2. Similar situations occurring in different functional areas are handled in a consistent manner by the functional managers;

3. The time spent by functional managers in decision-making is reduced as plans lay down clearly what is to be done and policies provide the discretionary framework within which decisions need to be taken; and
4. Coordination acorss the different functions take place where necessary.

Development of Functional Policies

The development of functional plans is aimed at making the strategies—formulated at the top management level practically feasible at the functional level. Strategies need to be segregated into viable functional plans and policies that are compatible with each other in this way, strategies can be implemented by the functional managers.

The process of development of functional policies may range from the formal to informal. Larger and more complex organisations may be several hundred policies related to every major aspect. Many of these policies could have been formulated through the formal process and laid down in company manuals and documents. Smaller organisations with simpler businesses may operate with a few policies most of which could be informal and understood rather than written down.

The process of development of functional policies—whether formal or informal—is similar to that for strategy formulation. Environmental factors relevant to each functional area have an impact of the choice of plans and policies. Organisation plans and policies affect the choice of functional plans and policies. Finally, the actual process of choice is influenced by objective as well as subjective factors. Functional plans and policies affect, and are affected by the resource allocation decisions.

PREPARING A PRODUCT STRATEGIES

One of the most important areas is new products or services since these, more than any other single factor, will determine what a company or other enterprise is or will be. The key questions in this area may be summarized as follows:

1. What do Our Customers Want? An effective strategy must be based on knowning what customers want. Do they want price, value, quality, availability, service? The success of the Hughes Tool Company, for example, has been based largely on making a shrewd analysis of what oil-and gas-well drillers wanted and furnishing them the exact drill but they wanted, of a high quality, in the place the bit was needed, and with adequate service to support the product. Likewise, International Business Machines (IBM) leadership in business computers has in large part been due to knowing what its customers wanted and needed, supplying it, maintaining advancement of product design, having a family of computers, and running a strong service organisation.

2. What is Our Business? This classic question might also be phrased in terms of what is not our business. It is also well to ask. What is our industry? Are we a single product-line industry, such as shoes or furniture? Or are we a process industry, such as chemicals or electronic components? Or are we an end-use indutry, such as transportation or retailing?

3. Who are Our Customers? To furher identify what kinds of business we are in and to give meaning to a product or service strategy, this is an especially key question. Peter Drucker has long said that the purpose of a business is to "create a customer," although he could hardly have meant to create customers without regard to profits. In answering this question, it is important to avoid too great an attachment to present customers and products.

4. What is Existing and Potential Competition? In deciding on a product strategy, it is important to assess realistically the nature and strength of existing competition. If a competitor in a field has tremendous strength in new products, marketing, and service, as IBM has had in the computer field, a company should carefully consider whether it has a change to enter the field effectively.

5. How far can we go in Serving Customer Needs? Product strategy formulation must consider this question. There are ofen important limitations. One is, of course, financial, and company must consider whether it has the financial resources to support necessary product research, manufacturing facilities, inventory and receivables, advertising and marketing, and a requisite service competence.

Legal limitations may also be important, as Procter and Gamble found when it was forced by the antirust laws to divest itself of its acquisition of the Clorox Company (makers of household bleach).

6. What Profit Margins can we Expect? A company naturally wants to be in a business where it can make an attractive profit. One of the keys is the gross profit margin, that profit above operating expenses which will carry overhead and administrative expenses and yield a desired profit before taxes.

7. What Basic form should Our Strategy Take? In formulating a product or service strategy, a company should determine the direction it wishes to go in terms of intensive or extensive product diversification. If it follows an intensive strategy, it might move in the direction of market penetration—going further in present product markets. Or it might decide on one of market development—going into markets it has not been in.

H. What Advantages do we have in Serving Customer Needs? This is a difficult and important question. Most companies like to have a product or service that competitors cannot very easily duplicate. Some larger companies look only for products that require a high capital investment in tooling and machinery, heavy advertising, strong engineering, expensive service organisations, and similar characteristics that tend to discourage the entry of smaller competitors into a market.

9. Do we Wish to Develop Our Own New Product? Here again, a company must address itself to the question of whether it is better for it to develop its own new products, whether it should rely on innovation by competitors to show the way, or whether it should lean heavily on product development by materials suppliers.

10. Do we Wish to be a Product Leader? This may seem to be a question with an obvious answer. Bu it is not, developing and marketing their products, some companies owe their success to being a close second in product leadership. The product leader will often have an advantage in reaching a market firm, but such a company may incur heavy costs of developing and attemtping to market products which do not become commercial successes as well as those which do. One of the major airlines, for exmple, prided itself for years on being the leader in acquiring and putting into service new aircraft. But after undergoing extensive "debugging" of several new planes, and suffering financial losses as a result, the company adopted the strategy of letting someone else be the leader and of becoming a close second.

11. How Much will not Customers Buy at What Price? This is a matter of what customers think they are buying; what they consider value, and what they will pay for it will determine what a business is, what it should produce, and whether it will prosper. Being able to answer this kind of question, particularly after identifying a business and who its customers really are, will be a major key to a product or service strategy.

THE FACTORS CONSIDERED IN FORMULATING MARKETING STRATEGY

Marketing as a body of resources allocated to the process of sale and distribution of product or services is not an end in itself. On the other hand, it is a means to an end, *i.e.*, obtaining the objectives of the firm. To contribute substantially to the firm's objectives, it is very necessary for marketing executives to chalk out their markeing programme and marketing policies well in advance. But the field of marketing is very sensitive and responsive to the environment. If a market fails to understand the realities of the particular environment he will make poor—perhaps disastrous—decisions and performance. Departure from convention, experimentation and innovation are frequently essential to business success, and even survival. Likewise, grasp of his marketing environment must underlie that marketer's decisions. Hence, adjustment in marketing programme and policies from time to time is a must. A firm can react to market environment in two ways: by adopting a natural policy of showing indifference to the changes or by adjusting its own marketing policy to the changed circumstances. An efficient manager who is desrious of success in future will always prefer the latter alternative. Hence, the need for marketing strategy arises in this context.

In the words of Philip Kotler. "Marketing strategy is the technique which a firm adopts to contract market changes. Thus, marketing strategy is a changing variable which changes according to market environment. It is the heart core of a marketing plan. Marketing strategy is a functional strategy and a part of grand corporate strategy. It is a consistent appropriate and feasible set of principles through which a particular company hopes to achieve its long-term marketing objective and profitability". In other words, markting strategy is a comprehensive plan of action design to meet the needs of the certain enterprise operating in a particular environment. It is based on overall corporate marekting objectives and is implemented by a co-ordinate marketing programme through the firm's marketing-mix the ideal marketing strategy would achieve optimum utilisation of all resources of the firm.

Factors

1. Synergistic Potential of Marketing Inputs. Some marketing inputs have mutually reinforcing power and this fact should be taken into account while working out an optimum overall marketing strategy. For example, advertising and displays repeat the advertising message at the time when the consumer is an outlet where the product is on sale.

2. Input Elasticity. Different marketing inputs vary in their effects on demand which should be considered in selecting the bet combination of marketing inputs. For example, a marketer may have to make several pricing decisions for a single product and his choice of the best combination depends partly on his analysis of price elasticity and demand. This will be possibly only through repeated tests and exercises.

3. Productivity of Marketing Inputs. The marketing executives should also recognise that all marketing inputs have equal productivity at various levels of use before they begin to have noticeable effects. So marketer should have an optimum combination of marketing inputs.

4. Substitutability of Marketing Inputs. Various marketing inputs can be mutually substituted by one another. This attribute brings flexibility and utility in marketing strategy. Hence, this factor should also be taken into account while considering marketing strategy.

5. Competitor's Counter Moves. The company has to estimate and forecast the competitor's counter moves with different marketing inputs and has to assess the relative effectiveness of those counter-moves. Price reduction, attractive gift schemes, improvement in packing may be an example of such countermoves. According to Coundiff and Still, "A marketer desiring to improve the 'hitting power' of his marketing strategy should give first consideration to those moves involving inputs that are least subject to effective retaliatory actions of competitors."

FINANCIAL MANAGEMENT

Financial management is concerned with managerial activities related to procurement and utilisation of funds for business purposes. It deals with planning, organisation, directing and controlling financial activities of the enterprise. Financial activities should not be merely restricted to raising of capital, but also to other aspects of financing like assessing the needs for capital, raising sufficient funds, cost of financing, budgeting, maintaining liquidity, lending and borrowing policies and distribution of profits.

In order to ensure the continuous availability of sufficient finance, financial management assesses the needs of the business in advance and then sets itself into motion to procure funds. Procurement of funds is a complex problem as choice of sources of finance is based on complex factors like risk, period, control and cost. Various sources of finance like shares, debentures, banks and other financial institutions, public deposits, etc., have to be compared in the light of these factors. After the funds have been procured, their effective utilisation is another major task of financial management. Funds should not be allowed to remain idle as they involve many costs. Funds should be put into those channels which generate an income higher than the costs of procuring them.

Since financing is one of the functional areas of any business enterprise, the objectives of financial management should be in tune with the overall objectives of the enterprise. The main objectives of a business enterprise is to earn sufficient profits so that a reasonable rate of return is paid on the capital employed and a part of the profit is ploughed back into the business to make it a stronger enterprise so that it may bear all the ups and downs in the business. The finance department can play an important role for the realisation of this objective. The objective of the finance department should be so devised that they contribute directly towards the achievement of the overall organisational objectives. Following is the list of the objectives of financial management of big enterprises:

(i) Ensuring better utilisation of capital by following the principles of liquidity, profitability and safety;

(ii) Ensuring regular and sufficient supply of capital to the business;

(iii) Co-ordinating the activities of the finance department with those of the other departments of the enterprise;

(iv) Ensuring a fair rate of return to the suppliers of capital.

Maximisation of profits is generally regarded as the objective of a business undertaking. Should this objective be followed in financial decision making? Modern authors on financial management have criticised the goal of profit maximisation and have advocated 'wealth maximisation' as the goal of financial decision making. Any financial action which creates wealth or which has a net worth above zero is a desirable one and should be undertaken. The rationale is using wealth maximisation concept as an operating financial management goal is that it reflects the most efficient use of society's economic resources and thus leads to maximisation of society's economic wealth.

The objections raised against profit maximisation as an objective of financial management are listed below:

(a) It does not consider the risk or uncertainty or prospective earnings stream. The prospective earnings stream would be more uncertain if the investment projects undertaken are more risky as compared to others.

(b) It does not specify the timing of expected returns. Few shareholders may like to invest in a project that promises its first return after 25 years or so. For most of the shareholders, the size of the total returns is not as important as the time patterns of returns.

(c) It does not take into consideration the interest of workers, consumers, government and other segments of the society. Thus, it is too narrowly centred. In practice, the goal of a business enterprise cannot be to maximise profits but to attain a certain level of profit, holding a certain share of the market or a certain volume of sales. The concept of social responsibility has also gained wide acceptance by the business houses these days.

(d) It does not allow for the effect of dividend policy on the market price of the share. The goal of profit maximisation prevents management to pay dividends so as to maximise earnings. "To the extent payment of dividends can affect the market price of the stock (or share), the maximisation of earnings per share will not be a satisfactory objective by itself", said Ezra Solomon. It should also be noted that the objectives of maximising earnings per share may not be the same as maximising market price per share.

The above mentioned reasons show that the objective of 'profit maximisation' or maximisation of earning per share' does not take care of the investment, financing and dividend decisions of the business. Ezra Solomon has made a good case for the adoption of the objective of "wealth maximisation." He has pleaded for a distinction between profit and profitability. Maximisation of profits in the sense of maximising shareholders' wealth is clearly an unreal objective. But profitability maximisation in the sense of using resources to yield economic values higher than the joint values of inputs required is a useful objective and it involves a 'different set of considerations. "In fact, achievement of wealth maximisation also maximises the achievement of the other objectives. To conclude, therefore, maximisation of wealth is the operating objective by which financial decisions should be guided."

SCOPE OF FINANCIAL MANAGEMENT

In order to realise the objective of financial management, the finance manager of a business enterprise has to manage various aspects of finance function which determine the scope of his duties. These aspects are explained below:

(a) Determining the Structure of Capital. By capital structure we mean the kind and proportion of different securities for raising finance for the business. Once the requirement of capital funds has been determined, a decision regarding the kind and proportion of various sources of capital has to be taken. For this, financial manager has to determine the proper mix of equity and debt and short-term and long-term debt ratio. These decisions have to be taken in the light of costs of raising finance from different sources, period for which funds are required and several other factors.

(b) Estimating the Requirements of Capital. The requirements of capital must be carefully estimated. A business requires funds both for long-term and for short-term. Estimating the requirements of funds involves the use of techniques of long-range planning. The financial management must also prepare budget of various activities to estimate the financial requirements of the business. If proper thought is not given to the financial requirements of the business, there will be either deficiency or surplus of funds. If the business has insufficiency of capital, it will not be able to meet its commitments in time. And if it has surplus funds, the management may become extravagant in spending.

(c) Investment decisions. The funds procured from various sources are to be prudently invested in various assets so as to optimise the return on investment. The investment of long-term funds requires a careful assessment of various alternatives through capital budgeting and opportunity cost analysis. A part of the long-term funds has to be invested in the working capital of the company.

(d) Choice of Sources of Finance. The management can raise finance from various sources like shareholders, debentureholders, banks and other financial institutions, public deposits, etc. The choice of the source or sources of finance should be done very carefully as they involve different costs and conditions. For instance, public deposits, though carry higher rates of interest than on debentures, do not involve any security of the assets of the company. A company may like this source if it does not want to create a change over its assets.

(e) Disposal of Surplus. The management has to decide how much to retain for ploughing back and how much to distribute as dividend to shareholders out of the surplus of the company. The factors which influence these decisions include the trend of earnings of the company, the trend of the market price of its shares, the requirements of funds for self-financing, the future prospects and so on.

(f) Management of Cash Flow. Cash is required to pay off creditors, purchase stock of materials, pay to labour and to meet day-to-day expenses. These should not be shortage of cash any time as it will damage credit-worthiness of the enterprise. It is also to be seen that there is no excess cash. Excess cash may be invested in near-cash assets which may be converted into cash quickly when needed.

Role of the Financial Management

Recent developments in business have placed the financial manager in a central position in the business enterprise. Financial manager is incharge of the management of the funds of the enterprise. He is concerned with the determination of requirements of funds, selecting and tapping various sources of funds and allocation of funds to particular assets—fixed and current.

Financial management is concerned with three types of decisions: *(i)* investment decisions—financial plan, capital budgeting, etc., *(ii)* financing decision—formulations of capital structure of financing mix; and *(iii)* dividend decision—dividend policy. Since most business activities involve the use of funds, financial management has come to occupy an important place in the modern business enterprises. Ezra Solomon has summed up the role of financial management in the following words: "Financial management is properly viewed as an integral part of overall management rather than as a staff specially concerned with fund raising operations. In this broader view, the central issue of financial policy is the wise use of funds and the central process involved is a rational matching of the advantage of potential uses against the cost of alternative potential sources so as to achieve the broad financial goals which an enterprise sets for itself."

FINANCIAL PLANNING

Financial planning is an important part of the overall planning of any business enterprise. This task is done by the promoters at the time of floating the business and by the financial manager and the top management after that. A considerable thought has to be given to evolve a financial plan for any business venture. If a business is started with inadequate capital, it may not be able to function smoothly because of its inability to meet its commitments in time. Thus, survival of the business may be in danger. If, on the other hand, it has more capital than is required, the earnings will have to be spread over an unnecessarily greater amount of capital and there may be a temptation of wasteful expenditure.

Financial planning involves three functions which are as follows:

(a) Determination of capital structure or form and proportion of different types of secuirities, namely, equity share, preference shares and debentures.

(b) Determination of amount of capital required. This depends upon many factors like promotional expenses, cost of fixed and current assets, cost of raising finance, and future needs.

(c) Laying down the financial policies in regard to cash control, borrowing and lending, and other areas of financial management.

FACTORS IN FINANCIAL PLANNING

At the time of formulating the financial plans, the following points should be given due consideration:

(a) **Present and Future Requirements.** A good financial planning system should be based on imagination and foresightedness. It should take care of not only the present requirements of the business but also the future requirements of the business. It should also make a provision for various contingencies which may arise in future.

(b) **Objectives.** The objectives of financial management should be consistent with the objectives of the enterprise. The main objectives of the financial department are raising of funds at the cheapest cost and utilisation of funds in the best possible manner.

(c) **Independence.** Financial planning should aim at sufficient return on investment so that the business enterprise may retain a part of earnings for ploughing back into the business every year. This will enable it to reduce dependence on outsiders which is necessary if the management does not want any interference by the outsiders with the internal working of the company.

(d) **Solvency and Liquidity.** The financial plans should be so devised that they do not jeopardise the survival of the enterprise. The enterprise should be solvent and liquid both in the short and long-run. The funds should be invested in those ventures which are likely to give sufficient return on investment. At the same time, it is also essential that adequate cash is always available with the business to purchase the current assets and meet the current expenses.

(e) **Flexibility.** Many times, business conditions change drastically and financial readjusments become essential. The financial plans must be easily adjustable to such changes. Thus, financial planning should be flexible to allow the diversion of funds into more profitable channels. It should also make provision for raising more funds at a short notice.

CHARACTERISTICS OF A SOUND FINANCIAL PLAN

Second financial planning is essential for the success of any business enterprise. It will provide policies and procedures to achieve closer coordination between the various functional areas of business. This will lead to minimisation of waste of resources. Management can follow an integrated approach to financial policies, procedures and programmes only if there is a sound financial plan. While preparing the plan of capitalisation in a company, the following factors should be given due consideration:

(a) **Flexibility.** Financial re-adjustments become necessary quite often. The financial plan must be easily adjustable to them. A rigid capital structure will limit the scope of initiative by the management. The company should be in a position to finance its expansion programmes without much difficulty. This can be achieved only when the financial plan is dynamic in nature.

(b) **Foresight.** Financial planning should be based on vision and foresightendness of the management. These should be systematic forecasting of various contingencies. It should be decided well in advance the level of liquidity to be maintained in the enterprise.

(c) **Simplicity.** A sound financial plan should provide simple financial structure which could be managed easily. It is not always necessary to include all type of securities in the capital structure.

(d) **Optimum Use of Funds.** It may prove very costly to keep idle funds. These should be optimum utilisation of available financial resources. If this is not done, the profitability will suffer. There should be a proper balance between the fixed capital and the working capital.

(e) **Liquidity.** The financial plan must provide sufficient financial liquidity. This will be possible only when there is adequate net working capital a major portion of which is represented usually by share capital, reserves and long-term loans. The degree of liquidity to be maintained is determined by the size of the company, its age, its credit standing, nature of its business, etc.

(f) Anticipation of Contingencies. The finance department should anticipate various contingencies which it may have to face. This may lead to keeping the same idle capital for meeting some unforeseen events. It will be much better if these contingencies are anticipated in advance.

Financial aspect of business activities deals primarily with raising, administering and distribution of funds by the organisation for the purpose of business operations. Thus financial policies have three major dimensions: *(i)* determination of the total amount of funds to be used by the organisation; *(ii)* determination of what specific assets the organisation should acquire, or allocation of funds among various assets in an efficient manner; and *(iii)* determination of how the needed funds should be financed or obtained the best mix of financing with relation to the overall valuation of the organisation. Accounting policies will be established to deal with questions as how to treat inventories, which accounts to capitalise, and how to treat expenses and cost. These policies affect the organisation's appearance of success or failure. Thus major policy decisions in the area of finance and accounting are as follows:

1. **Level of Dividend Payment.** Dividend payment history, the stability of earnings, rate of growth and profit levels, liquidity positions, ability to borrow, debt contract restrictions, legal constraints.
2. **Capital Structure.** Nature of business operations, nature of capital market, cash generation capacity, tax savings.
3. **Level of Working Capital.** Uncertainty of cash receipts and disbursements, borrowing capacity, efficiency of cash management, volume of credit sales, reasonability of sales, credit policies.

The basic criterion in financial policies is that the funds needed are available at the right time and at the lowest possible costs.

SOURCES OF POLICIES AND STRATEGIES

To understand how strategies and policies come about in a typical organisation, it might be well to review their major sources. These may be classified as follows:

1. Externally Imposed. To a rapidly increasing extent, strategy or policy is being externally imposed by government, trade unions, and trade associations. Whether in the form of direct regulation, the competition of government-owned or government-supported business, or the many conditions for accepting government aids or contracts, the result is to circumscribe and dictate many aspects of strategy or policy. Strong national unions, operating through collection bargaining and detailed labour contracts, have also imposed policy upon managers. Besides, thousands of local, regional, and national associations have their effect in varying degrees on policy. Other social group-such as church, school, fraternal, social, and charitable organisation-may also mould or dictate an entrprise's strategy or policy.

2. Implied. It is not unusual for policy and even strategy to develop from actions which people see about them and believe to constitute them. Employees will readily understand what is real policy if they work for an enterprise that has published policies to product high-quality goods, to maintain plant cleanliness, or to promote from within, and yet permits contrary actions. Its real policies, or the lack of them, are implied.

For example, the top managers of a certain company earnestly solicited new product ideas, especially from its marketing and engineering groups. The response was generous. Each idea was subjected to complex investigatory procedures and was judged by conservative standards. Most were rejected, and no explanations were made. Even key people in the firm came to believe that it was company's policy to confine new products to low-risk items. This imputed policy, which was quite contrary to what the firm really wanted, became the guideline for new product decisions.

3. Originated. The most logical source of strategy or policy is top management, which originates it for the express purpose of guiding subordinates in the their operations. Originated strategy or policy flows from the objectives of the enterprise, as these are defined by the top executive authority. These may be broad in scope, allowing key subordinates to give them clearer definition, or they may be promulgated so completely as to leave little room for defintion and interpretation. The extent to which they are centralized or decentralized is obviously dependent upon the extent to which authority is concentrated or dispersed.

Characterizing a strategy or policy as originated does not necessarily imply that it is imposed by command. Many are the adroit managers who originate them and obtain compliance by making unobtrusive suggestions. In fact, some skillful managers originate strategy or policy and secure compliance by allowing subordinate managers to leave a conference believing that they themselves originated it. But often a strategy or policy is imposed upon subordinates with a force and clarity that permit no deviation. Thus, a company president might originate a policy of using sales agents on a commission basis, rather than full-time sales people, by merely making indirect suggestions along this line to a sales manager, or, in another instance, the president might be positive and blunt in stating a policy that the company will not engage in price-cutting to make a sale.

4. Appealed. Second source is appeal. In practice, perhaps most policy and even some strategies stem from appeal of exceptional cases up the hierarchy of managerial authority. If occasions for decision arise for executives who do not know whether they have sufficient authority or how the matter should be handled, they may appeal to their superior. As appeals are taken upward and decisions are made on them, a kind of common law is established. Precedents develop and become guides for future managerial action.

Policies or strategies developed from appeals are sometimes incomplete, uncoordinated, and confused. If decisions are made on a given set of facts without regard for their possible effects on other aspects of the operations, or if unintended precedents develop from them, the resulting policies may not guide the thought and action of subordinates as really desired by top managers. Moreover, policies, or even strategies, may be formulated that the top executives do not even know about. For example, in one company there existed a long-time strategy of marketing strictly on a quality basis and never engaging in price-cutting. In a particularly strong competitive period, the chief executive gave the sales manager the right to cut price to meet some aggressive competition. After permitting this on several occasions, he found that he had, for all intents and purposes, changed the company's marketing strategy to that of being an industry price-cutter.

TYPES OF PLANS

Basically plans are of two types: formal and informal. Formal planning is comprehensive and rational. Informal planning is exclusive to managers who develop plans, but they never formally put them on paper and may not even communicate them to others. The informal planning remains only within the minds of the managers as an image of what should or shall be done. It lacks definiteness, expression and even rationality in the sense that it is instinctive in nature and not systematic. However, it is interesting to note that at times informal plans are more significant than formal ones.

Formal plan can be further classified into several categories:

(i) **Strategic and Functional Planning.** In strategic planning, the top managers determine the general objectives of the enterprise and the steps to accomplish them in the light of resources currently available and likely to be available in future. Functional planning, on the other hand, is planning that covers some functional areas like production, marketing, finance and purchasing.

(ii) **Long-range and Short-range Planning.** Long-range planning sets long-term goals for the enterprise and formulates specific plans for attaining these goals. It involves an attempt to anticipate, analyse and make decisions about basic problems which have significant reaching well beyond the present operating horizon of the enterprise. Short-range planning, on the other hand, is concerned with the determination of short-term activities to accomplish long-term objectives. Short-range planning relates to a relatively short period and has to be consistent with the long-range plans.

(iii) Administrative and Operational Planning. Administrative planning is done by the middle-level managers and it provides the foundation for the operative plans. Operative plans are made by the lower level managers to put the administrative plans into practice.

(iv) Ad hoc and Standing Planning. Ad hoc plans are made for certain specific matters. But standing plans are designed to be used over and over again. They include organisational structure, standard procedures and standard methods.

PLANNING PROCESS OR TECHNIQUE

It was observed earlier that planning is basically an exercise in determining the ends (*i.e.*, objectives) and means to achieve them. Thus, planning process involves basically two phases, namely;

(1) Determination of objectives.

(2) Setting up of plans to achieve the determined objectives.

Objectives

Objectives are the ends towards which the activities of an enterprise are directed. They provide direction to various activities of the enterprise. They depict a future state of affairs which an organisation strives to realise. They lay down guidelines for various activities and also constitute a source of legitimacy which justify the various activities of an organisation and also its very existence. Objectives serve as bench-mark of measuring the performance of various people working in the organisation and the overall efffectiveness and efficiency of the organisation.

Objectives are key to effective planning in any business organisation. In fact, planning has no meaning unless it is related to certain well-defined objectives or goals. Objectives are not only useful in planning but also in other managerial functions like organising, directing and controlling. They are an important aid in decision-making in any area of business. Clear-cut objectives encourage consistency in decision-making in the long-run.

On the basis of above discussion, we can define objective as follows:

It is an end (purpose, mission, result, or goal) the organisation is expected to achieve, acquire, create, preserve or distribute and towards which managers direct their efforts. The achievement of objectives is a must for the survival and growth of any business organisation. Peter F. Drucker has suggested that objectives must be set up in the following key areas of business: marketing, innovation, human organisation, financial resources, physical resources, productivity, social responsibility and profit resources.

Significance of Objectives

The importance of clearly defined objectives is generally recognised as contributing to management function in a variety of ways:

(1) Objectives serve as reference point for keeping the efforts of the organisation on proper lines.

(2) Continuous reviewing of objectives helps the organisation to compete effectively with the rival firms.

(3) They are helpful in co-ordinating the activities undertaken by the organisation.

(4) Clearly defined objectives are analogous to the star system which acts as a watch-word for managers just as it is used by ships for navigation.

(5) Objectives serve as prerequisites to determine effective policies, procedures, methods, strategies and rules.

Well-defined and integrated objectives for various units and functional areas within the organisation have numerous advantages which are as follows:

(i) **Unity of Planning.** Managers at various levels in the organisation make plans of their own. Planning may lose its consistency unless plans have the same focus of attention.

(ii) **Means of Decentralisation.** Managerial work with appropriate authority and capacity for independent decision is shared by a large number of managers. This may lead to disintegration in place of decentralisation unless there is a comman goal. The objectives guide to coordinate and remove conflicts or misunderstanding between various individuals.

(iii) **Basis of Control.** Objectives provide the basis of control by clarifying the contribution of each position as well as each unit.

(iv) **Stimulate Motivation.** Objectives fit individual goals into overall organisation goals and make the job meaningful and worth-while and stimulate human motivation.

NATURE OF OBJECTIVES

Objectives are the action commitments through which the mission of a business organisation is to be carried out and the standards against which performance is to be measured. Effective objectives have the following characteristics:

(i) **Objectives are Realistic and Operational.** Objectives must be derived from "what our business is, what it will be and what it should be". They must be capable of being converted into specific targets and assignments, They must be capable of becoming the basis as well as the motivation for work.

(ii) **Objectives may be Long-range or Short-range.** Since a business organisation is a continuous entity, it must have both long-range and short-range objectives. Short-range objectives normally cover a period up to two years and long-range objectvies are to be achieved in the long-run. There must be an integral relationship between the short-range and long-range objectives of the enterprise.

(iii) **Objectives are Multiple in Nature.** There must be multiple objectives rather than a single objective. Objectives are needed in all areas of business on which its survival depends. Every department should have specific objectives which are directed towards the achievement of overall business objectives. Similarly, every position has certain objectives which are derived from the departmental objectives.

(iv) Objectives Follow a Hierarchy. The objectives of the organisation must have a hierarchy. A convenient way of structuring the objectives is first to view the organisation as a total entity with overall global goals. These goals provide the basis for setting them at the second level which in turn becomes the basis for goals of the third level and so on. The goals at the second level are the means used for achieving the goals or ends set at the level, and similarly, goals at third level become means to attain the objectives of second level. Thus, goals at various levels of organisation form an 'end-means' chain.

ORGANISATIONAL LEVEL	PARTIAL FUNCTIONAL ORGANISATION CHART		
TOP	MANAGING DIRECTOR		
FIRST	PRODUCATION	FINANCE	SALES
SECOND	PRODUCT A	PRODUCT B	PRODUCT C
THIRD	SHOP 1	SHOP 2	SHOP 3
LOWEST	OPERATIVE	OPERATIVE	OPERATIVE

This 'end-means' chain continues throughout the organistional structure. The goals at each level are derived more or less logically, from the levels immediately above, and they collectively form a hierarchy. The above figure illustrates the idea of goals following the hierarchy, through 'end-means' chain. The hierarchy of goals following the 'end-means' chain highlights two important aspects of the nature of objectives:

(1) Movement to lower levels of organisational hierarchy, results in narrowing the scope for goal setting at successive levels;

(2) The time perspective kept in view similarly shrinks as we move down to lower levels of the organisational hierarchy. While an operative worker may have goals for each day, say, the number of units to be produced, the time perspective of a departmental head, say Production Manager may be a year or so.

FEATURES OF VALID OBJECTIVES

If objectives are to serve as effective guides to action they must possess the following characteristics:

(1) Objectives Must be Concrete, Specific and Particular. If stated in the too general terms they may not successfully direct the efforts constructively. A company may say that it is in the business of producing air conditioners. However, since it will be in entirely different business if it chooses to make air conditioners for office buildings, or for home cooling, or for automobiles, the company must specify the kind of air conditioners it will produce.

(2) Objective Should be Verifiable. If progress cannot be measured against specific standards or goals they lose their value from the standponit of controlling. A goal 'to increase profits' is measurable in general sense but whether the increase is of 5 percent or 50 percent both will meet the goal. If, however, it is set " increase porfits by 10 percent," 'progress is measurable with greater specificity.

(3) **Objectives Should Encourage Higher Performance yet be Realistic.** The objectives should have an orientation towards bringing about growth, developement and improvement of the organisational performance at all levels, but they must not be set at so high a level that they discourage even a try on the part of the members of organisation not to talk of achieving them.

(4) **Objectives Should be Result-centred.** Goals should focus on results and not on activity. Activity is only a means to achieve the results or objectives. Taking the above example, if the management decides to increase sales by 20%, it is an activity in terms of increasing the sales. This activity may or may not achieve the results of realising 10% increase in profits because of increase in cost of distribution and taxes. Thus, increasing sales is a means and not an end in itself.

(5) **Objectives Must be Balanced.** Once a hierarchy of objectives has been established, there may be tendency for certain objectives to claim undue emphasis. Part of managers's role is to make sure that each objective gets only the due share of activity and resources.

(6) **Objectives Must Form a 'Network'.** They must be interconnected and mutually supportive, and cannot exist in isolation. For example, suppose that one unit of the company has the objective that will increase costs at the same time there is in effect a 'cost saving' programme, the two objectives will become conflicting, and obviously, such a situation will not work.

MANAGEMENT BY OBJECTIVES

A method of implementing compatible objectives at all organisational levels is management by objectives (M.B.O.). The thrust of MBO is on what must be accomplished (goals) rather than how it is to be accomplished (methods). Fundamental to the MBO is the mutual setting of objectives between each subordinate and his superior. It allows the subordinate plenty of room to make creative decisions on his own. The supervisor is available for advice, counsel, and direction, should the subordinate seek his assistance.These objectives are then used as standards for evaluating the performance of subordinates. Ideally, the process should begin at the top of the organisational hierarchy.These objectives are then used as guides to set goals at second level and so on. This process works in the fashion of 'end-means' chain discussed above. But, goal setting under MBO differs from other approaches because of its emphasis on measurable objectives, the specification of time period for the completion of objectives, and participation by superior and subordinate in goal setting process and the evaluation of performance. The process seems deceptively simple; in reality, it requires careful analysis of each position and its necessary contribution to overall organisational objectives. Moreover, it requires that top management makes special efforts to determine measurable objectives at all levels.

MBO has several advantages:

(1) It provides greater employee involvement and commitment. One works one's best to achieve goals set by self.

(2) Under M.B.O. objectives are more realistic because they are set by those who have to carry them out.

DEVELOPMENT OF PLANS

Once objectives are established, the logical sequence is to develop the plans to achieve them. The plans shall be developed along three lines:

(1) Establishing policies and strategies.

(2) Developing medium-range and short-range plans to implement the policies and strategies.

(3) Laying down procedures, schedules for carrying out the medium and short-term plans.

Before we detail the process how each of these three is shaped it is important to know the framwork within which they are to be developed:

(i) Developing the Planning Premises. It is important to identify the assumption on which plans will be based. Assumptions are the expected future setting on which all planning depends. As a matter of fact, each of us makes assumptions for everything we plan. For instance, we either take packed lunch or money to buy lunch even though we are not hungry when we leave for work in the morning.We do so on the simple assumption that we will be hungry again by noon. Similarly, managers draw up plans based on their assumptions or beliefs about the future events. It is important to point out that these assumptions need revision with the change in situation.

(ii) Reviewing Limitations. There is always the possibility of existence of certain limitations that could affect the ability of the work-group to reach its objectives. An intelligent manager must make plans anticipating the conditions of limitations that might restrict the smooth operation of the plans. Key areas for anticipation are power, machinery, inventories of material and parts, finance and labour availability. There are some of the important areas which must be given due weightage while making plans. A good manager must consider combinations of all possible limitations and make provisions for them.

(iii) Developing Alternatives. The planner must try to find all the possible alternatives plans of action. Without resorting to such a search, he is likely to be guided by his limited imagination. Usually, there are several alternatives for any problem. The planner should try to screen out the most unviable alternatives so that he has a limited number of alternatives for final choice. Contingency plans should also be developed in order to smooth out the effects of deviations in the original plan.

(iv) Evaluating Alternatives. The alternatives must be evaluated in terms of various factors like cost, risk, availability of funds etc. to choose the most feasible alternative.The reason for considering many alternatives is to know which plan offers the greatest chance of success in reaching the predetermined objectives. The planner may take the help of various quantitative techniques to evaluate the available alternatives. This exercise may lead to the conclusion that no one course of action is optimum; so the planner may decide to select two or more alternatives and combine them to have the most feasible plan.

The purpose of listing these steps is that before the managers set themselves to formulate plans they should do so with reference to the framework provided by these steps.

After the objectives have been laid, the formulation of policies and strategies constitutes the next step. Policies are broad guides to action. They prescribe the most desirable ways and means for the accomplishment of a given objective. For example, to meet the objectives of 'making prompt collections from creditors' the policy statement may be: "To extend credit after satisfactory investigation, in line with sound credit principles, and pursue the creditor delaying the payment beyond credit period".

Policies generally deal with recurring problems. They may apply to entire institution or to specific functional areas or to both. Policies may extend over long or short periods of time. They may be either broad or limited in scope. A policy simply sets guidelines or boundaries within which subsequent decisions are made. The purpose of policies is not to achieve absolute uniformity of action but to guide people who have to take decision in that connection. While objectives provide the end which a manager should try to achieve, the policies provide the guidelines which he should keep in mind while achieving the ends. Policies tend to predecide to avoid repeated analysis and give a unified structure to various types of planning.

PROCESS OF FORMULATING POLICIES

In formulating business policy, the first step is to specify clearly the areas needing policies. Relevant information should then be collected. The sources of information are past practices, stated objectives, government requirements, trade associations, unions and other sources. Once the information is collected, the top management should work on deciding the policies in consultation with the different levels of the organisation. The responsibility of laying down policies though lies with top management, the lower levels must be consulted and due weightage given to their advice. Participation by subordinates would ensure that policies are realistic because they possess the first hand knowledge of organisational climate. Secondly, since policies are to be used by subordinates, their participation in formulation process would encourage ready acceptance of these by them. While laying down the policy statements the management should take care that policies laid down possess following features:

(1) The policy should express the intention of management.

(2) The policy must be preceded by a brief description of subject-matter so that there may be a common understanding of what policy covers.

(3) The policy must be laid by top management only. It is only at this level that a total view of organisation can be taken.

(4) The policy must be broad, general and flexible. To be a guide to action or decision "generality" is necessary, or else it would become a decision in itself.

(5) The policy must be translated in writing; two reasons may be advanced for this:

Firstly, a policy will be vague unless it is written down. Secondly, if a policy is in writing, it will reveal the intentions of the top management clearly. Special skill is required to select and adhere to policy language which will state and synthesize the general principles and the scope for discretion. A policy should be finalised after consulting the persons who are supposed to use it. The reaction of such people should be analysed carefully. After a policy is framed it must be properly communicated to the people who are expected to use it. It is also necessary to appraise the policies after a certain period of time to know their effectiveness.

Kinds of Policies

Policies may be set up in the key areas of the enterprise like production, purchase, finance, personnel and marketing. If this is done, the policies will be classified by major functions of an enterprise. Policies may also be classified on the basis of source of the policy, *i.e.*, *(i)* internal, *(ii)* external, and *(iii)* appealed. Internal policies include those initiated by managers at various levels to guide the subordinates. External policies include those policies arising to meet the various pressures and requests of forces outside the enterprise, such as government, trade unions and trade associations. Appealed policies come into existence from the appeal of an exceptional problem by a subordinate to his superior regarding how to handle the problem.

There is one more classification of policies based on the organisational levels of managers. There may be policies which are used primarily by the top managers, other policies by the middle managers and still other policies which are applicable chiefly to the first line managers. The policies at these three levels may be termed as basic, general and departmental policies. Basic policies affect and relate to the topmost level of managerial hierarchy. General policies affect the middle level managers and are more specific than the basic policies. Departmental policies are highly specific and are applicable at the lowest level of management.

Benefits of Policies

Policies are set up to achieve the following benefits:

(i) By making policy decisions on frequently recurring problems the top management provides the guidelines to lower level managers. It will permit decisions to be made in case of similar problems without repeating the reasoning and expensive analysis required initially to state the policy or make the decision.

(ii) Policies help managers at various levels to act with confidence without the need for consulting the superiors every time. This will also ensure promptness of action.

(iii) Policies facilitate better administrative control. Policies provide the rational basis of evaluating the results. By setting up policies, the management ensures that decisions made will be consistent and in keeping with the objectives and interests of the enterprise.

Strategy

Having laid the policies, the other related task is to choose strategies. Strategy involves as to how available resources will be used to achieve objective, in the face of obstacles, which may be in form of competitive forces, government regulations, technical upheavals, social change etc. That is to say, the strategic planning pays special attention to relatively uncontrollable external factors. Emphasis is placed on predicting the future behaviour of external variables and the formulations of alternative courses of action in the light of future events. As such, the manager has to do a lot of forceasting before laying down the strategy. To illustrate the view point, in view of changing consumer tastes and technology the company may decide to change its product line. This decision would be termed as strategic. This illustration points to how the organisation is irrevocably committed to large expenditures once the decision is taken. A mistake in strategic planning may be disastrous.

Once the policies and strategies have been decided upon, the management's task is to specify the medium-range and short-range plans. Medium-range planning is the process whereby specific functional plans are laid for specific number of years incorporating the details of how strategies are to be carried out to achieve the long-range objectives. Normally, the planning period is five years. Medium range plans generally cover major functions only and are translated into financial term in the form of a proforma Balance Sheets and profoma Profit and Loss Statement.

The short-range plans are one or two year plans to carry on the actual work. They are very detailed and include budgets and programmes. These are explained below:

Programme

A Programme is a sequence of activities designed to implement policies directed towards the achievement of objectives. A programme lays down the definite steps which will be taken to accomplish a given task. It also lays down the time to be taken for the completion of each step. A programme might include such general activities as purchasing new machines that will enable to increase output or hiring work-force to operate new equipment or introduction of a new product in the market. Thus, a programme is a complex of objectives, policies, procedures, task assignments, steps to be taken, resources to be employed and other elements necessary to carry out a given course of action. The managers at different levels chalk out programmes describing the contents, and actions in their spheres of responsibility to contribute towards organisational objectives.

Budgets

A budget is a statement of expected results expressed in numerical terms like rupees, product units, and man hours. Since it is a statement of expected results it is also used as an instrument of managerial control. It provides a standard by which actual operations can be measured and by which variations can be checked. But it should not be forgotten that making a budget is clearly planning. A budget forces an enterprise to make in advance a numerical compilation of expected cash flow, expenses and revenues, capital outlays or machine hour utilisation. Budgeting is essential for control, but it cannot mechanise unless it reflects plans. As a means of effective planning, the process of budgeting may involve the preparation of budgets of sales, purchase, materials, labour and manufacturing expenses.

Budegting coordinates the activities of various departments of a business enterprise by adjusting the departmental budgets into the master budget. Every departmental head consciously plans the future operations of his department in tangible terms. Since budget portray verifiable and measurable goals to be reached within a period of one year, they inject a sense of clarity, direction and purpose in the activities of the organisation. However, to be effective means of planning, budgets should have functional flexibility. They should not be rigid instruments. They should be able to cope with unforeseen circumstances within a predictable range of activities.

Schedules and Procedures

The final step in planning process is to develop schedules and procedures to put into operation the short-range plans. Schedules are the timings fixed for completing the programmed operations. They lay down the timings when each step in a programme will be executed. Schedules are a necessary part of planning in order to ensure continuity in production to secure constant flow of product into the market and to avoid delay in various operations.

The procedures are sequence of steps in implementing various plans. According to G. R. Terry, a procedure is a series of related tasks that make up the chronological sequence and the established way of performing the work to be accomplished. It is a list of systematic steps for handling events that occur regularly. Procedures involve planned sequence of operations for handling recurring business operations uniformly and consistently. Procedures are genarally set up for processing an order, shipping the goods, handling claims, collection of payments and so forth.

Procedures should be distinguished from policies. A policy is a guide to thinking. But a procedure is a guide to action and it hardly leaves any room for judgement. Policies are specific guide-lines for managerial thinking towards certain issues. But procedures are systematic ways of handling regular events. They are operational guides to action and routinise the performance of repetitive jobs. Every procedure consists of various methods to accomplish each phase of work. A method is the manual or mechanical way by which each operation is performed. A method is more limited in scope than a procedure because it deals with a task that is only one step of a procedure.

❒

9

Coporate Structure

The concept of corporate planning has in recent years gained wide currency in management literature. Its connotation is somewhat overlapping with the concept of strategic planning. It is, therefore, necessary that the scope of corporate planning and strategic planning should be clearly understood.

Simply stated, corporate planning is comprehensive planning process which involves continued formulation of objectives and the guidance of affairs towards their attainment. It is a systematic and disciplined exercise designed to help identification of the objectives of an organisation or corporate body, determination of appropriate targets, and formulation of practical plans by which the objective could be achieved. It is undertaken by higher management for the firm as whole on a continuous basis for making entrepreneurial decisions systematically and with the best possible knowledge of their probable outcome and effects, organising systematically the efforts and resources needed to carry out the decisions, and measuring the results of these decisions against the expectations though systematic feedback.

The object of corporate planing is to identify new areas of investment and marketing. Initiating new projects, new courses of action, and analysing past experience are the subject-matter of corporate planning. Thus, it plies *(a)* the imposition of a planning discipline on the present operations of the business, and *(b)* a reappraisal of the business and of the direction in which it should be heading. The essence of corporate planning lies in the application of the company's resources and competencies to the most profitable uses. Innovation is the core of such planning. At the same time it ensures that managers are continually measuring their performance against the company's long-term profit and market objectives, evaluating alternative methods of reaching the goals, and keeping in touch with changes in the market and in technology.

The comprehensive nature of the corporate planning process lies in that operational planning, project planning and strategic planning are its constituents. These are now examined as follows.

It is essential for every business firm to manage its ongoing operations efficiently to keep the business afloat in the market with which it is familiar. Operational planning is necessary so as to ensure that changes in the market situation for the existing product line do not adversely affect the earnings for the firm. Thus, operational planning involves study of the market conditions for the existing range of products to maintain and improve the position of the form in the face of competition. It is essentially a short-term exercise and deals with the existing product, market and facilities. The degree of uncertainty in operational planning is of a low order; the time span of discretion is short; choice of alternatives is relatively simple. But the firm can ill afford to ignore long-term changes in the product markets. It has to look for new markets for the existing product, develop new products, create a market for the same and utilise the existing facilities and expertise to meet new requirements. Considerations such as these characterise project planning, which is a forward looking exercise concerned with new markets, new products and new facilities. Project planning is, therefore, to deal with a greater degree of uncertainty, and demands a high order of judgment on the part of strategist due to the risks involved.

Strategic planning refers to the formulation of a unified, comprehensive and integrated plan aimed at relating the strategic advantages of the firm to the challenges of the environment. It is concerned with appraising the environment in relation to the company, identifying the strategies to obtain sanction for one of the alternatives to be interpreted and communicated in an operationally useful manner. Thus, strategic planning provides the framework within which future activities of the company are expected to be carried out. Compared with project planning, the time span of discretion in strategic planning is much longer, the degree of uncertainty and corresponding risks involved are much greater, and judgement to be exercised is of more importance.

In as much as strategic planning determines the future direction of a company, corporate planning is essentially based on strategic planning, and at the same time takes care of project planning and operational planning. Thus, corporate planning is described as a formal systematic managerial process, organised by responsibility, time and information, to ensure that operational planning, project planning and strategic planning are carried out regularly to enable top management to direct and control the future of the enterprise. It follows that corporate planning is not synonymous with long-range planning. Corporate planning is concerned with determination of objectives and developing means to achieve the objectives. It may encompass both short periods as well as long periods. The tune span depends on how far ahead a company wants to forecast and to plan, which, in turn, depends upon the nature of business that the company wants to be in and commitment of resources required for it. For instance, in the modern heavy engineering industry, commitment of resources is generally required for a fairly long period to 15 or 20 years.

Thus corporate planning in an engineering enterprise will involve tong-term considerations regarding market demand, technology and such other factors. It will have a short time horizon in the case of garment industry. Long-range planning, however, necessarily connotes planning with a long-term horizon in view, generally five years or more. Corporate planning in capital intensive industries is always associated with long-range planning. Besides, corporate planning is concerned with the existing products in existing markets as well as new products and new markets.

Strategic Planning and Operational Planning

When comprehensive corporate planning is divided into strategic and operational planning, the sphere of activities is deemed on the basis of their objectives and scope in the total management process.

From this point of view the examples of strategic planning in an organisation may be: planned growth rate in sales, consideration of how much growth is to be achieved by internal development as opposed to mergers and acquisitions; planned diversification by technologies, types of products, customers and geographical areas; comparatively important planning activities in the areas of organising, staffing, finance, etc. which affect all major functions. As against strategic planning, operational planning can be defined as follows:

Operational planning is the process of deciding the most effective use of the resources already allocated and to develop a control mechanism to assure effective implementation of the actions so that organisational objectives are achieved. Operational planning taken in this way may include: adjustment of production, marketing and financial capacity of the organisation to the expected level of operations, in both the short term and long term; increasing the efficiency of operating activities through analysing past performance/budgeting future costs, developing control over costs and efficiency; programming the comprehensive and specific details of future short term operations. On the basis of the explanation of strategic and operational planning, following is the distinction between strategic planning & operational planning:

1. The type of environment between two types of planning is different. Strategic planning takes into account the external environment and tries to relate the organisation with it. It usually encampasses all the functional areas of the organisation and is effected within the existing and long term framework of economic, social, technical, and political factors. Operational planning focusses on internal organisational environment so as to make the effective use of given resources.
2. Strategic planning is usually conducted by top level management and other specified planning staff in the organisation. At this level, people can take overall view of the organisation and have necessary capability to relate the organisation with the external environment. Operational

planning is usually spread over a wide range within the organisation and is generally performed by operating managers with the help of the subordinate staff. Since two planning groups are widely separated in the organisation, some incompatibility may exist between two types of planning. Therefore, there is need for integrating these two in order to have better planning effects.

3. Strategic planning guides the choice among the broad directions in which the organisation seeks to move and cope the general planned allocations of its managerial, financial physical resources over future specified period of time. Operational planning, on the of the hand, focusses on the ways and means by which each of the individual functions may be programmed so that process may be made towards the attainment of organisational objectives. In performing a function, operational planning puts questions:

   (i) what objectives and conditions must be met? Within the framework of these questions, operational plans are-formulated. Usually the answers of operational planning tries to achieve ˜the results and actions suggested by the strategic planning.

   (ii) why is the action required?

   (iii) what are the results of the action required?

   (iv) where will the action accomplish?

   (v) what action is to be taken?

4. Strategic planning precedes the operational planning since the later is primarily the implementation of the former. Since strategic planning sets trends and direction for managerial actions, its time horizon is usually quite large say five years or so. Operational planning is heavily concerned with short term programmes implementing step by step progress towards basic organisational goals, organisational depth and tiancial resources. These restrictions

on the organisation's potential accomplishment are more prevalent in the short .term than over a long term; therefore, strategic planning must recognise the limits of what operational planning can realistically be undertaken in given time periods. Thus strategic planning is restricted by the practical limitations under which operational planning operates.

DIFFERENT PLANNING SYSTEMS

Management literature is replete with references to planning. It is discussed as function of management, categorised into different types and considered as a major set of techniques. Here, we direct our attention to a few types of planning systems relevant to business policy. Among these, we briefly discuss operational, project, management by objectives, contingency, short-range, long-range, corporate, and strategic planning.

Operational Planning

Operational planning is lower-level planning and is based on sub-goals derived from organisational objectives. The focus is on managing the day-to-day affairs of the company. The primary responsibility for implementation of operational plans rests on the operating level of management; middle-level executives or line managers, who are guided by the senior management with regard to the formulation of strategies. In managing the day-to-day affairs, operating managers are guided by a set of policies, procedures, rules, forecasts, targets and budgets. In this manner, all operating managers, in different functional areas, implement their respective plans. Operational plans, therefore, are parts of the overall organisational plan and work in tandem with each other. Operating plans and operating managers are to be distinguished from operations plans (which relate to the production function) and operations managers (who look after the production activities).

Management by Objectives

Management by objectives, *per se*, is not a type of planning system; it is a systems approach to managing by emphasising the role of objectives. Operationally, it facilitates planning and the implementation and control of plans. The organisational objectives are divided into divisional or departmental objectives which are further subdivided into individual objectives. Such an inter-locking system of the objectives serves as the basis for managing, evaluation and control of performance. Thus, management is concerned with setting of objectives, goals and targets which are a part of the planning function.

Project Planning

In a broader sense, project planning relates to planning for a clearly identified programme or a set of tasks such as construction project. Within organisations, and in a narrow sense, project planning refers to planning done for a specific task like product development. The nature of each project is unique and planning is done for each project individually. The emphasis in project planning is on working within set time and resource constraints. The form of organisation used is a temporary structure known as matrix organisation. Project planning derives its goals from the organisational objectives. An organisational strategy, for implementation, may require many plans and programmes; each programme includes several projects.

Short-term (Short Range) Planning

Deciding about the planning period-the number of years ahead for which planning is done is an important decision. There is no definite planning period on the basis of which plans could be classified as being of a short or long duration. It would depend, among other factors, on the uncertainty present in the future or the nature cut products. For companies in the oil exploration business, the planning period would be long-up to 20 years or more-while a fashion garments manufacturer may not plan for more than a year. A basis on which plans could be termed as short-or long-range is the commitment principle: "a period of time in the future necessary to foresee, as well as possible, the fulfillment or commitments involved in decisions made today." Ordinarily, plans for less than one year are termed as short-range and those for 3 to 5 years are long-range plans. Short-range planning involves making plans which are based on current data. These are the immediate goals to be achieved, present commitment of resources minor changes in schedules, policies and requirements, and midterm appraisals. Short-range plans operate within the framework of long-range plans. Sometimes, medium-range planning can also be undertaken which froms a linkage between the short and long-range plans.

Long-terms (Long Range) Planning

Long-range planning as the name indicates, deals with planning for a future period of time. The planning process involves a systematic identification of opportunities and threats so that managers may use the date to make current decisions in order to use the opportunities and avoid the threats. By consideration of the future developments, as manager can assess the futurity of current decisions-the likely impact that a decision taken now is going to make in the future-and make current decisions accordingly. In this manner, long-range planning deals with issues which are of the vital significance and have a long-term impact. There are many other terms used to planning which is for a long term is of vital significance, and is concerned with the futurity of current decisions.

Contingency Planning

The contingency approach rests on the premise that there is no one best way to solve a problem, the right approach depends on the situation. Environmental conditions, on which much of long-term planning rests, change so rapidly that policy makers are often constrained in making tenable assumptions regarding future developments. Too much formal planning does not seem to work under such conditions. A realistic approach, to contain these problems, is to adopt contingency planning. This involves taking action in incremental steps, reassessing strategies at each stage and reformulating plans in order to reach a predetermined goal.

For example, a company manufacturing refrigerators faces competition in the market as a result of which it modernises its operations. In the next stage, it raises capacity levels to take advantages of economics of scale. Further, in order to offset seasonal fluctuations, it starts making watches and, thus, diversifies into a new area. The three steps of modernisation, expansion and diversification, show that the company has reviewed its strategies at each stage and tries to ensure survival and profitability by adopting contingency planning. Had the conditions been different at any of the three stages, the company would have adopted a different approach. Such an approach would have been contingent on that situation.

Strategic Planning

Strategic planning is a process which, through an examination of external and internal factors for an organisation, results in a set of mission, purpose, objectives, policies, plans and programmes for implementation. In this manner, strategic planning results in action designed to implement a strategy. A view of strategic planning is that the objectives and goals, and the strategies designed to achieve them, give rise to two types of plans. These are the operating and strategic plans. The operating plans are implemented by the different units in an organisation while strategic plans are implemented through projects. Strategic planning is considered a part of wider system of managing through strategy *i.e.* strategic management.

Comprehensive or Systematic or Corporate Planning

Corporate planning is a term to denote a formal, comprehensive, and systematic appraisal of environmental and internal factors in order to evolve strategies to achieve organisational objectives. It is formal as it requires formulation of plans, strategies, and policies on the basis of documents and figures. It is comprehensive as it deals with all types of plans: short and long-range, corporate, divisional and functional, and strategic and operational plans. It is systematic as it covers the whole planning process in a logic and sequential manner. Due to its nature, corporate planning is also known as comprehensive corporate planning, comprehensive planning or systematic planning.

In practice, a team of corporate planners assists the senior managers in determining objectives and goals to be achieved, strengths and weaknesses of the company, the opportunities and threats operating in the environment, and the strategies and action plans to be adopted. The corporate planners are also involved in continuous monitoring of the implementation process of plans and the process taking place. On the basis of such an evaluation, the strategies and action plans are reviewed and reformulated, if necessary.

Corporate planning is a term often used synonymously with long-range planning and strategic planning. It is also a term rarely found in American, literature pertaining to business policy. But others including India books, often use the term 'corporate planning'. Some of the earlier books published in the area of business policy in India carried the title of Corporate Planning.

The term 'corporate planning' is also used extensively in management journals, popular business magazines, and in industry. Management courses in the area of business policy offered by institutions and Universities in India are also known as corporate planning courses. Notwithstanding the popular use of the term 'corporate planning', normally, it is taken to be synonymous with long-range planning and strategic planning.

Problem of Semantics in Terminology: Planning Terms

As in Section, we deal with the problem of semantics in terminology related to various planning terms that have been used above. For this purpose, we take up the following combinations of terms as examples.

(1) Long-range Planning—Corporate Planning—Strategic Planning. These three terms, in groups of two each at one time, have been considered above. Much of what has been stated is also valid for these three terms jointly. Individually, these terms do mean different things to different people. Historically, they have emerged at different times. Each of these terms has come to signify planning systems that have been invented in response a unique set of environmental factors. With regard to the literature in the area of business policy, writers have extolled the virtues of one planning system while treating the others as secondary. But the differences between them, as of today, are at best, academic.

Practitioners do not view them differently, many authors also adopt an approach of using them interchangeably. A reasonable approach, in our opinion, could be to consider the nature of planning involved. If the planning is done at a senior level of management, is sufficiently long-range, is valid for the company as a whole, and is of vital, pervasive or continuing importance, it can either be called long-range, corporate or strategic planning. The basic thrust in such planning has to be on the process of identification of opportunities and threats in the environment and their matching with the strengths and weaknesses of the company in order to formulate strategies to achieve the objectives, purpose and mission of the organisation.

(2) **Long-range Planning—Strategic Planning.** Ansoff differentiates long range planning ("Where future is expected to be predictable through extrapolation of the historical growth") and strategic planning ("...future is not necessarily expected to be an improvement over the past nor is assumed to be extrapolable") Steiner, Miner and Gray do not differentiate long-range (also corporate) planning and strategic planning stating that "strategic planning is the phrase most widely used today." Sometimes, strategic planning is considered an emerging term for corporate planning, which itself is thought to be a successor to long-range planning. For all practical purposes, however, both the terms are considered to be synonymous.

(3) **Corpprate Planning—Strategic Planning.** These terms are also mostly taken as being synonymous. But there of different view. "Although corporate planning and strategic planning are closely linked", says Argenti, "they are not synonymous either". Corporate planning can be divided into two parts, according to Agrenti. The first relates to decided the corporate objectives and the second to the determination of corporate strategies. So, "strategic planning is the second part of corporate planning". The present

trend is exemplified to consider both these terms, as well as long-range learning to be synonymous for all practice purposes.

(4) **Long-range Planning—Corporate Planning.** Some authors, specially the earlier ones, differentiate between these two terms. Argenti is of the opinion that not all long-range plans are corporate all corporate plans are necessarily long-range. Ansoff equates both and says that long-range planning is "sometimes called corporate planing." Sometimes, corporate planning is taken as learning for the whole company as contrasted with functional plans. Others do not consider corporate plans as simple aggregates of functional plans. Occasionally, corporate planning is thought to be a combination of long and short-range plans. However, the most accepted approach presently is to consider both long-range planning and corporate planning as synonymous for all practical purposes.

(5) **From Strategic Planning to Strategic Management.** While strategic planning helps to resolve the problem of strategy formulation on the basis of mission and objective-setting and the analysis of environmental and internal factors it falls short of taking into account a few relevant aspects. Asnoff *et al.* deal with these shortcomings in terms of three variables. First, with regard to managerial problems strategic planning considers there external linkages with the environment "under a basic assumption that the internal configuration will remain essentially unchanged". Second dealing with process of resolving managerial problems it covers only problem-solving (or planning) while assuming that implementation and control will follow. Thirdly the variables included in strategic planning analysis are exclusively "technological-economic informational while social and political dynamics both within and outside the organisation are assumed to be irrelevant and unaffected".

The sub-variablest which have been excluded from consideration have a major impact on resolving strategic problems. For instance it is essential to consider the impact that formulation of strategy, and changes in it, have on the organisation. Again-the solution of managerial problems can only be done through a comprehesive approach that not only considers formation but also implementation and control of strategy. Factors like psychosociological and political dimensions of policy-making are essential for diagnosing the myriad of problems faced by managers.

Strategic management a newer and broader concept of managing organisation straregically takes into account all the aspects of managerial.

RANGE OF STRATEGIC PLANNING

1. Following reasons may justify business policy formulation or strategic planning. One justification is that it has been found useful in practice. Research studies, based on the experience of companies and executive viewpoints, have indicated that strategic planning contributes positively to the performance of enterprises.
2. Different Studies reveal that companies which had undertaken formal strategic planning not only out performed the non-planners on most measures of sources (return on equity growth of sales, earning for shares, and value of the firms), but significantly outperformed their own past results/ as well; besides, the companies that used strategic planning were able to predict the outcome of planning much better than others.
3. Researches have shown that strategic planning can isolate the key factors in an industry and thus help companies plan their strategies more effectively.
4. With changing environment of business of product-market conditions technology, economic, climate—strategic planning is the only means by which future opportunities and problems can be anticipated by company executives.

5. It enables executives to provide necessary direction for the enterprise, take full advantage of new opportunities and minimise the attendant risks.
6. Strategic planning is beneficial particularly in organisations when there is a long time lag between managerial decisions and the results thereof.
7. Strategic planning enables management to improve the chances of making decisions which will stand the test of time and revising the strategy on the basis of monitoring the progress of R & D and the changes in product-market conditions.
8. With clear goals and direction provided for the future, employees in general and managers in particular can better perceive the ways of achieving the corporate objectives consistently with the individual and group aspirations. This is conducive to greater harmony and goal congruence.
9. Formal strategic planning focuses on problems of the total enterprise, not just functional problems in the marketing, finance or personnel areas. Persons exposed to strategy formation thus develop a breadth of understanding and undergo change of attitudes in the process.

LIMITATIONS OF STRATEGIC PLANNING

Strategic Planning in management is essential but there are practical limitations to its use. The reasons why people fall in strategic planning emphasise the practical difficulties encountered in planning.

A number of limits within which planning has to operate make this undertaking difficult. Following are the limitations:

(1) Problems of Change. The above factor works more as limiting factor in the light of changes in future conditions. In a complex and rapidly changing environment, the succession of new problems is often magnified by implications that make planning most difficult. The problem of change is more complex in long-range planning. Present conditions tend to weigh heavily in planning, and by overshadowing future needs, may sometimes results in error of judgment. Such factors as changing technology, consumer tastes and desires, business conditions, and many others change rapidly and often unpredically. In such conditions, planning activities taken in one period may not be relevant for another period because the conditions in two periods are quite different.

(2) Failure of People. There are many reasons why people fail in planning, both at the formulation level as well as implementation level. Some of the major failures are lack of commitment to planning, failure to develop, sound strategies, lack of clear and meaningful objectives, tendency to overlook planning premises, failure to see the scope of the plan, failure to see planning as a rational approach, excessive reliance on the past experience, failure to use the principles of limiting factors, lack of top management support lack of delegation of authority, lack of adequate control techniques, and resistance to change. These factors are responsible for either inadequate planning or wrong planning in the organisations concerned.

(3) Lack of Accurate Information. The first basic limitation of strategic planning is the lack of accurate information and facts relating to future., Planning concerns future activity and its quality will be determined by the quality of forecast of future events. As no manager can predict completely and accurately the events of future, the planning may pose problems in operation. This problem is further, increased by lack of formulating accurate premises. Many times, managers may not be aware about the various conditions within which they have to formulate their planning activities.

(4) Inflexibilities. Manager while going through the strategic planning process have to work in a set of given variables. These variables may be more in terms of organisational or external. These often provide considerably less flexibility in planning action.

(A) ***Internal.*** Major internal inflexibilities that may limit planning are related to the an psychology. Organisatonal policies and procedures, and long-term capital investment. The first internal inflexibility is in the form of human psychology in that most of the people have regard for the present rather

than for future. The present is not only more certain than future, it is also more desirable, and more real. Thus, resistance to change is a basic factor which works against planning because planning often depends on the changes. People may have feelings that if planning is soft-pedalled, the changes and the possible danger of future will be minimised. For them, planning tends to accelerate change and unrest.

Second type of internal inflexibility emerges because of organisationnal policies and procedures once these are established, they are difficult to change. Though these policies, procedures, and, rules are meant to facilitate managerial functions by, providing guidelines, they often are too numerous and exacting that they leave very little scope for managerial initiative and flexibility. Since managers have to plan for future which is not static but changing, they often find themselves in great constraints. Such problems are more common in bureaucratic organisations where rules and procedures are the matters of prime concerns.

Third type of internal inflexibility comes because of long-term capital investment. Long-term planning is not a process of making future decisions, but a means of reflecting the future in todays decisions. If the organisation has taken a long-term investment, it is committed by that and future actions have to be takin in the light of the investment. Thus managerial planning is limited to that extent.

(B) ***External.*** Beside the internal inflexibilities, managers are contronted with many external inflexibilities and they do not have control over these. These factors may be social, technological, legal, labour union, geographically and economic. The managers have to formulate their plans keeping in view the demand of these factors. Thus their scope of action is limited making planning in effective in many cases.

(5) Time and Cost. While going 'through the strategic planning process managers should also take into account both time and cost factors. The various steps of planning may go as for as possible because there is no limit of precision in planning tools. But planning suffers because of time and cost factors. Time is a limiting factor for every manager in the organisation on, and if they are busy in preparing elaborate reports and instructions beyond certain level, they are risking their effectiveness. Excessive time spent on securing information and trying to fit all of it into a compact plans is dysfunctional in the organisation.

(6) Rigidity. Often people feel that planning provides rigidity in managerial action. Many types of internal inflexibilities, discussed above, may be results of planning itself. The planning stifles employee initiative and forces managers into rigid or straitjacket mode of executing their work. In fact, rigidity may make managerial work more difficult than it need be. This may result in it delay in work performance, lack of intiative, and lack of adjustment with changing environment. Many people feel that planning is limited in value because best results can be obtained by a muddling through types of operation in which each situation is tackled when and if it appears pertinent to the immediate problem. Though this factor of rigidity of planning is limiting factor but without planning, it is really difficult to operate particularly in large organisations.

The planning also involves cost on the part of the orgartisation. The various factors analysed above contribute to the limitations of strategic planing, either making planing ineffective or making lesser degree of planned work.

CONFLICTS BETWEEN STRATEGIC PLANNING AND OPERATIONAL PLANNING

There are certain conflicts between strategic and operational planning. These conflicts may be generated because of the different nature of two types of planning or because of the different groups of people involved in them. Most of the common conflicts between strategic and operational planning are as follows:

(1) First source of conflict between strategic and operational planning may be period of futurity. Strategic planners think in terms of long term future of the organisation, sometimes even at the cost of immediate gains. On the other hand, operational planners may concentrate more on near future. Strategic planners may think in terms of long term profitability as new projects may affect short term profitability adversely because of their long gestation period.

(2) Strategic planning is likely to proceed at a more leisurely pace than operational planning. Operational planners focus on their present resources, have major day-to-day operating responsibilities and are under pressure to immediately accomplish a higher level of activity at lower cost. They have to meet the more specific targets in the organisation on which their survival in organization is determined. Under such circumstances, each group may exaggerate its importance in the organisation and combining the two types of planning may become even necessary.

(3) Strategic planners are more prone to change while operational planners may not relish changes. For example, the growth prospects of an organisation can best be served by broadening or shifting the base into areas with more potential for development. Such shifts, however, are likely to decrease efficiency as new products with which the organisation has had little or no experience are scheduled to be developed and manufactured. The *status quo* therefore, as far as product lines are concerned, may be more attractive organisational policy for functional managers.

The above factors may lead to conflicts between strategic and operational planning. However, since operational planning contributes to strategic planning, it is essential that both are properly integrated. Corporate planning makes an attempt for this integration.

REASONS FOR INADEQUATE PLANNING IN INDIA

There are many factors which affect the corporate planning and are not quite conducive to Indian organisations. The need for an extent of corporate planning within any economy is governed basically by the following factors:

(a) Scarcity of resources

(b) Government policy and control

(c) Competition facing the firm

(d) Size of the firm.

There is substantial interdependence among these factors and the intensity of impact of each one of these factors may vary from country to country from firm to firm within the same country, or from time to time within the same organisation. A study related to the cross-cultural management philosophy, practices and effectiveness with particular reference to India have suggested the following propositions:

All other factors being the same, the higher a firm's score on the management philosophy (*i.e.*, attitudes toward various components of society internal and external to the firm) index, the greater will be its concern for long-range planning.

The greater the degree of competition, the greater will be the need for long-range planning by the individual company.

The greater the degree of economic and political instability, the lesser the likelihood that private industrial enterprises will undertake systematic long-range planning.

The greater the degree of government control over prices and the availability of raw materials, the lesser the likelihood that the firm will undertake systematic long range planning.

The greater the degree of governemental hostility toward the business community, the lesser the likelihood that a firm will undertake systematic long-range planning.

The implication of the above propositions is given usually low score on management philosophy among Indian organisations: these constraints are likely to be stronger enough to subdue the passion for long-range planning, apart from management philosophy. Following characteristics of Indian environment work against formulation of the plans by Indian organisations:

(1) As regards the size of the organisation, the Monopolies and Restrictive Trade Practices Act, 1969, sets constraints on expansion and diversification strategy through the limits on assets size (Rs. 20 crores) and market share (33.3 per cent). Thus area of expansion and diversification-most important area of LRP for larger organisations is defined by Government regulations. Further constraints are out on organisations, with foreign-majority equity holding and public sector organisations, though there is a basic difference. The former organisations area of business is determined by Government, thus narrowing the scope of discretionary planning. In the case of the latter, business goals in terms of areas of activity are pretty clear and stable.

(2) There is not enough degree of competition among sellers because of sellers market conditions. Though in some consumer goods, the conditions of the market have changed, there is high rate of returns. Thus for most organisations, a fair amount of rate of return is assured. The market is further accentuated by growing population and market size, fairly stable consumer tastes, progressive deeming of areas of business by Government in which organisations can go. As such many organisations do not see any need for systematic planning. This is supported by non-existence of separate planning division in most of the organisations.

(3) Lack of resources, in general also creates barriers in formulation and implementation of plans. There is a competition for claims for resources—specially materials, infrastructural facilities, such as, power transport finance, managerial manpower. Since many of these resources are canalised and controlled through Government agencies, there is no competition in the supply resources. It verges more on monopoly-rationing supplies to a large number of competing organisations. Many of the organisations view that constraining forces in effective plan implementation are the Government policy, licensing policy, delay in procurement of

machinery and equipment, erratic supply of raw materials, shortcomings in transport and communication facilities, and delay in implementation of projects in other sectors.

Thus either because of lack of appreciation of need for planning or because of prevailing conditions working against effective formulation and implementation of plans, some organisations do not make attempts to look beyond a year and others accept the conditions as constraints in their attempt at planning. The factors—degree of competence, ownership professional training of management, and perception of Government attitude towards the companies—may account to some extent for the difference in attitudes.

FACTORS OF MAKING STRATEGIC PLANNING EFFECTIVE

It is not sufficient to say that managers must take actions to make strategic planning effective, but they must be clear as to what actions can be taken in this direction. Following factors are important for making planning effective:

(1) **An Open Systems Approach.** The problems of planning should be dealt through open systems approach. It suggests that managers must take into account interactions with their total environment in every respect of planning. Open systems approach makes it necessary on the part of the managers that they take into account the environmental variable such as, technological, social, cultural, legal, political, and economic. Further, they must also take into account the internal interaction pattern that is, how their planning process is affecting others and is affected by others. When managers take all these factors into account is affected by others. When managers take all these factors into account, they are in better positions to plan and execute their actions.

(2) **Participation in Planning.** As discussed above, planning progress should be a joint one. The best planning is likely to be done when managers are given an opportunity to

contribute to plans affecting the area over which they have authority. Participation in planning affecting managers areas of authority at any level through their being informed contributing suggestions and being consulted, leads to good planning commitment, loyalty, and managerial effectiveness.

The various methods of participation in planning process may be followed in the organisations depending upon their requirements and understanding of the people.

(3) **Integration of Long-term and Short-term Plans.** Managers often focus their attention only on very short - term plans, even if they plan. As discussed earlier, a good planning process involves integration of long-term and short-term plans. A short-term plan contributes towards the achievement of the long-term plan. Thus, if a manager is planning for very short period, he must take into account his long-term plans also. He must constantly watch and review that his short-term plans contribute to his long-term plans. If this is not the situation, he must modify his course of action which may include modification in both long-term and short-term plans.

(4) **Communication of Planning.** Many planning efforts fail because managers do not adequately emphasise the role of communicating various planning elements, such as, goals, strategies, policies, and planning premises. If these are communicated clearly, adequately, and timely, the managers are motivated and initiated to take planning process. Which may be necessary for them. When a manager understands the various aspects of planning he is in a better position to foresee his future course of action and may develop a habit of planning every course of future action.

(5) **Initiative.** Planning to be effective must have the initiative and support of top level management. It is the top level which is responsible for success or failure of any

organisational process, and planning is no exception. The basic objectives which are set at the top level must be two-way process which involves people at other levels also. Further, when top management rigorously reviews subordinates programmes, it naturally stimulates planning interest throughout the organisation. The planning action by top management does not suggest in everything will come from the top and subordinates will do nothing, rather the planning process should be a joint one.

(6) **Establishing a Climate.** The managers should try to establish a climate where every person in the organisation takes planning action. Every superior managers should remove obstacles to planning and present facilities for planning of his can be done by setting clear goals, establishing and publishing applicable significant planning premises, involving all managers in planning process, reviewing subordinate plans and their performance, and assuring appropriate staff assistance and information at all levies of management.

ORGANISATIONAL OBJECTIVES

Organisational objectives seek to direct the efforts of all members of a team while personal goals are motives of people working in the team. Efficiency is high when the two types of objectives are mutually supportive or compatible. Organisational objectives are the goals established to guide the efforts of the company and each of its components. Objectives are variously referred to as purposes, goals, missions, or targets. The establishment of objectives is a very important step in planning. Planning can be effective only if objectives are carefully selected. A clear statement of purpose understood by one and all is the best guarantee of effective management. Objectives must be actionable, that is, meaningful to the manager who is to achieve them. Objectives or goals must be specific and capable of accomplishment. They must be identified in such a way that ultimate success or failure can be determined.

The above description reveals the following characteristics of organisational objectives:

1. Every organisation has number of economic, social and human objectives rather than a single aim. As stated earlier, objectives are required in every area of business where the success and survival of the business is important. Every department or division has its own objectives in addition to the overall objectives of the organisation. Different objectives should be balanced with one another. A business firm has both general and specific objectives are narrow in scope *e.g.*, to reduce absenteeism. Organisational goals are sometimes divided into *(a)* maintenance goals, and *(b)* productivity goals. Maintenance goals are the expression of the desire to ensure the existence of the enterprise, while productivity goals aim at improvements in performance.
2. Objectives are the ultimate ends or results towards which an organisation and its members strive at all times. All activities and, resources of an enterprise are directed towards the achievement of common and specified objectives.
3. Objectives are the standing plans which recurringly guide action. They are the basis of other plans such as policies; procedure programmes, etc. Objectives are the concrete expressions of the purposes of an enterprises. Primary or major objectives provide the principal reasons for the establishment of the enterprise while collateral objectives supplement and contribute to the primary objectives. Organisational objectives are the basis of long range planning whereas departmental objectives provide the basis for short range planning. Different organisations have different objectives and there is no universal set of objectives. Objectives must, however, be practicable, consistent and clear cut. There must be proper coordination between major and derivative goals and between long range and short range objectives. Objectives should be specific,

verifiable and well planned. There must be active participation of all concerned in the determination of objectives.

4. Objectives are arranged in a hierarchy which is known as the 'Ends and Means Chain.' Objectives of a lower order act as the means for the achievement of higher level objectives. For instance, the organisational objectives are more basic than the departmental objectives.

5. Objectives may be long-term or short-term. Long-term objectives refer to the objectives to be achieved over a long period of time while short-term objectives are to be achieved within a period of one to two years. Short-run objectives are steps towards long-term objectives.

Impact on Strategic Planning Programme

(a) Clear and specific objectives avoid conflicts and misunderstanding. They facilitate unified action and integration of efforts on the part of members of the organisation. When objectives are clearly defined and there is agreement on them, every individual tries to adjust his actions and this leads to voluntary coordination. Thus objectives serve as the important tool of management. They define excellence in organisational performance. Without objectives, the manager possesses no tools for deciding whether performance is satisfactory or disappointing. By delimiting the course of the operations, objectives help to avoid misdirecting of the resources and to ensure maximum utilisation of the assets of the firm.

(b) Well-defined objectives help in effective delegation and decentralisation of authority. By providing clear-cut guidelines for action, they avoid the need for detailed and specific guidance on the part of management. Knowledge of objectives helps to transform random behaviour into systematic efforts. Goals are vital links in planning process.

(c) As there exists an ends and means relationship between objectives, objectives make for consistent and unified planning. Objectives provide the common denominator for different types of plans. The entire process of management concerns itself with means to achieve objectives.

(d) Objectives serve as the standards with which actual performance can be evaluated. They are also helpful in fixing responsibility. In this way, objectives provide the basis for control. Performance can continually be evaluated in terms of how well the organisation is moving in the direction of its objectives.

(e) Objectives provide a sense of purpose. They improve the motivation and morale of members of the organisation by making the job meaningful and worthwhile. They serve as guide-posts to action and efforts. Objectives are key to effective planning as plans have no meaning unless they are designed to achieve certain well defined objectives. By defining objectives, management establishes the image or character of the firm.

In the words of Ordway Tead, "it is difficult to overstress the notion of the purpose, aim, objective or goal of the organisation as fundamental to every view of or element in administration."

Planning can be a useful managerial function only if objectives are properly spelled out. Therefore, every enterprise should state its of objectives precisely and clearly.

❐

10

Strategic Value Analysis

One of the most difficult tasks that any of us face is the analysis of our own values. As managers in an organization it is especially hard because of the conflict that is the result of the various roles that we have, as manager, parent, citizen, "expert" or whatever. Each role gives rise to different sets of behaviour in terms of those groups or individuals with whom we interact. A cursory examination of our behaviour with others reveals the difficulty of finding consistency. Our behaviour towards one group in often inconsistent with our behaviour towards another group. Yet, if consistency is possible it is because there is something that underlies each of the social roles which we play. If Freud taught us anything it is that what is on the surface is not always what is real. Yet this attempt to "get behind the curtain" and carefully examine our values is fraught with difficulty. Revealing our hopes and dream and desires involves a great deal of personal risk and relies on our ability to trust those companions who undergo this process with us. The "quickie" values analysis of sensitivity training and other methods show how easy and costly mistakes are.

The analysis of ethical values has become a "hot" topic in business more recently. In the wake of alleged "corporate scandals" in Watergate, the Ford Pinto case and other newsworthy items, several corporations have begun to develop codes of ethics. Business schools have instituted courses in business ethics, and other courses have been questioned on their ethical component. Yet all questions of values are not questions of moral values. While a concern for ethics is a necessary ingredient to the analysis of "what do we stand for," it is not in itself sufficient. How, then, are we to understand the dominant values that are present in organizations? First, we need to be more precise about the nature of values. Second, we need to understand how personal values and organizational values fit together. Finally we need to know how organizational values fit among several different organizations. By trying to answer questions at each of these levels of analysis we can begin the process of values-clarification.

Values come in many flavours, sizes and shapes. There are aesthetic values about what things are beautiful or what is good art. There are social values about what kinds of institutions are good and just. There are religious values about the worthiness of beliefs in god. There are moral values about the goodness or rightness of certain kinds of actions which affect our fellow persons. There are values about all kinds of things such as what makes an apple a good apple, or what makes a strategic plan a good strategic plan, or what makes a managerial decision a good one, etc. It may help us to sort through this jungle if we distinguish two kinds of values, those which are intrinsic and those which are instrumental. Intrinsic values are basic. Things which are intrinsically valuable are good in and of themselves. Intrinsic values are to be pursued of their own account and worth. Unless two intrinsic values conflict, we do not usually compromise on them.

For some, being able to maximize their own or their family's happiness is an intrinsic value, yet another way of putting it, is that intrinsic value. Yet another way of putting it, is that intrinsic values represent the "bottom line" of life and its pursuits. Instrumental values are means to intrinsic values. We place instrumental value on those things which lead us toward the attainment of things, actions or states of mind which are intrinsically valuable. Religious rituals or services which lead us toward our belief in a supreme being may be of instrumental value.

Constitutions which guarantee freedom of action have instrumental value to those who see freedom of action as intrinsically valuable. For some, the creative or artistic process has instrumental value in so far as it leads to the creation of works of art. For some, work itself has instrumental value in so far as it leads to the ability to maximize happiness, or to self-fulfillment, etc. Therefore, activities which help to bring about intrinsic values also have value which we have called "instrumental value."

However, these activities do not have value in and of themselves, but they have value only so far as they contribute to the achievement of intrinsic values. It is easy to see how activities which originally have instrumental value gain intrinsic value.

As we get more caught up in the process of work. We give it intrinsic value regardless of the outcome. Workaholics abound in organizations. It is easy to replace intrinsic values with instrumental values, over a long period of time. Once values are intrinsic they are difficult to change, for we see those activities as good in themselves, and it does not matter if they lead to the original outcome. Instrumental values are relatively easier to change, for if a time honored method of activity can be shown not to lead to the desired result which is intrinsically valuable, then a new method must be tried.

Many of the activities in which an organization engages daily are instrumentally valuable, because they lead to the attainment of the instrinsic values of the organization and its members. Yet another useful distinction to make, if we are to understand the tangle of values in which we live, is that between the values of an individual and those of the organization. Organizations exist through time and span generations of members. Culture, tradition, purpose and personality of leaders all help to shape the values of an organization. However, it is not necessary for the values of an organization to be identical with the values of any member of the organization. Even the ultimate "organization man" may not completely and totally identify with his organization.

Organizational values will reflect history, will be slow to change over time and may be the amalgamation of the values of many individuals. Thus, organizational values may "fit" more or less well with the values of the individuals who are members of the organization. Executives in an organization should, however, be able to articulate the most important values of the organization, and there should be a high degree of congruence between their personal values and the values of the organization.

This analysis of organizational values is not specific to the business organization and can be applied to virtually any organization. However, it is easy to see why there are so many disagreements among an organization and its stakeholders. If there is dissonance between the values of an organization and its members, and dissonance between the values of "stakeholder organization" and its members, then it is a small wonder that successful transactions every occur. Several managers in XYZ company began to discuss organizational values in a management development seminar.

One group of managers insisted that the dominant value must be "survival of the firm" while another group insisted with equal vehemence that the dominant value must be "customer service." A third group believed that "profitability" was the key business value, while a fourth focused on "employee satisfaction." These managers spent a good deal of time trying to clarify- the meaning of these values and how their beliefs in them affected their firm. Needless to say, XYZ was undergoing a protracted period of organizational realignment where it was not clear that the old values were still appropriate for organizational survival. As it goes through the slow process of determining its organizational values, much of which cannot be done explicitly, XYZ runs the risk of alienating a large number of its stakeholders.

The first task in the process of "values analysis," is to explicate the intrinsic values of the executives in the organization, and to separate the intrinsic values of the executives in the organization, and to separate those values from the instrumental values, or activities which achieve intrinsic values. The second task is to explicate the intrinsic values of the organization itself, and to separate those values from the methods that have evolved to achieve those values. The third task is to analyze the differences between the personal values and organization values. The fourth task is to be explicit about where there are conflicts and inconsistencies, recognizing that changes may be hard to undertake. The fifth task is to analyze the intrinsic values of important stakeholder groups and to separate these values from the methods those groups use to attain them.

Social Issues Analysis

Given that managers understand the stakeholders in their organization, and understand their own and their stakeholders' values, it is necessary to understand the social context of the organization. That is, what are the major issues facing society today? What are the major issues facing our society in the next 5 to 10 years? What are the central differences between these two sets of issues? Again it might be useful to apply the schema developed earlier and divide these issues into economic, technological, political, social and managerial. The process of thinking through these two lists of issues helps to understand the place of the firm in society as it currently stands and helps to understand where it might lead, or at least what the assumptions are that managers make about where it might lead. Naturally the analysis will contain errors, and 10 years from now it might look silly. However, to formulate strategy at the enterprise level it is just as necessary to look at the future, as it is in forecasting the length of the product life-cycle at the product strategy level.

The analysis of social issues can be combined with stakeholder analysis to look at the impact of current and future social issues on the stakeholders of the firm. Continued acceleration of the micro-chip technology, together with the increased need for business-government cooperation may well give rise to a concern with privacy. The road to "telescreens" and "two-minute-hates" is not so distant as when Orwell wrote of them. The technology, together with the political climate, may well yield a scenario where individual freedom is threatened. If projections of the current state of the art in computer technology are remotely plausible, then it will be possible for every home to be wired together in a nationwide computer network. A computer system is like a bank vault in some sense. If something can be put into it, it can be taken out of it, and not always by the persons authorized to do so it is not hard to imagine the emergence of stakeholder groups concerned with the safeguarding of citizens privacy, given the current technology. Any computer company worth its salt must be worried about privacy, now, before there is a crisis. Several decisions could be taken to be prepared for the issue and stakeholders that will emerge. The first is for executives in major computer companies such as Digital Equipment, IBM, Control Data, etc. to individually decide how the privacy issue affects their firm, now and into the future. The second would be to sponsor joint research on the concept of privacy, to find out how current stakeholders feel.

Finally, we could initiate programs of development and education to find solutions to commonly voiced concerns. These decisions are necessary now, before some Luddite backlash emerges, and regulations are passed which limit the beneficial uses of computer technology; however, they should only be made within the context of a careful understanding of what an individual business stands for in terms of its values on issues such as privacy. The purpose of these pieces of analysis is to lay the groundwork for the formulation of enterprise level strategy, or a statement of "what do we stand for." By combining an understanding of the stakeholders in an organization, the values of the organization and an account of the social issues which affect the firm now and in the future, we can articulate a statement of either, where the organization currently is, with respect to its enterprise strategy, or we can formulate a new direction for the enterprise.

A Typology Enterprise Strategy

There are many ways to put these pieces of analysis together into a statement of enterprise level strategy. Stakeholders, values and social issues are all important ingredients and can be mixed together in a variety of proportions. However they are put together the outcome should be some sort of "fit" with the society in which managers find themselves. Organizations which do not have an appropriate enterprise strategy over time are not socially viable, and experience a great deal of both internal and external turbulence. What the organization stands for is not consistent with the values of its members causing internal stress, and is not consistent with the needs of its stakeholders or the social issues of the time causing external stress. There are at least five generic enterprise level strategies which can be seen as achieving "fit" among stakeholders, values and social issue . Each of these strategies represents a whole set of particular responses and action to the circumstances facing an individual firm. Hence, these generic strategies are broad descriptions of answers to "what do we stand for," and involve tradeoffs about the relative importance of stakeholder concerns, values and social issues. We shall briefly discuss each of the following:

(1) specific stakeholder strategy

(2) stockholder strategy

(3) utilitarian strategy

(4) Rawlsian strategy

(5) social harmony strategy.

Other enterprise level strategies are possible in addition to those mentioned here, which has been singled out to be of particular interest.

Narrow Stakeholder Strategy

– Maximize benefits to one or a small set of stakeholders

Stockholder Strategy

– Maximize benefits to stockholders

– Maximize benefits to stakeholders

Utilitarian Strategy

– Maximize benefits to all stakeholders (greatest good for greatest number)

– Maximize average welfare level of all stakeholders

– Maximize benefits

– to society

– Rawlsian strategy

– Act to raise the level of the worst-off stakeholder

Social Harmony Strategy

– Act to maintain or create social harmony

– Act to gain consensus from society

Specific Stakeholder Strategy

One response to "what do we stand for" is to concentrate the efforts of the firm towards satisfying the needs of a small number of specific stakeholder groups, of the needs of one or two generic stakeholder groups. For example, if "Customer Service" and "Employee Welfare" are the basic values for a particular organization, and if everything the firm does is aimed at achieving these intrinsic values, then in some realistic sense that firm stands for improving the welfare of customers and employees. Since these are but two of many stakeholders, we have dubbed this kind of enterprise strategy, "specific stakeholder strategy." To adopt such a strategy is to try and maximize the benefits of the firm to a relatively narrow group of stakeholders.

The concept of "specific stakeholder strategy" leads to the following hypothesis:

> "If the actions of the firm have a relatively narrow range of effects on a relatively small number of stakeholders, and if the values of the managers of the firm are closely aligned with the values of these stakeholders, and if there is little relevant social change, then the firm is likely to adopt a specific stakeholder strategy of maximizing the returns to a small set of stakeholders. An example of firms adopting specific stakeholder strategies would appear to be several firms in the computer business who align themselves almost totally with the customer. Hewlett-Packard, IBM and Digital Equipment are almost legendary for their customer relationships."

From published accounts it is difficult to tell if this customer alignment is an end in itself or a means to an end, but there is some evidence that it is an end in itself. The history of the industry involved creating a demand for its products. The resulting attention to customer needs and customer service has become the criterion for success and leadership in the industry. We could hypothesize that as managers come up through the ranks in a company oriented towards sô much that it would be impossible to change the orientation of the company. Social issues have had little effect on these companies as they have developed. Perhaps with the advent of the personal computer and large computer network available to the public for little cost, the impact of social issues such as privacy and "1984" will increase, thereby necessitating a re-examination of the enterprise level strategies of these firms.

The second type of enterprise strategy is really a special case of the specific stakeholder strategy However, it so pervades our way of thinking that we can list it separately. It is the concentration of effort by managers towards satisfying the needs of the stockholders of the firm. The stockholder strategy is perceived to be so pervasive as to warrant extra attention, even though its logic is identical with that of the narrow stakeholder strategy where "stockholder" is substituted for "narrow range of stakeholders." The essence of the stockholder strategy is "to maximize returns to stockholders," or if interpreted more broadly, "to maximize the market value of the firm." Executives in firms who adopt the stockholder strategy usually believe that they have a fiduciary obligation to stockholders, that is, they must always seek to act in the interests of the stockholders. However, it must be noted that the legal concept of management as bearing fiduciary obligation to stockholders is undergoing some change.

Taken to its logical extreme, such an enterprise strategy could involve actions which are immoral or unethical, as well as illegal. When questioned about payments to the Committee to re-elect the President in 1972, one Chief Executive respond that he was doing what was necessary to protect the interests of the company and its stockholders. A closely related variant of the stockholder strategy might be called "the financial stakeholder strategy." This version relies on satisfying the interests of the set of stakeholders who have who have financial stakes in the firm, or who can heavily influence those stakeholders who have financial stakes. Thus, management actions are aimed towards stockholders, banks, other holders of debt, investment analysts, etc. The values of management in this case must dictate that "financial stake" counts for more than other kinds of interests. Management recognizes that "ownership" needs to be broadened to include any group who is risking its capital in the firm.

One hypothesis suggested by the above analysis is:

> If the actions of a firm have effects which are perceived by its managers to be primarily economic, and if the values of management are oriented towards satisfying a fiduciary obligation to the owners of the firm, and if the relevant social issues are perceived by managers to be economic growth and prosperity, then the firm will adopt a stockholder strategy, to maximize the returns to stockholders or to maximize the market value of the firm.

Examples of the stockholder strategy are abundant. Firms who pride themselves on the increase in the quarterly dividend .above all else, who pay constant attention to short term measures of performance and who run their businesses as if the corporation were an investment company with its businesses as its portfolio of stocks are all candidates for the stockholder strategy.

A third enterprise level strategy is one that tries to improve the general quality of life in society. Actions are undertaken which raise the general welfare of society. Such firms answer "what do we stand for" with "improving society," or "doing something that is socially useful" Managers in these firms usually believe that the firm does have a wide range of effects on stakeholder groups. They believe that the purpose of the corporation is to produce the greatest good for the greatest number of people in society, that business is fundamentally a social institution and thereby incurs obligations which must be discharged by seeking to produce social good. Such firms will be responsive to social issues and will seek to contribute to the development of these issues. Thus, our hypothesis is:

"If the actions of a firm are perceived by its managers to have a wide range of effects on stakeholders, and if the managers have utilitarian values, *i.e.*, that they should maximize the social welfare as far as is possible and if there are a wide range of social issues that affect the firm, then the firm will adopt a utilitarian strategy to maximize the welfare of as many stakeholders as possible."

One example of this strategy might be AT&T's development and implementation of "Universal service" as a guiding principle for managing the telephone business. "Universal Service" means that telephone service is made available to as many people as possible because the telephone is socially desirable. Policies, including pricing, are adopted to make telephone service available to everyone regardless of income level or location.

Accounting practices, service organizations, internal measurements are all oriented towards maximizing the availability of the telephone and thereby raising the general quality of life in society. It can be argued that AT &T adopted such a strategy in its early days to appease the government officials worried about anti-trust, etc. But, this does not invalidate the strategy, if AT&T is genuinely concerned with "universal service" as a method for improving social welfare and if such a concern has become the guiding intrinsic value for its managers.

A fourth generic strategy at the enterprise level is for the managers of a firm to see themselves as agents of social change. In particular in the U.S. they might see themselves as seeking to bring about true equality of opportunity or seeking to maximize the amount of freedom that individuals have to live their own gives. Rawls has argued that social institutions are just only in so far as they insure individual liberties that are compatible with "a like liberty for all," and that the offices and privileges are open to anyone regardless of race, sex, etc. Rawls argues further that inequalities in the distribution of goods and services in a society are justified only if the inequalities raise the level of the least well-off social groups. A crude application of Rawls's theory to the issue at hand, the development of enterprise level strategy, would possibly dictate that a firm seek to raise the level of its least well-off stakeholder and to insure that its employment and promotion practices encourage equal opportunity to all social groups. In order for a Rawlsian strategy to be appropriate managers must share the values which underlie the theory; namely, they must believe that the just society does not discriminate among social classes in its allocation of basic goods and services. Furthermore, managers must believe that the corporation can have some effect in correcting current inequalities if any exist, and these basic values of equality of opportunity and freedom underlie a host of current and future social issues. Thus, our hypothesis is:

> If the actions of a firm are perceived to have a wide range of effects on stakeholders of differing social positions, and if the values of the managers are oriented towards freedom and equality of oppodunity for all members in society and if social issues which affect the firm are concerned with freedom and equality of opportunity, then the firm will adopt a Rawlsian strategy, *i.e.*, it will seek to raise the welfare of the least well-off stakeholder groups and to insure that the positions in the firm are open to all members .of society. One example of a Rawlsian strategy might well be Control Data's undertaking to improve the lot of inner cities through their City Venture subsidiary. Projects are undertaken which help to renovate portions of the inner core of decaying cities, usually as a subcontractor, to, or in conjunction with, government. Additionally, Control Data has undertaken to train and employ the "hardcore" unemployed in several cities. In short they have looked for business opportunities which are not only profitable but which raise the level of the least advantage groups in society.

A fifth generic strategy comes from a cursory analysis of some other societies and the methods businesses have in aligning themselves very closely with the local communities. It is possible to adopt an enterprise strategy based on the principle of social harmony, that is, to insure that whatever action is taken, it is agreable to and supported by a large, near unanimous group of stakeholders. The emphasis on social harmony comes from the basic values of communitarianism, where we value being a respected member of the community over all else. Under such a strategy, the company gets its essential identity from the community, and is unwilling to go along a divergent path. When conflict arises with stakeholders, major efforts are undertaken to resolve the conflict to the "mutual understanding" of all parties.

During an executive development program with several Japanese managers question was posed as to what they would do when a conflict arose between their company and the local community. One manager replied, "we would talk with them until we reached a mutual understanding." Upon further probing and asking what would happen if no such understanding were achieved. He replied, "we would talk some more until we reached a mutual understanding." One then asked him what would be done if the company's interest was diametrically opposed to the community's interest. And, he replied once again, "we would talk until we reached a mutual understanding of our interests." Such an approach depends on values very much like those described in a harmony strategy.

Necessity of Enterprise Strategy

It is very easy to misinterpret the foregoing analysis as yet another call for corporate social responsibility or business ethics. While these issues are important in their own right, enterprise level strategy is a different concept. We need to worry about enterprise level strategy for the simple fact that corporate survival depends in part one there being some "fit" between the values of the corporation and its managers, the expectations of stakeholders in the firm and the societal issues which will determine the ability of the firm to sell its products. For instance, if we are to be able to innovate with new technology and bring new products to market, we must understand how such changes affect the people in our business, as well as whether it helps us to meet continuing expectations of stakeholders.

To return to our earlier example, if Bell wishes to survive, its managers must understand the changes in their values that are necessary to compete in the new tele-communications environment. Whether such changes are socially responsible or morally praiseworthy is an important question, but it is yet a further question which an analysis of enterprise strategy does not address.

Enterprise strategy is concerned with the question of "consistency" among the key elements of a firm's relationship with its environment. The formulation of enterprise strategy helps us to begin to clearly articulate corporate values, and to insure that they are in touch with the expectations of those groups who have a stake in the firm. Corporate strategists have ignored this level of strategic thinking for too long. It can be the difference between success and failure in today's business environment. By addressing the issues in an "upfront and tough-minded" manner, we can avoid the worst case that is prevalent in many firms: self-deception. Self-deception occurs when we do not honestly ask the tough questions, and do not accurately assess our own values and the stakeholder picture that we face. It involves saying one thing and acting on another. Self-deception is the difference between those values that we espouse and those that are really in force, and is one of the main reasons for a credibility ap between management and its stakeholders. Here are a few examples:

1. XYZ Company espoused quality of work life in its brochures and other communications to its employees. The president of XYZ made a speech in which he articulated "the moral responsibility" of XYZ to its employees, and commended the employee body of XYZ for serving the company well during its history. However, soon afterwards the company began to offer early retirement in an effort to reduce the number of employees, and later began to layoff employees. The actions of the company did not match its words.
2. ABC Company espoused the need to work closely with a particular government agency to find ways of regulation

that benefited ABC, the agency and the local community. Yet resources were not allocated and time was not spent to deal with the agency. "Good intentions" led no where, and the company was slow to deal with a non-productive adversarial relationship with the government.

3. JKL Company espoused the value of doing what was in the shareholder's best interests. The management of JKL made many public statements, and quite probably private ones to each other, about the need to work for the shareholder. Yet when a merger proposal was put on the table by another company which would give JKL shareholders roughly a 300% premium over the current value of the stock, it was turned down by management as "not in the shareholder's interest." Self-deception, on a large scale, had occurred.

Each of the enterprise strategies outlined above holds possibilities for self-deception. With the separation of ownership and control, it is easy for the intrinsic value involved in carrying out this fiduciary obligation to take on less and less importance over time. One "bad faith" variation of the stockholder strategy is described by Burnham whereby managers maximize the control that they can exert over the affairs of the firm, regardless of the effect on the interests of the stockholders. Williamson has investigated the conditions under which such managerial discretion arises and becomes pervasive. "Acting in the interests of the stockholders" becomes the rationalization for exerting control over the affairs of the corporation. Tender offers which appear to increase the stockholders returns will be rejected. Joint ventures which have potentially high payoffs will be spurned when they require a sharing of control.

Management will act defensively to regulatory attempts to change the practices of the firm, and it will ignore social issues and critics as inappropriate and as not in the interests of the stockholders. Bad faith versions of utilitarian strategies are possible as well. Here, we could claim that whatever is done in the interests of the stockholders is automatically in the interests of society. Therefore, since our basic values are utilitarian, every action must be evaluated in terms of being in the interests of the stockholders. An even more deceiving situation can occur if our basic values are really oriented towards control of the affairs of the corporation. A double bind resulting from the deceptive version of the stockholder strategy occurs whereby almost any action can be justified in either the interests of the stockholders or the interests of society, or in short in the interests of any group other than management, which is of course the real group in whose interests the action is undertaken. There is, of course, a similar version of the Rawlsian strategy, for it is possible to exploit the least well off groups in society under the guise of making them better off. We might believe that sweat shops, below subsistence wages, selling inferior quality products in ghettos, making non-nutritional food available in poor areas, etc. are examples of business practices which are possible to rationalize through an application of Rawlsian principles.

It is also possible to argue, albeit not logically, that raising the level of the least well off groups occurs when there is more for everyone, *i.e.*, when we try to maximize the greatest good for the greatest number of stakeholders, and that more for everyone is accomplished only when actions are taken which maximize the interests of the owners of the firm. Here we are right back to the original pathology in the stockholder strategy, but with a level of rationalization and rhetoric possible to confuse even the most enlightened stockholder. The harmony strategy presents equally thorny problems, for we can use the unwillingness of the community to change as an excuse for not finding alternative methods of accomplishing our goals. The harmony strategy can act as a rationalization for the status quo, when in reality we need to work very hard at "reaching a mutual understanding."

Socrates said that the unexamined life is not worth living and that the secrets of life are knowable only if "know thyself" is followed. We believe that Socrates advice is applicable to us as managers. Only by understanding "what we stand for" can we clearly articulate business issues which are important and address those issues in a manner which is rational. It is easy for us to deceive ourselves, whether we are making decisions about beginning a personal exercise program or launching a new subsidiary.

The purpose of analyzing enterprise level strategy and claiming that there are at least five generic strategies which can be consistently or inconsistently applied from the analysis of stakeholders, values and social issues has not been to argue for one or another of the five strategies. Rather, one believes that it is important for us to understand honestly whatever our enterprise strategy happens to be. So little is known about the values as they exist in organizational life that one believes it is premature to argue for the' preference of one strategy over another.

By attempting to articulate enterprise level strategies, executives set the context for the next round of development of corporate level strategies, and the organization moves slowly towards a unified purpose that both produces bottom line results and serves the purposes and values of executives and other organizational members and stakeholders. Enterprise level strategy is no panacea. But, it is necessary if we are -to survive in the world as it exist today.

A more traditional approach to setting direction for the corporation involves answering the corporate level questions. At least two methods have evolved in the literature and in practice for analyzing the business, or set of businesses, in which a firm competes. Each of these methods seeks to determine the "proper" set of businesses for the firm, and each has been used in most major V.S. corporations. Following Andrews and Christens on, Andrews and Bower situational analysis identifies "the pattern of purpose and policies defining the company and its businesses. Strengths, weaknesses, opportunities and threats are determined, corporate resources are analyzed, and a rigorous set of questions is answered, including, "Where are we now," "What can we do" "What do we want to do," and "What should we do." The bottom line to situational analysis is that many different factors are important in determining the strategic position of a firm, and the set of relevant factors may depend on the industries in which the firm has historically competed, the individual strengths of the managers and other contingencies.

An alternative approach to setting direction at the corporate level is the use of a "portfolio approach," whereby the individual business elements of a multi-business firm are plotted on a grid which measures relative market share versus industry growth. The idea behind portfolio theory is that at the corporate level the strategic task is to achieve a balanced portfolio, where "balanced" is to be understood as "smooth overall cash flow" or "the achievement of a maximum overall return for a given level of risk" or an acceptable level of overall growth. Resources are allocated among the corporation's set of businesses according to how each "fits" with the overall portfolio.

We noted that neither of these approaches is sufficient, in and of itself, to take account of the business environment that most executives face today. They do not automatically account for, nor measure, the influence of multiple stakeholders effects on the firm. It is easy to overlook the stakeholders in the firm using only situation analysis; however, we might explicitly add more questions to make the analysis even more complex and to collect and analyze a host of data on stakeholder influences. The major concern with situational analysis is then compounded. It offers no systematic way to put the pieces of the analysis together.

On the other hand, portfolio theory simply ignores, or at least discounts, the ability of non-marketplace stakeholders to affect the businesses of the firm. Hence, if rigidly followed, portfolio theory leads to decisions to invest in businesses which, give little incentive to a firm's stakeholders to offer their support for the firm. Both of these methods of setting corporate direction can be enriched to yield a better understanding ,of the firms's stakeholders. One such process that has been developed is the "stakeholder audit." Just as the financial audit creates and certifies a financial roadmap for the firm, so does a stakeholder audit create and certify a roadmap of the external environment of the firm. The stakeholder audit process builds on the analytical techniques developed of identifying the stakeholders and their stakes in the firm, as well as the analysis conducted in setting direction at the enterprise level.

However, the stakeholder audit process does not assume that a firm has a carefully articulated enterprise strategy, nor does it assume that a firm has a good idea of who its stakeholders actually are? Rather, in keeping with the framework developed, this type of audit assumes that there are stakeholders in the external environment of the firm whether its manager are aware of them or not. This is similar to the fact that a financial audit can be done, albeit with difficulty, whether a business follows generally accepted accounting principles or not. One such "stakeholder audit" process consisting of four; main strategic tasks: *(1)* stating the corporate mission; *(2)* identifying stakeholder issues and concerns; *(3)* assessing corporate strategies for stakeholders; and *(4)* adjusting stakeholder priorities. In addition, there are several feedback loops in the process. This process can be tailor-mad depending on the particular situation of a firm, and thus it should not be viewed as a rigid set of steps to be followed at all costs. Rather, it is meant to serve as a conceptual guideline for managers who want to understand their environments in stakeholder terms. A brief discussion to each of these tasks and feedback loops and some examples of how this process can be used follows:

Task 1: Stating the Corporate Mission. Many hours of executive trime have been spent trying to formulate a statement of corporate purpose which is both meaningful and acceptable to a majority of the top executives in the firm. Often times it is simply impossible for them to agree on the definition of the firm's business. Such conflict is good for the organization as long as it is productive and dealt with openly. The stakeholder audit process begins with a provisional statement of the mission as it appears in the annual report, has been articulated in the business press or has been explained in the corporate planning process or to financial analysis. From this provisional statement of mission the businesses of the corporation are identified, again, as they have been traditionally arranged. Thus, a company whose mission is to achieve a dominant position in the micro-computer business, may have several distinct business areas such as "business software," "games," "computers" and "peripherals." These businesses mayor may not be segmented by strategic business units, again depending on the degree of sophistication of the company's planning system.

From the analysis of mission, business and generic stakeholder a matrix similar to this exhibit can be constructed which shows in grid form the importance of each class of stakeholder to achieving success in each business. This generic stakeholder /business success matrix is useful, not only in initially thinking through the relative importance of each stakeholder category, but it organizes the information in a way that allows executives to readily determine which stakeholders will have an impact on the implementation of specific business goals and objectives.

Task 2: Identifying Stakeholder Issues and Concerns. Once the generic stakeholder analysis has been completed, specific stakeholder groups for each business need to be identified. Here a stakeholder map for each business can be drawn. Again, a ranking procedure may be used to deduce importance of particular stakeholder groups for success in a business. From the analysis of specific stakeholders, several versions of the stakes of each group can be deduced. The degree of detail should vary by the depth of understanding that managers have *vis-a-vis* stakeholders. The degree of detail need not be uniform for all stakeholders, with more effort spent on those groups which managers feel they understand relatively less well.

Once this initial analysis is completed a list of key concerns or issues must be developed for each stakeholder group. In many cases the information required to complete this steps will be readily available from historical records and the experiences of individual managers. In some cases, however, the information must be systematically gathered by interviewing individual stakeholders, briefing session with managers who are "stakeholder experts" or "boundary spanners" responsible for a particular stakeholder relationship and by an analysis of the public record to determine positions of stakeholders on key issues.

This information can be aggregated at the corporate level and displayed in a matrix of stakeholders *vs.* issues and concerns.

Completion of a stakeholders issues matrix enables the managers involved in the audit process to orient themselves externally towards the issues and concerns of key external groups. The managers can identify the sensitivity points in their external environment and pinpoint the issues or concerns which must be resolved if success in particular businesses can be achieved. The matrix also allows an aggregate look across businesses at the concerns of employees, consumer advocates or local communities, enabling managers to think about the strategies which the firm as a whole may have with these stakeholder groups.

Task 3: Assessing Corporate Strategies for Stakeholders. Task 1 and 2 create an external view of the firm by analyzing stakeholders and the key concerns of each. The purpose of Task 3 is to identify how the firm is currently meeting the needs of its stakeholders, *i.e.*, what is the current strategy of the firm with regard to each stakeholder or group of stakeholders. This strategy statement must not only include what the firm is currently doing with respect to a stakeholder but how the firm is accomplishing the strategy or the process of achievement, and what organizational unit within the firm has responsibility. Identifying existing stakeholder strategies can normally be accomplished by a review process with the SBU, division or functional managers responsible. However, in large and complex organizations it may be the case that no one is responsible for a particular stakeholder group at the corporate level, with responsibility residing at the "strategy center" level.

Corporate staff in public relations or public affairs may have functional responsibility for non-traditional stakeholder groups such as consumer advocates, the media and government, and may be formulating programs in virtual isolation from the strategy center managers. It will be difficult, in such cases to articulate a strategy for the corporation as a whole towards a particular stakeholder or set of stakeholders. Also, the corporate strategy may well be inconsistent with the programs undertaken at the lower levels in the firm. Once a statement of purpose and an action plan for each stakeholder has been identified at the business and corporate level, the response of stakeholder groups can be determined. Again, interview with stakeholders or internal experts, as well as searching the public record needs to be undertaken. The effectiveness of each strategy can then be rated on a simple scale of effective, somewhat effective, somewhat ineffective, in effective and undetermined. A stakeholder strategy matrix to display this information for the firm as a whole.

Task 4: Adjusting Corporate Priorities. Obviously, the desired result in the stakeholder audit process is to readjust the corporate priorities to more closely align the firm with satisfying stakeholder need, or towards changing the mission of the firm. Given the assessment of firms environment and the effectiveness of current strategies in dealing with stakeholders in Tasks 1-3, the senior managers conducting the audit must decide where to put the firm's priorities. Ideally, the enterprise level strategy will set the context for this analysis, but realistically, many firms have not articulated their strategy at such an abstract level.

Thus, particular corporate level strategies may need revision giving rise to Loop 1 and the need to reassess the position of a particular business and the programs it is using to achieve success with its stakeholders. Or, if there are enough ineffective or questionable strategies, then the executives need to travel down Loop-2 and to re-examine the mission of the firm. By undertaking a stakeholder audit on a regular basis managers can gain a good understanding of how effectively the firm is meeting the requirements of its environment and meeting the stated mission of the firm.

The length of time to complete an audit varies by size and degree of complexity of the firm. However, it should be relatively easy to integrate the process into the front end of the planning cycle. Alternatively, the audit can be performed as a one-time snapshot of how well the organization is meeting stakeholder concerns. The latterprocess is more in the mode of validation, and should be undertaken only if the firm has some idea of its entire array of stakeholders.

Tailor Making the Stakeholder Audit

CD Insurance Co

CD Insurance Co. is a relatively small insurance company whose primary business is health insurance. CD writes both group and individual policies, and is in a few other peripheral businesses which are a small part of its total sales. A limited number of large customers account for a high proportion of CD's business. CD operates in a limited geographical area and for the most part has a very good reputation in this area as a good corporate citizen. In fact, the enterprise level strategy can probably be classified as utilitarian, as CD managers were quite conscious of promoting the welfare ,of the community, as well as the health of its policyholders. A new CEO at CD became worried about the changes that the insurance industry in general, and the health care industry in particular, were undergoing. The new CEO also began to change the enterprise level strategy towards spreading what he perceived the financial risks to be, and hence more towards a stockholder strategy.

High inflation and the availability of other financial, instruments made the workers of the industry the individual life policy, virtually obsolete. At the same time corporate customers began to see the need for broader services involving employee benefits, health coverage, group life and even corporate financial services which large data processing oriented companies could provide. Large insurance companies were beginning to offer a full product line which would compete with CD's market niche, in terms of both products and geographies. Some large firms were beginning to move into data processing, communications and business services, threatening to make CD's group insurance business obsolete.

Aetna and IBM had formed a partnership to operate Satellite Business Systems. American Express and its Fireman's Fund subsidiary were clearly in the same "complete business services" market: Other large firms such, as Prudential, Connecticut General, etc. were experimenting with innovations such as group legal, dental and even group auto insurance in efforts to who large corporate clients. Within the context of the health care industry the recent regulatory pressure began to drastically affect the cost of health care medicare and Medicaid programs were increasingly going to the "low cost producer" and the ability to win those contracts was based on the efficiency of a company's data-processing operations. New technological advances in data-processing were beginning to outstrip the availability of systems, therefore firms who could afford substantial capital investment had an advantage.

Thus, the competitive structure of the industry began to change. New stakeholders emerged, as well as new issues, and the picture of the external environment of traditionally staid and conservative insurance companies began to radically shift. As a relatively small player, CD needed to take stock of this environment and attempt to position itself favourably for the future. Executives at CD saw its mission as maintaining its current position in .the market, while seeking to find a niche in some other industry for the future. A stakèholder analysis of CD showed five major generic groups of stakeholders, or five separate environments, in which CD could possibly operate. These five areas were (in the order of importance): *(1)* Health Insurance; *(2)* Other Insurance; *(3)* Local Community; *(4)* Financial Services; and *(5)* Data Processing. East set of stakeholders yielded several major issues and a set of questions for CD managers to answer in terms of the strengths and weaknesses of the company in dealing with the issues and stakeholders in a particular area such as data processing, as well as the opportunities and threats which that area held for the company. The net result of this stakeholder audit process, tailor-made to examine the further stakeholder environment, of CD was the formulation of several alternative corporate missions. The alternatives considered included: *(1)* becoming a data processing consulting firm in the local community; *(2)* developing a more complete line of insurance products; *(3)* opening an BMa, and going into the "wellness" business; *(4)* expanding the health insurance business into other markets; and *(5)* looking for a merger partner. The generation of these options caused a great deal of conflict at CD. The CEO and his top management team had to choose a path to follow.

They picked they relatively safe alternatives of opening an HMO and expanding into some new markets, while keeping an eye open, for a merger partner. Such alternatives were not acceptable to all managers, and some did leave the company. While the managers at CD are still in the process of shifting the priorities in the company to achieve a shift in corporate direction, their stakeholder audit helped them to better understand how the external environment was changing, and the strategic options, that were available to them.

SVA Methodology

The name "Strategic Value Analysis" stems from the idea that the strategic value of information and information technology must be understood in order to identify and evaluate opportunities and derive a meaningful plan. This goal is accomplished by linking information and systems capabilities to the strategic objectives of the organization in a clear and concise manner. The nature of this linkage will be explained in the following sections. Before proceeding with an overview of the SVA methodology, we need to clarify the conditions under which it is applicable, and those for which it is not. It will become clear that the proposed method represents a serious and costly undertaking by any organization, and cannot be successful unless it has senior management understanding and support. The methodology does not apply to short-term planning situations with narrow scopes; it is best geared to long time horizons and broad scopes. It also applies best to situations in which a fundamental examination of information systems technology can have payoffs; some reasons to believe this is true should exist beforehand. For example, competitors might be improving their operations, the existing automated systems might be very outdated, or perhaps everyone just believes there is great potential.

There are valid reasons why the methodology is not applicable. One is a belief that the existing systems reflect the most modern business practices. Or the business, while large, is so simple that information flows and systems have been easily rationalized and modernized. And of course, if the business is not in a stable or growth position, but rather is declining, then it usually does not make sense to make heavy investments in a fundamental modernization program. In these situations, other modes and methods of information-systems planning are appropriate.

Planning Task Force

The complete SVA methodology is carried out as a 10-step process. While the flow of activities is generally as depicted, some of the steps can be worked on concurrently. These steps are undertaken by a task force of representatives from the functional areas of the organization included within the scope of the planning exercise, along with key informational-systems personnel. The make-up of the planning task force is critical to the success of the planning project, and to the quality of the resulting plan. An underlying theme to the SVA approach is the need to challenge the *status quo*, not only with respect to information systems, but relative to everyday business practices as well. Persons with limited parochial viewpoints, who cannot conceive of doing things differently, are not the proper participants for the planning task force. Nor are the anarchists who criticize everything but have no constructive opinions of their own. Rather, the best people for the task force are those who can think of alternatives to current ways of doing things, who are deeply knowledgeable about the needs of the .functional areas they represent yet have an overall company viewpoint, and who can deal at a conceptual level. The task-force representatives should be recognized by both senior management and their own peers as knowledgeable and influential members of the firm. This is important, because one of the benefits of the heavy user participation in the task force is the creation of grass-roots support for the plan by those who will have to make it work.

The kinds of people required to sustain the SVA methodology are precisely those who the organization can spare the least. But, there is no alternative. Typical task force make-up ranges from 6-15 persons, working from one-quarters to three-quarters of their time for periods ranging from 2-5 months. The temptation to accept personnel who are more available but less desirable should be resisted. The quality of participation, not the quantity, is what matters. It is important that the core members of the planning task force cover all of the functional areas included within the scope of the planning exercise. Several members should be representatives from the information-system organization, but in general more users than systems personnel are needed. The task force can also reach out to those with particular knowledge or viewpoints as required. The use of outside consultants on the task force has proven valuable. Consultants can provide a neutral viewpoint to the diversity of opinion, can bear much of the administrative and project management duties of the team, and can bring new ideas and a broader experience to the undertaking. They can also ask the difficult "why" and "why not" questions.

The first step in the Strategic Value Analysis approach is a review of strategic business plans. If no formal strategic planning is done within the organization, then some effort needs to be expended to develop a set of business objectives prior to launching the systems planning exercise. The SVA method is driven by the set of business objectives and cannot be utilized without them. The planning task force must thoroughly understand the strategic business objectives and their relative importance. Discussions with corporate planning representatives and senior management may be useful in gaining an understanding of the plans and objectives beyond that available from a review of written documents.

The business objectives should be ranked to reflect their relative significance, both to understand their importance and because in some causes the objectives can be contradictory. For example, common business goals, such as to reduce product cost and increase product quality, can some-times pe contradictory. If we can conceive of ways to do both, fine. But if, for instance, a proposed change increases quality by x at an increase in product cost by y, then is it worthwhile? To insure that the relative importance of business objectives is understood, assign them a percentage factor. The percentages of all objectives must total 100 per cent. The interpretation is as follows: If management had $100.00 to spend in achieving these objectives, how would the money be allocated (assuming each dollar would have the same effect on any objective)? Sometimes a breakdown of the objective can be made based on operating data. For instance, if the objective to reduce direct product costs has been assigned 30 per cent, and we know that material consumes two-thirds of the direct cost while labour consumes one-third,. then we might identify sub-objectives of:

Reduce direct material costs—20 per cent

Reduce direct labour costs—10 per cent

The next step in the methodology is the most critical and time consuming. It involves analyzing the business in a top-down fashion using data-flow diagrams. A major output of this step is a process model of the business. Which can serve as a framework for a variety of systems design and implementation activities.

The technique presented here is based on the structured systems analysis method, very similar to the approach employed by Cane and Sarson, DeMarco, Ross and Schoman, Ross et al and others. Basically, the idea is to analyze and describe the business operations and information flow in ever increasing levels of detail. The point of view is a functional one and not related to organizational structure. Typically, the analysis is performed in two ways. First, the "as is" or current situation is depicted, followed by the "to be" situations, which incorporates improvements and enhancements. In the SVA methodology, the emphasis is on the "to be" description of the business. The differences between the "as is" and the "to be" analyses are proposed by the planning task force in order to:

- Rationalize business practices which no longer make sense
- Unify business practices across factories or departments
- Help achieve a strategic business objective
- Make effective use of information systems and technology

The structured analysis approach is sometimes referred to as "functional decomposition," because it breaks down business functions into lower levels of detail. Strategic value Analysis also breaks down the business objectives into lower levels of detail, reflecting the breakdown of the functions. At each level, a set of sub-objectives is produced that identifies how that function can achieve the higher-level objectives. This is a powerful technique for forcing the examination of objectives at each function of the business and in increasing levels of detail. It establishes linkage between strategic plans and actual business operations.

The context developed is ideal for identifying new methods of doing business, improved information flows, and the need for information systems, all in support of the stated business objectives. Conversely, it brings to light ongoing programs and projects that are not in support of business objectives. Depicts the concept of functional decomposition along with decomposition of business objectives. The third step in SVA involves a review of existing information-systems support, and usually proceeds in parallel with a number of other activities. Not all members of the task force have the same level of knowledge relative to the company's ongoing information-systems activities and this step helps to insure that each member has a common base of understanding.

There are a number of reasons why this understanding is important to the planning effort. First, the relative assessment of information requirements should take into account the current level of support; in other words, the task force evaluates opportunities that can help to achieve business objectives over and above what is already in place. Second, when it comes to developing an implementation plan, existing systems must be taken into account as interfaces and as sources of data. The implementation plan that emerges from the planning study must be realistic in terms of the organization's ability to carry it out. Thus, some understanding is required of the hardware, software, personnel, and other resources currently available. These resources can represent opportunities to capitalize on or constraints to overcome.

The fourth proceeds to identify information-system capabilities that can help achieve the business objectives. These are developed for each of the lower-level processes, and are described from a functional and not a system viewpoint. For example, consider level 2 function of "Assemble Products". It has an objective to lower line inventory that is derived from the objective to lower material costs associated with its higher level function ("Manufacture Products"). Information system capabilities that could help achieve this objective might be:

- A daily (instead of weekly) replenishment system for production line inventory.
- A system to drive an automated conveyor to feed line inventory.
- An improved line-balancing program for better inventory usage projections rather than mini max.

The importance of these capabilities is evaluated in terms of their contribution to the stated business objectives.

In step 5, the logical data base to support the "to be" data flows and needed capabilities is designed. The methodology for this step is one that has evolved over the past 15 years and has been applied to more than 100 data-planning and design situations. It is an easy-to-learn technique, and can be mastered without having any technical computer science background. The emphasis is on coming to grips with how the organization should define and structure its information concepts in a way that can accommodate the needs of all functions. It also formalizes the conceptual framework that is usually informal and often inconsistent as previously described.

Next, the capabilities that were delineated in step 4 are synthesized into systems in step 6. Capabilities recall are stated in terms of business needs; for example, "the ability to track those vendors who are regularly shipping material late." This capability, along with others, might be provided by a comprehensive "Vendor-rating system." Several capabilities can be satisfied by one system, or a capability can stand alone as a single system.

Step 7 involves the specification of the long-range logical and physical system architect that is needed to meet the needs of the systems and data base. It might cover major hardware and system software selection, communations facilities, and overall architectural issues, such as centralized or decentralized processing location of data, and types of remote and local-interconnections. The purpose is not to develop detailed configurations, but rather to explore the overall long-term architectural issues in light of the entire set of required systems.

The combination of Steps 5, 6 and 7 provides the long-range goals for data, application systems, and hardware/software environments needed to meet the firm's business objectives. In step 8, specific projects are defined to put these into place. Each project should be well-defined and limited in scope. For example, one project might:

- select and install an application package; or
- design and implement an application system, or part of an application; or
- install new hardware; or
- develop a detailed plan for tying systems together; or
- extend a system to a new number of users; or
- develop a prototype of a new system.

The resources and time required to complete each project are estimated, and then, in Step 9, alternative plans are developed.

Direction-setting Decisions

Direction-setting decisions are not one-time decisions to enter a market. They affect every level of the corporation-by shifts in policy, reallocation of resources and changing the nature of the corporation's stakeholder map. New entrepreneurs decide on direction with the decision to enter a particular business, and ongoing businesses can change current direction or explicitly set a direction by examining the businesses they are in and want to be in. Such decisions may represent shifts in the underlying values of the corporation and its managers. New businesses sometimes require new ways of thinking about how to compete in the business, as well as whether the new business fits with the values and beliefs of employees. Decisions to divest or de-emphasize a particular business which has long historical roots in the company can also signal that a snift in values has occurred. Perhaps the current direction of the business has proven to be unprofitable, or even illegal. It is critical for us to carefully examine where the corporation is headed.

Decisions to enter new areas of business, or to revise corporate goals, or to emphasize a particular function or strategic issue form the context out of which other strategic tasks can be undertaken and accomplished. For mulating new organizational structures and systems, or trying to get a handle on how well the corporation is performing make little sense without an understanding of the direction of the firm. Strategic decisions are intentional actions which are designed to exert some measure of control over the future state of the corporation. Too often we take too narrow a view of strategy.

For instance, viewing the direction-setting task as merely plotting the businesses of a firm on a product/ market grid and ignoring the corporate culture and values has led many a firm down the primrose path of portfolio madness, with many unrelated and unmanageable businesses. Conversely, by paying attention only to culture and values and ignoring the "bottom line" implications of the culture, many firms have paved the way to their own obsolescence. AT&T's recent agreement with the Department of Justice, modifying the 1957 Consent Decree preventing AT&T from entering data processing businesses, is an example of the largest corporation in the world setting a new direction.

By agreeing to divest the Bell Operating Companies, AT&T got out of the local telephone exchange business to concentrate on the long distance, terminal equipment and data network businesses. Long standing corporate policies have been called into question with this decision, in particular the way that AT&T accounts for its costs and the way that the Bell Operating Companies charge customers for basic telephone service. Resources will be allocated differently based on the nature of the new businesses.

New relationships with key stakeholder groups-including the FCC, state public service commissions, customer segments, competitors and other-will have to be charted. The underlying values of AT&T employees as provides of a public service will need to change, as the business enters new competitive markets. The changes in these values and relationships with stakeholders will form a new context, or culture, for the AT &T of the future. AT & T's dramatic settlement with the Department of Justice on January 8, 1982 leaves no doubt as to whether the action was intentional. However, the consequences of the act will be felt for years to come, and will be watched as a dramatic example of a direction setting decision. IBM's decision to enter the personal computer business is another example of a large corporation undertaking a shift in its strategy and reversing the course of earlier policies.

IBM's decision may have far reaching effects on others in the market, as well as on its own mix of products and services. The related decision to make IBM Personal Computers compatible with other industry products 'reverses a long standing tradition of setting' industry standards at IBM. IBM gains a new set of stakeholders by entering this market, *i.e.*, the morass of software, hardware and other micro-computer vendors, manufacturers, users and home computer "freaks" who previously had little to do with the acknowledged "computer industry leader." Companies in the V.S. automobile industry have recently gone through changes in direction, induced primarily by competition from Japan and Europe. Chrysler has begun to execute a turnaround from the brink of bankruptcy, and in so doing has changed direction by reallocating resources to the US. from its worldwide subsidiaries, and by focusing on the auto business and getting out of the defense and credit businesses. GM and Ford have set new directions by focusing on the development of the so-called "world car," and by paying attention, at least in Ford's case to the need to change management philosophy and values regarding how to enable workers to be more productive. Direction setting has consisted of defining the business or businesses of the corporation, traditionally. From the dramatic pronouncements of management consultants ("you're in the packaging business, not the can business") to the more recent scholarly analysis of business, definition by Abell setting direction has included answering the question. The complicated nature of the modern corporation entails that we address these questions at several levels. It makes sense to set direction for the corporation as a whole, just as it makes sense to set direction for a division and for a particular organizational subset of a division.

Traditional Direction Setting Questions

Corporate Level Questions

- What is our Business?
- What Businesses are we in?
- What Businesses do we want to be in? - What Businesses should we be in?

Division Level Questions

- What are the synergies among the division's businesses?
- What is our division's Portfolio?
- How do we succeed in this "family of businesses"?

Business Level Questions

- How do we succeed in this business (or with these products)?
- Where are we going with this business?
- Should we be a "low cost producer," or should we "find a niche"?

Management theorists have usually divided questions of strategic management into three levels: corporate, division and business unit. There are direction-setting questions at each level. The answers to direction-setting questions at the corporate level will form the context for answers at the division level. The answers to division-level questions will serve as context, or possibly constraints, on how to compete in a particular business. What then serves as context for the answer to the corporate-level questions, and how can corporate mission statements be formulated to have real meaning? At least two separate sets of questions need to be addressed in formulating a statement of mission for the corporation. The first concerns a broad set of issues around values, social issues and stakeholder expectations of the firm. This level of analysis, is called "Enterprise Strategy."

The second set of issues, is that given a broad statement of what the corporation, and we as its managers stand for, we can begin to articulate the range of business opportunities that are available to us. This level of analysis is usually called "Corporate Strategy." We shall see that it rests on an understanding of how the stakeholders of the corporation can affect each business area. A process called "Stakeholder Audit" is discussed to help us formulate concrete corporate-level strategy. Most of these studies are touched in an idiom that is explicitly critical of the overreliance on the analytical techniques of strategic management. However, what the authors really point out is that strategic management must be interpreted more broadly to encompass the diverse realm of values. Every manager knows that value judgments are a primary ingredient of a successful strategy. Not only must values be taken into consideration when formulating strategy, but if the strategy is to be implemented the values of those affected by it must also be factored into the equation. When values are shared throughout an organization, implementation or strategy execution is relatively simple. None of these ideas in new.

Military and religious organizations have practiced and virtually perfected the principle of depending on the shared values of their constituents. However, the idea is quite novel when we apply it to the conscious formulation of corporate strategy, since by its very nature the corporation is "impersonal" and "logical and rational" rather than "value-laden." Also, the prevailing idiom of strategic management has focused on the 'hard facts' available from such disciplines as finance and accounting, economies and marketing.

In the strategy literature, Schendel and Hofer and Hofer *et al.* have identified a level of strategy called "enterprise strategy" which identifies the relationship of the from the research on the social responsibility of business, enterprise strategy, as formulated by these researchers answers the question, "What should we do?" In part enterprise strategy, on this interpretation, represents the moral or ethical component to strategic management which was identified by the early researchers in the field but which has been largely ignored, except as an addition to the "business" concerns of the firm. A suggested distinction between" social responsibility" and "business issues" was not useful in a world where there are multiple demands and stakeholder groups. We need to begin to think about integrating both of these concerns into a notion of "effective management," and we saw how the stakeholder concept can give us a start on this task. Given the importance of values and management style, as well as the shifts in the business environment, we can redefine the notion of enterprise level strategy to more closely align "social and ethical concerns" with traditional "business concerns." Part of the difficulty in setting direction for a company is understanding the impact of changes in business strategy on the underlying values of the firm, and to understand the new stakeholder relationships which will be charted as a result. Major changes in direction cannot be accomplished without an understanding of the impact on stakeholders, especially those groups which are very "close" to the managers such as employees, unions, customers, etc. Direction setting is inherently tied to understanding what the managers and employees of a corporation stand for. We propose to define enterprise level strategy as an answer to the question "WHAT DO WE STAND FOR?" At the enterprise level, the task of setting direction involves understanding the role of a particular firm as a whole, and its relationships to other social institutions. Appropriate questions are "what is the role of our organization in society," "what role do we want to play in society," "how is our organization qua organization perceived by our stakeholders," "what principles or values does our organization represent," "what obligations do we have to society at large," and "what are the implications for our current mix of businesses and allocation of resources."

Enterprise level strategy does not necessitate a particular set of values, nor does it require that a corporation be "socially responsive" in a certain way. It does examine the need, however, for an explicit and intentional attempt to answer the question "what do we stand for." The need for thinking about strategy at the enterprise level is reinforced by the analysis of the changing nature of the stakeholder map of many large organizations, and the complexity of organizational life.

If this analysis has any merit at all, then the attempt to understand the context of the firm and how this context relates to more traditional direction setting questions must be made. By explicitly examining the enterprise strategy of a firm, it is believed that intentional actions to change can be made which will yield a "fit" with the other levels of analysis. Questions of enterprise level strategy have a long history at least as far back as Berle and Means and perhaps to Adam Smith. However, there is little research which proposes both how to address the question of enterprise strategy and what kinds of strategies are a available, in a systematic fashion. There is a great deal of research on individual questions which need to be answered' if enterprise strategy is to be formulated, but no systematic account of both strategic process and content. The followings are a proposed process for formulating enterprise strategy: *(1)* Stakeholder Analysis, *(2)* Values Analysis, and *(3)* Societal Issues Analysis, must form the foundation for the articulation of enterprise level strategy. Let us look at each briefly, and then describe a range of several alternative enterprise strategies.

Stakeholder Analysis

Managers must seek to gain a more accurate and detailed account of the external environment of which their organizations are a part. In particular, the stakeholder concept can be used to better understand, at the rational level, exactly who are the groups and individuals that can affect or are affected by the achievement of an organization's purpose. In using this analysis to better understand the enterprise strategy of the firm, it is sometimes necessary to take the analysis of "Stakes" one step further, and to give it several dimensions. A particular stakeholder may have" economic" effects on the firm, *i.e.*, its action may affect the profitability, the cash flow or the stock price of the firm. Conversely, actions of the firm may affect the economic well-being of a particular stakeholder, as for instance, when that stakeholder has an economic stake of marketplace power. However, a firm may have economic effects on other stakeholder groups, such as government or activists groups, in terms of their budgets, their ability to raise funds, etc. Customers and suppliers have economic effects on a business. If raw materials are not of a sufficient quality or price, a manufacturing firm will not be able to attain its normal quality standards. If customers become dissatisfied with a firm's product they can go elsewhere, or find a substitute. More subtly, regulatory agencies can have economic effects on a business by passing rules which involve spending resources to comply, or by preventing competition and allowing a small group of firms to effectively control the price in an industry.

A particular stakeholder group may have "technological" effects on the firm by enabling or preventing the firm from using core technologies, developing new technologies, bringing existing technologies to market or by constraining what technologies can be "produced" by the firm. The converse is also true, especially if we define "technology" in rather broad terms to include some of the group's "software." The microcomputer industry is fraught with new technologies. The introduction of one technology by an IBM can make another technology obsolete almost overnight. Software firms dependent on the old technology can be made to go bankrupt quite rapidly. A particular stakeholder may have "social" effects on the firm, by altering the position of the firm in society, changing the opinion of the public about the firm, or allowing or constraining what the firm is able to do with "society's permission." The firm may have social effects on a particular stakeholder as well by helping or constraining the stakeholder to engage in certain activities, or by giving the stakeholder a "cause" around which to rally. Assessments of the impact of products such as automobiles and telephones reveal that they have had a remarkable impact on the way that we communicate with each other, and the way that we think about our lives and careers. These social effects often translate into "political" effects on the firm. Stakeholder actions often involve the political process in order to achieve some social purpose. Conversely, the firm may have political effects on a stakeholder group by helping or hurting its chances of success in the political realm. Business groups have lobbied in recent years against the formation of a national consumer advocate agency in the government, an agenda item that many consumer leaders feel is necessary to the achievement of their long range goals of making business more responsive to consumer needs.

A stakeholder may have "managerial" effects on the firm by forcing it to change its management systems and processes, and even its managerial style and values. Managerial effects may well be the most important in terms of a firm's ability to understand its relationships with certain groups and to take these groups into account on a routine basis. The converse is equally true here. Consumer advisory panels have "forced" several utilities to alter their methods of filing rate cases, by having the firm make presentations and enter into negotiations with the consumers before filing the case with the state regulatory commissions. As a result, we would expect the companies to gradually change their beliefs about the consumer groups over a long period of time, from one of "irrational, pain in the... to one of "those folks can help us avoid stumbling blocks with the state commissions and our customers." By further analyzing the stakes of groups into "economic," "technological," "poll heal," "social" and "managerial" we can understand in more detail the cause and effect relation. The most difficult problem with the analysis portrayed is that it represents the perceptions of the analysis or the senior executives doing the analysis. How can managers be certain that their readings of stakeholders perceptions are correct? We have already shown that to assume that a consumer advocate perceives only an economic stake in the firm may well be mistaken. It is necessary to undertake a validation process using interviews, surveys, the public record, interviews with internal boundary spanners who are stakeholder experts, etc. In cases where we are formulating enterprise strategy for the first time, or where the external environment has changed sufficiently, we many need to undertake an explicit process of verification of the inputs into enterprise strategy. At the very minimum managers must use stakeholder analysis to lay bare their own beliefs about the stakes of each important stakeholder group.

❒

11

Alternative Strategy

Whatever the approaches managers adopt for identifying the strategic alternatives, they will result into a number of strategies. There are various ways of classifying the strategies.

(i) These can be classified on the basis of their scope. In such a case, the strategies may be classified as master strategies, also called as grand or root strategies, and programme strategies. The former deal with the overall strategic action while latter deal with strategies which may be devised to implement programme.

(ii) The classification may be based on the level of organization wherein the strategies can be classified as headquarter strategies and divisional strategies If the latter is developed in pursuit of the former, they may be called substrategies also.

(iii) The classification may be based on purpose and functions of the organisation and various strategies may be master strategies and functional strategies. Functional strategies may be for production, marketing, finance, personnel, and so on.

Even if we take master strategies for an organization, there can be various alternatives. There may be three categories of master strategies which an organization can follow. These are stability strategy, growth strategy, and retrenchment strategy. A combination of two or more strategies can also be followed simultaneously. A discussion of these strategies gives ideas about them.

1. Growth Strategy

Growth strategy is the much-talked and published in the present Indian environment. If we look at the corporate performance in the recent years, we find how the various organisations have grown both in terms of sales and profit as well as assets.

In fact, in life of any organization, growth is necessary at some point of time. However, it is not necessary that the various stages will be uniform for all organisations. For example, many organisations may not decline even after a considerable period of time while many may die very soon even before passing through regeneration stage. This is evident by the high mortality rate of small organisations. On the other hand Tata Iron and Steel established in 1907 is still the corporate leader. It suggests then that the strategies followed by the organisations will determine the application of various stages. If the organisations are going through growth strategy at appropriate time, they can avoid declining and regeneration stages. Growth strategy can be defined as follow:

> 'A growth strategy is one that an enterprise pursues when it increases its level of objectives upward in significant increment, much higher that an exploration of its 'past' achievement level. The most frequent increase indicating a growth strategy is to raise the market share and or sales objectives upward significantly.'

Growth under growth strategy can be differentiate from normal growth which an organization can achieve through its normal learning curve. A normal learning curve suggests that organisations will grow both in terms of sales and profitability by gaining experience of various functions the rate of growth under such case quite low and falls on a trend line which can be consistent throughout a period, of time. However, when the organization reaches at the level of maturity, its sales and profit may stabilise In this growth strategy, the rate of growth is much faster than the list years owing to additional operational facilities in the organization.

2. Stability Strategy

Stability strategy, though most frequently used by most of the organisations, often presents a confusing nomenclature. In fact, most of such organizations look: for growth and do not remain stable over the long period of time. However, when they adopt some changes in their strategy postures, they try to stabilise in a particular area which is consistent with their strengths. Thus basic approach in the stability strategy is 'to maintain present course.' Stability strategy can be defined as follow:

> 'In an effective stability strategy, companies will concentrate their resources where the company presently has or can rapidly develop a meaningful competitive advantage in the narrowest possible product-market scope consistent with the firm's are sources and market requirements.'

3. Turnaround Strategy, Divestment & Liquidation Strategies

(i) Turnaround Strategy. Turnaround strategy also known as cutback strategy, has the basic philosophy: 'hold the present business and cut the cost'. This situation is needed as no organisations is immune from internal hard time-stagnation or declining performance-no matter what the state of economy is. Traditionally, turnaround situations have been discussed either in terms of the areas of organisational performance to be improved or the time criticality of the turnaround actions. Thus the most frequent turnaround situations have been those involving improvement in declining organisational profitability coupled with decline in sales or market share. However, with increasing impact of inflation and capital cost, much attention is being given to turnaround involving improve asset utilisation. Thus turnaround strategy can be deemed as follows:

> Turnaround strategy involves that strategic action which an organization takes to complete in the same business in, turnaround situations. Turnaround situations may be improvement in organisational lower

performance caused by downward trend which is not controllable by present actions of management.

(ii) Divestment Strategies. Divestment (also called divestiture or cutback) strategy involves the sale or liquidation of a portion of business, or a major division, profit centre or SBU. Divestment is usually a part of rehabilitation or restructuring plan and is adopted when a turnaround has been attempted but has proved to be unsuccessful. The option of a turnaround may even be ignored if it is obvious that divestment is the only answer.

(iii) Liquidation Strategies. A retrenchment strategy considered the most extereme and unattractive is liquidation strategy, which involves closing down a firm and selling its assets. It is considered as the last resort because it leads to serious consequences such as loss of employment for workers and other employees, termination of opportunities where a firm could pursue any future activities, and the stigma of failure.

Why is Liquidation Difficult. Many small-scale units, proprietorship firms, and partnership ventures liquidate frequently but medium-and large-sized companies rarely liquidate in India. This is due to a variety of factors. The company management, government, and financial institutions, trade unions, and creditors and other agencies are reluctant to take a decision, or ask, for liquidation. Each party has its own reasons for doing so. While the management may hesitate to liquidate due to the fear of failure, the government may not easily allow liquidation due to the political and other risks involved. Trade unions would naturally resist the loss of employment of workers. Ceasing operations does not mean that a firm is freed from its contractual obligations to the suppliers unless of course, it is declared insolvent or bankrupt selling assets for implementing a liquidation strategy may also be difficult as buyers as difficult to find. Moreover, the firm cannot expect adequate compensation as most assets, being unusable, are considered, as scrap. Besides the practical difficulties in liquidation, there is also a psychological aspect which cannot be overlooked. The prospects of liquidation create a bad impact on the company's (or business group's) reputation. For many executives who are closely associated with firms, liquidation may be traumata experience. Despite the hesitancy on the part of all conformed with a company that intends to liquidate and the difficulties in the process of liquidation sometimes a firm may be forced to liquidate.

Planned Liquidation. Liquidation strategy may be unpleasant as strategic: alternative but when a "dead business is worth more than alive", it is a good proposition. When liquidation is evident, an abandonment plan is desirable. Planned liquidation would involve a systematic plan to reap the maximum benefits for the firm and its shareholders through the process of liquidation.

4. Retrenchment Strategy

Retrenchment strategy, though less frequently used and publicised, has been pursued by various companies successfuly. Even many experts do not agree with the present nomenclature of the strategy because of wise scôpe of action in this strategy. Retrenchment, as used in the field of personnel management, denotes separation of employees mainly due to decreased amount of work owing to recession or reorganisation of work. The same word is used in the field of strategic management with a slightly different emphasis because retrenchment strategy does/not always involve getting off the business. Retrenchment strategy can be defined as follow:

A retrenchment strategy is one that an enterprise pursues when it decides to improve its performance in reaching its objectives by : *(a)* focussing on functional improvement, specially reduction in cost; *(b)* reducing the number of the products and markets it serves up to and including liquidation of the business; *(c)* reducing the number of function it performs by becoming a captive company.'

5. Merger, Joint Venture and Takeover

(i) Merger and takeover or a acquisition strategies basically involve the external approach to expansion. Basically two, or occasionally more than two firms are involved. There is not much difference in the three terms used for such types of strategies and they are frequently used synonymously. But a subtle distinction can be made. While mergers take place when the objectives of the buyer firm and, the seller firm are matched to a large extent, takeovers or acquisitions usually are based on the strong motivation of the buyer firm to acquire.

(ii) ***Joint Venture.*** It is effective strategy when development costs have to be shared, risks spread out, and expertise combined to make effective use of resources.

Types of Joint Ventures. Joint ventures are common within industries and in various countries. But they are specially useful for entering international markets. From the point of view of Indian organisations, the following types of joint ventures are possible:

A. Between an Indian firm and a foreign company in third country;

B. Between an Indian firm and a foreign company in that foreign country;

C. Between two firms across different industries; and

D. Between an Indian firm and a foreign company in India.

Strategic Issues. It offers the advantages of achieving objectives mutually by the participating firms. Eliminating, controlling, or reducing competition may be of strategic importance and can be brought about through joint ventures. Increasing the market share can also be achieved.

Diversification strategies may be adopted by participating firm if a joint venture is planned across different industries. If technology is a critical variable in strategy, then joint venture with foreign companies can be feasible. If legal and regulatory hurdles come in the way of external expansion, they could be subverted through a joint venture strategy of combining with a foreign firm in that foreign country or in a third country. Environmental treats within the country or opportunities abroad may close firms to undertake joint ventures.

Strategic advantages are important for joint ventures to be set up and sustained.

(iii) Takeover Strategies. Takeover or acquisition is currently the popular strategy being adopted by Indian companies. During the three decades after Independence, the normal route of growth was through licensing and setting up new projects. The current decade has seen an increasing use of takeover strategies (or simple takeovers) as the means of rapid growth.

How Takeovers Take Plan. Certain guidelines can be proposed for takeovers to take place systematically. For instance following procedure is recommended for acquisition.

1. Treat people with dignity and concern.
2. Spell out the objective.
3. Anticipate and solve problems early.
4. Assess managerial quality.
5. Check the compatibility of business styles.
6. Indicate how the objective would be achieved.

6. Diversification and Integration Strategies

Diversification is a much-used and much-talked about strategy. In reality, it is not a strategy but a set of strategies. These strategies involve all the dimensions of strategic alternatives. Diversification may involve internal or external, related or unrelated, horizontal or vertical, and active or passive dimensions-either singly or collectively.

Essentially, diversification involves a change in business definition either in terms of customer functions, customer groups, or alternative technologies.

Different Types of Diversification Strategies

The different types of diversification strategies are as follows:

(i) ***Vertical Integration.*** When an organization starts making new products that serve its own needs, vertical integration takes place. In other words, any new activity undertaken with the purpose of either supplying inputs or serving as a costomer for outputs is vertical integration.

Vertical integration could be of two types backward and forward integration. Backward-integration means moving towards the source of raw materials while forward integration involves up activities that will bring the organization nearer to the ultimate customers.

(ii) ***Horizontal Integration.*** When an organization takes up the same types of products at the same level of production or market no process, it is said to follow a strategy of horizontal integration. When a luggage company takes over its rival luggage company it is horizontal, integration (or merger). Horizontal integration strategy may be frequently adopted with a view to geographically expand by taking up a competitor in another area, to increase the market share, and to benefit from economies of scale.

(iii) ***Concentric Diversification.*** When an organization takes up an activity in such a manner that it is related to its existing business definition either in terms of customer groups, customers functions, or alternative technologies, it is concentric diversification. Concentric diversification may be of three types.

A. When a similar type of products is offered with the help of unrelated technology, *e.g.* a company in the sewing machine business diversifies into kitchen ware and household appliances, which are sold through a chain of retail stores to housewives.

B. When a similar type of product (or service) is provided with the help of related technology, *e.g.* a raincoat manufacturer makes other rubber-based items such as waterproof shoes and rubber gloves sold through the same retail outlets.

C. When a new type of product or service is provided with the help of related technology, *e.g.* a leasing firm offers hire-purchase services to institutional customers and consumer financing for purchase of durables to individual customers.

(iv) Conglomerate Diversification. When an organization adopts a strategy which requires taking up those activities which are unrelated to its existing business definition-either in terms of customer groups, customer functions or alternative technologies, it is conglomerate diversification. Frequently such companies are referred to as conglomerates.

7. Modernisation Strategies

In developing countries like India, technology is often employed as a strategic and competitive tool. Modernisation, which basically involves technological upgradation, is used to achieve organisational, objectives such as increased production, lower costs, efficiency, productivity. Here, modernisation is dealt with, not in an operational manner indicating technological upgradation, but in a strategic sense. With respect to the classification of strategic alternatives, modernisation could be considered as:

A. Internal stability strategy if the pace of modernisation is low to moderate, internal expansion strategy if the pace of modernisation is high.

B. External retrenchment if part of the organization is divested or liquidated with the aim of modernisation.

C. External expansion strategy if the organisation merges with or acquires another company for the purpose of modernisation.

Internal retrenchment strategy if resources are redirected from one area to another with the aim of modernisation.

Reasons for Adopting Modernisation Strategies

Modernisation strategies are used for different reasons. As we pointed out earlier, some of these are increasing production, lowering costs, improving efficiency and productivity, etc. Most of these objectives apparently seem to be aimed at improving the overall performance but they may also be aimed at increasing thy competitive ability.

Consider these examples:

* National Organic Chemicals Industries Ltd. (NOCIL), a major manufacturer of petrochemicals in the private sector, undertook as Rs 100 crore modernisation plan in order to compete effectively.
* Modi Industries Ltd. has planned to invest Rs 30 crore for technological upgradation of its steel unit, primarily for widening its product range.
* The corporate planning team at Steel Authority of India Ltd. (SAIL) envisages as Rs 15,000 crore capital, spending programme spread over seven years to modernise its steel plants with a variety of objectives such as lower costs, energy saving higher capacity utilisation closing down unprofitable units, etc.

Modernisation could be used for different purposes as can be seen from the above examples. Some of these could be operational but most modernisation programmes involve a huge amount of resources and are aimed at gaining competitive and strategic strengths. Some organisations, in fact, build their strategies around technology.

8. Combination Strategies

An introduction to combination strategies is essentially a combination strategies. These are mixture of stability, expansion or retrenchment strategies applied either simultaneously (as that same time in different business) or sequentially.

It would be difficult to find any organization that has survived and grown by adopting a single 'pure' strategy. The complexity of doing business demand that different strategies be adopted to suit the situational demands made upon the organization. An organization which has followed a stability strategy for quite sometime has to think of expansion. Any organization which has, been on an expansion path for long has to pause to consolidate its businesses. Multi-business organisations—as most large and medium Indian companies are now-have to follow multiple strategies either sequentially or simultaneously.

When and Why to Pursue Growth Strategy

As pointed out earlier, growth is the necessary phenomenon of organisational life. However, it is not always beneficial to grow. For example, if a small organization grows beyond a size and it does not remain small according to the definition by the Government, it loses many benefits and incentives which are meant for such organisations. Inspite of these, the organisations take up growth activities because this is the only way of survival in the long-run. Following are given some specifications in which organisations should look for growth strategy.

1. Notwithstanding above, the organization can grow only when the environment permits. For example, in Indian business environment, there are numerous opportunities for growth because of general growth pattern of the economy but it offers more constraints certain categories of organisations particularly those covered by MRTP Act, FERA, licensing etc. Keeping in view all these aspects, an organization has to think for its growth much ahead to avoid delay because of certain constraints. Therefore, if

the opportunity comes for the growth, the organization should capitalise it.

2. The environment offers various concessions and incentives for growth in certain industries in certain areas. For example, the government gives various concessions to priority sector industries and industries in backward areas. Whenever such opportunities exist, the organization can go for growth. Moreover in order to take the advantages of investment allowance reserve, the organization has to invest the amount kept under this reserve. Therefore, the growth is almost a necessary condition for this.

3. When the organisation has been stabilised after the various growth or other strategies, it can look for growth either in the same field or in diversified field. For such an organisation, growth becomes the way of life: growth-stabilising-growth-stabilising and so on. However, an organisation should adopt growth strategy to the extent it is manageable.

REASONS FOR PURSUING GROWTH STRATEGY

The question is: why do the organization follow growth strategy? This question becomes more pertinent specially when growth strategy, particularly through diversification, is more risky while stability strategy is less risky. The answer can be that there are several reasons why the organisations opt for growth, the reasons for growth are as follows:

(i) Growth offers many economies because of large scale of operations. The per unit cost of production can be very low at appropriate level of operations. This is possible because fixed costs are appropriated over large number of units. Moreover, the economies of increasing scale also afford and enhance deeper and deeper degrees of specialisation. With more people available to do the different kinds of work, greater penetration can be made into the competitive fine points of products, market segmentation applications, and marketing policies and programmes. These eventually lead to certain strategic advantages to the organization concerned.

(ii) There are certain intangible advantages of growth. These may be in the from of increased prestige of the organization, satisfaction to employees and social benefits. The growing organisations have always been preferred by investors of various kind. The prestige of the organization itself is advantageous in various ways. Growing organisations offer satisfaction to their employees by offering them more promotional avenues from within stagnation in the hierachical promotion is avoided. Thus availability of promotional avenues are motivating factor for the personnel in the organisations. Growth strategy can be adopted in the form of expansion, vertical integration, diversification, merger, acquisition and joint venture. The basic objective in all these cases is growth but the basic problem in each case is significantly different which needs more elaborate discussion.

(iii) Growth strategy is taken up because of managerial motivation to do so. Managers with high degree of achievement and recognition always prefer to grow. The needs on the part of managers push them to think as to how they can achieve their need satisfaction. The answer lies in the continuous growth of the organization for the group of organisations as a whole. For example, managers first want recognition in a limited area. When this is achieved, they look forward for a broader area. When this is also achieved, they look for still broader area. This is never-ending chain which compels the managers to think in terms of continues growth.

(iv) In the long-run, growth is necessary for the very survival of the organisations themselves, particularly when the environment is quite volatile. The organization that does not grow may be pushed out of the business because of the new entrants in the field. If the organization is stabilised for very long time, it may lose its profitability because the costs may go on increasing due to higher wages, higher costs of other inputs, and lower level of efficiency because of certain obsolescence in plant and machinery, while there may not be corresponding increase in the revenue from the present products.

Reasons for Adopting Stability Strategy

Though most of the organisations follow stability strategy for a period of time, some organisations follow it for much longer than others. It has been observed that as the companies get older, they become more conservative and more likely to pursue a stability strategy. Following are some important factors which suggest why the organization follow stability strategy:

(a) If the organisation's past history is full of change, it will like to adopt stability so as to become efficient and manageable and to reap the rich harvest of all such past changes. In fact, stability strategy should always be followed after the growth strategy to take the best advantages of the situation.

(b) If the organisation's strategic advantages lie in the present business and market, it pursues stability strategy. For example, if organization has high market share, it can continue in the same business and should concentrate on the internal operational efficiency.

(c) A stability is less risky in that it offers the safe .business to the organization unless there is major environmental change. If management prefers to take less risk, it can continue stability strategy.

(d) The nature of environment affects the extent to which the organization can follow alternative strategies. For example, if the organization wants to grow either through expansion or diversification, it has not only to appraise the environment but it has to get licence from the government for the purpose. If such a licence is not available, "there is no alternative for the organization and the organization has to go through stability strategy. For example, the government has refused the expansion applications of various companies on the ground that they are dominant undertakings. Thus they have no alternative to choose. Many of the organisations have been forced to pursue stability strategy because of the regulatory measures of the government. Similarly if the total environmental forces are not excessively volatile, the organization can pursue stability strategy.

(e) Some organisations are slow to change or resistant to change. Since stability strategy fits in their total framework, they often prefer not to change. Generally larger is the organization and the more successful it has been, the greater is the resistance to change. Such organisations react to forces of environment and will change strategies only in extraordinary times.

(f) Perception of management about the performance of the organization may motivate them to pursue stability strategy. If the managers are satisfied with present performance, they will like to continue with the same. Management may not always be sure of what combination of decisions is responsible for this and, therefore, they may decide to continue the way the results are being achieved.

The stability strategy is basically defensive in its approach. It may be pursued to protect certain present organisational strength. There is not much functional change in any part of the organisation. However, it does not mean that there is not change in organisations structure and processes also. There can be organisational changes in these directions in order to bring efficiency in operation.

REASON OF ADOPTING DIVERSIFICATION STRATEGIES

There are many reasons why organisations adopt diversification strategies. The three basic and important reasons are :

A. Diversification may be the only way out if growth in existing businesses is blocked due to environmental and regulatory factors.

B. Diversification strategies are adopted to minimise risk by spreading it over several businesses.

C. Diversification may used to capitalise on organisational strength or minimise weaknesses.

The different types of diversification strategies described above (vertical, horizontal, concentric and conglomerate diversification) each have their own advantages and disadvantages. These are as follows:

	Merits	*Limitation*
A. Horizontal	Eliminating competitors	* Increase in risk
	* Access to new markets	* Reduces flexibility
B. Vertical	1. Economiesing Operations	* Risk of Unfamiliar business
	2. Access to and control of Supply or demand	* Less flexibility due to more commitment to a line of business.
C. Congomerate	* Better management and Allocation of cash flows	* Diversion of resources Leading to lack of Concentration
	Reducing risk by spreading investment	* Risks of managing new business.
D. Concentric	* Attain synergy by exchange of resources and skills	* Additional investment in new technology
	* Economies of scale and Tax benefits	* Untried Technologies

TURNAROUND STRATEGY

Once the organisation has decided on the type of broad turnaround strategy it should use, it needs to begin to shape the more specific aspects of its chosen turnaround strategy. These action plans will depend not only on the current strategic and operating health of the organisation but also on the exact nature of the industry in which it competes and on its strengths and weaknesses *vis-a-vis* other competitors in the same industry. When an organisation takes up turnaround actions usually, it involves following stages:

A. Designing Operating Turnarounds. Operating turnarounds focus on internal efficiency. The strategy an organisation can adopt in this case may be to make itself efficient in everything it does. For this purpose, there can be four alternatives-revenue-generating, cost-cutting, asset reduction, and combination strategies.

(i) Asset-Reduction Strategy. Asset-reduction strategy can be adopted if the organisation's operation is quite low as compared to its break even, say 30 to 40 per cent. In such cases, the basic question is: what assets should be sold and what should be retained. The answer will depend on the organisation's present/future strategy and saleability of different assets. As a general rule, those assets should be kept which the organisations are using currently or will be using after a year or so. However, sale of assets should not be taken in haste otherwise the assets may not fetch appropriate price. The choice of asset-reduction strategy depends primarily on the long-term prospects of the business of the organisation after the turnaround is completed.

(ii) Revenue-Generating Strategy. In a typical revenue-generating strategy, the organisation would focus primarily on its existing line of products, although it might be possible that these products are supplemented by products it used to make but has discontinued, provided that these products could be introduced quickly and profitably. In addition, the organisation may also take up the production of other products on a short-term basis to utilise its additional capacity but such products may not form the product line for it on a long-term basis. The greater emphasis is put on more resource-generating products. Some major efforts such as price cutting, increased advertising and increased direct sales efforts would be undertaken to stimulate the current sales level. At the same time, R & D expenditure will be low or moderate and staffing at low level as compared to sales. These are all short-term measures. However, the organisation should indentify the resources and skills that it will need in order to implement its long-term strategy so that these can be protected during the short-term programme that will follow.

(iii) ***Combination Effort Strategy.*** Under combination strategy, the organisation pursues all three strategies discussed above simultaneously in relative balanced proportions. The reason for this combination effort is that the cash flow produced by a balanced effort will be sufficiently higher than that which would be produced by a narrowly focussed strategy. A combination is preferable specially when the organisation is operating quite close to its break even. If a combination strategy is adopted, it increases the complexity of managerial jobs. Therefore, it should be used only when the potential payoff more than adequately compensates for the additional "managerial complexity and operational difficulties" it entails.

(iv) ***Cost-Cutting Strategy.*** If the organisation is working close to the level of break even point and it has high direct labour costs, high fixed expenses, or limited financial resources, it can adopt cost-cutting strategy. Cost-cutting is quite possible and produces results in the short-term as compared to revenue generating strategy. In fact, many companies have adopted to overcome the problem of high direct labour costs by offering voluntary retrenchment to workers on attractive compensation to take long-term advantages. Similarly, advertising costs can be cut by changing the nature of advertising from institutional to product, R & D costs can be suitably cut, personnel development costs can be mininused.

B. Change in Top Management. Before any turnaround action is to be taken, it is desirable to identify whether the present management is suitable for such an action. Though it is not necessary that the present top management can not take up such actions, a change in top management can not take up such actions, a change in top management is desirable specially if it has such a strong set of beliefs about how to run the business in question and many of which are wrong. Whether the present top management should continue or change depends on the types of qualities it possesses. It has been observed that different general managers have skills of different types of managerial tasks. Consequently if the present management does not have these qualities, it should be changed. Similarly, a hard-nosed, experienced cost-cutter will be required if an operating turnaround with a major cost reduction is to be pursued.

C. Designing Strategic Turnarounds. Strategic turnarounds are needed when the business has a strong current operating health but the organisation has lost its position strategically. Most turnarounds involve circumstances in which there has been a major decline in sales and/or market share position. Consequently the principle method of differentiating among turnarounds is determined according to the magnitude of the sales and share reversal sought. Usually, three alternatives are available:

(i) Two level increase in share position, that is, movement from a dropout position to a competitor position or from a follower position to a leader position.

(ii) Maintenance or even reduction of share accompanied by the focussing on one or more defensible product/market segment or niches.

(iii) One-level increase in share position, that is, movement from a dropout position to a follower position; from a follower position to a competitor position or from competitor position to leader position.

Why to Adopt Turnaround Strategy?

Turnaround strategy, though a negative connotation of growth, is always preferable when the business is passing through, lean trot. In fact, many famous organisations have adopted this strategy to overcome some of their problems. Therefore, this strategy should not be looked merely as negative one, rather than a framework for pursuing growth strategy when the organisations overcome some basic problems both external and internal.

Downtrend in organisational performance is caused by both internal factors-management actions which are largely controllable and external factors which are incontrollable. Therefore, in order to find out what turnaround strategy an organisation should follow, the following questions are more considering.

If the business is worth saving, the other questions is: What is the state of current operating health as well as strategic health? This requires a detailed analysis of organisational strengths and weaknesses. Once this exercise has been taken and completed, the organisation can turn to the task of selecting the type of turnaround strategy to be pursued. It may be mentioned here that an organisation adopts two types of turnarounds: strategic and operating. Turnaround strategy involves the change in the organisation's strategy to compete in the present business. It may involve determination of organisation's share in the market-no change in the market share or change of market share by certain percentages. In the case of functional areas, most turnarounds are built around key skills in marketing production engineering, etc.

Is the business worth saving, or is it better to liquidate it now? If the answer of the former is yes, the organisation should go further for identifying what turnaround strategy it can pursue. The basic consideration in analysing this question is that the going concern value of the firm is more than its liquidated value. If the liquidated value is more, it is preferable to adopt divestment or liquidation strategy rather than to invest the substantial energies required by a turnaround for only a marginal payoff.

❒

12

Strategy of Foreign Collaboration

Collaboration with foreign companies has been found to have special appeal as a growth strategy particularly in developing countries. Depending on the purpose in view, such collaborations may be classified as: Managerial, Technical and Financial. There are many advantages which a firm in the host country can derive from the collaboration deal:

1. Improving competitive abilities for domestic and export marketing;
2. Enlarging the scale of operations and reducing costs;
3. Developing indigenous production of components and spare parts;
4. Upgradation of existing technology or introduction of advanced technology, acquiring technical know-how, and facilitating transfer of technology;
5. Fostering cultural changes with respect to work ethos, attitude towards discipline, etc.;
6. Securing foreign equity investment as a part of risk capital and enhancing the potential ability to raise necessary funds from the domestic capital market;
7. Deriving the benefits of import substitution and increased foreign exchange earning;
8. Developing the brand image of products more quickly.

Benefits which may accrue to the foreign collaborators are:

1. Return on financial outlay;
2. Earnings by way of royalty and fees for technological collaboration, supply of drawings and documents technical and managerial know-how;
3. Tax benefits derived in low-tax host countries. Royalties, technical fees, and service charges are taxed at a lower rate than profits;
4. Market expansion in countries restricting hard currency imports.

Examples of Foreign Collaborations in India

The growth of many enterprises in India is attributable to the strategy of foreign collaboration. In recent years, a number of companies have decided to join hands with foreign companies providing for technical financial and managerial collaboration. Some of these are mentioned below:

Maruti Udyog tie up with Suzuki of Japan for the manufacture of passenger cars and vans;

Technical collaboration of Nirup Synchrome Ltd., with Acna Chimica Organica S.P A., a division of Montedison, Italy, for the manufacture of synthetic dyes;

Hindustan Teleprinters Ltd., tie up with Olivetti of Italy to make electro-mechanical teleprinters and electric typewriters. Financial and technical collaboration of TISCO. UK promoting Tata Robins-Fraser Ltd., a company manufacturing material handling equipments of various kinds and undertaking 'system contracts' for such equipments.

Financial and technical collaboration of Bajaj Tempo Ltd., with West German Daimler-Benz AG;

Joint ventures promoted during the last four years by DCM, Hyderabad Allwyn, Punjab Tractors, and Eicher Motors in collaboration with Japanese companies—Toyota,

Nissan, Mazda, and Missubishi respectively, to manufacture light commercial vehicles;

Technical collaboration of Noduran Founders Maharashtra Ltd., with SKF-GISAG of East Germany (GDR).

In addition to this 'orientation' of foreign collaborations, they also suffered from a number of other disadvantages.

1. The practice of multiple collaborations led to the introduction of standards of various countries (in raw materials, spare parts, designs, specifications, and even terms of measurement) into the Indian industry even for very similar products or within the same firm. This multiplicity led to large inventory accumulation and uneconomic locking up of working capital. It also hindered standardisation and variety reduction which are so essential for raising industrial productivity;
2. Foreign collaborations have helped the growth of monopolies and concentration. They joined hands with the big business houses and the latter were only too eager to enter into understanding with them since the presence of foreign links often conferred certain strategic advantages (patent, resources, foreign exchange, etc.) enabling the big business houses to diversify and expand;
3. The government permitted multiple collaborations, *i.e.* repetitive import of the same or similar technology. This resulted in repetitive payments without additing to the stock of technical knowledge in the country;
4. The most important part related to the presence of various restrictive clauses in the agreements. Some restrictions imposed were: *(i)* the technology cannot be passed on to anyone else, in some cases even after the expiry of the agreement; *(ii)* manufacturing is to be carried out according to the specifications laid down by the collaborator and no local adaptations can be made; *(iii)* control over overseas purchase was exercised through the provision that it had to

be made directly or indirectly through the collaborator; *(iv)* production was tightly controlled at times through the posting of foreign technicians; *(v)* controls over the pricing and marketing of the products were exercised by requiring that a part of the production was to be sold to the collaborator's subsidiary in India at a fixed commission or that specified firms were to be made the sole selling agents; and *(vi)* right to export was also restricted by provision that exports could be done only to specific countries or or certain preconditions.

5. The terms of agreements were mostly weighted in favour of the foreign collaborators and were against Indian interests. This arose on account of the lack of bargaining power in the Indian side and the government's eagerness to acquire foreign participation in the face of foreign exchange shortage;

6. The terms of payment were also drawn up so as to squeeze out the maximum payment under one head or other. Generally 5 per cent of the annual turnover for 10 years as royalty plus 5 per cent of the imported plant cost as technical fees in the case of royality-cum-technical fees, or 10 per cent of the issued capital as lumpsum payment for technical fees alone, were the limits of official policy. However, these tended to become routine;

7. Since the responsibility of specification and supply of equipment was entrusted to the foreign collaborators, there was close tie-up between the designers and suppliers resulting not only in price mark-up but also in over-import of equipment. Sometimes equipments were imported even when they were available locally, sometimes they remained idle for want of spares.

REGULATORY CONDITIONS GOVERNING THE SETTING UP OR INDIAN JOINT VENTURE ABROAD

(A) Formation of a limited company is a must for participation in a joint venture abroad; only corporate bodies are allowed such participation as per the Guidelines of the Government of India.

Under Sec. 27 of the Foreign Exchange Regulation Act, 1973 (FERA) approval is required to be obtained for the proposed venture *(a)* from the Ministry of Commerce, GOI, in Case of industrial joint ventures, *(b)* from the Ministry of Finance (Deptt. of Economic Affairs) in the case of non-industrial joint ventures.

After approval of the Ministry concerned a formal approval for the project is to be obtained from the Reserve Bank of India (Exchange Control Deptt.) Application for this purpose should be accompanied by: *(i)* Copies of the application with annexures submitted to the Ministry and approval received; *(ii)* Copy of the project/feasibility study report of the project: and *(iii)* Copies of the Memorandum and Articles of Association as well as of the Certificate of Registration of the overseas joint venture company.

Also under Sec. 27 of FERA, permission must be obtained by Indian residents to accept appointment as Directors on the Board of the joint venture company, for which application has to be made to the Ministry of Finance (Deptt. of Economic Affairs). Approval is generally given for a period of two years, which may be renewed on application. The permission so granted is to be submitted for approval of the Reserve Bank of India.

(B) The joint venture agreement finalised and executed on consultation with the solicitors should be submitted to the Ministry of Commerce for approval: and a copy of the agreement, as approved by the Ministry, submitted to the concerned office of the Reserve Bank.

(C) For entitlement of deduction of certain payments received from the overseas joint venture company u/s 80-O of the Income Tax Act, 1961, an application in the prescribed form along with the copy of joint venture agreement has to be submitted to the Central Broad of Direct Taxes, New

Delhi, on or before the last day of October of the relevant assessment year.

(D) Prior approval has to be obtained front the Ministry of Industry (Deptt. of Company Affairs) for investment in the shares of the overseas joint venture company under Sec. 372 (4) of the Companies Act. The time specified in the approval for such investment must be adhered to, and if it is likely to be delayed suitable extension of times should be applied.

(E) Permission for export of machinery to the joint venture company against equity participation has to be obtained from the Commerce Ministry. On application .giving details of each item of such machinery including FOB value in Indian Rupees price in foreign currency break up of FOB value against a lakh shares will be issued by the joint venture company and the balance value if any, to be received by the Indian company.

(F) Registration with the related Export Promotion Council to avail of export incentive, excise duty concession, etc., and enrolment with the Regional JCCI & E for cash compensatory support and REP licence the also necessary.

(G) Half yearly progress reports have to be submitted to the Ministry of Commerce till the project is fully implemented and a copy of the same submitted to the RBI.

(H) After the project is fully implemented, annual performance report in the prescribed format is to be submitted every year to the Ministry of Commerce together with the copy of audited Balance Sheet and Profit and Loss Account of the joint-venture company, and a copy of the report with annexures is to be sent to RBI.

INDIAN GOVT. POLICY ON FOREIGN COLLABORATION

The inflow of foreign private investment and the import of foreign technology have been subject to Government regulation in most developing countries. This has been so essentially for two reasons.

(A) To ensure industrial growth in conformity with national priorities. The contribution of foreign capital and foreign technical collaboration in different respects having been found to be of significance also prompted governments in third world countries to be less enthusiastic about foreign participation. Indian Government policy in this respect has changed over time.

(B) To prevent the continuation and emergence of foreign vested interests.

The regulatory framework and Government policy with respect to foreign investment and collaboration were spelt out in July 1980 along with the industrial policy statement presented in Parliament. The policy was modified in May 1990, and a new policy initiative announced in July 1980.

Policy Statement, July 1980

Advanced Technology for Economics of Scale: In a number of cases Indian industry has not been able to compete in markets abroad because the scale of output which is related to the level of domestic demand is too small to give them the advantage of modem technology and economies of scale. In cases where a larger production base would increase the competitiveness of Indian industry abroad, Government will consider favourably the induction of advanced technology, and will permit creation of capcity large enough to make it competitive in world fiarkets.Provided substantial exports are likely. The purpose of introducing such a policy would be not only to encourage exports but also to enable industry to produce better quality products at lower cost which will ultimately benefit the consumer in terms of price and quality.

The Indian industry must earmark substantial resources for R & D to constantly update technologies with a view to optional utilisation of scarce resources, better service to the consumer achieving greater exports. We also have to lay greater emphasis on bringing the benefit of the latest R & D to the medium and small Units.

There has already been considerable simplification and streamlining of licensing procedures. Nevertheless, there is scope for further improvement in reducing the period of time taken for disposal of applications for the creation of new capacities, proposals for substantial expansion and the production of new items. It is proposed to speed up the processes of examination and decision-making and also to examine the possibilities of further rationalisation and simplification of the system of industrial licensing.

The industries where no foreign collaboration, is considered necessary are specified. The import of technology may be considered by Government even in these fields if they conform to the guidelines referred to in the statement on Industrial Policy.

Government will take active measures to facilitate the transfer of technology from efficiently operating units to new units. Companies which have well established R & D organisations, and have demonstrated their ability to absorb, adapt and disseminate Modern technology will be permitted to import such technology, as will increase their efficiency and cost effectiveness. This will not only lead to saving of foreign exchange but would also ensure self-sufficiency and higher exchange earnings.

Guidelines for Approval. The following are some of the important guidelines for approval of proposals for foreign collaboration (financial and or technical):

1. ***Equity Participation.*** Government's policy towards permitting foreign equity participation will continue to be selective. Such participation has to be justified having regard to factors such as the priority of the industry, the nature of the technology involved, whether it will enable or promote exports which may not otherwise take place, and the alternative terms available for securing the same or similar technological transfer. The ceiling for foreign equity participation is 40 per cent although exceptions can be considered on merit.

   The foreign share capital should be by way of cash without being linked to tied imports of machinery and equipment or to payment for know-blow, trade marks, brand names, etc.

Keeping in view the need to provide additional facilities to promote investment in the country from Oil Exporting, Developing countries, which have large financial resources but not the type of technology that the country needs, it base been decided that foreign proposals from these countries need not be associated with transfer of technology from the equity holders, and that such investment may be of a portfolio nature. Within the framework of the investment policy of the Government, it has been decided to provide the following facilities:

(a) Investment of the aforesaid pattern may be allowed in hotels.

(b) Investment may also be allowed in new hospital projects and such hospitals should have adequate provision for outdoor and emergency medical service to the general public, and also for a minimum percentage of occupancy by Indian public.

(c) Loans should also be allowed to be raised abroad for such joint ventures provided the terms are reasonable.

(d) Investment from oil-exporting developing countries may be permitted in new companies even if it is in the nature of portfolio investment.

(e) Such investments should not exceed 40 per cent in the equity.

(f) The new companies should be export-oriented or should undertake manufacturing activities covered under Appendix-I of the press Note of 2nd February, 1973.

2. ***Renewal of Collaboration Agreement.*** Applications for extension of collaboration agreements are scrutinised carefully and extensions are agreed to only in those cas s where Government is satisfied that there is need for them.

Application for extension may be considered in the following circumstances:

(a) If the collaboration agreement involves the manufacture of a large number of items and the Indian party could start manufacturing some of the items only at a later stage. In such cases, extension is granted only in respect of these few items the manufacture of which started later;

(b) If the item of manufacture is sophisticated and it is necessary that the period of collaboration should be extended for a short period to enable the Indian party to fully absorb the know-how;

(c) If it is felt that such extension would be in the interest of exports of the manufactured products. Even where extensions are considered and granted, every effort is made to reduce the rate of royalty payable, with regard to the nature of the product and the period of extension.

3. ***Technical Collaboration.*** Technical collaborations are considered on the basis of annual royalty payments, which are linked with the value of actual production. The percentage of royalty will depend on the nature of technology but should not ordinarily exceed 5 per cent. Royalty is calculated on the basis of ex-factory selling price of the product net of excise duties minus the cost of standard bought out components and landed cost of imported components. Royalty payments are subject to Indian taxes. Wherever appropriate, payment of a fixed amount of royalty per unit of production will be preferred.

Lumpsum payments may also be considered in appropriate cases for the import of drawings, documentation and other forms of know-how. In deciding on the reasonableness of such payments, account will be taken of the value of production so that the lumpsum and the recurring royalty, if any, is an acceptable proportion of the value of production. Such payments will be subject to applicable Indian taxes. The lumpsum payments should be phased out as follows:

1/3rd after agreement has been taken Oil record,

1/3rd to be paid on the transfer of documentation, etc., and

1/3rd to be paid at the commencement of production or after completion of 48 months of the signing of the foreign collaboration agreement whichever is earlier.

Policy, May 1990

While making certain changes in the industrial licensing policy in May 1990, the government also announced certain decision with respect to foreign investment and collaborations with the object of attracting inflow of technology more effectively. Foreign investment up to 40 p.c. equity was decided to be allowed on an automatic basis. The landed value of imported capital goods in such cases was to be allowed up to 30 p.c. of the value of plant and machinery. As regards transfer of technology, if import of technology was considered essential they would be free to conclude an agreement with the foreign collaborator without obtaining any clearnance from the Government. Two conditions were laid down in that connection; *(i)* Royalty payment should not exceed 5 p.c. on domestic sales and 8 p.c. on exports; *(ii)* If lumpsum payment was involved in technology import, the proposal must be submitted for clearance lay Government, but decisions would be communicated to the entrepreneur within 30 days.

ACQUISITION OF TECHNOLOGY THROUGH FOREIGN COLLABORATION

Foreign technical collaboration may involve agreement for supply of technical know-how, engineering services in respect of specific projects, patent or trade mark agreement, and agreement for supply of plant, machinery and other equipment. The technology policy of the Government of India announced on 3rd January 1983 envisaged import of technology in selected areas for its efficient absorption and adaptation appropriate to national priorities and research. In accordance with this policy, acquisition of technical know-how or services is governed by the following principles:

(i) There shall be a firm commitment for absorption, adaptation and subsequent development of imported know-how through adequate investment in R and D by importers of technology.

(ii) The collaboration agreement should necessarily provide for horizontal transfer of technology.

(iii) The company importing technology trust built up its engineering and R and D centre to assimilate, update and indigenise the technology in defect improvements as required within the shortest possible time.

To give effect to the objectives underlying its technology policy, the Government passed the Research and Development Cess Act, 1986, and notified the Rules framed thereunder in October 1987 to be effective from 1st December 1987. The Act and. Rules provide for the levy and collection of a cess at the rate of 5% on all payments made for the import of technology with a view to encouraging the commercial application of indigenously developed technology and adapting imported technology wider domestic application. The cess is payable on payments for import of technology, including:

(i) Payments made towards the cost of drawings and designs, publications and services of technical personnel.

(ii) Payments made towards import of technical know-how approved by Central Government in terms of any foreign collaboration agreement.

(iii) Payments made to foreign collaborators or to any other person for or in connection with deportation of technical personnel to India in accordance with the approval granted by the Central Government or the Reserve Bank of India. If the technology package includes supply of plant and machinery, and acquisition of patent and trade marks, payment for the same will also be regarded as payment towards or in connection with import of technology and hence will be liable to the levy of cess.

HARMFUL EFFECT'S OF THE OPERATIONS OF MNCs ON INDIAN ECONOMY

The operations of MNCs open up the possibilities of interference in the industrial (and other) activities of the recipient country and are thus resented by the 'nationalist' thinkers. Their arguments against the operations of. MNCs can be summed up as follow:

1. **Payment of Dividends and Royalty.** A large sum of money flow out of the country in terms of payment of dividends, profits, royalties, technical fees and interest to the foreign investors. For instance, remittance made abroad by private sector companies stood at Rs. 72.26 crores in 1969-70. This rose to Rs. 398.9 crores in 1981-82 and further to Rs. 8135 crores.

   It would be revealing to point out that Caltex which had a total investment of Rs. 16.92 crores in India, remitted profits, amounting to Rs. 43 crores in the period 1968-70. ESSO with a total investment of Rs. 29.58 crores remitted profits totaling Rs. 83 crores during the same period.

2. **Political Interference.** Because of their immense financial technical power, the MNCs have gained the necessary strength to influence the decision making processes in underdeveloped countries. Though they do help in transferring technology to underdeveloped countries, it has been often found that models and patterns of industrial development and technologies transferred are not in harmony with the interests of the host countries. The governments of underdeveloped countries have also felt threatened by the direct and indirect interference of MNCs in their internal affairs. The autonomy and sovereignty of the host countries is in danger. Because of these reasons, the governments of various countries have sought to restrict the activities of MNCs in their economies through a battery of administrative controls and legal provisions.

3. **Technology Transfer not Necessarily Conducive to Development.** As far as transfer of technology to underdeveloped countries is concerned, the behaviour pattern of MNCs reveals that they do not engage in R and D activities within the underdeveloped countries. Their R and D efforts are concentrated in laboratories in the home country or in other industrialised countries. Though R and D activities continue to be centralized in the parent country, the host countries have to bear the bulk of their costs since the affiliates of the MNCs in these countries remit payments on this account generally in relation to their sales volume. Such payments by the affiliates are generally over and above those remitted in the form of royalties and technical fees to the parent firm. The satisfaction expressed on technology transfer is partly misconceived also on account of the fact that MNCs which generally command a semi-monopolistic position in their product lines do not transfer their first-line or most advanced technology until foreign firms compel them to do so. In many cases, the technology transferred is of a capital-intensive nature which is not useful from the point of view of a labour surplus economy. In fact, continued insistence on the import of such technology can have serious consequences for the economy of the host country since unemployment will increase. Also, market will fail to grow and this constraint alone would suffice to restrain the rate of growth from increasing.
4. **Distortion of Economic Structure.** MNCs can inflict heavy damage on the host country in various forms such as suppression of domestic entrepreneurship, extension of oligopolistic practices (such as unnecessary product differentiation, heavy advertising, or excessive profit taking), supplying the economy with unsuitable technology and unsuitable products, worsening of income distribution by distorting the production structure to meet the requirements of high-income elites, etc. Modern Marxist economists (Paul Baran, for example) argue that foreign investment

(especially through multinational corporations) opens up the doors of 'neoimperialism' and 'exploitation'.

CONCESSIONS GRANTED BY GOVT. TO FOREIGN COLLBORATION

Policy Initiative, July 1991

As a part of the changes in industrial policy announced on 24 July 1991, the Government also initiated changes in its policy relating to foreign investment and foreign collaboration agreements. In sum the decisions are as follows:

1. In respect of industries other than the high priority industries, automatic permission would be given subject to the same guidelines as above if no free foreign exchange is required for any payments.
2. All other proposals will need specific approval under the general procedures in force.
3. No permission would be necessary for hiring of foreign technicians, foreign testing of indigeneously developed technologies. Payment may be made from blanket permits or free foreign exchange according to RBI guidelines.
4. To provide access to international markets, majority of foreign equity holding up to 51 p.c. equity would be allowed for trading companies primarily engaged in export activities. While the thrust would be on export activities, such trading houses shall be at par with domestic trading and export houses in accordance with the Import-Export policy.
5. Automatic permission would be given for foreign technology agreements in high priority industries up to a lumpsum payment of Rs. 1 crore, 5 p.c. royalty for domestic sales and 8 p.c. for exports, to total payment of 8 p.c. of sales over a 10 year period from date of agreement or 7 years from commencement of production. The prescribed royalty rates are net of taxes and would be calculated according to standard procedures.

6. Approval would be given for direct foreign investment upto 51 p.c. foreign equity in high priority industries There shall be no bottlenecks of any kind in this process. Such clearance would be available if foreign equity covers the foreign exchange requirement for imported capital goods.

7. While the import of components, raw materials and intermediate goods, and payment of know how fees and royalties would be governed by the general policy applicable to other domestic units, the payment of dividends would be monitored through the Reserve Bank of India so as to ensure that outflows on account of dividend payments are balanced by export earnings over a period of time.

8. Other foreign equity proposals, including proposals involving 51 p.c. foreign equity which do not meet the criteria under *(i)* above, will continue to need prior clearance. Foreign equity proposals need not necessarily be accompanied by foreign technology agreements.

FOREIGN COLLABORATION AND MNCs

A common form of MNC participation in Indian industry is through entering into collaboration with Indian industrialists. Foreign collaboration agreements are made between Indian companies and foreign parties, involving sale of technology, as well as use of foreign brand names for the final products. The enormity of Foreign collaborations entered into by the Indian companies would be clear from the fact that in nearly all of the new industries in the large or medium size group, privately or publicly owned, set up after independence, some collaboration agreement was present. Trends of liberalisation in the 1980s' gave substantial spurt to foreign collaborations. This would be clear from the fact that the annual average number of foreign collaboration approvals by the Government witnessed a big jump from 319 during the period 1975 to 1980 to over 771 between 1981 and 1988. In fact, of the total 12,760 foreign collaboration agreements approved in 40 years between 1948 and 1988. As many as 6,165 (*i.e.* 48.3 per cent) have been approved during the eight years between 1981 and 1988. This is a direct result of the liberal policy on technology imports being pursued by the government in recent years.

While there have been collaboration agreements with a number of countries, the largest number of collaborations has been with the U.S.A. followed by the West Germany and the U.K. In recent years there has been a spurt in collaboration agreements with Japan. Of the total of 6,165 collaborations approved between 1981 and 1988, the USA accounted for 1,245 followed by West Germany 997, the UK 963 and Japan 600. The other important countries are France (315), Switzerland (265), Italy (232), Sweden (155) and Neatherlands (130).

Study of these foreign collaborations reveals certain interesting results. Thus, a large number of agreements were concluded for the manufacture of products which were non-essential or which could be produced with help of local technology. These items included vaccum flasks, lipstick, toothpaste, cosmetics, brassiers, ice-cream, gin, beer, biscuits, dry batteries and readymade garments. Not only were collaborations granted for these products, they were often in multiple numbers and were renewed on expiry. Clearly such collaborations were often directed to serve the needs of high income groups and to take advantage of a foreign brand name.

Characteristics of Multinational Corporations

The MNCs have certain characteristics, among which the more important are as follows:

1. ***Giant Size.*** The assets and sales of MNCs run into billions of dollars and they also make supernormal profits. For example, the General Motors' yearly operating revenues exceed gross national product of all but a dozen or so countries. It has more than 40 subsidiaries in 26 countries, with its centralised decision-making apparatus being located in the United States. The IBM's physical assets are worth round 7 billion dollars. ITT has 708 subsidiaries in 67 countries on 6 continents. It is the biggest multinational, accounting for USA's one-third balance of payments. Such is the enormous size of MNCs.

2. ***International Operations.*** In such a corporation control resides in the hands of a single institution. But its interests and operations sprawl across national boundaries. An MNC operates through a parent corporation in the home country. It may assume the form of a branch or a subsidiary in the home country. If it is a branch, it acts for the parent corporation without any local capital or management assistance. If it is a subsiiliary, the majority control is still exercised by the foreign parent company, although it is incorporated in the home country. The foreign control may range anywhere between the minimum of 51 per cent to the full 100 per cent. An MNC thus combines ownership with control The branches and subsidiaries of an MNC operate under the united control of the parent company.
3. ***Spontaneous Evolution.*** MNCs usually grow in a spontaneous and unconscious manner. Very often they develop through creeping incrementalism. Many films have become international by accident. At times, firms have also established subsidiaries abroad due to wage differentials and better opportunities prevailing in the home country.
4. ***Oligopolistic Structure.*** Through the process of merger- and takeover, etc., in course of time an MNC acquires awesome power. This coupled with its giant size make it oligopolistic in character.
5. ***Collective Transfer of Resources.*** An MNC facilitates a multilateral transfer of resources. Usually this transfer takes place in the form of a "package" which includes technical know-how, equipments and machinery, raw materials, finished product, managerial services, and so on. MNCs are composed of a complex of wodely varied modern technology ranging from protraction and marketing to management and finance.

Regulation or Multinational Corporations

In view of that fact the MNCs do possess a potential that can be gainfully exploited, most of the underdeveloped economics have chosen to regulate their activities rather than to dispense with them altogether.

1. The government may allow collaboration in certain selected industries or certain selected regions where the operations of MNC is felt highly suitable.
2. The threat of nationalisation is an effective tool of regulation. Although nationalisation should be resorted to only its the extreme situations, the very fact that it on be exercised makes the corporations act in a disciplined manner.
3. The host country may lay down certain export criteria.
4. A multi-tax system may be followed by the government. The MNCs be taxed at a higher rate.
5. MNCs may be allowed to invest for specific periods. Thus, after a certain period of time restrictions may be imposed on foreign holdings, or there may be provision for gradual disinvestment.

Finally, MNCs may be asked to carry out a minimum fixed share of their total research and development activities within the host countries.

Reasons for the growth of multinationals are manifold, the important ones being as follows:

1. **Technological Superiorities.** The main reason why MNCs have been encouraged by the underdeveloped countries to participate in their industrial development is on account of the technological superiorities which these firms possess as compared to national companies. The underdeveloped countries regard transfer of technology from MNCs useful on account of the following reasons: *(a)* Industrialization represents the most important way out of underdevelopment and the resources of these countries are insufficient to sustain the industrial progress on their own; *(b)* Local manpower rematerials local capital equipment etc. have to be optimally exploited and these countries are unable to accomplish this; *(c)* Depending totally on local companies

would require heavy imports of raw materials capital equipment machinery and technical knowledge whereas MNCs bring these on their own; and *(d)* The underdeveloped countries have to face stiff competition for selling their products in international markets. Unless their goods meet international standards and quality specifications, they cannot sell. MNCs help them in producing such goods.

2. **Product Innovations.** MNCs have Research Development Departments engaged in the task of developing new products and superior designs of existing products. Therefore their production opportunities are far greater as compared to national companies.
3. **Marketing Superiorities.** A multinational firm enjoys a number of marketing superiorities over the national firms: *(a)* It possesses a more reliable and uptodate market information system; *(b)* It enjoys market reputation and faces less difficulty in selling its products; *(c)* It adopts more effective advertising and sales promotion techniques; and *(d)* It has efficient warehousing facilities due to lower inventory requirements.
4. **Financial Superiorties.** A multinational firm enjoys the following financial superiorities over the national firm: *(a)* It has change financial resources with which it can easily turn all circumstances in its favour; *(b)* It maintains a high level of funds utilization by generating funds in one country and using them in another; *(c)* It has easier access to external capital markets; and *(d)* Because of its international reputation it is able to raise more international resources. Even investors and banks of the host country are eager to invest in it.
5. **Expansion of Market Territory.** As the operations of a large-sized firm expand and as its international image builds up it seeks more and more extension of its activities beyond the physical boundaries of the country in which it is incorporated.

❐

13

Strategic Issues in International Management

The world is changing so fast that many companies find it difficult to keep up. Global competition is the name of the game. Firms must formulate, successfully implement, and control global strategies in order to survive and prosper in the future. The global company is becoming the most viable force in world trade and international relations. The strategic aspects of managing multinational corporations is the focus of this chapter. Hence, our approaches in this chapter is to view the strategic analysis process and international strategy issues as orthogonal to each other. We first review the strategic analysis process, then identify issues of international strategy, and examine these issues in developing a strategy and a structure to operate in the global market. The chapter also covers an integrated strategy of MNCs and the approach of such companies in dealing with the restriction and guidelines put forth by host nations.

INTERNATIONAL STRATEGIC MANAGEMENT: ANALYTICAL FRAMEWORK

Strategic management can be defined as the process of assessing a corporation and its environment in terms of meeting the long-term objectives of the firm, so that it can conform to its environment and take advantage of the opportunities in the market to be best of its ability. Next, the term international must be defined in order to fully understand the phenomenon of international strategic management. International may be defined as activities that involve two or more countries. Thus, the concept international strategic management can be defined as the effect and interaction of strategic management between two or more nations.

The major aspects of strategy analysis include: setting goals and objectives, performing competitive and industry analysis, analysing resources and capabilities, developing strategic options, choosing a strategy, and implementing that strategy, with feedback loops among all the processes. Figure-l shows this in simplified model.

International business involves a specific set of issues whose strategic resolution ties into the generic strategic analysis framework in Figure-l. These international strategy issues are presented in Figure-2 and involve *(1)* increasing geographic spread (often referred to as 'internationalisation'), *(2)* achieving local adaptation (often referred to as 'responsiveness'), *(3)* building global integration (sometimes referred to as 'globalisation' or 'global strategy'), and *(4)* multi-business, multi-country and often multi-firm issues such as international strategic alliances and global merger and acquisitions.

FIGURE-1

THE STRATEGIC ANALYSIS PROCESS

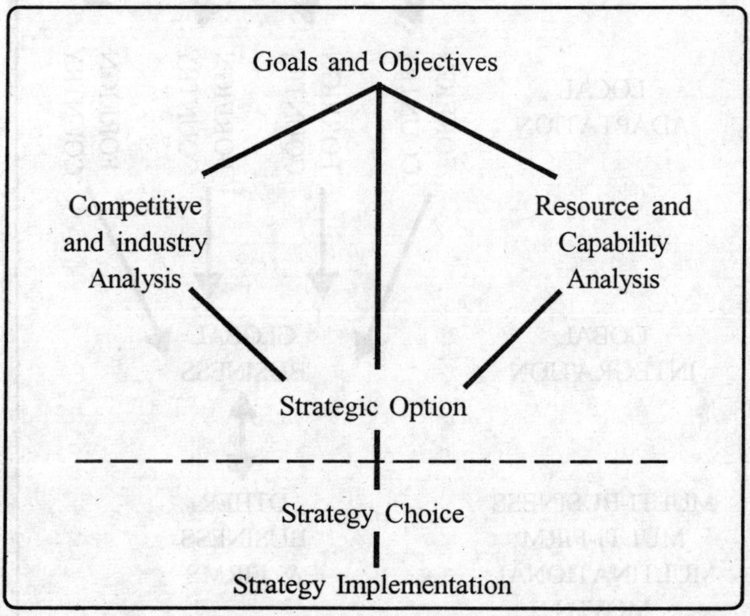

In general, the more basic issues in international strategy requires more use of the more basic issues in strategy analysis, as illustrated in Figure-3, although that last international issues of multi-business/multi-firm/multinational moves tends to require heavy emphasis on all five strategic analysis processes. We see heavy reliance on goal setting, industry analysis, and resource assessment as firm expand internationally. Adaptation and integration are driven largely by issues developed through competitive analysis and resource assessment, while integration must also consider issues revealed by different means of assessing strategic conditions and opportunities.

FIGURE-2

INTERNATIONAL STRATEGY ISSUES

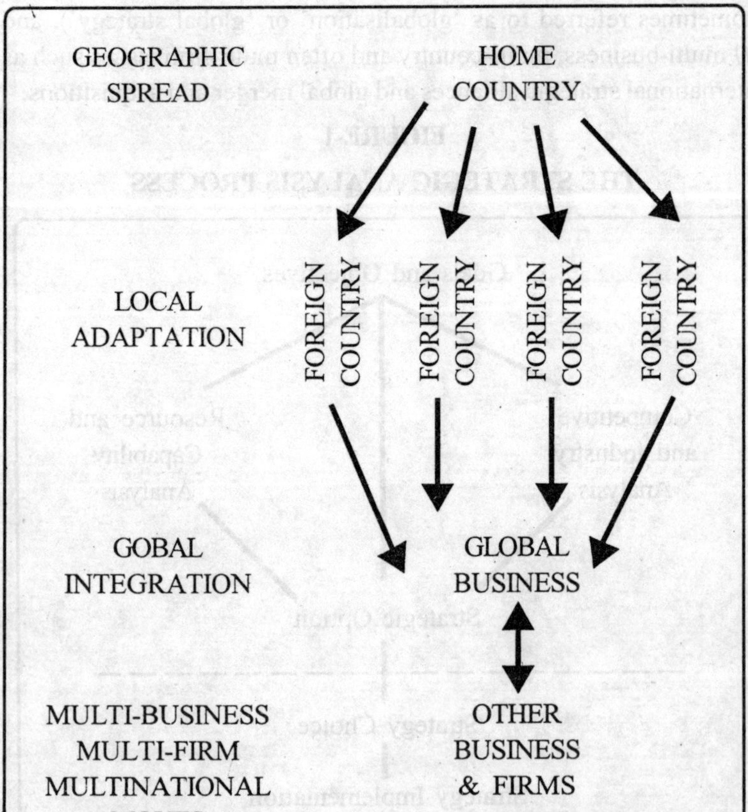

THE STRATEGIC MANAGEMENT PROCESS

Strategic management is the function of top management in running an organisation successfully. The process involves three basic components: *(i)* Strategy formulation and planning; *(ii)* Strategy implementation; and *(iii)* Evaluation and control.

FIGURE-3

MAPPING OF INTERNATIONAL STRATEGY ISSUES AND THE STRATEGIC ANALYSIS PROCESS

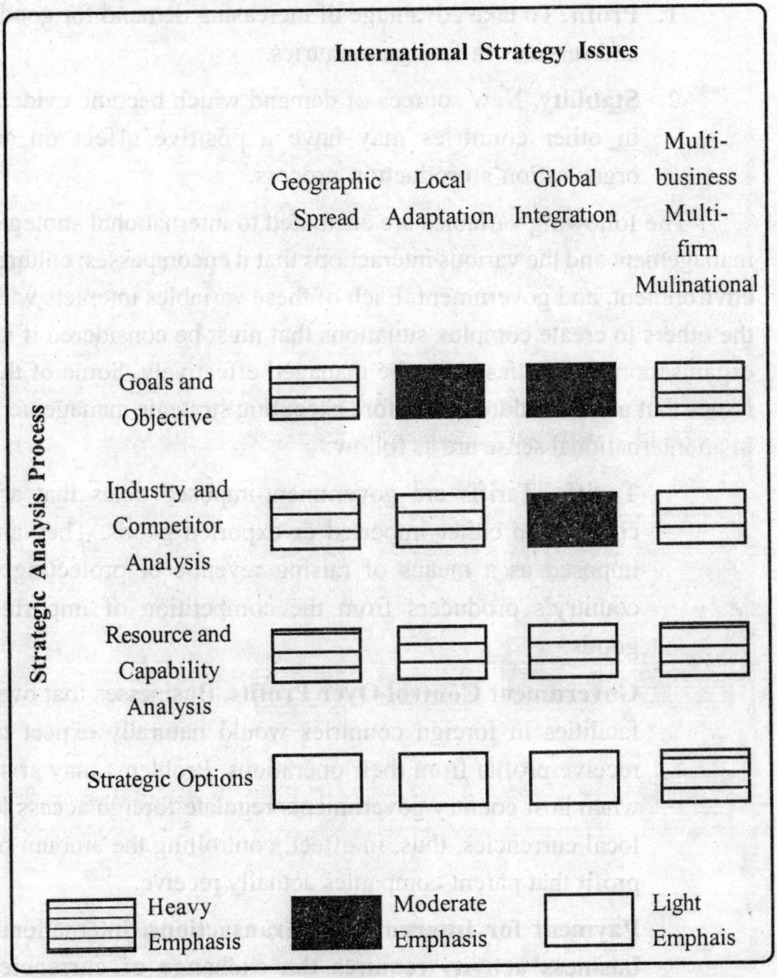

When business activities are extended to be international in scope, new challenges and opportunities are presented to management. Management must first understand the decision to pursue business activities on an international level. Management must also carefully examine the interaction of variables that constitute international strategic management.

Two objectives motivate an organisation to extend its operations to other countries:

1. **Profit.** To take advantage of increasing demand for goods and services in foreign countries.
2. **Stability.** New sources of demand which become evident in other countries may have a positive effect on an organisation's production process.

The following variables are attributed to international strategic management and the various interactions that it encompasses: culture, environment, and government. Each of these variables interacts with the others to create complex situations that must be considered if an organisation's activities are to be managed effectively. Some of the issues that must be addressed before executing strategic management in an international sense are as follow:

Tariffs. Tariffs are government-imposed taxes that are charged on either imported or exported goods. They are imposed as a means of raising revenue or protecting a country's producers from the competition of imported goods.

Government Control Over Profits. Businesses that own facilities in foreign countries would naturally expect to receive profits from their operations. Problems may arise when host country governments regulate foreign access to local currencies, thus, in effect, controlling the amount of profit that parent companies actually receive.

Payment for International Transactions. International business activity requires the exchange of currencies between countries. Problems may arise relative to foreign exchange rates, as they tend to fluctuate in value.

Culture. Different cultures are brought together through international business activity. Complex problems may arise as the result of language barriers and differences in cultural values, tastes, and attitudes.

Taxation. Businesses conducting operations in foreign countries are subject to the laws and regulations of those countries. Local taxes may be very high due to the lack of other sources of revenue, thus shifting the tax burden to multinational corporations.

Each of these issues and their associated variables must be carefully considered in order to ensure effective international strategic management.

Strategic Planning *Versus* Long-Range Planning

In a sense, all strategic planning involves long-range planning, but not all long-range planning involves strategic thinking. In defining strategic planning, it is important to recognise that there is a difference between strategic planning and long-range planning. Long-range planning fails to recognise the changing environment and simply extends present trends into the future. Strategic planning, on the other hand, addresses the wants and needs of an organisation; in other words, it considers a firm's mission. This approach enables a firm to identify its strengths and weaknesses and helps determine what to do in order to get the job done.

Strategic planning provides direction and clarity and identifies where a firm should be three to five years down the road. Strategic planning is not about mechanical data analysis, predictions, and economic forecasts; it is a way of thinking and structuring business ideas-like a game of chess.

The problem with long-range planning is that it is not a way of thinking, but rather a way of formulating a plan to organise, realise, or achieve something, without considering the changing environment.

The typical socialist five-year plan is a good example of long-range planning, and it proves the dangers of ignoring economic and political changes.

Multinational Firms and the Environment

The importance of strategic management in a multinational firm cannot be overemphasised. The fall of the Berlin Wall (which was followed by reduced tariffs for developing, non-industrial nations) and improvements in transportation technology are two examples of recent developments that have caused decision makers in multinational corporations to review their procedures for identifying optimal investment sites abroad. Companies looking to expand into these economic areas face several issues.

One consideration is which market to penetrate. For example, a company needs to understand the restrictions to trade in various regions (*i.e.*, tariffs, quotas, etc.). A community is larger than just one country; it may consist of a group of countries that have aligned themselves for efficiency. These communities are constantly changing, and companies must stay well informed to ensure the competitive advantage of international expansion. Multinational prospects must also consider the long-range implications of international business, one of which is the relationship between the member states of the regional blocs.

The foreign exchange rate can present problems in international markets. Fluctuations in the exchange rate affect the foreign cost structure of products within three to six months. Although this may present gains as well as losses, a company must ask itself if its competencies lie in manipulating different currency positions or are based on certain skills and transferable assets. The foreign exchange rate can have a significant impact on where an organisation will expand.

Multinational expansion provides companies entry to certain regions of the world which have a distinct advantage in terms of tax and wage differentials. Management must exercise careful judgment in evaluating the different types and amounts of incentives. Incentives to companies locating in specific areas take a variety of forms, such as programmes for training and housing.

Companies that seek new markets in foreign countries must do an environmental analysis, both internal and external. The most common environments that organisations evaluate are the economic, technological, societal, political, and ecological. The economic environment is the most critical and also the most difficult to analyse because it deals with the national economic scene. A number of economic trends are of particular interest to businesses, including the stability of the currency the projected growth in the gross national product, the expected growth in the consumer price index, and changes in the tax structure.

In many cases, the technological environment may be the deciding factor in expansion. The success of a business can depend on its ability to stay on the cutting edge of technology. Several technological trends that may interest a firm are micro-circuits, solar heating and other alternative energy sources, and metal alloys.

The political environment, which includes regulations, is an extremely critical variable in the long-term efficiency and success of a firm. Firms in regulated industries need to pay special attention to environmental trends in order to be able to predict future courses of action. Significant issues in the political environment include corporate taxes, retirement age, public interest groups, and government permits.

Finally, the ecological environment must be recognised. This area has come under severe scrutiny as people seek to make the earth a safer place. Today, firms must carefully plan projects so as not to have an adverse impact on the environment. Issues in the ecological environment that are of broad interest include clean water requirements, emission standards, bans on certain types of businesses, and noise and air pollution requirements.

Strategic Planning

Management sets the course for an organisation through the formulation of organisational plans. Organisations are attempting to respond to the growing need to anticipate changes in the environment-both internal and external-through organisational planning. Although this type of effective planning has dominated outstanding organisational performance, the complexity of change has increased so dramatically that additional planning has become fundamentally important.

A strategy is the "big picture" in terms of what a firm is capable of doing. A strategic plan is made up of a strategy and the time-related details for carrying out that strategy. It should include: *(i)* Marketing mix (the target market); *(ii)* Drain on company resources; *(iii)* Anticipated sales and profits; and *(iv)* Control procedures to ensure that the plan is following its intended course.

Strategic planning does not take place in a vacuum. The plan is used by marketing, accounting, production, human resources, and all the other specialists. A strategic plan lets everybody in the firm know what they are trying to accomplish and it gives direction to the whole business effort. Effective strategic planning requires that all aspects of the plan are carried out efficiently at all levels of operation. Every departmental decision is capable of casting a shadow on the final outcome of the strategic plan; therefore, all levels of operation must carry out their assignments completely.

Planning has been defined as drawing from the past to decide in the present what to do in the future. When a company implements strategic planning, it must first analyse its present situation and then formulate and implement those strategies that will be most beneficial in the long run. Extreme care and precision are required to match resources with market opportunities over the long term. Strategic planning differs from day-to-day operational planning in that it is very long term in purpose and direction.

Solid commitment to the strategic plan and its anticipated outcome must be built from the top level of management all the way down through the operational levels. Unlike operational day-to-day planning, where one change after another may be implemented to facilitate an outcome, the final outcome of a strategic plan may take years to realise. Without proper guidelines (policies), a strategic plan may not have the flexibility to achieve its final outcome, which is why it is critical to select a plan that has been well thought out and focuses on the very best interest of the company. Everyone in a company will feel the consequences of a poorly constructed strategic plan. An operational plan ensures the smooth flow of work on a day-do-day basis; in contrast, a strategic plan indicates a company's present position as well as what its position is destined to be in the future.

Basic Stages of Strategic Planning

Step 1: Assess Corporate Strategy. This process requires a firm to assess its own position relative to its environment. In doing so, an organisation must include a SWOT (strengths, weaknesses, opportunities, or threats) analysis to determine its strengths and weaknesses. After analysing its strengths and weaknesses, an organisation must evaluate its potential and identify where the opportunities and threats lie in the external environment. Strategic analysis allows an organisation to define its range of strategic alternatives and choose the one most appropriate for its present external environment.

Step 2: Strategy Formulation. In the process of strategy formulation, an organisation first creates and set of realistic and comprehensive goals and objectives. An appropriate strategy is then selected based on the result that the organisation wants to accomplish. Strategy formulation allows an organisation to identify the strategy that can best meet its realistic goals.

Step 3: Strategy Implementation. This is the most important step in strategic planning.. A plan that is formulated perfectly 'but implemented incorrectly will not produce the desired result. The implementation strategy must have an operational plan that can organise and move resources when they are needed. To do this effectively, such variables as culture, personnel, and the structure and design of the organisation must be assessed.

Many companies find the consequences of not planning adequately and then not implementing correctly extremely hazardous. With the arrival of the computer age, the external and internal environments at most companies are constantly changing. Technology is constantly improving, government regulations are constantly changing, and management policies and personnel are constantly being replaced. This view is even more apparent in the world market. Those who cannot plan in a multicultural mode will lose market share in the global economy. Those who cannot adapt to new technology, changes in foreign policy, and cultural differences will be dropped from the world market as others who plan and implement better strategies take their place. Lack of planning in the global market can mean loss of profits or even failure to survive.

A UNIFIED MODEL FOR INTERNATIONAL PURPOSES

Countries differ socially, economically, technically, and politically. In order to be successful in the international business environment, it is essential that these differences be recognised and taken into consideration in managing international activities. Several basic questions should be asked when considering opportunities in foreign market . Should we go international? In what parts of the world should we look for such opportunities? How soon should we begin our venture in the international market? What are the best means to exploit these opportunities? In deciding whether to enter foreign markets, management should:

1. Evaluate the opportunities for the firm's products and services in foreign markets, as well as the potential threats, problems, and risks associated with such opportunities.
2. Evaluate the strengths and weaknesses of the firm's managerial, material, technical, and operational (finance, marketing, etc.) capabilities to determine whether the necessary resources are available to successfully exploit potential opportunities in foreign markets.

Two basic steps are used in developing a model for international strategy: an environmental analysis and an internal resources audit. The general focus of the environmental analysis is on the discovery and evaluation of business opportunities and threats and the associated problems and risks. In an international sense, three different levels of environmental analysis should be considered: *(1)* multinational,

(2) regional, and *(3)* country. Multinational environmental analysis consists of broadly identifying, forecasting, and monitoring critical factors in the world environment. It involves the study of global technological developments, various trends in government intervention, and changes in overall values and life-styles. These items are evaluated in terms of their degree of impact, both now and in the future. Regional environmental analysis focuses on a more detailed study of the critical factors within a definite geographic area (*e.g.*, Western Europe, the Middle East). This level is directed toward identifying marketing opportunities for a company's products, services, and/or technology in a specific region. The third level, country environmental analysis, involves an even more refined examination of the critical environmental factors. This level continues to focus on the economic, legal, political, and cultural factors in an even smaller number or refined group of countries. This analysis, however, must be oriented toward the specific strategy to enter each individual market in order ensure successful planning.

The second step which aids in the development of an international strategy is the internal resources audit. The primary purpose of this audit is to appropriately match a company's managerial, technical, material, and financial resources with those required for successful operation. This audit is related to the business rather than the environment. It focuses on key business success factors, which are simply defined as the key factors essential for success in a particular business. This audit is also considered to be country related in that the amount of resources required will vary relative to the country involved.

Hence, formulating a unified model for international purposes must include:

(i) Evaluating international opportunities, threats, problems, and risks;

(ii) Evaluating a firm's strengths and weaknesses in order to exploit opportunities in foreign markets;

(iii) Defining a firm's scope relative to international business involvement;

(iv) Formulating a firm's international corporate objectives; and

(v) Developing specific corporate strategies for a firm as a whole-an international corporate strategy.

AN INTEGRATED STRATEGY

The multinational corporation (MNC) is the first institution in human history to plan on a global scale. Its purpose is to organise and integrate economic activity around the world in order to maximise profit. Its failures and successes are measured through growth in global profit and market share. International trade usually benefits all parties involved. The basic assumption in such trade is that the growth of the whole strengthens the welfare of all. The overall focus is increased efficiency. International companies now have significant influence on world productivity and technological advancement. Their influence has grown so vast that it affects all aspects of society. Furthermore, the average rate of growth of the most successful MNCs is two to three times higher than that of most advanced countries.

Manufacturing Firms

Manufacturing firms usually follow a four-step process to enter the international environment:

1. A corporation exports goods requested by foreign customers.
2. A firm initiates marketing activities abroad.
3. A firm establishes other functional activities overseas, such as manufacturing. Firms in this stage are called multinationals.
4. A firm is characterised by widespread operation and is no longer identified with just one particular country. Firms in this stage are called transnationals.

The revenues of these transnational corporations exceed the gross national product of many of the countries in which they operate.

Going International

Modern corporations are trying to grain and advantage over their competitors. Most are finding that a good way to do so is through the complex process of going international. By going international, corporations can extend their product lines to other cultures. They can also save money on labour costs by taking advantage of the lower standard of living in some countries. One big advantages of doing business in foreign countries, particularly developing countries, is that high unemployment rates provide inexpensive and vast labour pools. This helps companies to generate more capital and, therefore, bring in more revenue. These countries are ideal for industrial companies in labour-intensive industries. Many U.S. manufacturing firms have found that they incur lower input costs by locating their manufacturing facilities outside the United States and thus can export their products at lower prices than if those same products were manufactured at home. The maquiladora in Mexico is a case in point; by sending parts to Mexican plants for assembly, manufacturers can save on labour costs. By going international, a company can make and save money simultaneously, depending on the geographic area.

Several factors both influence the decision to go international and make the move feasible. The ever-pressing need to get ahead of the competition may be a good reason to go abroad. In underdeveloped nations, labour is inexpensive, which means that a company pays less to get the same job done. Another reason for going abroad is rapid expansion, in an effort to keep up with product demand. A home-based company may be expanding rapidly, but not rapidly enough to keep up with market demand. An overseas facility can satisfy such demand. A final reason for going international is the absence of trade barriers vital to many economies throughout the world. This trend is reflected in the increased efforts of many countries to promote international trade.

Strategy Formulation

Objectives and strategies are formulated by considering mission, strategic policy and information. When a firm operates outside its home country, its strategic objectives and overall strategy change. To adjust its strategy to its various environments, a firm can implement a number of options. Depending on the type of change required, it can choose either expansion or expansion and diversification. However, a firm that chooses expansion as its strategy to achieve corporate development and efficient use of existing resources for higher profits will soon find that it needs to diversify to maintain systematic growth. In the diversification strategy, a firm has two alternatives for expansion:

1. **Geography (the International Route).** A strategy is prepared to weight the pros and cons of developing foreign markets and the implications of the decision.
2. **Product.** A firm can choose a move into a new business as an alternative to going international or as a way to enter foreign markets. A company can also purchase another business that operates in a foreign environment.

The stages of strategy formulation can be categorised as follows: *(1)* decision preparation stage (also called long-term planning), *(2)* matching stage (also called intermediate-term planning), and *(3)* implementation stage (also called short-term planning). In the preparation stage, strategists gather questions and ideas and develop ways to measure and determine feasibility. Other activities include establishing a more objective view of the company's future and setting policies to aid in achieving corporate objectives. It also involves the preparation of a timetable for supplementary decisions. The strategists at this stage plan for the efficient use of corporate resources to the greatest possible advantage and design a system to manage the constant flow of information. When the basic decisions about strategy have been made, a corporation is ready to undertake the next step. The matching stage involves the development of systematic guidelines to forecast opportunities and threats, along with setting deadlines to measure progress and establishing mechanisms to cope with possible problems. The strategists develop a structure for international logistics to purchase raw materials and distribute products. Then the strategists select methods to integrate and compromise between the company's resources and the design of the decision system. In the third stage, tasks and available machinery are assigned to each operating unit for implementation. Other activities in this stage include developing efficient inventory procedures, financial practices, and the flexibility to accommodate delays when a part of the program runs late.

MNCs are highly dependent on a strategic advantage, as are most organisations. Many multinational firms key in on the superiority of some resource, such as capital, labour, or technology. Capitalising on an advantage can compensate for a weakness. Strategy formulation gives a company a competitive advantage in that it improves quality and reduces costs. It also facilitates innovation through open lines of communication among team members.

A key factor for success in going multinational is a strong integrated strategy. An integrated strategy should always include costs and margins. A corporation that wants to be strong in the international arena must consider competitive advantage. In a long-range strategic plan, it would be senseless to operate an international subsidiary whose costs exceed its profits. The same is true in integrated strategy.

Two assumptions are connected with a successful multinational integration strategy: *(1)* integration provides a MNC with an advantage over its competitors and *(2)* an organisation can trade off some proceeds of its competitive advantage with host governments. Once these assumptions have been implemented, a company must pay close attention to economies of scale and the economic situation in the countries to which it expands.

Another function of integration is supplier partnership, which facilitates better communication with suppliers and can prove to be valuable in product design.

Implementing an integrated strategy usually requires several compromises with the host country. These usually involve sharing the economic benefits of the new subsidiary or branch of the MNC. Laws and regulations, whether domestic or international, also need to be considered, because they differ from country to country.

An integrated strategy should also consider customer needs and tastes, which vary from culture to culture. An integrated strategy allows a company that is going international to adjust its product line to suit a variety of customers and cultures. It also allows room for improvements, such as new distribution channels, for optimal international commercial practices.

A strong integrated strategy includes logistic management, which is the central operational task. Logistic strategy analysis must start with economic factors, because the production-marketing system exists to implement the resource transmission capabilities rooted in these factors. The major factors are economic differentials and the efficiencies available through a unified global system. However, analysis based on economic factors must be modified by other influences, including government actions and corporate characteristics. Logistics strategy for a MNC has three main goals:

1. To efficiently transmit resources so as to maximise their flow in a natural direction as determined by economic differentials and government actions.
2. To utilise the potential and make maximum use of the special advantages of a MNC as a global organisation.
3. To effectively implement resource transmission, with special regard to communication as a critical factor.

MNCs use logistics systems to keep production balanced and to check inconsistencies in the schedules of integrated plants. At monthly meetings, key managers and company experts schedule production, lines and corporate goals for the up coming month. A key topic is generally inventory control.

Unfortunately, many companies fail due to inconsistencies. Decisions in the expansion of an integrated system are more complicated than the daily operations of a domestic corporation. Efficiency of operation and flexibility of supply must be carefully monitored on a daily basis. The number of integrated plants should be kept at a limited or optimal level in order to avoid unnecessary complexities. For example, when Volkswagen invested in the United

States, it did not realise the magnitude of the risk involved. First, the cost of labour was extremely high. Then, when the dollar rose dramatically, the cost of operation was affected by the exchange rate, which made the integration obsolete. Integration strategies and logistic play an important role in the expansion process, not only for U.S. based companies but for growing companies throughout the world.

Host Country Controls and Regulations

Companies must adhere to different rules in international marketing and therefore, strategies must also be altered. Indeed, the governments of different countries impose different regulations on MNCs, in varying- degrees. Host countries often restrict the following:

(i) **Ownership.** Host countries typically require that a local firm own a majority or controlling interest;

(ii) **Employment.** Almost all host countries demand that certain managerial and technological positions he held by host country nationals;

(iii) **Profits and Fees.** Profits and fees are typically set at some maximum level;

(iv) **Internal Debt Capital.** Internal debt capital is often set according to a preestablished formula;

(v) **Training and Development.** Insistence on training and development for host country nationals is common;

(vi) **Host Country Markets.** Most host countries demand development of their exports;

(vii) **Technological Bases.** Most host countries seek technology-based industries rather than extractive industries.

Setting objectives is also significantly affected by a multinational environment because growth may he legislatively limited; efficiency may be held to an undesirably low level by extra costs as dictated by governments; use of resources may be set at specified levels; contribution to owners (profits) is usually set at arbitrary levels; contribution to customers may be modified to meet government-established levels; contribution to employees focuses on technical training and often includes guaranteed employment as opposed to true development; contribution to society is stressed by the government's involvement in all areas.

A basic strategy of Japanese companies is to diversify early in their history. US. firms do not diversify quite as early, and European firms tend to diversify later still. Japanese companies pay closer attention than any other country to quality in production. Japanese management philosophy is oriented toward the group or team. In virtually all countries, negotiation with the government is becoming increasingly more critical than it has in the United States and Canada. While objectives and strategies will vary, the basics of strategy are the same. The differences in the basic strategies of MNCs can be traced to cultural/historical factors.

Strategies at Strategic Business Units

The factors that affect strategy at the strategic business unit (SBU) level are significantly modified in multinational operations. All of the factors involved in the marketing mix are affected in some way by the international environment, competition, institutions, and the legal systems. The product itself is very important. Design, packaging, and special needs to accommodate certain sizes and dimensions for consumers in different countries are very important. Promotion is also governed by local practices. Price is frequently determined by cultural customs that influence the amount of money that should be spent on a product. Distribution is affected by, among other things, availability of roads and other transportation channels. A firm must consider all of these factors in order to be successful.

Financial strategies should address currency exchange rates. Fluctuations in exchange rates can cause many problems in terms of profits. Production strategies must cope with the logistical problems that accompany inadequate transportation systems, a dearth of suppliers, and a largely unskilled work force. Personnel strategies should consider laws and customs in regulating work and authority.

The specifics of management functions vary among countries. Managers have different expectations in terms of motivation and leadership style. Different countries have different management hierarchies, motivational techniques, and long-range planning priorities. Control strategies are very important to multinational firms, as are functional strategies, such as communication habits and decision-making skills. If a multinational organisation is to survive and prosper, it must be able to adapt.

One of the most important factors that affects MNCs is the host country's culture. People in different parts of the world have different beliefs. Language is also an important consideration. The same word can take on a different meaning in a different culture. Before a company plans to integrate into another country, extensive research must be done on the area's culture. An important cultural factor that affects management is how competition is viewed. This can influence motivation, leadership style, the compensation system, and the type of people hired.

An additional factor in the success of MNCs is the use of comparative management, which is defined as the analysis of cross-cultural management practices and techniques. Many international managers fail because they are unfamiliar with patterns in the local culture. The American way of doing things is not always the proper way in other cultures. Combining cultures in managerial decisions promotes understanding. To work effectively in a foreign country, a manager must understand the culture of the host country. For example, AT&T representatives at the company's first privately held exhibit in Tokyo were well prepared. In addition to .language skills, they had also acquired information about the shared knowledge, beliefs, and values of potential Japanese customers, as well as their ways of interacting and conducting business.

A corporation should also consider local attitudes and beliefs in terms of time value, punctuality or promptness, achievement, work, and change. These factors have a major influence on the business functions of a MNC and may require adaptation.

Sociocultural components include religion, folklore, music, and art. Advertising a product in a commercial with music in the background may not be appropriate in certain cultures. Americans may enjoy the music, but other cultures may find it distasteful or even sacrilegious.

Material culture involves technology and how a product will interact in a specific culture. For example, what if all Ford automobiles sold in India had the steering wheel on the left side? They would be unsuccessful because most Indians drive on the right side of the vehicle. This would be both a cultural and a technological error.

Education plays a major role in the success of a MNC. A company can both improve product quality and achieve its goals by sharing technology and information. Implementing this idea in a multicultural research and development programme can improve a company's product line. When a product that is successful in the United States needs to be adjusted to suit a new region, both cultures can work together to create a suitable product. Participants in a multinational venture need to sit down and communicate their differences. For example, exchanging gifts is customary in some countries, whereas in the United States it is seen as bribery. Differences in language must also be addressed. These differences should be discussed before a programme begins.

There are so many differences between cultures that it is impossible to cover them all at once. The point is that in order to be successful, a manager of a MNC should be sensitive to and aware of these differences. A manager will gain the respect of his or her employees by trying to understand what they stand for and what their beliefs are, and the same is true for the employees. By understanding the differences in other cultures, a MNC fosters better employee relations, which in turn affects output and the operation in general in a foreign region. Many companies have failed in the past due to a lack of knowledge about other cultures. It is important for a MNC to gain an advantage over its competitors, and one way to do so is by understanding the culture of its host country.

While learning about a host country's culture, it is also important to build excellent communication channels. In the international market, a complex pattern of communication is often created by the combination of diversity of activities, spread of operations, pressures of environment and competition, and individual characteristics of the panics involved.

All top-level managers in an integrated multinational business need channels for communication and information. These channels are important in keeping subsidiary managers from developing self—serving arguments against integration. All the branches of a MNC should be for used on the same goals. Communication channels have a strong influence on the overall integrated strategy. A functional channel provides feedback on market performance of existing products, requests for new products and review of development projects. Functional channels are limited when communication on a key competitive issue is misinterpreted which is usually due to a lack of knowledge about the host country.

Global strategic decisions affect the entire company. Managers value input from subsidiaries and work back and forth with top executives in decision making. This type of dialogue requires open lines of communication, even at lower levels. It also means that a company must learn to trust and respect the decisions of lower level managers.

Two-way communication can sometimes result in heated debates. As people split into factions, they begin to distrust one another. Moreover, when subsidiary managers participate in global strategic decision making, they come to view the decisions as their own. This leads to debate over who is right, as people defend their decisions. When information and ideas are exchanged freely, global strategic decision making can be both informative and productive. It allows managers at all levels to express their opinions and hear the opinions of others. When managers feel that their views are taken into consideration, they are likely to be satisfied with the strategic decisions made.

The communication channel that involves interface with senior management can be formal or informal. It includes programme plans and possible environmental strategies. These plans involve a specific purpose and are aimed at a specific area in need of improvement. The programme discussed well in advance and involves a specific purpose. An environmental strategy is a response to important conditions or issues in the natural environment, such as worker codetermination. Here, a subsidiary manager brings the problem to the attention of corporate management at headquarters, although sometimes it is better for a subsidiary to act autonomously and depart from corporate patterns.

When top management cannot resolve or deal directly with an issue that affects an operation in the integrated network, the corporate managing committee has the final decision in the issue resolution process. For example, a subsidiary that feels that its budget is insufficient can approach the corporate managing committee with a request to have it increased. Some integrated companies assign key senior executives as local advocates. They represent key subsidiary or regional interests at corporate headquarters in order to facilitate communication. A strong global market requires strong localism. The integrated strategies for communication must be brought to the attention of the performance of the strategic business units. Thus, a balance must be struck between decision making and communication.

❒